Visual Basic™—
Game Programming
for Windows™

Visual Basic™—
Game Programming
for Windows™

Microsoft
P R E S S

® **Michael J. Young**

PUBLISHED BY
Microsoft Press
A Division of Microsoft Corporation
One Microsoft Way
Redmond, Washington 98052-6399

Library of Congress Cataloging-in-Publication Data
Young, Michael J.
    Visual Basic—game programming for Windows / Michael J. Young.
       p. cm.
    Includes index.
    ISBN 1-55615-503-4
    1. Windows (Computer programs) 2. Microsoft Visual BASIC.
    3. Computer games. I. Title.
    QA76.76.W56Y685   1992
    794.8'15262--dc20   92-24249
                                                                CIP

Printed and bound in the United States of America.

1 2 3 4 5 6 7 8 9 MLML 7 6 5 4 3 2

Distributed to the book trade in Canada by Macmillan of Canada, a division of Canada Publishing Corporation.

Distributed to the book trade outside the United States and Canada by Penguin Books Ltd.

Penguin Books Ltd., Harmondsworth, Middlesex, England
Penguin Books Australia Ltd., Ringwood, Victoria, Australia
Penguin Books N.Z. Ltd., 182–190 Wairau Road, Auckland 10, New Zealand

British Cataloging-in-Publication Data available.

Acquisitions Editor: Michael Halvorson
Project Editor: Jack Litewka
Technical Editor: Jim Fuchs

C O N T E N T S

ACKNOWLEDGMENTS

I want to thank all the people at Microsoft Press who made developing this book one of my most enjoyable writing experiences. In particular, I want to express my gratitude to Mike Halvorson, who converted an offhand idea of mine into an exciting book concept. I greatly appreciate his continued enthusiasm, support, and positive feedback.

It was also a pleasure working with Jack Litewka, who handled my manuscript with insight and sensitivity. He did a great job of improving the syntax and style while preserving the semantic content.

I need to thank Jim Fuchs for improving the semantic content. He not only enhanced the technical accuracy and the consistency of the terminology but also discovered more than one "unexpected feature" in the game programs.

Additionally, I want to thank Eric Stroo, who provided constructive and encouraging comments during the early stages of the project, and all the other people at Microsoft Press who worked on the book.

Finally, I would like to compliment the developers of Visual Basic for creating a truly innovative and elegant development system. The ease of programming with Visual Basic allowed me to continually keep ahead of schedule.

INTRODUCTION

The success of Microsoft Windows has brought with it a resurgence of interest in computer games. One reason for the popularity of Windows games is undoubtedly the superb device-independent graphics that this environment supports. Perhaps another reason is that the windowed screen permits the user to unobtrusively run a small game alongside a spreadsheet or other serious application, making it available for an instant break. Probably the most important underlying reason for the popularity of Windows is that Windows is simply more *fun* than previous PC environments. Witness the recent abundance of light-hearted Windows software, such as cartoon calendars, flying-toaster screen savers, and gaudy wallpaper backgrounds.

Although Windows games have always been fun for the player, they have not always been much fun for the programmer. The complex interface and slow development cycle of the original software tools made graphics programming difficult and inhibited creativity and experimentation. With Visual Basic, however, the interactive tools, the simplicity of the source code, and the almost instantaneous development cycle can make programming games as much fun as playing them.

This book–disk package is written for several audiences:

- For the computer-game enthusiast, it provides 12 new ready-to-run Windows games and fractals.

- For the aspiring or experienced game developer, it explains many general techniques and principles for writing effective computer-game programs.

- For the Visual Basic programmer, it offers a wealth of techniques that are not covered in the manuals or in introductory books, and it serves as an ideal next step after learning the fundamentals.

What the Package Provides

The book–disk package for *Visual Basic—Game Programming for Windows* contains the following components.

■ The disk contains 12 ready-to-run Windows games and fractals, complete with online help. These games are designed to entertain, challenge, and amuse. The collection includes popular games with an original twist (such as Peg Solitaire, Fractal Puzzle, and TriPack), original games (such as Grid War), and several classic games you might not have seen before (such as Ludo, Ringo, and Boule).

■ The disk provides all the source files you need to create each of the games in Visual Basic, so you can modify and enhance the games or use the code as the starting point for writing your own games. (Note: Long program lines in this book have been wrapped to the next line and indented one space.)

■ For each game, the book provides historical notes (where applicable) and interesting facts, complete playing instructions, and a section on strategy to help you become a better player. For each game, the book also presents the complete source code, detailed explanations on how the game is programmed, and suggestions for enhancements that you might want to write yourself.

What You Need

To run the games or to work with the game source code in Visual Basic, you need two hardware items in addition to the minimal requirements for running Microsoft Windows version 3.0: You must have a machine capable of running Windows in standard or enhanced mode, and you must have a mouse, trackball, or other cursor-control device. Also a 386-based computer and an EGA or better color monitor is strongly recommended.

The software requirements are simple: You must have Microsoft Windows version 3.0 or later and Visual Basic version 1.0 or later. If you would like to create or edit the online help, you will need the Microsoft Help Compiler.

To understand the programming techniques presented in this book, you do not need any books or materials in addition to the manuals supplied with Visual Basic. Before reading the programming sections in this book, however, you should become familiar with the programming fundamentals by reading through either the Visual Basic *Programmer's Guide* or the online tutorial included with the Visual Basic product.

An Overview of the Book

This overview helps you to get the most out of the information presented in the book.

Part I: The Basics

Chapters 1 and 2 focus on introductory material and general techniques that will be used throughout the book. The remaining chapters in the book (Chapters 3 through 13) each present a single computer game.

Part II: Puzzles

Chapters 3 through 7 present computer games and fractals—Peg Solitaire, Deduce, Word Squares, Queens, and Fractal Puzzle and Fractal Generator—that challenge you to solve a variety of puzzles.

The programs for these games introduce the basic techniques for creating game graphics and demonstrate several of the easiest methods for moving playing pieces with the mouse.

Part III: Strategic Board Games

Chapters 8, 9, and 10 present games of strategy—Tic Tac Toe, Ludo, and Ringo. These games involve skill as well as luck. Your opponent is the computer.

The programs in this part of the book employ more sophisticated drawing techniques than the games in previous parts and use more advanced methods for moving objects with the mouse. They also include routines for calculating optimal game moves and for hit-testing within nonrectangular areas (that is, for determining the playing area containing the mouse pointer).

Part IV: Action and Gambling Games

The action games presented in Chapters 11 and 12—TriPack and Grid War—challenge your sense of timing and spatial relationships, and the gambling game presented in Chapter 13—Boule—tests your luck.

The programs for these games use the most advanced animation techniques in the book. You will learn how to move objects automatically, in response to timer events, and how to plot complex paths for these objects to follow.

How to Use the Book

After reading this Introduction and Chapters 1 and 2, you can read the remaining chapters selectively and in any order. You should, however, keep two things in mind:

- The chapters toward the end of the book tend to present more advanced programming techniques.

- A given programming technique is fully explained only when it is first used in a game; therefore, you might need to refer to a previous chapter to fully understand a technique used in a particular game.

The chapters devoted to games are designed so that you can easily locate the kind of information you want. Each chapter begins with general information and proceeds toward greater levels of detail. If you are interested only in playing the game, you can read the first few sections, which provide a brief history of the game, detailed playing instructions, and hints on effective strategy.

If you have a general interest in how the game is programmed, you can read the section on coding (for example, "Coding Peg Solitaire"), which briefly discusses the programming techniques used in the game and provides an overview of the flow of program control. If you want a detailed explanation and analysis of one or more specific areas of the program, you can read the appropriate sections following the overview.

Although all the source code for each game is listed in the book, you might also want to load the source code for the game you are studying into Visual Basic. This will allow you to directly examine and experiment with each of the features discussed in the text. (Information on loading the source code is given in Chapter 1.)

Finally, please note that all the Windows API functions that appear in the chapters also appear in the Appendix in alphabetic order. (The API functions are discussed in Chapter 2.) The Appendix makes it easy to locate and review the API functions whenever the need arises.

PART I

THE BASICS

CHAPTER ONE

GETTING STARTED

In this chapter, you will first learn how to install the companion disk and run the games, so you can begin playing as soon as possible. You will then learn how to use the source-code listings printed in the book and how to load and modify the source-code files provided on the companion disk.

Installing the Companion Disk

The companion disk packaged with this book contains all the games and game help files as well as all the source files needed to create the games in Visual Basic. Because the files on the disk are compressed, you must run the Install program to copy them to your hard disk.

To run the Install program, perform the following steps from within Windows:

1. Place the companion disk in a floppy-disk drive.

2. Activate the Windows Program Manager or the Windows File Manager.

3. Choose the Run command from the File menu. The Run dialog box appears.

4. Type the following into the Command Line text box: the letter of the floppy drive that contains the companion disk, a colon, a backslash (\), and the word *install*. For example, if the companion disk is in drive A, you would type

   ```
   a:\install
   ```

5. Click the OK button. (The Install program starts.)

6. Choose *one* or *both* of the Installation Options displayed in the Install program window. These options are:

   ■ Install the games and game help files.

   ■ Install the program source files.

7. By default, the Install program copies the files to the directory *C:\VBGAMES*. If you want to specify a different directory, enter the full directory path into the Target Directory text box. If the specified directory does not exist, the Install program creates it.

8. Click OK.

If you select *Install the games and game help files*, the Install program copies the executable (EXE) files and help (HLP) files for each game in the \VBGAMES directory. (If you specified a different directory name, substitute that name for *\VBGAMES* throughout this description.) The Install program also creates a new group in your Program Manager window titled "VB Games." This group contains an icon for each of the games, so you can easily run the programs.

If you select *Install the program source files*, the Install program copies the source files for each game to a separate subdirectory within the \VBGAMES directory. The following table lists the names of the executable and help files (in alphabetic order) for each game as well as the names of the subdirectories used to store the source files.

Game (Chapter)	Executable and Help Files (in \VBGAMES)	Source-File Directory
Boule (Chapter 13)	BL.EXE, BL.HLP	\VBGAMES\BL
Deduce (Chapter 4)	DD.EXE, DD.HLP	\VBGAMES\DD
Fractal Puzzle (Chapter 7)	FP.EXE, FP.HLP	\VBGAMES\FP
Fractal Generator (Chapter 7)	FRACTAL.EXE	\VBGAMES
Grid War (Chapter 12)	GW.EXE, GW.HLP	\VBGAMES\GW
Ludo (Chapter 9)	LD.EXE, LD.HLP	\VBGAMES\LD
Peg Solitaire (Chapter 3)	PS.EXE, PS.HLP	\VBGAMES\PS
Queens (Chapter 6)	QP.EXE, QP.HLP	\VBGAMES\QP
Ringo (Chapter 10)	RG.EXE, RG.HLP	\VBGAMES\RG
TriPack (Chapter 11)	TP.EXE, TP.HLP	\VBGAMES\TP
Tic Tac Toe (Chapter 8)	TT.EXE, TT.HLP	\VBGAMES\TT
Word Squares (Chapter 5)	WS.EXE, WS.HLP	\VBGAMES\WS

If you decide not to install one of the components (the games or the source files), you can run the Install program again at any time to install the missing component.

Playing the Games

After you run the Install program, you can start a game by simply double-clicking the game icon within the newly created "VB Games" group in your Program Manager window. Complete instructions for playing each game are included in the chapter that presents the game. The playing instructions are also available as online help. To access online help, either press F1 to see the help index or choose a specific topic from the Help menu. Online help also includes illustrations as well as information on using each menu command.

The Source Information in the Book

The coding section in each chapter (for example, "Coding Ludo") contains a complete set of source listings and figures for the game presented in that chapter. You could create the game by entering this information directly into Visual Basic (although it would certainly be much easier to load it from the source files provided on the companion disk, as described in the next section). The primary purpose for including this information is to provide a convenient printed reference you can use while reading about how the program is coded.

The source information for each game consists of of six parts:

- A labeled image of the main form at design time, giving the name of the form and the names of all controls assigned to the form.

- A table listing all the *nondefault* properties assigned to the main form and each of its controls. The table includes only those property settings assigned at design time, not those assigned at runtime through program statements. It also includes only those properties explicitly set by using the Visual Basic properties bar or by directly sizing or moving objects on the screen; it does not include property settings that Visual Basic automatically assigns. (For example, if you change the setting of the Height property, Visual Basic

5

adjusts the ScaleHeight property to the correct corresponding value; in this case, the table includes only the Height property.) Finally, notice that the property table also includes the form grid spacings (set through the Grid Settings command on the Edit menu), even though these values are not actually properties.

- A table describing the form's menu design. You create a menu by selecting the form and then opening the Menu Design Window dialog box. (Choose the Menu Design Window command from Visual Basic's Window menu.) For each menu item, the first column in the table gives the caption, which you enter into the Caption text box in the Menu Design Window dialog box; four dots preceding the caption indicate that the menu item is indented one level. The second column in the table gives the name of the menu item, which you enter into the CtlName text box of the Menu Design Window dialog box. The third column in the table indicates any *nondefault* settings assigned to the menu item. For example, the menu item might be assigned an accelerator key (through the Accelerator drop-down list box), it might be checked (by choosing the Checked option), or it might be disabled (by turning off the Enabled option).

- A labeled image of the ABOUT form, giving the name of the form and the names of all controls assigned to the form. (For information on creating this form, see the section titled "Displaying an About Dialog Box" in Chapter 2.)

- A table listing all the *nondefault* properties assigned to the ABOUT form and each of its controls. (This table is similar to the one showing nondefault properties assigned to the main form, described above.)

- The Visual Basic source code for the program. The source-code listing is divided into several parts: the global module (if present), the code for the main form, and the code for the ABOUT form. Within each of these parts, the code is listed in the same order in which it appears in the Visual Basic code window: the declarations, followed by the general procedures in alphabetic order, followed by the event procedures in alphabetic order.

Loading and Modifying the Source Files

Playing the games is only part of the fun and challenge provided by the programs in this book. After you have played a game for a while and have read through the chapter explaining how the game is programmed, you can begin adding features and enhancements: The last section in each chapter recommends enhancements you might make. For example, if you find a game too easy, you can make it more difficult.

Because the companion disk provides freestanding EXE files for all the games, you do not need to load a game into Visual Basic merely to play it. However, if you want to examine a game's source code, make changes to the game, or add enhancements, you must first load the source files.

If you have not yet installed the source files on your hard disk, follow the installation instructions provided earlier in this chapter. To load the source files for a particular game, choose the Open Project command from Visual Basic's File menu, and then select the name of the project file for that game. The project file is named using the two-letter abbreviation for the game, followed by the MAK filename extension. The name of the directory containing the source files—including the project file—for each game is provided in the table on page 4.

For example, to load the source files for the Peg Solitaire game, you would specify the file

```
C:\VBGAMES\PS\PS.MAK
```

assuming that you have installed the disk files in the \VBGAMES directory on drive C. When you open a project file, Visual Basic loads all the source files that constitute the program. After the source files are loaded, you can examine or modify any source file by choosing that file in the Project window.

The following table briefly describes the source files that are provided on the companion disk.

Source File	Purpose
GLOBAL??.BAS (GLOBALBL.BAS, GLOBALFP.BAS, and so on)	Global modules, containing global type definitions and variable declarations.
??.FRM (BL.FRM, DD.FRM, and so on)	The files that define the main forms and the controls contained in them.

(continued)

continued

Source File	Purpose
??ABOUT.FRM (BLABOUT.FRM, DDABOUT.FRM, and so on)	The files that define the About dialog boxes and the controls contained in them.
??.MAK (BL.MAK, DD.MAK, and so on)	The project files for the programs. A project file stores a list of the source files that constitute a program.
*.BMP (for example, BL.BMP and TILE.BMP)	Bitmap graphics files, created in Windows Paintbrush. The graphics in these files are assigned to the Picture property of forms and picture boxes.
*.ICO (for example, BL.ICO, DD.ICO, and DD1.ICO)	Icon graphics files. The graphics in these file are assigned to the Picture property of picture boxes (like the BMP files) or to the Icon property of forms (to create the program icons).

Remember: Unlike the other source files, the BMP and ICO graphics files are *not* loaded into Visual Basic when you open the project file because the data in these files has already been incorporated within the form (that is, the graphics data is stored within the FRM file). These files are provided on the disk in case you want to edit an image and then replace the original graphics in the form. You can edit a BMP file using Windows Paintbrush, and you can edit an ICO file using the Icon Works program included with Visual Basic or any other icon-designing utility. (Complete instructions for incorporating graphics into a program are given in the chapters that follow.)

CHAPTER TWO

GENERAL PROGRAMMING TECHNIQUES

Three fundamental programming techniques presented in this chapter are used in all the game programs presented in this book. The three techniques allow you to

- Display an About dialog box from a Visual Basic program

- Extend Visual Basic by calling Windows API functions

- Create an online help system

Displaying an About Dialog Box

An About dialog box is a standard feature of a Windows program. It can be used to display the name of the author of the program, a copyright notice, the program version and serial number, and other information. Each of the game programs presented in this book displays a simple About dialog box when the user chooses the About command from the game's Help menu.

The About dialog box includes the name of the game, the author's name, the program icon, and an OK button that the user clicks to close the dialog box. An example of an About dialog box is shown in Figure 2-1 (taken from the Peg Solitaire game, presented in Chapter 3).

Figure 2-1.
The About dialog box for the Peg Solitaire game.

The first step in adding an About dialog box to a program is to choose the New Form command from Visual Basic's File menu. When you do so, Visual Basic creates a new form, assigning it a default name. You can then add controls, set form and control properties, and attach code using the same methods that you use to define the main form. To conform to Windows programming conventions, however, a form used as a dialog box should contain the property settings listed in the following table.

Property	Setting
BorderStyle	3 - Fixed Double
ControlBox	True
Icon	(None)
MaxButton	False
MinButton	False
WindowState	0 - Normal

The full list of properties and controls assigned to the About dialog box for each game is given in the chapter describing the game.

Loading the About Dialog Box

In all the programs presented in this book, the About menu item is named MenuAbout (the name is assigned in the Menu Design Window dialog box), and the ABOUT form is named FormAbout. Accordingly, whenever the user chooses the About menu command at runtime, control passes to the *MenuAbout_Click* event procedure, which is part of the code attached to the main form. This procedure then displays the dialog box using the *Show* method, as follows:

```
Sub MenuAbout_Click ()
    FormAbout.Show 1
End Sub
```

T I P

You should normally create a dialog box *after* defining the main form. If you create the dialog box first, you will have to choose the Set Startup Form command from the Run menu and then select the main form so that Visual Basic will load this form first.

The *1* parameter value passed to *Show* indicates that the dialog box is to be modal, meaning that once the dialog box has been displayed, the user cannot perform any actions in the program until clicking the dialog box's OK button to close the dialog box. According to convention, About dialog boxes are modal.

Unloading the About Dialog Box

When the user clicks the OK button within the About dialog box, program control passes to the *Command1_Click* event procedure, which is attached to the dialog box form. This procedure closes the dialog box by calling the *Unload* method, as follows:

```
Sub Command1_Click ()
    Unload FormAbout
End Sub
```

Calling Windows API Functions

You can greatly extend the capabilities of Visual Basic by directly calling the functions provided by the underlying Windows system. These functions are collectively termed the Windows Application Programming Interface, or API.

Because the API functions are not an integral part of Visual Basic, you must explicitly declare an API function before calling it. The declaration can be placed within the (declarations) section of the module from which it is called, or it can be placed within the global module (in which case, you can call the function from any form or module in the program). After you have declared the function, you can call it in the same manner as you would a native Visual Basic function or statement or a procedure that you have written.

All the games presented in this book call one or more API functions. The first time a function is used, the chapter provides a figure that lists the function declaration, describes each of the parameters, and explains how to use the function. For example, the *BitBlt* API function is first used in Chapter 7 (in the Fractal Puzzle game); accordingly, Chapter 7 provides a figure explaining this function. You can then refer back to this figure whenever you encounter *BitBlt* in later chapters. Or, for easy reference, you can turn to the Appendix, where all the API functions used in this book are grouped in alphabetic order.

Note: The Visual Basic manuals do not provide the declarations for the API functions, nor do they explain the use of these functions. However, if you want to use API functions not described in this book, you can obtain the necessary information by purchasing *Microsoft Windows Programmer's Reference*. (*Microsoft Visual Basic Professional Toolkit* also contains API reference material.)

The API function descriptions in this book differ from the function documentation you might see elsewhere. One difference is that the descriptions have been simplified and focus on the features that are most useful for Visual Basic programming. Also, some of the API functions that actually return values are declared as Visual Basic Sub procedures (which do not provide return values); this is done to simplify the declaration and the function call when the return value is not used. (An example is the API function *SetCapture*.) Finally, the functions are described using Visual Basic terminology rather than standard Windows programming terminology; for example, the descriptions use the term "form" rather than "window" and the term "event" rather than "message."

Creating an Online Help System

All the games in this book provide online help containing complete instructions for playing the game and using the program commands. These help systems make use of the help utility provided by Windows.

Developing an online help system using the Windows help facility requires two main steps. First, you must create a HLP file that contains the help information you want to display; this file is distributed with your program. Second, you must add code to your program to call the Windows help facility.

Creating a HLP File

The companion disk included with this book provides ready-to-use HLP files for all the games. Creating your own HLP files, however, requires several tools that are not included with the Visual Basic package. You must have the Windows Help Compiler; and you must have a word processor, such as Microsoft Word for Windows, that is capable of producing documents in "rich text format" (RTF).

Note: The Help Compiler is available as a separate product from Microsoft Corporation. In addition, *Microsoft Visual Basic Professional Toolkit* includes the Windows 3.0 Help Compiler and a kit for creating setup programs.

The main steps for producing a HLP file are as follows:

1. Using a word processor, create a document containing the help text and graphics. By applying appropriate formatting codes, you can establish hypertext links between topics and link words to definitions. By adding footnotes, you can assign identifiers to topics (so that they can be referenced from your program) and specify keywords to be used by Help's Search command.

2. Save the document in RTF format.

3. Create a help project file. This is a standard text file but with an HPJ extension. It tells the Help Compiler the name(s) of the RTF document(s) containing the help text. (Note: You can combine more than one document in a single help system.) The project file also provides other information needed to properly compile the help file.

4. Run the Help Compiler, specifying the name of the help project file. If the compile is successful, the Help Compiler creates the HLP file. For example, the following command would run the compiler and create the file PS.HLP:

```
HC PS.HPJ
```

Coding the Help System

At runtime, the program displays the help information contained in the HLP file by calling the Windows help utility. The help utility is accessed through a single Windows API function, *WinHelp*, which is described in Figure 2-2 on the following page.

Windows API Function: *WinHelp*

Purpose Calls the Windows help facility either to display a help topic or to remove the help window when the program has finished displaying help.

Declaration
```
Declare Sub WinHelp Lib "USER" (ByVal hWnd As Integer,
 ByVal lpHelpFile As String, ByVal wCommand As Integer,
 ByVal dwData As Long)
```

Parameter	Description
hWnd	The hWnd property of the main form.
lpHelpFile	A string containing the name of the HLP file with the help information you want to display. The string must include the full path if the file is neither in the current directory nor in the Windows directory.
wCommand	A code indicating the action wanted. The following are among the values you can pass:

Constant	Value	Meaning
HELP_CONTEXT	1	Display the topic indicated by the *dwData* parameter.
HELP_HELPONHELP	4	Display help on using the help system.
HELP_INDEX	3	Display the help index.
HELP_QUIT	2	Remove the help window.

dwData	If the *wCommand* parameter is set to HELP_CONTEXT, this parameter supplies the identifier of the specific help topic you want to see. (Identifiers are assigned to each help topic when the HLP file is created.) If *wCommand* is not set to HELP_CONTEXT, you should assign *0* to this parameter.

Figure 2-2.
The WinHelp *Windows API function.*

14

All the programs in this book include a uniform help menu, as shown in Figure 2-3.

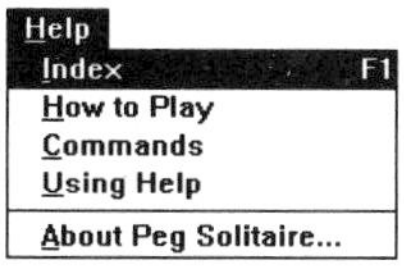

Figure 2-3.
The Help menu.

When the player chooses a command other than the About command from the Help menu, the event procedure for the command calls *WinHelp* to display the appropriate help topic.

F Y I

The event procedure that processes a specific menu command is named according to the identifier that was entered into the CtlName text box in the Menu Design Window dialog box.

Specifically, when the user chooses the Index command or presses the F1 key (which is the accelerator keystroke assigned to this menu item), the *MenuIndex_Click* event procedure calls *WinHelp* as follows:

```
WinHelp hWnd, HELP_FILE, HELP_INDEX, 0
```

The first parameter, *hWnd*, supplies the handle of the main form. The second parameter, *HELP_FILE*, provides the name of the help file. For example, in the Peg Solitaire program, the constant HELP_FILE is defined as follows:

```
Const HELP_FILE = "PS.HLP"
```

T I P

You do not need to specify the full path of the help file if it is contained in the current directory when the program is run or if it is in the Windows directory.

The value passed as the third parameter, *HELP_INDEX,* causes the help utility to display the index; you identify the index topic when you create the help file.

Similarly, when the user chooses the Using Help command, the *MenuUsingHelp_Click* event procedure calls *WinHelp* to display the standard information (supplied by the help utility itself) about using the help system:

```
WinHelp hWnd, HELP_FILE, HELP_HELPONHELP, 0
```

When the user chooses the How To Play command, the *Menu-HowTo_Click* event procedure calls *WinHelp*:

```
WinHelp hWnd, HELP_FILE, HELP_CONTEXT, HelpHowToPlay
```

The value passed as the third parameter, *HELP_CONTEXT,* causes the help facility to display a topic other than one of the standard help topics. (The index and the information about using help are standard help topics.) In this case, the fourth parameter, *HelpHowToPlay,* supplies the identifier (which you assigned when you created the help file) of the topic you want.

When the user chooses the Commands menu command, the *MenuCommands_Click* event procedure calls *WinHelp* in the same fashion:

```
WinHelp hWnd, HELP_FILE, HELP_CONTEXT, HELP_COMMANDS
```

Finally, before the program exits, it must call *WinHelp* one last time to remove the help window. If the program fails to do this, the help window will be left on the screen until the user manually removes it. Accordingly, when the user chooses the Exit command from the File menu, the *MenuExit_Click* event procedure calls *WinHelp* immediately before terminating the program:

```
Sub MenuExit_Click ()
    WinHelp hWnd, HELP_FILE, HELP_QUIT, 0
    End
End Sub
```

Passing the value *HELP_QUIT* as the third parameter causes the help system to remove the help window. Actually, the window is removed after *all* applications using the help utility have passed HELP_QUIT to *WinHelp.*

If the user terminates the program through the control-menu box (the box in the upper left corner of the window), the *Form_Unload* procedure also calls *WinHelp* to remove the help window:

```
Sub Form_Unload (Cancel As Integer)
    WinHelp hWnd, HELP_FILE, HELP_QUIT, 0
End Sub
```

Note: If the help window is not currently displayed, the call to *WinHelp* is unnecessary, but harmless.

PART II

PUZZLES

C H A P T E R   T H R E E

PEG SOLITAIRE

The game Peg Solitaire is a computer version of an eighteenth-century game. You will learn a little about the history of the traditional game and how to play this new version of it. You will also learn how the game is coded. Among the Visual Basic programming techniques introduced in this chapter, two are especially important: creating graphics for a game using bitmaps and picture boxes, and using Visual Basic's drag-and-drop feature to generate simple animation.

About Peg Solitaire

Peg solitaire, sometimes known as board solitaire, is a well-known game that takes many forms. It is played with a board containing an array of holes, some of which are initially filled with pegs (or marbles). The objective of the game is to remove pegs and leave a single peg—or a specific pattern of pegs—remaining on the board. A peg is removed when one peg "jumps" over another peg and into an empty hole on the other side.

The game originated in France, purportedly the invention of a prisoner in the Bastille. It later became popular in England and other parts of the world.

The conventional French board is octagonal and contains 37 holes, as shown in Figure 3-1; it is played with pegs. The standard English board is round and contains 33 indentations; it is played with marbles that fit into the indentations.

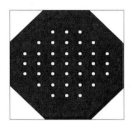

Figure 3-1.
The French peg solitaire board.

The basic game begins with all the holes filled except for one; the player chooses the initial empty hole. The player then attempts to remove all the pegs except for a single predesignated peg, by jumping pegs in a horizontal or vertical direction.

The traditional game can be varied by beginning with a specific pattern of pegs (such as a cross) rather than with a full board. It can also be varied by attempting to remove pegs so that a chosen pattern of pegs—rather than a single peg—remains on the board.

Playing Peg Solitaire

The Peg Solitaire program presented in this chapter is closest to the French (37-peg) version of the game. It is played with only 17 pegs, however, and the holes are arranged along diagonal and vertical lines rather than in horizontal rows.

Chapter 1 explains how to install and run the games presented in this book, all of which are included on the companion disk. Peg Solitaire is contained in the file PS.EXE. When you run this file, the program starts a game. You can start a new game at any time (even before the current game is completed) by choosing the New Game command from the Game menu. The program displays the opening window shown in Figure 3-2.

Figure 3-2.
Peg Solitaire at the beginning of a game.

At the beginning of a game, all the holes are filled with pegs. The objective of the game is to remove all pegs except for the one at the top center of the board.

To begin play, you first click on a peg to remove it from the board. You can remove any peg. (Varying your choice from game to game will alter the strategy required to win the game and will add variety to your playing.)

After the first peg, you remove pegs by jumping over them. To do this, use the mouse click-and-drag procedure to remove a peg from its hole, have it "jump" over an adjacent peg, and then drop the peg into the empty hole on the far side of the peg you want to remove. When you do this, the computer eliminates the jumped peg. If you drop a peg at an invalid position, the program returns the peg to its hole.

Note: You can click and drag using either mouse button.

When no more moves are possible, the computer ends the game and displays the number of pegs remaining. The program also rates your performance: If a single peg remains at the top center position, as shown in Figure 3-3, you see the message "genius!" displayed in the game's message area. A single peg remaining at another position is rated as "outstanding!" Other final arrangements are rated with diminishing degrees of acclaim.

Figure 3-3.
A winning final position in a game of Peg Solitaire.

Strategy and Hints

You will probably develop your own strategy for playing Peg Solitaire. If you are strongly left-brained, you might be able to choose an optimal move by planning two or three moves ahead. If you are strongly right-brained, you might do better by playing rather quickly and observing the pattern of the pegs. In general, try to avoid leaving isolated pegs. One approach is to work from one edge toward the opposite edge, without leaving any pegs behind.

Coding Peg Solitaire

The source code for the Peg Solitaire program is contained in the files listed in the following table.

File	Purpose
GLOBALPS.BAS	Contains a global type definition (RECT)
PS.FRM	Defines the main form, FormMain, and the controls it contains
PSABOUT.FRM	Defines the ABOUT form, FormAbout, and the controls it contains
PS.MAK	Contains the Peg Solitaire project file

All these files are included on the companion disk provided with this book. Chapter 1 explains how to install the files on your hard disk and how to load them into Visual Basic if you want to examine or modify them.

Figures 3-4 through 3-8 provide all the information needed to create the Peg Solitaire program. Figure 3-4 illustrates the main form (FormMain, defined in the file PS.FRM) as it appears at design time. Figure 3-5 lists the form and control property settings defined in PS.FRM. Figure 3-6 lists all the menu items assigned to the PS.FRM form through Visual Basic's Menu Design Window dialog box. Figure 3-7 illustrates the ABOUT form (FormAbout, defined in the file PSABOUT.FRM) as it appears at design time, and Figure 3-8 lists the properties assigned to PSABOUT.FRM. There is no menu on this form.

Finally, Figure 3-9 lists all the source code in PS.FRM and PSABOUT.FRM.

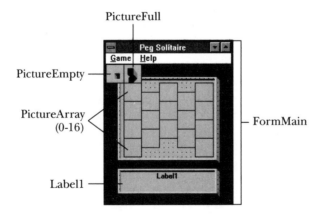
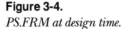

Figure 3-4.
PS.FRM at design time.

Object Name	Object Type	Property	Setting
FormMain	Form	BackColor	&H00800000 [dark blue]
		BorderStyle	1 - Fixed Single
		Caption	Peg Solitaire
		FormName	FormMain
		Grid Height	8 [pixels]
		Grid Width	8 [pixels]
		Height	4335 [twips]
		Icon	(Icon) [PS.ICO]
		Left	990 [twips]
		MaxButton	False
		Picture	(Bitmap) [PS.BMP]
		ScaleMode	3 - Pixel
		Top	1080 [twips]
		Width	3480 [twips]
Label1	Label	Alignment	2 - Center
		BackColor	&H0000FFFF& [yellow]
		BorderStyle	0 - None
		ForeColor	&H00000000& [black]
		Height	34 [pixels]
		Left	27 [pixels]
		Top	187 [pixels]
		Width	168 [pixels]
PictureArray	Array of picture boxes	BackColor	&H0000FFFF& [yellow]
		CtlName	PictureArray
		Height	33 [pixels]
		Index	0 - 16
		Left	[varies]
		Top	[varies]
		Width	33 [pixels]

Figure 3-5. *(continued)*

PS.FRM form and control properties.

Figure 3-5 *continued*

Object Name	Object Type	Property	Setting
PictureEmpty	Picture box	CtlName	PictureEmpty
		Height	33 [pixels]
		Left	0 [pixels]
		Picture	(Icon) [PS1.ICO]
		Top	0 [pixels]
		Visible	False
		Width	33 [pixels]
PictureFull	Picture box	CtlName	PictureFull
		DragIcon	(Icon) [PS3.ICO]
		Height	33 [pixels]
		Left	32 [pixels]
		Picture	(Icon) [PS2.ICO]
		Top	0 [pixels]
		Visible	False
		Width	33 [pixels]

Indentation/Caption	Control Name	Other Features
&Game	MenuGame	
....&New Game	MenuNew	
....-	MenuSep1	
....E&xit	MenuExit	
&Help	MenuHelp	
....&Index	MenuIndex	Accelerator = F1
....&How to Play	MenuHowTo	
....&Commands	MenuCommands	
....&Using Help	MenuUsingHelp	
....-	MenuSep2	
....&About Peg Solitaire...	MenuAbout	

Figure 3-6.
PS.FRM menu design.

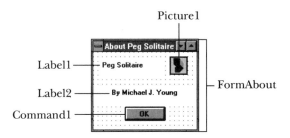

Figure 3-7.
PSABOUT.FRM at design time.

Object Name	Object Type	Property	Setting
Command1	Command button	Caption	OK
		Default	True
		Height	375 [twips]
		Left	840 [twips]
		Top	1440 [twips]
		Width	1095 [twips]
FormAbout	Form	BorderStyle	3 - Fixed Double
		Caption	About Peg Solitaire
		FormName	FormAbout
		Grid Height	120 [twips]
		Grid Width	120 [twips]
		Height	2445 [twips]
		Left	1140 [twips]
		MaxButton	False
		MinButton	False
		Top	1440 [twips]
		Width	2880 [twips]
Label1	Label	Caption	Peg Solitaire
		Height	375 [twips]
		Left	240 [twips]
		Top	240 [twips]
		Width	1575 [twips]

Figure 3-8.   *(continued)*
PSABOUT.FRM form and control properties.

Figure 3-8 *continued*

Object Name	Object Type	Property	Setting
Label2	Label	Alignment	2 - Center
		Caption	By Michael J. Young
		Height	375 [twips]
		Left	0 [twips]
		Top	960 [twips]
		Width	2745 [twips]
Picture1	Picture box	AutoSize	True
		BorderStyle	0 - None
		Height	480 [twips]
		Left	2040 [twips]
		Picture	(Icon) [PS.ICO]
		Top	120 [twips]
		Width	480 [twips]

GLOBALPS.BAS code

```
Type RECT
    Left As Integer
    Top As Integer
    Right As Integer
    Bottom As Interger
End Type
```

PS.FRM code

```
'Help Section:
Const HELP_FILE = "PS.HLP"
'WinHelp wCommand values:
Const HELP_CONTEXT = &H1
Const HELP_HELPONHELP = &H4
Const HELP_INDEX = &H3
Const HELP_QUIT = &H2
```

Figure 3-9.   *(continued)*

Source code for the Peg Solitaire program. (Notice that long program lines are wrapped to the next line and indented one space.)

Figure 3-9 *continued*

```
'WinHelp dwData values (help topics):
Const HELP_HOWTOPLAY = 10&
Const HELP_COMMANDS = 20&
'Windows help API:
Declare Sub WinHelp Lib "USER" (ByVal hWnd As Integer, ByVal
  lpHelpFile As String, ByVal wCommand As Integer, ByVal dwData
  As Long)

Const CLIENTBOTTOM = 242
Const CLIENTRIGHT = 223

Dim DragSource As Integer
Dim GameStarted As Integer
Dim I As Integer

Const WS_CAPTION = &HC00000
Const WS_THICKFRAME = &H40000
Declare Sub AdjustWindowRect Lib "USER" (lpRect As RECT, ByVal
  dwStyle&, ByVal bMenu%)

Const LOGPIXELSX = 88
Const LOGPIXELSY = 90
Declare Function GetDeviceCaps Lib "GDI" (ByVal hDC%, ByVal
  Index%) As Integer

Sub InitNewGame ()
    For I = 0 To 16
        PictureArray(I).Picture = PictureFull.Picture
    Next I
    Label1.Caption = "click to remove first peg..."
    GameStarted = 0
End Sub

Function JumpOK (Idx1 As Integer, Idx2 As Integer, Idx3 As
  Integer) As Integer
    If PictureArray(Idx1).Picture = PictureEmpty.Picture Then
        JumpOK = 0
    ElseIf PictureArray(Idx2).Picture = PictureEmpty.Picture
Then
        JumpOK = 0
    ElseIf PictureArray(Idx3).Picture = PictureFull.Picture
Then
        JumpOK = 0
```

(continued)

29

Figure 3-9 *continued*

```
    Else
        JumpOK = -1
    End If
End Function

Function MovePossible () As Integer
    If JumpOK(0, 5, 10) Or JumpOK(0, 3, 6) Then
        MovePossible = -1
    ElseIf JumpOK(1, 3, 5) Or JumpOK(1, 6, 11) Or JumpOK(1, 4,
7) Then
        MovePossible = -1
    ElseIf JumpOK(2, 4, 6) Or JumpOK(2, 7, 12) Then
        MovePossible = -1
    ElseIf JumpOK(3, 8, 13) Or JumpOK(3, 6, 9) Then
        MovePossible = -1
    ElseIf JumpOK(4, 6, 8) Or JumpOK(4, 9, 14) Then
        MovePossible = -1
    ElseIf JumpOK(5, 3, 1) Or JumpOK(5, 8, 11) Or JumpOK(5,
10, 15) Then
        MovePossible = -1
    ElseIf JumpOK(6, 3, 0) Or JumpOK(6, 8, 10) Or JumpOK(6,
4, 2) Or JumpOK(6, 9, 12) Then
        MovePossible = -1
    ElseIf JumpOK(7, 4, 1) Or JumpOK(7, 9, 11) Or JumpOK(7,
12, 16) Then
        MovePossible = -1
    ElseIf JumpOK(8, 6, 4) Or JumpOK(8, 11, 14) Then
        MovePossible = -1
    ElseIf JumpOK(9, 6, 3) Or JumpOK(9, 11, 13) Then
        MovePossible = -1
    ElseIf JumpOK(10, 5, 0) Or JumpOK(10, 8, 6) Then
        MovePossible = -1
    ElseIf JumpOK(11, 8, 5) Or JumpOK(11, 13, 15) Or JumpOK(11,
6, 1) Or JumpOK(11, 9, 7) Or JumpOK(11, 14, 16) Then
        MovePossible = -1
    ElseIf JumpOK(12, 9, 6) Or JumpOK(12, 7, 2) Then
        MovePossible = -1
    ElseIf JumpOK(13, 8, 3) Or JumpOK(13, 11, 9) Then
        MovePossible = -1
    ElseIf JumpOK(14, 11, 8) Or JumpOK(14, 9, 4) Then
        MovePossible = -1
    ElseIf JumpOK(15, 10, 5) Or JumpOK(15, 13, 11) Then
        MovePossible = -1
```

(continued)

Figure 3-9 *continued*

```
    ElseIf JumpOK(16, 14, 11) Or JumpOK(16, 12, 7) Then
        MovePossible = -1
    Else
        MovePossible = 0
    End If
End Function

Sub Form_DragDrop (Source As Control, X As Single,
 Y As Single)
    Source.Picture = PictureFull.Picture
    DragSource = -1
End Sub

Sub Form_Load ()
    Dim I As Integer
    Dim Rec As RECT

    Rec.Left = 0
    Rec.Top = 0
    Rec.Right = CLIENTRIGHT
    Rec.Bottom = CLIENTBOTTOM
    AdjustWindowRect Rec, WS_CAPTION, -1
    FormMain.Width = (Rec.Right - Rec.Left + 1) * (1440 /
GetDeviceCaps(hDC, LOGPIXELSX))
    FormMain.Height = (Rec.Bottom - Rec.Top + 1) * (1440 /
GetDeviceCaps(hDC, LOGPIXELSY))

    For I = 0 To 16
        PictureArray(I).Width = 33
        PictureArray(I).Height = 33
        PictureArray(I).BorderStyle = 0
        PictureArray(I).DragIcon = PictureFull.DragIcon
    Next I
    PictureArray(0).Left = 32:    PictureArray(0).Top = 32
    PictureArray(1).Left = 96:    PictureArray(1).Top = 32
    PictureArray(2).Left = 160:   PictureArray(2).Top = 32
    PictureArray(3).Left = 64:    PictureArray(3).Top = 48
    PictureArray(4).Left = 128:   PictureArray(4).Top = 48
    PictureArray(5).Left = 32:    PictureArray(5).Top = 64
    PictureArray(6).Left = 96:    PictureArray(6).Top = 64
    PictureArray(7).Left = 160:   PictureArray(7).Top = 64
    PictureArray(8).Left = 64:    PictureArray(8).Top = 80
    PictureArray(9).Left = 128:   PictureArray(9).Top = 80
```

(continued)

Figure 3-9 *continued*

```
    PictureArray(10).Left = 32:  PictureArray(10).Top = 96
    PictureArray(11).Left = 96:  PictureArray(11).Top = 96
    PictureArray(12).Left = 160: PictureArray(12).Top = 96
    PictureArray(13).Left = 64:  PictureArray(13).Top = 112
    PictureArray(14).Left = 128: PictureArray(14).Top = 112
    PictureArray(15).Left = 32:  PictureArray(15).Top = 128
    PictureArray(16).Left = 160: PictureArray(16).Top = 128
    Label1.Left = 27: Label1.Top = 187: Label1.Width = 168:
Label1.Height = 34

    DragSource = -1
    InitNewGame
End Sub

Sub Form_MouseMove (Button As Integer, Shift As Integer,
 X As Single, Y As Single)
    If DragSource < -1 Then
        PictureArray(DragSource).Picture = PictureFull.Picture
        DragSource = -1
    End If
End Sub

Sub Form_Unload (Cancel As Integer)
    WinHelp hWnd, HELP_FILE, HELP_QUIT, 0
End Sub

Sub Label1_DragDrop (Source As Control, X As Single,
 Y As Single)
    Source.Picture = PictureFull.Picture
    DragSource = -1
End Sub

Sub MenuAbout_Click ()
    FormAbout.Show 1
End Sub

Sub MenuCommands_Click ()
    WinHelp hWnd, HELP_FILE, HELP_CONTEXT, HELP_COMMANDS
End Sub

Sub MenuExit_Click ()
    WinHelp hWnd, HELP_FILE, HELP_QUIT, 0
    End
End Sub
```

(continued)

Figure 3-9 *continued*

```
Sub MenuHowTo_Click ()
    WinHelp hWnd, HELP_FILE, HELP_CONTEXT, HELP_HOWTOPLAY
End Sub

Sub MenuIndex_Click ()
    WinHelp hWnd, HELP_FILE, HELP_INDEX, 0
End Sub

Sub MenuNew_Click ()
    InitNewGame
End Sub

Sub MenuUsingHelp_Click ()
    WinHelp hWnd, HELP_FILE, HELP_HELPONHELP, 0
End Sub

Sub PictureArray_Click (Index As Integer)
    If Not GameStarted Then
        PictureArray(Index).Picture = PictureEmpty.Picture
        GameStarted = -1
        Label1.Caption = "game in progress"
    End If
End Sub

Sub PictureArray_DragDrop (Index As Integer, Source As
 Control, X As Single, Y As Single)
    Dim Cancel As Integer
    Dim Message As String
    Dim PegCount As Integer

    DragSource = -1
    If PictureArray(Index).Picture = PictureFull.Picture Then
        Source.Picture = PictureFull.Picture
        Exit Sub
    End If
    Select Case Index
        Case 0
            If Source.Index = 10 And PictureArray(5).Picture =
PictureFull.Picture Then
                PictureArray(5).Picture = PictureEmpty.Picture
                PictureArray(0).Picture = PictureFull.Picture
            ElseIf Source.Index = 6 And PictureArray(3).Picture
```

(continued)

Figure 3-9 *continued*

```
= PictureFull.Picture Then
            PictureArray(3).Picture = PictureEmpty.Picture
            PictureArray(0).Picture = PictureFull.Picture
        Else
            Source.Picture = PictureFull.Picture
            Cancel = -1
        End If
    Case 1
        If Source.Index = 5 And PictureArray(3).Picture =
PictureFull.Picture Then
            PictureArray(3).Picture = PictureEmpty.Picture
            PictureArray(1).Picture = PictureFull.Picture
        ElseIf Source.Index = 11 And PictureArray(6).Picture
= PictureFull.Picture Then
            PictureArray(6).Picture = PictureEmpty.Picture
            PictureArray(1).Picture = PictureFull.Picture
        ElseIf Source.Index = 7 And PictureArray(4).Picture
= PictureFull.Picture Then
            PictureArray(4).Picture = PictureEmpty.Picture
            PictureArray(1).Picture = PictureFull.Picture
        Else
            Source.Picture = PictureFull.Picture
            Cancel = -1
        End If
    Case 2
        If Source.Index = 6 And PictureArray(4).Picture =
PictureFull.Picture Then
            PictureArray(4).Picture = PictureEmpty.Picture
            PictureArray(2).Picture = PictureFull.Picture
        ElseIf Source.Index = 12 And PictureArray(7).Picture
= PictureFull.Picture Then
            PictureArray(7).Picture = PictureEmpty.Picture
            PictureArray(2).Picture = PictureFull.Picture
        Else
            Source.Picture = PictureFull.Picture
            Cancel = -1
        End If
    Case 3
        If Source.Index = 13 And PictureArray(8).Picture =
PictureFull.Picture Then
            PictureArray(8).Picture = PictureEmpty.Picture
            PictureArray(3).Picture = PictureFull.Picture
        ElseIf Source.Index = 9 And PictureArray(6).Picture
```

(continued)

Figure 3-9 *continued*

```
= PictureFull.Picture Then
                PictureArray(6).Picture = PictureEmpty.Picture
                PictureArray(3).Picture = PictureFull.Picture
        Else
                Source.Picture = PictureFull.Picture
                Cancel = -1
        End If
    Case 4
        If Source.Index = 8 And PictureArray(6).Picture =
PictureFull.Picture Then
                PictureArray(6).Picture = PictureEmpty.Picture
                PictureArray(4).Picture = PictureFull.Picture
        ElseIf Source.Index = 14 And PictureArray(9).Picture
= PictureFull.Picture Then
                PictureArray(9).Picture = PictureEmpty.Picture
                PictureArray(4).Picture = PictureFull.Picture
        Else
                Source.Picture = PictureFull.Picture
                Cancel = -1
        End If
    Case 5
        If Source.Index = 15 And PictureArray(10).Picture =
PictureFull.Picture Then
                PictureArray(10).Picture = PictureEmpty.Picture
                PictureArray(5).Picture = PictureFull.Picture
        ElseIf Source.Index = 11 And PictureArray(8).Picture
= PictureFull.Picture Then
                PictureArray(8).Picture = PictureEmpty.Picture
                PictureArray(5).Picture = PictureFull.Picture
        ElseIf Source.Index = 1 And PictureArray(3).Picture
= PictureFull.Picture Then
                PictureArray(3).Picture = PictureEmpty.Picture
                PictureArray(5).Picture = PictureFull.Picture
        Else
                Source.Picture = PictureFull.Picture
                Cancel = -1
        End If
    Case 6
        If Source.Index = 0 And PictureArray(3).Picture =
PictureFull.Picture Then
                PictureArray(3).Picture = PictureEmpty.Picture
                PictureArray(6).Picture = PictureFull.Picture
        ElseIf Source.Index = 10 And PictureArray(8).Picture
```

(continued)

Figure 3-9 *continued*

```
= PictureFull.Picture Then
                PictureArray(8).Picture = PictureEmpty.Picture
                PictureArray(6).Picture = PictureFull.Picture
            ElseIf Source.Index = 2 And PictureArray(4).Picture
= PictureFull.Picture Then
                PictureArray(4).Picture = PictureEmpty.Picture
                PictureArray(6).Picture = PictureFull.Picture
            ElseIf Source.Index = 12 And
PictureArray(9).Picture = PictureFull.Picture Then
                PictureArray(9).Picture = PictureEmpty.Picture
                PictureArray(6).Picture = PictureFull.Picture
            Else
                Source.Picture = PictureFull.Picture
                Cancel = -1
            End If
        Case 7
            If Source.Index = 1 And PictureArray(4).Picture =
PictureFull.Picture Then
                PictureArray(4).Picture = PictureEmpty.Picture
                PictureArray(7).Picture = PictureFull.Picture
            ElseIf Source.Index = 11 And PictureArray(9).Picture
= PictureFull.Picture Then
                PictureArray(9).Picture = PictureEmpty.Picture
                PictureArray(7).Picture = PictureFull.Picture
            ElseIf Source.Index = 16 And
PictureArray(12).Picture = PictureFull.Picture Then
                PictureArray(12).Picture = PictureEmpty.Picture
                PictureArray(7).Picture = PictureFull.Picture
            Else
                Source.Picture = PictureFull.Picture
                Cancel = -1
            End If
        Case 8
            If Source.Index = 4 And PictureArray(6).Picture =
PictureFull.Picture Then
                PictureArray(6).Picture = PictureEmpty.Picture
                PictureArray(8).Picture = PictureFull.Picture
            ElseIf Source.Index = 14 And
PictureArray(11).Picture = PictureFull.Picture Then
                PictureArray(11).Picture = PictureEmpty.Picture
                PictureArray(8).Picture = PictureFull.Picture
```

(continued)

Figure 3-9 *continued*

```
            Else
                Source.Picture = PictureFull.Picture
                Cancel = -1
            End If
        Case 9
            If Source.Index = 3 And PictureArray(6).Picture =
PictureFull.Picture Then
                PictureArray(6).Picture = PictureEmpty.Picture
                PictureArray(9).Picture = PictureFull.Picture
            ElseIf Source.Index = 13 And
PictureArray(11).Picture = PictureFull.Picture Then
                PictureArray(11).Picture = PictureEmpty.Picture
                PictureArray(9).Picture = PictureFull.Picture
            Else
                Source.Picture = PictureFull.Picture
                Cancel = -1
            End If
        Case 10
            If Source.Index = 0 And PictureArray(5).Picture =
PictureFull.Picture Then
                PictureArray(5).Picture = PictureEmpty.Picture
                PictureArray(10).Picture = PictureFull.Picture
            ElseIf Source.Index = 6 And PictureArray(8).Picture
= PictureFull.Picture Then
                PictureArray(8).Picture = PictureEmpty.Picture
                PictureArray(10).Picture = PictureFull.Picture
            Else
                Source.Picture = PictureFull.Picture
                Cancel = -1
            End If
        Case 11
            If Source.Index = 5 And PictureArray(8).Picture =
PictureFull.Picture Then
                PictureArray(8).Picture = PictureEmpty.Picture
                PictureArray(11).Picture = PictureFull.Picture
            ElseIf Source.Index = 15 And
PictureArray(13).Picture = PictureFull.Picture Then
                PictureArray(13).Picture = PictureEmpty.Picture
                PictureArray(11).Picture = PictureFull.Picture
            ElseIf Source.Index = 1 And
PictureArray(6).Picture = PictureFull.Picture Then
                PictureArray(6).Picture = PictureEmpty.Picture
                PictureArray(11).Picture = PictureFull.Picture
            ElseIf Source.Index = 7 And
```

(continued)

Figure 3-9 *continued*

```
PictureArray(9).Picture = PictureFull.Picture Then
            PictureArray(9).Picture = PictureEmpty.Picture
            PictureArray(11).Picture = PictureFull.Picture
        ElseIf Source.Index = 16 And
PictureArray(14).Picture = PictureFull.Picture Then
            PictureArray(14).Picture = PictureEmpty.Picture
            PictureArray(11).Picture = PictureFull.Picture
        Else
            Source.Picture = PictureFull.Picture
            Cancel = -1
        End If
    Case 12
        If Source.Index = 6 And PictureArray(9).Picture =
PictureFull.Picture Then
            PictureArray(9).Picture = PictureEmpty.Picture
            PictureArray(12).Picture = PictureFull.Picture
        ElseIf Source.Index = 2 And PictureArray(7).Picture
= PictureFull.Picture Then
            PictureArray(7).Picture = PictureEmpty.Picture
            PictureArray(12).Picture = PictureFull.Picture
        Else
            Source.Picture = PictureFull.Picture
            Cancel = -1
        End If
    Case 13
        If Source.Index = 3 And PictureArray(8).Picture =
PictureFull.Picture Then
            PictureArray(8).Picture = PictureEmpty.Picture
            PictureArray(13).Picture = PictureFull.Picture
        ElseIf Source.Index = 9 And PictureArray(11).Picture
= PictureFull.Picture Then
            PictureArray(11).Picture = PictureEmpty.Picture
            PictureArray(13).Picture = PictureFull.Picture
        Else
            Source.Picture = PictureFull.Picture
            Cancel = -1
        End If
    Case 14
        If Source.Index = 8 And PictureArray(11).Picture =
PictureFull.Picture Then
            PictureArray(11).Picture = PictureEmpty.Picture
            PictureArray(14).Picture = PictureFull.Picture
        ElseIf Source.Index = 4 And PictureArray(9).Picture
```

(continued)

Figure 3-9 *continued*

```
= PictureFull.Picture Then
            PictureArray(9).Picture = PictureEmpty.Picture
            PictureArray(14).Picture = PictureFull.Picture
        Else
            Source.Picture = PictureFull.Picture
            Cancel = -1
        End If
    Case 15
        If Source.Index = 5 And PictureArray(10).Picture =
PictureFull.Picture Then
            PictureArray(10).Picture = PictureEmpty.Picture
            PictureArray(15).Picture = PictureFull.Picture
        ElseIf Source.Index = 11 And
PictureArray(13).Picture = PictureFull.Picture Then
            PictureArray(13).Picture = PictureEmpty.Picture
            PictureArray(15).Picture = PictureFull.Picture
        Else
            Source.Picture = PictureFull.Picture
            Cancel = -1
        End If
    Case 16
        If Source.Index = 11 And PictureArray(14).Picture =
PictureFull.Picture Then
            PictureArray(14).Picture = PictureEmpty.Picture
            PictureArray(16).Picture = PictureFull.Picture
        ElseIf Source.Index = 7 And PictureArray(12).Picture
= PictureFull.Picture Then
            PictureArray(12).Picture = PictureEmpty.Picture
            PictureArray(16).Picture = PictureFull.Picture
        Else
            Source.Picture = PictureFull.Picture
            Cancel = -1
        End If
End Select

If Cancel Then Exit Sub

If Not MovePossible() Then
    Beep
    For I = 0 To 16
        If PictureArray(I).Picture = PictureFull.Picture
Then
            PegCount = PegCount + 1
        End If
```

(continued)

Figure 3-9 *continued*

```
        Next I
        Select Case PegCount
            Case 1
                If PictureArray(1).Picture = PictureFull.Picture
Then
                    Message = "genius!"
                Else
                    Message = "outstanding!"
                End If
            Case 2
                Message = "very good!"
            Case 3
                Message = "good!"
            Case 4
                Message = "not bad!"
            Case Else
                Message = "try again!"
        End Select
        If PegCount = 1 Then
            Label1.Caption = "game over! " + Chr$(13) + Chr$(10)
+ " 1 Peg Left:  " + Message
        Else
            Label1.Caption = "game over! " + Chr$(13) + Chr$(10)
+ Str$(PegCount) + " Pegs Left:  " + Message
        End If
    End If
End Sub

Sub PictureArray_MouseDown (Index As Integer, Button As Integer,
Shift As Integer, X As Single, Y As Single)
    If GameStarted And PictureArray(Index).Picture =
PictureFull.Picture Then
        PictureArray(Index).Picture = PictureEmpty.Picture
        DragSource = Index
        PictureArray(Index).Drag 1
    End If
End Sub
```

PSABOUT.FRM code

```
Sub Command1_Click ()
    Unload FormAbout
End Sub
```

Programming Techniques

The background drawing for the Peg Solitaire game was created in Microsoft Paintbrush, which is included with Microsoft Windows. The image was saved in a file, which was then loaded into the form at design time. This technique is used in most of the games in this book and allows you to create precise, detailed drawings that are easy to modify.

Each of the Peg Solitaire playing objects (either a peg or an empty hole) was created by assigning an icon to a picture box. The icons were designed in the Icon Works program that is supplied with Visual Basic. Using a separate picture box for each playing object makes it simple to determine the location of the mouse pointer when the player clicks one of the pegs. This method also makes it possible to quickly change the appearance of a playing object (for example, to convert a peg to an empty hole) by assigning a different icon to it.

As you will see, however, one of the problems caused by using Paintbrush drawings or icons in a program is that these objects tend to make the appearance of the game dependent on the specific video mode. A section later in this chapter, "Coding for Device Independence," describes techniques for avoiding this problem.

Finally, the player is allowed to drag the pegs within the form by means of the Visual Basic drag-and-drop facility. This is the easiest method for moving an object in response to mouse movements. In later chapters, you will learn more sophisticated techniques that overcome some of the limitations of the drag-and-drop method.

Program Overview

Here is a summary of the main sequence of events in the Peg Solitaire program.

- When the program starts, the *Form_Load* event procedure performs all the initialization tasks that need to be completed once only, at the beginning of the program. It then calls the general procedure, *InitNewGame*, to start a new game.

- Whenever the player chooses the New Game command from the Game menu, the *MenuNew_Click* event procedure also calls *InitNewGame* to start a new game.

- The *InitNewGame* general procedure performs the initialization tasks required for each new game, including setting the *GameStarted* flag to FALSE.

- If the player clicks a peg while the *GameStarted* flag is set to FALSE, the *PictureArray_Click* event procedure removes the peg and sets *GameStarted* to TRUE. This process allows the player to remove the initial peg at the beginning of a game.

- If the player presses the mouse button while the pointer is over a peg, the *PictureArray_MouseDown* event procedure starts a drag operation (permitting the player to move the peg within the form), provided that *GameStarted* is TRUE.

- If the player drops the peg at a valid position, the *PictureArray_DragDrop* event procedure permanently moves the peg to the new position and removes the jumped peg. If no more moves are possible, it also displays the results and ends the game. If the player drops the peg at an invalid position, the *PictureArray_DragDrop* event procedure (or a *DragDrop* event procedure for another object) returns the peg to its origin.

Creating the Background Graphics

The drawing that serves as the background for the main Peg Solitaire program was created using the Microsoft Paintbrush program. This drawing consists of the playing board at the top of the form and the message area below it; it does not include the pegs or holes.

The following are the specific steps I used to transfer this drawing from Paintbrush to the Visual Basic form:

1. When the drawing was completed, I selected the desired portion of the drawing using the Pick tool, as shown in Figure 3-10. Keep in mind that you must select the *exact portion of the drawing* that you want to display in the form because you cannot adjust the size or position of a drawing after it has been added to a form. Also, you should select only that portion of the drawing that you actually want to display; otherwise, you will unnecessarily increase the size of your program.

2. I chose the Copy To command from the Paintbrush Edit menu to save the selected portion of the drawing in a bit-map file. (The name of this file is PS.BMP, and it is included on the companion disk accompanying this book.)

Figure 3-10.
Selecting the Paintbrush drawing to be transferred to Visual Basic.

Note: I did *not* use the File menu's Save command to create the graphics file because this command would save the entire drawing, generating a bitmap file that is much larger than necessary. Adding this bitmap file to the form would unnecessarily increase the size of the program and the time required to load it.

3. I activated Visual Basic, selected the main form (by clicking on a position within the form not occupied by a control), and chose the Picture item in the Visual Basic properties drop-down list box. I then clicked the "..." button located to the right of the settings text box to open the Load Picture dialog box and specified the file containing the drawing, PS.BMP. The drawing appeared within the form, positioned at the upper left corner.

When you assign a drawing to a form's Picture property, the upper left corner of the drawing is always placed at the upper left corner of the form. If you need to adjust the position of the bitmap or make any other changes to the drawing, do the following:

1. Open the graphics file in Paintbrush (PS.BMP, for the Peg Solitaire drawing), and edit the drawing as needed.

2. Save the file. (This time, you can use the normal Save command because the file has already been reduced to the minimum size.)

3. Load the file into the form again, as described in step 3 of the procedure outlined on the preceding page.

You can assign only a *single* drawing to a form. Each time you load a drawing, it replaces the previous bitmap. (In the next section, you will learn how to add multiple drawings to a form by placing each drawing in a separate picture box.)

You can also assign a drawing to a Visual Basic picture box, using the methods described in this section.

F Y I

The drawing used for the Peg Solitaire background does not fill the entire form (because the drawing was kept to the minimal size to avoid unnecessarily increasing the size of the program). Accordingly, the background color of the form (that is, the BackColor property) is assigned the *same* color as the background of the drawing created in Paintbrush (dark blue, which has the numeric value &H00800000&). The drawing thus blends into the background of the form.

The Pros and Cons of Using Bitmaps

After loading a Paintbrush drawing into a form, Visual Basic assigns the (Bitmap) setting to the form's Picture property, meaning that the drawing is stored as a bitmap. A bitmap records the exact position and color of each pixel used to create the drawing. By creating a bitmap in Paintbrush and adding it to a form, you can easily generate a very precise and effective graphic image. You can even use Paintbrush's Zoom In command on the View menu to edit individual pixels, making your drawing more precise.

Using a bitmap to create a drawing in Visual Basic, however, has the following disadvantages.

- Adding a bitmap to a form consumes a large amount of memory, making the program larger and slower loading.

- A bitmap has a fixed size. Therefore, the drawing cannot easily be enlarged or reduced in size if the user changes the size of the form. Accordingly, the BorderStyle property of the main Peg Solitaire form is assigned the *1 - Fixed Single* setting, creating a window that cannot be changed in size when the user runs the program.

- Using bitmaps can cause unexpected results when the program is run under various graphics resolutions. This problem is addressed later in this chapter, in the section titled ''Coding for Device Independence.''

In Chapter 6, you will learn how to use Visual Basic drawing commands to create background graphics for a form. As you will see, using drawing commands instead of a bitmap results in a smaller, faster-loading program and produces graphics that can be easily scaled. However, you will also discover that graphics produced in this manner can be tedious to code and difficult to modify.

Adding the Picture Boxes

The bitmap used for the Peg Solitaire background, described in the previous section, depicts the playing board but does not include the holes and pegs. Rather than including them in the bitmap, the images for the holes and pegs are placed in an array of picture boxes so that the images can be easily changed and the locations of mouse events readily determined as the game is played. The images contained in the picture boxes *overlay* the underlying bitmap.

The array of picture boxes is named PictureArray, and has 17 elements, one element for each hole on the playing board. The array elements have indexes ranging from 0 through 16 and are arranged as shown in Figure 3-11. (Indexes are used to identify individual elements of a control array.)

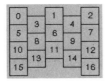

Figure 3-11.
The elements of PictureArray.

The easiest way to add an array of picture boxes to a form is to create a single picture box and *assign to it all the properties you want.* Then use the Copy and Paste commands to make additional copies of the picture box. (Before inserting the first copy, Visual Basic will ask you if you want to create a control array; answer *Yes.* Also, be sure to select the form itself before issuing the Paste command; if you select an existing picture box, the new picture box will be inserted inside it!) Each of the copies becomes a member of an array, and Visual Basic assigns to it the same properties as the original picture box. The elements of this array will automatically be assigned sequential indexes.

> **T I P**
>
> To facilitate positioning the elements of the array, as well as other controls, you might want to adjust the spacing of the grid lines by using the Grid Settings command on the Edit menu.

The background color of the picture boxes is set to the same color as the playing board (that is, the BackColor property is set to the value *&H0000FFFF&*, for bright yellow). Also, at runtime, the picture box borders are removed by setting their BorderStyle properties to *0 - None.* Consequently, when the game is played, the picture boxes blend into the background bitmap, and only the images within the boxes are visible.

No drawings are actually assigned to the PictureArray elements at design time. Rather, the drawings are stored within two separate picture boxes, named PictureEmpty and PictureFull, and are later copied to the PictureArray elements as needed at runtime. PictureEmpty and Picture-Full are stored in the upper left corner of the main form. (See Figure 3-4.) Their Visible properties are set to False so that they will not be seen when the program is running.

As the names imply, PictureEmpty stores an image of an empty hole, and PictureFull stores an image of a hole containing a peg. These

> **F Y I**
>
> At design time, the BorderStyle properties of the picture boxes are left at the default setting, *1 - Fixed Single*, to make it easier to see the locations and sizes of the boxes.

images are contained in the icon files PS1.ICO and PS2.ICO, which are included on the disk provided with this book. An icon is assigned by choosing the Picture property of the picture box from Visual Basic's Properties drop-down list box, clicking the "..." button, and then specifying the name of the icon file when prompted. The DragIcon property of the PictureFull picture box is also assigned an icon (the icon contained in PS3.ICO, which depicts a simple peg). The use of this "drag icon" will be explained later in the chapter.

A fourth icon, in the file PS.ICO, is assigned to the Icon property of the main form itself; Windows displays this icon whenever the form is minimized (at design or runtime). The four icons used for Peg Solitaire are shown in Figure 3-12.

PS1.ICO   PS2.ICO

PS3.ICO   PS4.ICO

Figure 3-12.
The icons used in the Peg Solitaire game.

A label named Label1 is the final control placed within the main form. This label is used to display messages to the user during the game.

T I P

The custom icons for Peg Solitaire were created using the excellent Icon Works program that is supplied with Visual Basic. Visual Basic also provides an extensive collection of ready-to-use icons that you can assign to forms or picture boxes. They are contained in the ICONS subdirectory of the directory in which you installed Visual Basic.

Coding for Device Independence

As you have seen, the Peg Solitaire form is constructed by assigning a background bitmap to the form itself and then placing picture boxes and a label at precise positions on top of this bitmap. The problem with this basic technique, however, is that it is *not* device independent.

To illustrate the problem, consider what would happen if you designed a form using a VGA adapter but later ran the program on an EGA system. The bitmap is always displayed using a fixed number of pixels. VGA and EGA systems have the same number of pixels in the horizontal direction (640); however, VGA has 480 pixels in the vertical direction, while EGA has only 350. An EGA pixel is therefore taller than a VGA pixel. Accordingly, the relative height of the bitmap on the screen would *increase* when the program was run under EGA.

In contrast, the positions and sizes of picture boxes, as well as the size of the form itself, are specified, by default, in twips. A twip is equal to $\frac{1}{1440}$ of an inch, and is a device independent unit. In other words, a control that is assigned a height of 1440 twips will always be 1 logical inch high on the screen, regardless of the graphics mode. To maintain this constant height, the control will encompass a greater number of pixels in the vertical direction on a VGA system than it will on an EGA system.

You can now see what would happen to a form that was carefully designed on a VGA system: When run on an EGA system, all bitmaps and icons (which also contain a fixed number of pixels) would become taller—but the size of the form, as well as the sizes and locations of the picture boxes and other controls, would remain the same! As a result, controls would not align with the underlying bitmap. Furthermore, a given bitmap or icon might no longer fit into the form or picture box that contains it.

Nevertheless, the Peg Solitaire program maintains device independence, despite its use of bitmaps and controls, through some additional coding. The ScaleMode property of the main form is assigned the *3 - Pixel* setting (rather than the default *1 - Twip* setting). As a result, the sizes and positions assigned to the controls are interpreted as actual screen pixels.

T I P

If you want a picture box to be just large enough to contain the bitmap that is assigned to it, regardless of the video mode, you can set the picture box's AutoSize property to True. Enabling the AutoSize feature, however, does not prevent the possible misalignment of a picture box with an underlying bitmap. Also, forms do not have an AutoSize property.

It might seem that this step would be sufficient to properly align the form and the controls with the bitmap and the icons. Unfortunately, however, Visual Basic freely changes measurements assigned at design time according to the particular video mode under which you are editing or running the program. Suppose, for example, that you are designing a program on a VGA system and that you assign a picture box a width of 32 pixels and a height of 32 pixels, to ensure that an icon will fit within it. (Icons are 32 pixels square.) If you later load the program on an EGA system, you will notice that Visual Basic has reduced the height measurement of the picture box, presumably so that it still appears square on the screen. However, the icon will no longer fit within it.

Fortunately, Visual Basic does not alter measurements assigned at runtime through program statements. Consequently, the *Form_Load* event procedure of PS.FRM explicitly assigns positions and sizes to all controls contained in the form. (See Figure 3-9.)

Note: Visual Basic calls the *Form_Load* event procedure for the main form when the program is first run. This procedure should therefore contain any required initialization statements.

For example, the statements

```
PictureArray(I).Width = 33
PictureArray(I).Height = 33
```

assign the *I*th element of *PictureArray* a size of 33 pixels by 33 pixels. (The statements are placed inside a For loop, where *I* varies from 0 to 16, to size all members of the array.) Also, the statements

```
PictureArray(0).Left = 32: PictureArray(0).Top = 32
```

place the upper left corner of the first element of *PictureArray* exactly 32 pixels from the top and left edges of the form. The specific numbers are easily obtained by selecting each control and then reading the position and dimensions directly from the settings box on Visual Basic's Properties bar. These values are *hard-coded* into the program: Visual Basic will not alter them when the video mode changes. Thus, the controls will always be placed at the appropriate pixel positions on the bitmap, and the icons will always fit within the picture boxes.

Assigning the correct dimensions to the *form* is not as easy. At design time, you can determine the dimensions of the *inside* of the form *in pixels* required to accommodate the contents of the form. (To do this, use the mouse to adjust the form to the size you want, and then read the resulting values of the ScaleWidth and ScaleHeight properties, which give the width and height of the inside of the form in pixels.) To set the size of the form at runtime, however, you must assign the appropriate dimensions of the *outside* of the form *in twips* to the Width and Height form properties.

Note: You cannot change the size of a form at runtime by simply assigning pixel dimensions of the inside of the form to the ScaleWidth and ScaleHeight properties. Adjusting these properties changes the coordinate system without altering the size of the form.

Accordingly, the initialization code must first convert the inside measurements of the form to the outside measurements and then convert the resulting values from pixels to twips. The *Form_Load* procedure accomplishes the first conversion by calling the Windows API function *AdjustWindowRect* (described in Figure 3-13), as follows:

```
Dim Rec As RECT          'RECT is defined in GLOBALPS.FRM.

Rec.Left = 0             'Horizontal coordinate of
                         'upper left corner of inside of form.
Rec.Top = 0              'Vertical coordinate of
                         'upper left corner of inside of form.
Rec.Right = CLIENTRIGHT  'Horizontal coordinate of
                         'lower right corner of inside of form.
Rec.Bottom = CLIENTBOTTOM 'Vertical coordinate of
                         'lower right corner of inside of form.
AdjustWindowRect Rec, WS_CAPTION, -1
```

Before calling *AdjustWindowRect*, the pixel coordinates of the inside of the form are assigned to the fields of the RECT structure Rec. (RECT is defined in the global module.) Rec is then passed to *AdjustWindowRect*, which changes the coordinates in this structure to those of the outside of the form. The second two parameters passed to *AdjustWindowRect* specify the features of the form and are explained in Figure 3-13.

Windows API Function: *AdjustWindowRect*

Purpose Supplies the outside coordinates of a form based upon the specified inside coordinates.

Declaration
```
Declare Sub AdjustWindowRect Lib "USER" (lpRect As RECT,
ByVal dwStyle&, ByVal bMenu%)
```

Parameter	Description

lpRect	A RECT type variable containing the coordinates of the inside of the form. *AdjustWindowRect* supplies the coordinates of the outside of the form by updating the fields of this variable. RECT has the following form:
	
	```Type RECT```
	``` Left As Integer```
	``` Top As Integer```
	``` Right As Integer```
	``` Bottom As Integer```
	```End Type```

dwStyle&	A code indicating the style of the window. If you have already set the form's BorderStyle property to *1 - Fixed Single*, you should assign *dwStyle* the value
	
	```WS_CAPTION```
	
	If you have already set the BorderStyle property to *2 - Sizable*, you should assign *dwStyle* the value
	
	```WS_CAPTION or WS_THICKFRAME```
	
	WS_CAPTION and WS_THICKFRAME are constants defined in your program; WS_CAPTION should be set to &HC00000 and WS_THICKFRAME to &H40000.

bMenu %	A flag that should be set to TRUE if the form has a menu.

Comments The "inside" area refers to the portion of the form inside the borders, title bar, and menu (if present). It is also known as the "client" area.

Figure 3-13.
The AdjustWindowRect *Windows API function.*

Note: See Chapter 2 for a general discussion on calling Windows API functions from Visual Basic programs.

Form_Load accomplishes the second conversion by calling the Windows API function *GetDeviceCaps* (described in Figure 3-14). This function returns the number of horizontal or vertical pixels per inch under the current graphics mode. *Form_Load* converts the values returned by *GetDeviceCaps* to the number of twips per pixel, using the fact that 1440 twips equal 1 inch. It then uses the resulting values to convert the twip coordinates of the outside of the form to pixels, and it assigns the final values to the FormWidth and FormHeight properties, as follows:

```
FormMain.Width = (Rec.Right - Rec.Left + 1) * (1440 /
 GetDeviceCaps(hDC, LOGPIXELSX))
FormMain.Height = (Rec.Bottom - Rec.Top + 1) * (1440 /
 GetDeviceCaps(hDC, LOGPIXELSY))
```

Windows API Function: *GetDeviceCaps*

Purpose Supplies device-specific information on a display device.

Declaration
```
Declare Function GetDeviceCaps Lib "GDI"
 (ByVal hDC%, ByVal Index%) As Integer
```

Parameter	Description
hDC%	Handle to the device context.
Index%	Indicates the type of information desired. The following table contains some of the values you can assign to *Index*:

Constant	Value	Meaning
LOGPIXELSX	88	Number of pixels per logical inch in the horizontal direction.
LOGPIXELSY	90	Number of pixels per logical inch in the vertical direction.

Figure 3-14.
The GetDeviceCaps *Windows API function.*

In some of the games presented later in the book, the *position* of the form on the screen is also adjusted at runtime.

The techniques given in this section maintain the proper alignment of bitmaps, icons, forms, and controls, regardless of the video mode. They do not, however, guarantee that squares will remain square or circles will remain circular. Image distortion is a problem inherent in using bitmaps. If maintaining exact proportions is an important feature for your program, you can create graphics at runtime using the device-independent twip scale mode, in conjunction with Visual Basic drawing methods. Chapter 6 introduces the use of Visual Basic drawing methods, and Chapter 10 shows how to use these methods together with the twip scale mode to create device-independent graphics.

Initializing the Program

Following the code for device independence, the *Form_Load* procedure calls the procedure *InitNewGame*, which is contained in the (general) section of PS.FRM:

```
Sub InitNewGame ()
    For I = 0 To 16
        PictureArray(I).Picture = PictureFull.Picture
    Next I
    Label1.Caption = "click to remove first peg..."
    GameStarted = 0
End Sub
```

This procedure initializes a new game. *InitNewGame* is also called by the *MenuNew_Click* event procedure, which is called each time the player chooses the New Game command from the Game menu.

InitNewGame first copies the image stored in the picture box PictureFull (depicting a hole filled with a peg) to all members of PictureArray. Therefore, the game begins with all 17 holes filled with pegs. *InitNewGame* also displays the initial message in Label1 *(click to remove first peg...)* and assigns FALSE (0) to the form-level variable *GameStarted* to indicate that the player has not yet removed the first peg.

Processing the First Click

To start a game, the player must click on one of the pegs. Because the pegs are located within the elements of PictureArray, clicking on a peg causes Visual Basic to call the *PictureArray_Click* event procedure and to pass the index of the clicked element as the parameter *Index*:

```
Sub PictureArray_Click (Index As Integer)
    If Not GameStarted Then
        PictureArray(Index).Picture = PictureEmpty.Picture
        GameStarted = -1
        Label1.Caption = "game in progress."
    End If
End Sub
```

PictureArray_Click copies the picture contained in PictureEmpty (depicting an empty hole) into the clicked member of PictureArray, effectively removing the initial peg. The procedure also displays a new message in Label1 *(game in progress)* and sets the variable *GameStarted* to −1 (the Visual Basic value for a TRUE condition), indicating that the player has removed the initial peg and is ready to start jumping pegs. Notice that after *GameStarted* is set to TRUE, *PictureArray_Click* ignores further click events by means of the *If* statement at the beginning of the procedure.

At this point, the program waits for the player to begin a jump operation.

Processing the MouseDown Event

After the initial peg has been removed, the player must remove the next peg by jumping—that is, by dragging a peg from its hole on the near side of the to-be-jumped peg and dropping it into a hole on the far side. To drag a peg, the player first places the pointer over the peg and presses the mouse button. When this occurs, Visual Basic calls the *PictureArray_MouseDown* event procedure, passing the index of the array member under the mouse pointer as the parameter *Index*:

```
Sub PictureArray_MouseDown (Index As Integer,
 Button As Integer, Shift As Integer,
 X As Single, Y As Single)
    If GameStarted And PictureArray(Index).Picture
```

```
    = PictureFull.Picture Then
        PictureArray(Index).Picture = PictureEmpty.Picture
        DragSource = Index
        PictureArray(Index).Drag 1
    End If
End Sub
```

The procedure begins by determining whether a game has begun (by checking the *GameStarted* variable) and whether the clicked element of PictureArray currently contains a peg (by comparing its Picture property to the Picture property of PictureFull). If both of these conditions are met, *PictureArray_MouseDown* performs the following three actions:

- It copies the picture contained in PictureEmpty (an empty hole) into the PictureArray element under the mouse pointer, effectively removing the peg from the hole.

- It assigns the index of the PictureArray element (*Index*) to the variable *DragSource*. (The use of this variable will be explained in the next section.)

- It initiates a drag operation for the PictureArray element under the mouse pointer.

Note: The procedure does not test whether a valid move is possible. As you will see later, this test occurs when the user attempts to drop the peg at a new location.

The drag operation is started by invoking the Visual Basic *Drag* method, passing *1* as a parameter:

```
PictureArray(Index).Drag 1
```

When the drag operation starts, Visual Basic replaces the normal mouse pointer with the *drag icon* assigned to the PictureArray element under the mouse pointer (that is, the icon assigned to the DragIcon property). As you saw previously in the chapter, the icon contained in the file PS3.ICO, which depicts a simple peg without a hole, is assigned at design time to the DragIcon property of the invisible picture box PictureFull. At runtime, the initialization code in the *Form_Load* procedure copies this drag icon to each member of PictureArray:

```
PictureArray(I).DragIcon = PictureFull.DragIcon   'I varies
                                                  'from 0 to 16
```

> ### T I P
>
> The background of the peg in PS3.ICO was created using the *Screen* color (rather than a solid color) so that the peg alone would appear on the screen.

As the player moves the mouse while holding down the button, the drag icon is moved across the form in the same manner as a normal mouse pointer. Visual Basic and Windows handle all the details of moving the icon across the screen. The drag process terminates when the player releases the button; Visual Basic then restores the normal mouse pointer and generates a DragDrop event (described in the next section).

The overall effect of the *PictureArray_MouseDown* procedure, therefore, is to make it appear that the peg has jumped out of the hole, leaving an empty hole behind, and is moving across the game board in response to the movement of the mouse.

The Visual Basic drag-and-drop facility is thus a simple way to animate a graphic object; however, you need to be aware of several important limitations. First, the drag icon is always displayed in black and white, even if the icon from which it is derived consists of many colors. As you can see when you play Peg Solitaire, the drag icon is not as realistic as the stationary icon depicting the peg in the hole. Second, you cannot change the size of the drag icon (without assigning an entirely new icon); thus, it would be difficult to scale the graphic elements contained in the form as the player changes the size of the form on the screen. Also, the size of an icon is limited to 32 pixels by 32 pixels.

> ### F Y I
>
> The DragMode properties of the PictureArray elements are assigned the default *Manual* setting. If the DragMode properties were set to *Automatic*, Visual Basic would initiate the drag operation as soon as the mouse button was pressed, *without* calling the *MouseDown* procedure. In this case, the program would not be able to remove the peg and set the *DragSource* variable.

In the following chapters, you will learn more sophisticated ways to animate objects (in response to mouse movements or timer events), which overcome these limitations.

Note: The *DragDrop* procedure does not test the *Button* parameter to determine which mouse button was pressed. The player, therefore, can use either button to drag the peg.

Processing the DragDrop Event

When the player releases the mouse button during a drag operation, Visual Basic restores the normal mouse pointer and calls the *DragDrop* event procedure for the form or control that is under the pointer when the button is released. When a DragDrop event occurs, the Peg Solitaire program performs one of two actions:

- If the peg is dropped at an invalid position, the program places the peg back in its original hole.

- If the peg is dropped on an empty hole at a valid position, the program adds the peg to the hole and removes the peg that was jumped.

Determining whether the peg has been dropped at a valid position requires a bit of program logic. Dropping the peg on the form itself, or on the Label1 control, is obviously invalid. Therefore, the *DragDrop* procedures for both these objects restore the peg to its original hole. Here is the code for the *Form_DragDrop* event procedure:

```
Sub Form_DragDrop (Source As Control, X As Single, Y As Single)
    Source.Picture = PictureFull.Picture
    DragSource = -1
End Sub
```

The *Source* parameter passed to the *DragDrop* procedure indicates the control that was being dragged, which in this case is one of the elements of PictureArray. The peg is restored to the original picture box by copying the Picture property of PictureFull to the Picture property of the source control. The procedure also assigns *DragSource* the value −1 to indicate that no picture is currently being dragged. (The use of Drag-Source will be explained later in this section.) The *Label1_DragDrop* event procedure is coded identically.

F Y I

You do not need to attach code to the *DragDrop* event procedures for the picture boxes PictureEmpty and PictureFull because these controls are *invisible* and therefore never receive DragDrop events. (If the player drops the icon on one of these forms, Visual Basic calls the *DragDrop* event procedure for the form itself.)

The *DragDrop* event procedure for PictureArray must determine whether the peg has been dropped on a valid member of the array. Visual Basic passes the index of the particular member of the array as the parameter *Index*:

```
Sub PictureArray_DragDrop (Index As Integer,
  Source As Control, X As Single, Y As Single)
```

The procedure begins by setting *DragSource* to −1 (explained later) and then checking whether the target picture box already contains a peg (which would immediately disqualify the move). If it does, the dragged peg is immediately sent home, and the procedure terminates:

```
DragSource = -1
If PictureArray(Index).Picture = PictureFull.Picture Then
    Source.Picture = PictureFull.Picture
    Exit Sub
End If
```

If the target picture box contains an empty hole, the procedure goes on to determine whether the move is valid. The criteria for a valid move depends on the specific target picture box; therefore, the procedure uses a large *Select* statement to branch to the appropriate test:

```
Select Case Index
    Case 0:
        [code for first PictureArray element]
    Case 1:
        [code for second PictureArray element]
    [Case 2 through Case 16]
End Case
```

The move is valid if the source picture box is two holes away and if the peg has jumped over a hole containing a peg. For example, the test for the first PictureArray element must look in two directions:

```
Case 0
    If Source.Index = 10 And PictureArray(5).Picture
= PictureFull.Picture Then
        PictureArray(5).Picture = PictureEmpty.Picture
        PictureArray(0).Picture = PictureFull.Picture
    ElseIf Source.Index = 6 And PictureArray(3).Picture
= PictureFull.Picture Then
        PictureArray(3).Picture = PictureEmpty.Picture
        PictureArray(0).Picture = PictureFull.Picture
    Else
        Source.Picture = PictureFull.Picture
        Cancel = -1
    End If
```

The specific numbers will make sense if you examine Figure 3-11, which shows the arrangement of the PictureArray elements. If the move is valid, the routine places a peg in the target hole and removes the peg from the jumped position. Otherwise, it replaces the peg in the source picture box and sets the variable *Cancel* to −1.

Following the *Select* statement, the procedure terminates if *Cancel* has been set to −1. If *Cancel* equals 0, then a move has been completed, and the code calls the function *MovePossible* to determine whether any moves are possible.

MovePossible is declared in the (general) section of PS.FRM. (See Figure 3-9 on page 28.) It examines each element of PictureArray, checking whether it contains a peg that could be jumped over a neighboring peg. The validity of each possible jump from a given source picture box is checked by calling another function declared in the (general) section, *JumpOK*. Again, refer to Figure 3-11 to make sense of the specific index numbers used in these functions.

Meanwhile, back in the *PictureArray_DragDrop* event procedure, if *MovePossible* returns FALSE (0), indicating that the game is over, the procedure beeps, counts the number of pegs remaining on the board, and displays a message in Label1 indicating that the game is over and rating the player's performance based on the number of pegs left.

Dropping an Icon Outside the Form

What happens if the player drops the peg icon outside the form? Visual Basic converts the drag icon to the special "Don't Drop" icon shown in Figure 3-15 on the following page, indicating that the peg icon should not be dropped. As soon as it is dragged back into the form, it resumes its original shape and no harm has been done. If, however, the player ignores this warning and drops the icon outside the form, Visual Basic terminates the drag operation *without calling a* DragDrop *event procedure.* The program, therefore, does not know that the peg icon was dropped on an invalid location. Consequently, the peg is never restored to its original hole.

Figure 3-15.
The "Don't Drop" icon.

When I first wrote Peg Solitaire, it was easy to cheat by dragging the pegs outside the program form and dropping them there; pegs could thus be quickly removed without making valid moves. The solution to this problem is worth describing because you will probably encounter the same problem when writing games that use the drag-and-drop facility.

The code for avoiding this problem uses the form-level variable *DragSource.* This variable is initialized to −1 at the beginning of the program. Then, before the *PictureArray_MouseDown* procedure initiates a drag operation, it sets *DragSource* to the index of the PictureArray element that is being dragged:

```
DragSource = Index
```

Subsequently, when a *DragDrop* event procedure is called, indicating the drag operation has been terminated, *DragSource* is set back to −1:

```
DragSource = -1
```

As you have seen, this statement is included in all the *DragDrop* procedures.

If, however, the player has mischievously dropped the icon outside the form, Visual Basic terminates the drag operation *without calling a* DragDrop *procedure,* and *DragSource* remains set to a value other than −1.

Fortunately, there is another way for the program to ascertain that a drag operation is not taking place. Normally, as the player moves the mouse over a form or control, Visual Basic repeatedly calls the *Mouse-Move* event procedure belonging to the object under the pointer. When a drag operation is in progress, however, Visual Basic does *not* call the *MouseMove* event procedure. The *MouseMove* event procedure for the main form takes advantage of this fact:

```
Sub Form_MouseMove (Button As Integer,
 Shift As Integer, X As Single, Y As Single)
    If DragSource <> -1 Then
        PictureArray(DragSource).Picture = PictureFull.Picture
        DragSource = -1
    End If
End Sub
```

When the event procedure is called, it knows that a drag operation is not taking place. If, however, the variable *DragSource* is equal to a value other than −1, Visual Basic must have terminated a drag operation without calling a *DragDrop* event procedure; otherwise, *DragSource* would have been restored to −1. The only explanation is that the player has dropped the icon outside the form. Accordingly, the event procedure restores the peg to its original location and then sets *DragSource* to −1.

As a result, when you play Peg Solitaire you can freely drop a peg outside the form. However, as soon as you move the pointer back into the form to resume playing, the peg that you tried to discard pops back into its original hole!

Implementing the Help Menu Commands

The Help menu on the main form follows the standard format used for all the games presented in this book. The first four commands on this menu access the Windows Help utility. The final command, About Peg Solitaire, displays the program's About dialog box. (See Chapter 2 for a complete description of how to create and display an About dialog box and how to access Windows Help.)

Enhancing the Game

Here are some suggestions for enhancing the Peg Solitaire game:

- Add an Undo command to the Game menu, which would allow a player to reverse the previous move.

- Alter the number or arrangement of holes on the board. As mentioned at the beginning of the chapter, traditional peg solitaire boards have either 37 or 33 holes, arranged in horizontal rows.

- Allow the user to choose various starting peg arrangements (rather than always filling all the holes except one).

- Vary the objective of the game. Rather than trying to remove all pegs except one, the player can try to create
  various patterns of pegs.

- Experiment with different background drawings or icons,
  which you can create using Paintbrush and a utility for icon
  design. You can easily alter the program drawings because
  they are simply pasted into the various objects and are not
  hard-coded into the program.

CHAPTER FOUR

DEDUCE

In the game Deduce, the player attempts to deduce a hidden sequence of numbers by making repeated guesses, guided by clues from the computer. The code for Deduce reveals the power of Visual Basic controls; the game is created entirely using standard control objects—picture boxes, labels, a command button, a scroll bar, and a timer. The game also illustrates the use of the Visual Basic random-number generator for creating varied number sequences.

Playing Deduce

When you run Deduce (DD.EXE), the program starts a game. You can later begin a new game at any time—even before the current game is completed—by choosing the New Game command from the Game menu. Figure 4-1 shows the Deduce window at the beginning of a game.

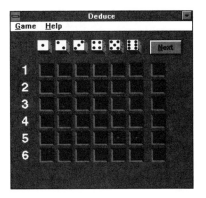

Figure 4-1.
Deduce at the beginning of a game.

When the program starts a game, it generates a random arrangement of the numbers 1 through 6, which it keeps "hidden." The object of the game is to deduce this sequence in as few attempts (guesses) as possible.

Each number in the hidden sequence occurs one time only. Therefore, the following are possible sequences:

425316   631452

while the following are *not* possible sequences:

232641   324364

Mathematically, the sequence is termed a permutation of six items taken six at a time.

In Deduce, sequences are represented using six dice. You begin by placing your first guess within the row labeled *1*. Drag each of the dice from the top of the window to a position within this row. You can freely rearrange the dice as often as you want. When you are satisfied with your arrangement, click the Next button or press Enter. The program now displays a die in the column under the Next button; the number shown on the die indicates the number of dice that you positioned correctly in row 1. If none of the dice is in the correct position, the program displays a blank die to the right of the row. The program also places a new set of six dice at the top of the window.

Note: After you click the Next button or press Enter, you cannot undo your move.

Now enter your second guess by dragging each of the dice from the top of the window to a position within row 2. Click Next (or press Enter) when you are done. The program displays a die at the far right of the row, indicating the number of dice positioned correctly. Figure 4-2 shows a game after two guesses, in which the hidden sequence is as follows:

421365

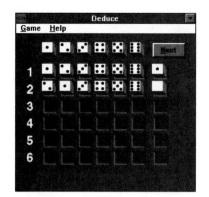

Figure 4-2.
A Deduce game after two guesses.

Continue in this manner until you have guessed the correct sequence. When you succeed, the computer displays a 6 on the die to the right of the row, and a message flashes at the bottom of the screen. Your score is indicated by the number of the row containing your final guess (the correct one).

Only six rows are displayed at a time. If you make six or more guesses, only the current row plus your five most recent guesses will be visible, and the program will display a vertical scroll bar (as shown in Figure 4-3). To view previous guesses that are not shown, use the scroll bar to move up and down through the rows.

Note: The maximum number of guesses you can make is 18.

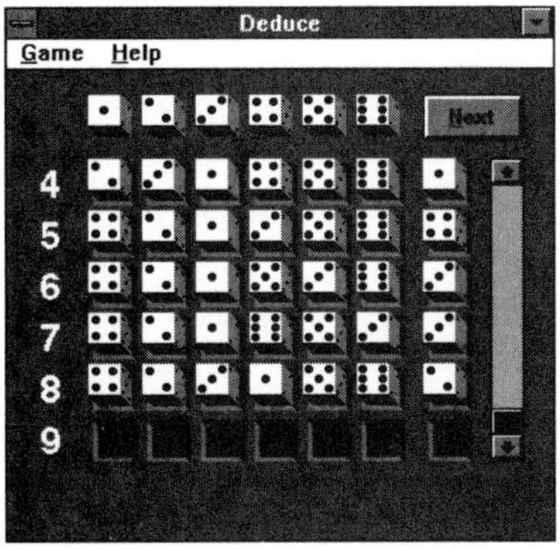

Figure 4-3.
A Deduce game after eight guesses.

Strategy and Hints

Your first move is pure guesswork, so the number of dice you place correctly is strictly a matter of luck. Beginning with the second move, however, your arrangements should be influenced by the previous moves and the scores obtained from them. You can use the information obtained from previous moves to eliminate many of the possible arrangements. If you ignore this evidence and simply continue to try random arrangements until you get lucky, the game could—in theory—require as many as 720 unique guesses! (Six items have 720 permutations. However, the game allows you to make only 18 guesses.)

Coding Deduce

The source code for the Deduce program is contained in files listed in the following table.

File	Purpose
GLOBALDD.BAS	Contains a global type definition (RECT)
DD.FRM	Defines the main form, FormMain, and the controls it contains
DDABOUT.FRM	Defines the ABOUT form, FormAbout, and the controls it contains
DD.MAK	Contains the Deduce project file

After you have installed these files (see Chapter 1 for instructions), you can load them into Visual Basic by choosing the Open Project command from the File menu, and when prompted, by specifying the project file DD.MAK.

Figures 4-4 through 4-9 present the form designs, properties, menu commands, and source code for the Deduce program.

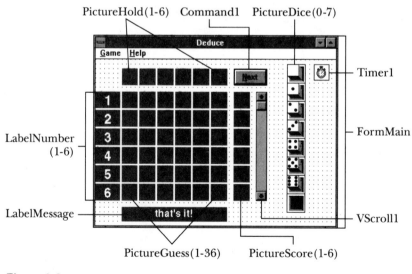

Figure 4-4.
DD.FRM at design time.

Object Name	Object Type	Property	Setting
Command1	Command button	Caption	&Next
		Default	True
		Enabled	False
		FontSize	9.75
		Height	29 [pixels]
		Left	248 [pixels]
		Top	16 [pixels]
		Width	60 [pixels]
FormMain	Form	BackColor	&H00FFFFFF& [white]
		BorderStyle	1 - Fixed Single
		Caption	Deduce
		FormName	FormMain
		Grid Height	8 [pixels]
		Grid Width	8 [pixels]
		Height	5010 [twips]
		Icon	(Icon) [DD.ICO]
		Left	1005 [twips]
		MaxButton	False
		Top	1095 [twips]
		Width	6600 [twips]
LabelMessage	Label	Alignment	2 - Center
		BackColor	&H00808000& [dark cyan]
		BorderStyle	0 - None
		Caption	that's it!
		CtlName	LabelMessage
		FontSize	13.5
		ForeColor	&H00FFFFFF& [white]
		Height	25 [pixels]
		Left	48 [pixels]
		Top	256 [pixels]
		Visible	False
		Width	189 [pixels]

Figure 4-5.
DD.FRM form and control properties.

(continued)

Figure 4-5 *continued*

Object Name	Object Type	Property	Setting	
LabelNumber	Array of labels	Alignment	2 - Center	
		BackColor	&H00808000& [dark cyan]	
		BorderStyle	0 - None	
		Caption	1 - 6	
		CtlName	LabelNumber	
		FontSize	18	
		ForeColor	&H00FFFFFF& [white]	
		Height	29 [pixels]	
		Index	1 - 6	
		Left	0 [pixels]	
		Top	56 - 216 [pixels]	
		Width	45 [pixels]	
PictureDice	Array of picture boxes	CtlName	PictureDice	
		DragIcon	*Index*	*Icon*
			0	[None]
			1	DD1D.ICO
			2	DD2D.ICO
			3	DD3D.ICO
			4	DD4D.ICO
			5	DD5D.ICO
			6	DD6D.ICO
			7	[None]
		Height	33 [pixels]	
		Index	0 - 7	
		Left	344 [pixels]	
		Picture	*Index*	*Icon*
			0	DD0.ICO
			1	DD1.ICO
			2	DD2.ICO
			3	DD3.ICO

(continued)

Figure 4-5 *continued*

Object Name	Object Type	Property	Setting	
			4	DD4.ICO
			5	DD5.ICO
			6	DD6.ICO
			7	DD7.ICO
		Top	[varies]	
		Visible	False	
		Width	33 [pixels]	
PictureGuess	Array of picture boxes	BackColor	&H00808000& [dark cyan]	
		BorderStyle	0 - None	
		CtlName	PictureGuess	
		Height	29 [pixels]	
		Index	1 - 36	
		Left	[varies]	
		Top	[varies]	
		Width	29 [pixels]	
PictureHold	Array of picture boxes	BackColor	&H00808000& [dark cyan]	
		BorderStyle	0 - None	
		CtlName	PictureHold	
		Height	29 [pixels]	
		Index	1 - 6	
		Left	[varies]	
		Top	16 [pixels]	
		Width	29 [pixels]	
PictureScore	Array of picture boxes	BackColor	&H00808000& [dark cyan]	
		BorderStyle	0 - None	
		CtlName	PictureScore	
		Height	29 [pixels]	
		Index	1 - 6	
		Left	248 [pixels]	
		Top	[varies]	
		Width	29 [pixels]	

(continued)

Figure 4-5 *continued*

Object Name	Object Type	Property	Setting
Timer1	Timer	Enabled	False
		Interval	300 [milliseconds]
VScroll1	Vertical scroll bar	Height	189 [pixels]
		LargeChange	6
		Left	288 [pixels]
		Top	56 [pixels]
		Visible	False
		Width	20 [pixels]

Indentation/Caption	Control Name	Other Features
&Game	MenuGame	
….&New Game	MenuNew	
….-	MenuSep1	
….E&xit	MenuExit	
&Help	MenuHelp	
….&Index	MenuIndex	Accelerator = F1
….&How to Play	MenuHowTo	
….&Commands	MenuCommands	
….&Using Help	MenuUsingHelp	
….-	MenuSep2	
….&About Deduce…	MenuAbout	

Figure 4-6.
DD.FRM menu design.

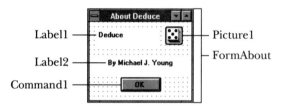

Figure 4-7.
DDABOUT.FRM at design time.

Object Name	Object Type	Property	Setting
Command1	Command button	Caption	OK
		Default	True
		Height	375 [twips]
		Left	840 [twips]
		Top	1440 [twips]
		Width	1095 [twips]
FormAbout	Form	BorderStyle	3 - Fixed Double
		Caption	About Deduce
		FormName	FormAbout
		Grid Height	120 [twips]
		Grid Width	120 [twips]
		Height	2445 [twips]
		Left	1140 [twips]
		MaxButton	False
		MinButton	False
		Top	1440 [twips]
		Width	2880 [twips]
Label1	Label	Caption	Deduce
		Height	375 [twips]
		Left	240 [twips]
		Top	240 [twips]
		Width	1575 [twips]
Label2	Label	Alignment	2 - Center
		Caption	By Michael J. Young
		Height	375 [twips]
		Left	0 [twips]
		Top	960 [twips]
		Width	2745 [twips]
Picture1	Picture box	AutoSize	True
		BorderStyle	0 - None
		Height	480 [twips]
		Left	2040 [twips]

Figure 4-8.
DDABOUT.FRM form and control properties.

(continued)

Figure 4-8 *continued*

Object Name	Object Type	Property	Setting
		Picture	(Icon) [DD.ICO]
		Top	120 [twips]
		Width	480 [twips]

GLOBALDD.BAS code

```
Type RECT
    Left As Integer
    Top As Integer
    Right As Integer
    Bottom As Integer
End Type
```

DD.FRM code

```
'Help Section:
'Help file:
Const HELP_FILE = "DD.HLP"
'WinHelp wCommand values:
Const HELP_CONTEXT = &H1
Const HELP_HELPONHELP = &H4
Const HELP_INDEX = &H3
Const HELP_QUIT = &H2
'WinHelp dwData values (help topics):
Const HELP_HOWTOPLAY = 10&
Const HELP_COMMANDS = 20&
'Windows help API:
Declare Sub WinHelp Lib "USER" (ByVal hWnd As Integer, ByVal
    lpHelpFile As String, ByVal wCommand As Integer, ByVal dwData
    As Long)

Const CLIENTBOTTOM = 288
Const CLIENTRIGHT = 318
Const HEIGHTPIX = 334
Const MAXPOS = 108
```

Figure 4-9.   *(continued)*

Source code for the Deduce program. (Notice that long program lines are wrapped to the next line and indented one space.)

Figure 4-9 *continued*

```
Const MAXROWS = MAXPOS \ 6
Const WIDTHPIX = 327

Dim Answer(1 To 6) As Integer
Dim DragSource As Integer
Dim GameOver As Integer
Dim GuessTable(1 To MAXPOS) As Integer
Dim IdxHi As Integer              'index of last PictureGuess element
                                  'in current row
Dim IdxLo As Integer              'index of first PictureGuess element
                                  'in current row
Dim IdxOffset As Integer
Dim ScoreTable(1 To MAXROWS) As Integer
Dim Scrolled As Integer

Const WS_CAPTION = &HC00000
Const WS_THICKFRAME = &H40000
Declare Sub AdjustWindowRect Lib "USER" (lpRect As RECT, ByVal
 dwStyle&, ByVal bMenu%)

Const LOGPIXELSX = 88
Const LOGPIXELSY = 90
Declare Function GetDeviceCaps Lib "GDI" (ByVal hDC%, ByVal
 Index%) As Integer

Sub InitNewGame ()
    Dim I As Integer, J As Integer
    Dim IdxTemp As Integer
    Static TempArray(1 To 6) As Integer
    Dim Top As Integer

    'Initialize controls:
    For I = 1 To 36
        PictureGuess(I).Picture = PictureDice(7).Picture
    Next I
    For I = 1 To 6
        PictureHold(I).Visible = -1
        PictureScore(I).Picture = PictureDice(7).Picture
        LabelNumber(I).Caption = Str$(I)
    Next I
    Command1.Enabled = 0
    VScroll1.Visible = 0
    LabelMessage.Visible = 0
```

(continued)

Figure 4-9 *continued*

```
    'Initialize variables:
    IdxLo = 1: IdxHi = 6
    For I = 1 To MAXPOS
        GuessTable(I) = 7
    Next I
    IdxOffset = 0
    For I = 1 To MAXPOS \ 6
        ScoreTable(I) = 7
    Next I
    Scrolled = 0
    GameOver = 0

    'Generate hidden random sequence:
    For I = 1 To 6
        TempArray(I) = I
    Next I
    Top = 6
    For I = 1 To 6
        IdxTemp = Int(Top * Rnd + 1)
        Answer(I) = TempArray(IdxTemp)
        For J = IdxTemp To Top - 1
            TempArray(J) = TempArray(J + 1)
        Next J
        Top = Top - 1
    Next I

    'Display the solution in Immediate Window for program
 testing:
    For I = 1 To 6
        Debug.Print Answer(I); " ";
    Next I
    Debug.Print
End Sub

Sub ScrollIt (RowOffset As Integer)
    Dim I As Integer
    Dim Offset As Integer

    For I = 1 To 6
        LabelNumber(I).Caption = Str$(RowOffset + I)
    Next I
    Offset = RowOffset * 6
    For I = 1 To 36
        PictureGuess(I).Picture = PictureDice(GuessTable(I +
```

(continued)

Figure 4-9 *continued*

```
 Offset)).Picture
    Next I
    If RowOffset = VScroll1.Max Then
        Scrolled = 0
    Else
        Scrolled = -1
    End If
    For I = 1 To 6
        PictureScore(I).Picture = PictureDice(ScoreTable(I +
 RowOffset)).Picture
    Next I
End Sub

Sub Command1_Click ()
    Dim Count As Integer
    Dim I As Integer, J As Integer

    For I = IdxLo To IdxHi
        J = J + 1
        If GuessTable(I + IdxOffset) = Answer(J) Then Count
 = Count + 1
    Next I
    PictureScore(IdxHi \ 6).Picture
 = PictureDice(Count).Picture
    ScoreTable(IdxHi \ 6 + IdxOffset \ 6) = Count
    Command1.Enabled = 0
    If Count = 6 Then
        GameOver = 1
        LabelMessage.Caption = "that's it!"
        LabelMessage.Visible = 1
        Timer1.Enabled = -1
        Exit Sub
    End If
    If IdxLo < 31 Then
        IdxLo = IdxLo + 6
        IdxHi = IdxHi + 6
    Else
        If IdxOffset >= MAXPOS - 36 Then
            Beep
            GameOver = 1
            LabelMessage.Caption = "no more guesses!"
            LabelMessage.Visible = 1
            Exit Sub
```

(continued)

Figure 4-9 *continued*

```
        End If
        IdxOffset = IdxOffset + 6
        VScroll1.Max = IdxOffset \ 6
        VScroll1.Value = VScroll1.Max
        VScroll1.Visible = -1
        ScrollIt IdxOffset \ 6
    End If
    For I = 1 To 6
        PictureHold(I).Visible = -1
    Next I
End Sub

Sub Command1_DragDrop (Source As Control, X As Single,
 Y As Single)
    PictureHold(DragSource).Visible = -1
    DragSource = 0
End Sub

Sub Form_DragDrop (Source As Control, X As Single,
 Y As Single)
    PictureHold(DragSource).Visible = -1
    DragSource = 0
End Sub

Sub Form_Load ()
    Dim I As Integer
    Dim Rec As RECT
    Dim Row As Integer, Col As Integer
    Dim X As Integer, Y As Integer

    'code for display device independence:
    Rec.Left = 0
    Rec.Top = 0
    Rec.Right = CLIENTRIGHT
    Rec.Bottom = CLIENTBOTTOM
    AdjustWindowRect Rec, WS_CAPTION, -1
    FormMain.Width = (Rec.Right - Rec.Left + 1) * (1440 /
GetDeviceCaps(hDC, LOGPIXELSX))
    FormMain.Height = (Rec.Bottom - Rec.Top + 1) * (1440 /
GetDeviceCaps(hDC, LOGPIXELSY))
    X = 48
    For Col = 1 To 6
        PictureHold(Col).Left = X: PictureHold(Col).Top = 16
```

(continued)

Figure 4-9 *continued*

```
        PictureHold(Col).Width = 29: PictureHold(Col).Height
= 29
        PictureHold(Col).Picture = PictureDice(Col).DragIcon
        PictureHold(Col).DragIcon = PictureDice(Col).DragIcon
        X = X + 32
    Next Col
    Y = 56
    For Row = 1 To 6
        LabelNumber(Row).Left = 0: LabelNumber(Row).Top = Y
        LabelNumber(Row).Width = 45: LabelNumber(Row).Height
= 29
        PictureScore(Row).Left = 248: PictureScore(Row).Top
= Y
        PictureScore(Row).Width = 29: PictureScore(Row).Height
= 29
        Y = Y + 32
    Next Row
    I = 1
    Y = 56
    For Row = 1 To 6
        X = 48
        For Col = 1 To 6
            PictureGuess(I).Left = X: PictureGuess(I).Top = Y
            PictureGuess(I).Width = 29: PictureGuess(I).Height
= 29
            X = X + 32
            I = I + 1
        Next Col
        Y = Y + 32
    Next Row
    Command1.Left = 248: Command1.Top = 16
    Command1.Width = 60: Command1.Height = 29
    VScroll1.Left = 288: VScroll1.Top = 56
    VScroll1.Width = 20: VScroll1.Height = 189
    LabelMessage.Left = 48: LabelMessage.Top = 256
    LabelMessage.Width = 189: LabelMessage.Height = 25

    Randomize
    BackColor = &H808000
    InitNewGame
End Sub

Sub Form_MouseMove (Button As Integer, Shift As Integer,
 X As Single, Y As Single)
```

(continued)

Figure 4-9 *continued*

```
    If DragSource <> 0 Then
        PictureHold(DragSource).Visible = -1
        DragSource = 0
    End If
End Sub

Sub Form_Unload (Cancel As Integer)
    WinHelp hWnd, HELP_FILE, HELP_QUIT, 0
End Sub

Sub LabelNumber_DragDrop (Index As Integer, Source As Control,
 X As Single, Y As Single)
    PictureHold(DragSource).Visible = -1
    DragSource = 0
End Sub

Sub MenuAbout_Click ()
    FormAbout.Show 1
End Sub

Sub MenuCommands_Click ()
    WinHelp hWnd, HELP_FILE, HELP_CONTEXT, HELP_COMMANDS
End Sub

Sub MenuExit_Click ()
    WinHelp hWnd, HELP_FILE, HELP_QUIT, 0
    End
End Sub

Sub MenuHowTo_Click ()
    WinHelp hWnd, HELP_FILE, HELP_CONTEXT, HELP_HOWTOPLAY
End Sub

Sub MenuIndex_Click ()
    WinHelp hWnd, HELP_FILE, HELP_INDEX, 0
End Sub

Sub MenuNew_Click ()
    InitNewGame
End Sub

Sub MenuUsingHelp_Click ()
    WinHelp hWnd, HELP_FILE, HELP_HELPONHELP, 0
End Sub
```

(continued)

Figure 4-9 *continued*

```
Sub PictureGuess_DragDrop (Index As Integer, Source As Control,
 X As Single, Y As Single)
    Dim Flag As Integer

    If Index >= IdxLo And Index <= IdxHi And GuessTable(Index
+ IdxOffset) = 7 Then
        PictureGuess(Index).Picture =
PictureDice(DragSource).Picture
        PictureGuess(Index).DragIcon =
PictureDice(DragSource).DragIcon
        GuessTable(Index + IdxOffset) = DragSource
        For I = IdxLo To IdxHi
            If GuessTable(I + IdxOffset) = 7 Then
                Flag = -1
                Exit For
            End If
        Next I
        If Not Flag Then Command1.Enabled = -1
    Else
        PictureHold(DragSource).Visible = -1
    End If
    DragSource = 0
End Sub

Sub PictureGuess_MouseDown (Index As Integer, Button As Integer,
 Shift As Integer, X As Single, Y As Single)
    If GameOver Or Scrolled Then Exit Sub
    If Index >= IdxLo And Index <= IdxHi And GuessTable(Index +
IdxOffset) <> 7 Then
        DragSource = GuessTable(Index + IdxOffset)
        GuessTable(Index + IdxOffset) = 7
        Command1.Enabled = 0
        PictureGuess(Index).Picture = PictureDice(7).Picture
        PictureGuess(Index).Drag 1
    End If
End Sub

Sub PictureHold_DragDrop (Index As Integer, Source As Control,
 X As Single, Y As Single)
    PictureHold(DragSource).Visible = -1
    DragSource = 0
End Sub
```

(continued)

79

Figure 4-9 *continued*

```
Sub PictureHold_MouseDown (Index As Integer, Button As Integer,
 Shift As Integer, X As Single, Y As Single)
    If GameOver Or Scrolled Then Exit Sub
    PictureHold(Index).Visible = 0
    PictureHold(Index).Drag 1
    DragSource = Index
End Sub

Sub PictureScore_DragDrop (Index As Integer, Source As Control,
 X As Single, Y As Single)
    PictureHold(DragSource).Visible = -1
    DragSource = 0
End Sub

Sub Timer1_Timer ()
    Static Count As Integer

    If Count > 3 Then
        Timer1.Enabled = 0
        Count = 0
        Exit Sub
    End If
    Beep
    If Count Mod 2 Then
        LabelMessage.Visible = -1
    Else
        LabelMessage.Visible = 0
    End If
    Count = Count + 1
End Sub

Sub VScroll1_Change ()
    ScrollIt CInt(VScroll1.Value)
End Sub
```

DDABOUT.FRM code

```
Sub Command1_Click ()
    Unload FormAbout
End Sub
```

Programming Techniques

You might have noticed that the form displayed in Figure 4-4 appears larger, and contains more controls, than the window actually displays when you are playing the game. This is because the Deduce game uses nine controls that are *not* part of the visible program display—the eight elements of PictureDice and Timerl. At design time, the form is left large enough to reveal these controls. At runtime, however, the form is explicitly sized so that it is just large enough to hold the visible controls (as shown in Figure 4-1).

The Deduce program uses many of the same coding techniques presented in the Peg Solitaire program in the preceding chapter. As with Peg Solitaire, the objects within the Deduce playing area are created using picture boxes, and changes to these objects are generated by assigning new Picture property settings. As with Peg Solitaire, Deduce game objects (in this case, dice) are animated in response to mouse movements using the Visual Basic drag-and-drop facility.

In addition to these previously demonstrated techniques, Deduce introduces the following new programming techniques:

- Using the Visual Basic random-number generator to create variable sequences of numbers.

- Incorporating a scroll bar to allow a player to view the picture boxes showing previous guesses.

- Including a command button so that a player can signal when a guess is complete. The button is enabled only when all dice are positioned in the current row.

- Using a timer control to flash a label and sound the speaker at regular intervals.

- Printing to the Debug object to provide information for checking that the program is working correctly.

Program Overview

Here is a summary of the sequence of events in the Deduce program.

- When the program starts, the *Form_Load* event procedure performs the required one-time initialization tasks and calls *InitNewGame* to begin a new game.

- When the player chooses the New Game command from the Game menu, the *NewGame_Click* event procedure also calls *InitNewGame* to start a new game.

- *InitNewGame* performs the initialization tasks required for each new game, including setting the *GameOver* flag to FALSE.

- If the player presses the mouse button while the pointer is over one of the dice at the top of the form, the *Picture-Hold_MouseDown* event procedure initiates a drag operation (permitting the player to move the die to a guess position), provided that *GameOver* is set to FALSE.

- If the player presses the mouse button while the pointer is over one of the dice in the row containing the current guess, the *PictureGuess_MouseDown* event procedure initiates a drag operation, permitting the player to change the position of the die.

- If the player drops the die on a valid position within the row containing the current guess, the *PictureGuess_DragDrop* event procedure moves the die to the new position. If all spaces in the row have been filled, it also enables the Next command button.

- If the player drops the die on an invalid position, the *PictureGuess_DragDrop* event procedure belonging to the object under the pointer returns the die to its original position at the top of the form.

- If the player clicks the Next command button (possible only when the current row has been filled), the *Command1_Click* event procedure displays the score. Also, if the correct sequence has been guessed, the procedure terminates the game and enables the timer.

- After the timer has been enabled, the *Timer1_Timer* event procedure begins receiving control every 300 milliseconds. It flashes the "that's it!" message at the bottom of the screen, beeps, and disables itself after four flashes of the message.

Designing the Form

The visual design of Deduce is created entirely by placing various controls within a blank form. Unlike Peg Solitaire, Deduce does not use a bitmap for the background. Rather, the color assigned to the BackColor property of the main form (&H00808000, dark cyan) serves as the background for the game window.

The controls used in the Deduce main form (FormMain, defined in DD.FRM) are listed in the following table.

Name of Control	Purpose
Command1	A command button, labeled Next, which the player clicks to move on to the next guess once the current guess has been completed.
LabelMessage	A label that displays "that's it!" when the player guesses the correct sequence.
LabelNumber	An array of labels, indexed from 1 through 6, used to number the rows.
PictureDice	An array of eight picture boxes used to store the images of the dice. PictureDice(0) stores the image of a blank die in a holder, PictureDice(1) through PictureDice(6) store the images of dice numbered from 1 through 6 in holders, and PictureDice(7) stores the image of an empty die holder. PictureDice(1) through PictureDice(6) also store drag icons, each of which is the image of the corresponding die *without* a holder.
PictureGuess	An array of picture boxes, indexed from 1 through 36, used to display the dice sequences arranged by the player.
PictureHold	An array of picture boxes, indexed from 1 through 6, used to display the dice at the top of the form. The player drags these dice down to the current row of PictureGuess to form a sequence.
PictureScore	An array of picture boxes, indexed from 1 through 6, used to display the dice that indicate the number of correctly placed dice in each row.
Timer1	A timer used to flash the "that's it!" message and repeatedly beep the speaker when the player guesses the sequence.
VScroll1	A vertical scroll bar that is displayed after the player has made six or more guesses. The player uses it to scroll through previous guesses.

83

The locations of these controls are illustrated in Figure 4-4 on page 66, and the nondefault properties assigned to them at design time are listed in Figure 4-5 on page 67.

The array of picture boxes, PictureDice, is used to store all the program icons. These are the only picture boxes that are assigned Picture or DragIcon properties at design time. At runtime, the pictures and drag icons are copied from the elements of PictureDice to other picture boxes, as they are needed.

At design time, the background color of each of the visible labels and picture boxes is set to dark cyan—that is, the BackColor property is assigned the value &H00808000. The background color of the form, however, is temporarily set to white to make it easier to view the sizes and positions of the controls (because the labels and picture boxes do not have borders). At runtime, the initialization routine changes the background color of the form to dark cyan, so the controls blend into the form background.

Initializing the Program

The program initialization code, in the *Form_Load* event procedure, first positions and sizes all the program objects to ensure that the form will be displayed properly—regardless of the current video mode. (See the Chapter 3 section titled "Coding for Device Independence" for a complete explanation of this technique.) Using the pixel scale mode and explicitly positioning program objects assures that all icons will fit within their picture boxes, that program controls will not overlap, and that the form will be large enough to hold all of its controls. It does not, however, prevent some distortion in the proportions of the icons. For example, the dice icons for Deduce were created using a VGA system; consequently, if the program is run on an EGA system, the dice are no longer square, but are slightly elongated in the vertical direction.

Form_Load also copies the appropriate icons into the elements of PictureHold, which are used to display the dice at the top of the window (with *Col* varying from 1 to 6):

```
PictureHold(Col).Picture = PictureDice(Col).DragIcon
PictureHold(Col).DragIcon = PictureDice(Col).DragIcon
```

This step is performed only once, at the beginning of the program, because the icons are not changed as the program is run and new games are started. The only property of these picture boxes that is changed is their visibility (that is, the Visible property). Notice that both the Picture property *and* the DragIcon property of the PictureHold elements are assigned drag icons stored within PictureDice (elements 1 through 6), because the drag icons depict plain dice without holders, as wanted.

Form_Load begins a new game by calling the general procedure *InitNewGame*. Whenever the player chooses the New Game command from the Game menu, the *MenuNew_Click* event procedure also calls *InitNewGame*.

The *InitNewGame* general procedure first prepares all the program controls for a new game, as follows:

- It copies the image stored within PictureDice(7), which represents an empty die holder, to all members of PictureGuess, in order to clear the playing area:

```
PictureGuess(I).Picture = PictureDice(7).Picture 'I varies
   from 1 to 36
```

- It makes all members of PictureHold visible, so that the six dice appear at the top of the window:

```
PictureHold(I).Visible = -1 'I varies from 1 to 6
```

- It copies the image from PictureDice(7), which depicts an empty die holder, to all elements of PictureScore (which are used to display the scores assigned to each guess):

```
PictureScore(I).Picture = PictureDice(7).Picture  'I varies
   from 1 to 6
```

- It numbers the rows (from 1 through 6) by setting the Caption properties of the LabelNumber elements:

```
LabelNumber(I).Caption = Str$(I) 'I varies from 1 to 6
```

- It disables the Next command button, hides the vertical scroll bar, and hides the label containing the message displayed when a game is won:

```
Command1.Enabled = 0
VScroll1.Visible = 0
LabelMessage.Visible = 0
```

The *InitNewGame* procedure next initializes program variables to prepare for a new game, as follows:

- It initializes *IdxLo* and *IdxHi*, which contain the indexes of the first and last elements of the *current* row of PictureGuess:

```
IdxLo = 1: IdxHi = 6
```

(The current row is the one in which the player is presently allowed to arrange dice.)

■ It assigns initial values to GuessTable:

```
For I = 1 To MAXPOS
GuessTable(I) = 7
Next I
```

GuessTable is an array of integers indexed from 1 through MAXPOS (108), used to store the number of each die that the player positions; the value 7 indicates that the player has not yet placed a die at the corresponding position. Because each guess requires positioning six dice, and the player is permitted a maximum of eighteen guesses, the table has 6 * 18 (or 108) elements.

■ It assigns an initial value to *IdxOffset*:

```
IdxOffset = 0
```

IdxOffset stores the index of the *first* element of GuessTable that is displayed on the form, in PictureGuess(1). In other words, it indicates how the elements of GuessTable are mapped onto the visible picture boxes of PictureGuess. Until the player completes six guesses, this value is 0, because *all* GuessTable elements are displayed. After the player has completed six or more guesses, however, 6 is added to *IdxOffset* with each guess, and some of the elements of GuessTable are no longer visible (unless the player explicitly scrolls, as explained later).

■ It initializes ScoreTable, which is an array of integers, indexed from 1 through 18, used for storing the number of correctly positioned dice in each sequence that the player has guessed:

```
For I = 1 To MAXPOS \ 6
ScoreTable(I) = 7
Next I
```

The value 7 means that the player has not yet placed a guess in the corresponding row. (Notice that 7 corresponds to the index of the blank die holder in PictureDice; later you will see how this correspondence is used.)

■ It sets the form-level variable *Scrolled* to FALSE:

```
Scrolled = 0
```

This variable is set to TRUE only when the player has completed six or more guesses and has used the scroll bar to view previous guesses. When *Scrolled* is TRUE, the current row is not visible, and the player is therefore not permitted to move dice.

■ Finally, the form-level variable *GameOver* is set to FALSE:

```
GameOver = 0
```

This variable is set to TRUE only after a game has been won. When it is TRUE, the player is not permitted to make further moves until choosing the New Game command.

Generating Random Sequences

The hidden sequences of dice are created by using the Visual Basic random-number generator. At the beginning of the program, the *Form_Load* event procedure calls the *Randomize* function, so the sequences of dice are different each time the program is run. Then, for each new game, *InitNewGame* uses the *Rnd* function to create a new hidden sequence of dice, as follows:

```
For I = 1 To 6
    TempArray(I) = I
Next I
Top = 6
For I = 1 To 6
    IdxTemp = Int(Top * Rnd + 1)
    Answer(I) = TempArray(IdxTemp)
    For J = IdxTemp To Top - 1
        TempArray(J) = TempArray(J + 1)
    Next J
    Top = Top - 1
Next I
```

TempArray is a procedure-level array of integers that initially stores the numbers 1 through 6; *Top* stores the index of the last element of this array (initially *6*). The *Rnd* function is used to pick a random element from this array; the value of this element is placed in the Answer array, which stores the hidden sequence. Notice that the expression

```
Int(Top * Rnd + 1)
```

returns a random integer ranging from *1* through *Top*.

After an element has been chosen from TempArray, it is deleted from the array by moving all the higher-indexed elements one position down and by decrementing *Top*. (Remember: A number cannot be used more than once.) This process is repeated five times to pick the remaining elements of Answer. (The last call to *Rnd* is unnecessary, but it simplifies the code.)

Displaying Testing Information

Before terminating, the *InitNewGame* procedure prints the hidden sequence of dice, stored in Answer, to the special Debug object:

```
For I = 1 To 6
    Debug.Print Answer(I); " ";
Next I
Debug.Print
```

If the game is run within the Visual Basic environment, this information appears within the Immediate Window and serves to help in testing the program as changes are made to the code. If the game is run from a freestanding EXE file, the solution is not printed; therefore, you do not need to remove this code, not even from the final version of the game.

Dragging and Dropping the Dice

After a new game has been initialized, the Deduce program waits for a MouseDown event signaling that the player wants to drag one of the dice. The player can drag any of the dice, which are stored in the members of PictureHold, from the top of the form. Accordingly, the *Picture-Hold_MouseDown* event procedure is coded as follows:

```
Sub PictureHold_MouseDown (Index As Integer, Button As Integer,
 Shift As Integer, X As Single, Y As Single)
    If GameOver Or Scrolled Then Exit Sub
    PictureHold(Index).Visible = 0
    PictureHold(Index).Drag 1
    DragSource = Index
End Sub
```

If the game has already been won (*GameOver* is TRUE) or if the player has scrolled to view previous guesses (*Scrolled* is TRUE), moves are not allowed and the procedure terminates immediately. Otherwise, the procedure calls the *Drag* method to initiate a drag operation and assigns the index of the dragged picture box to *DragSource*. Also, the procedure makes the dragged picture box invisible by assigning False to its Visible property, to create the illusion that the die has been removed; otherwise, both the original die and the drag icon would be visible.

Note: The code for dragging a picture box works in the same manner as the code in the Peg Solitaire game, which is fully described in Chapter 3. Accordingly, it is only briefly summarized here.

The player can also drag any of the dice that he has placed within the current row of PictureGuess. Similar code is attached to the *Picture-Guess_MouseDown* procedure to handle this event:

```
Sub PictureGuess_MouseDown (Index As Integer, Button As Integer,
 Shift As Integer, X As Single, Y As Single)
    If GameOver Or Scrolled Then Exit Sub
    If Index >= IdxLo And Index <= IdxHi And GuessTable(Index
 + IdxOffset) <> 7 Then
        DragSource = GuessTable(Index + IdxOffset)
        GuessTable(Index + IdxOffset) = 7
        Command1.Enabled = 0
        PictureGuess(Index).Picture = PictureDice(7).Picture
        PictureGuess(Index).Drag 1
    End If
End Sub
```

The drag operation is initiated only if the MouseDown event occurred within the current row of the PictureGuess array (*Index >= IdxLo And Index <= IdxHi*), and the current PictureGuess element contains a die (*GuessTable(Index + IdxOffset) <> 7*). Also, because a die is being removed from the current element, GuessTable must be updated to indicate the absence of a die (*GuessTable(Index + IdxOffset) = 7*), and the Next command button (Command1) must be disabled (just in case it was enabled).

Note: The Next button is enabled only when the current row of PictureGuess is full, and therefore ready to be scored.

Finally, the current element of PictureGuess is assigned the picture of the empty die holder, contained in PictureDice(7), to create the illusion that the dragged die is being removed.

After a drag operation has been initiated by either of these routines, the player is allowed to drop the die only on an empty position within the current row of PictureGuess. As in the Peg Solitaire game, the DragDrop event handlers attached to all other controls simply return the object to its home position. For example, if the player drops the die on the form, outside of a control, the following procedure is invoked:

```
Sub Form_DragDrop (Source As Control, X As Single, Y As Single)
    PictureHold(DragSource).Visible = -1
    DragSource = 0
End Sub
```

Also, as explained in Chapter 3 (in the section titled "Dropping an Icon Outside the Form"), the *Form_MouseMove* event procedure restores the icon to its home position if the user has dropped it outside the form.

The *PictureGuess_DragDrop* procedure tests whether the target picture box is within the current row of PictureGuess and whether the picture box is empty:

```
If Index >= IdxLo And Index <= IdxHi And GuessTable(Index +
 IdxOffset) = 7 Then
```

If both of these conditions are TRUE, the procedure assigns the appropriate picture and drag icon to the target picture box:

```
PictureGuess(Index).Picture = PictureDice(DragSource).Picture
PictureGuess(Index).DragIcon = PictureDice(DragSource).DragIcon
```

and updates GuessTable:

```
GuessTable(Index + IdxOffset) = DragSource
```

Then, if all six members of the current PictureGuess row are full, the procedure enables the Next command button:

```
For I = IdxLo To IdxHi
    If GuessTable(I + IdxOffset) = 7 Then
        Flag = -1
        Exit For
    End If
Next I
If Not Flag Then Command1.Enabled = -1
```

If the target member of PictureGuess is not in the current row or if the current row is full, the procedure returns the die to its home position:

```
Else
    PictureHold(DragSource).Visible = -1
```

Processing the Next Button Click

When the player clicks the Next button, the *Command1_Click* event procedure counts the number of correctly positioned dice, assigning the result to Count. It then places a die to the right of the row to indicate the value of Count, stores the value of Count permanently in ScoreTable, and disables the command button:

```
PictureScore(IdxHi \ 6).Picture = PictureDice(Count).Picture
ScoreTable(IdxHi \ 6 + IdxOffset \ 6) = Count
Command1.Enabled = 0
```

If Count contains the number 6, indicating that the player has solved the sequence, the procedure sets the *GameOver* flag to TRUE and displays a message in LabelMessage. The procedure also enables the timer, Timer1, and then exits. The purpose of the timer is to create a little fanfare in response to the player's success. After the timer has been enabled, the *Timer1_Timer* event procedure is called every 300 milliseconds. (At design time, the Interval property was set to 300.) *Timer1_Timer* calls *Beep* to sound the speaker, and it alternately hides and reveals the message in LabelMessage. After the message is displayed four times, the procedure disables Timer1, and the celebration ceases.

If the current row of PictureGuess is 1 through 5, the *Command1__Click* procedure simply adds 6 to the values of *IdxLo* and *IdxHi* to move on to the next row.

If, however, the current row is 6, the procedure must *scroll* to move the previous dice arrangements up by one row so that room is created for the next guess. (Remember: Only six rows are displayed on the form at a given time.) First, however, the procedure checks whether the maximum number of guesses has been reached; if the maximum has been reached, it displays the message "no more guesses!" and exits from the procedure rather than scrolling. (Scrolling is described in the next section.)

After scrolling, the *Command1_Click* event procedure restores the dice at the top of the form so that they are available for the next guess:

```
PictureHold(I).Visible = -1   'I varies from 1 to 6
```

Vertical Scrolling

The scrolling process is a bit complex. It involves Property settings made at design time as well as program statements and changes the player makes to the scroll bar at runtime.

At design time, the vertical scroll bar, VScroll1, is assigned the important property settings listed in the following table.

Property	Setting	Result
Min	0 (default)	The smallest possible setting of the scroll bar Value property is 0.
SmallChange	1 (default)	Visual Basic will change the Value property by 1 when the player clicks an arrow on the scroll bar (which will cause Deduce to scroll by 1 row).
LargeChange.	6	Visual Basic will change the Value property by 6 when the player clicks above or below the scroll box (which will cause Deduce to scroll by 6 rows, if possible).
Visible	False	The scroll bar is initially invisible.

To scroll the rows of dice arrangements, the *Command1_Click* event procedure first adds 6 to *IdxOffset*. (As explained previously, this is the index of the first member of GuessTable that is currently displayed.) It then assigns the property settings listed in the following table to the scroll bar.

Property	Setting	Result
Max	IdxOffset \ 6	The highest possible setting of the Value property equals the total number of hidden rows of guesses.
Value	VScroll1.Max	The scroll box is placed at the bottom end of the scroll bar.
Visible	−1 (True)	The scroll bar becomes visible (in case it was not already visible).

After the scroll bar has been adjusted, the *Command1_Click* event procedure calls the general procedure, *ScrollIt*, to actually move the pictures on the form:

```
ScrollIt IdxOffset \ 6
```

The parameter *IdxOffset \ 6* tells *ScrollIt* the row offset, from the beginning of GuessTable, of the dice the procedure should display. This call specifies the maximum offset.

ScrollIt is also called by the *VScroll1_Change* event procedure, which is called whenever the player directly manipulates the scroll bar:

```
Sub VScroll1_Change ()
    ScrollIt CInt(VScroll1.Value)
End Sub
```

The row offset specified in this call is based on the new Value property of the scroll bar.

To effect the scrolling, the *ScrollIt* general procedure remaps the dice values in GuessTable onto the members of PictureGuess:

```
Offset = RowOffset * 6
For I = 1 To 36
    PictureGuess(I).Picture = PictureDice(GuessTable(I +
 Offset)).Picture
Next I
```

and remaps the scores in ScoreTable onto the members of PictureScore:

```
For I = 1 To 6
    PictureScore(I).Picture = PictureDice(ScoreTable(I +
 RowOffset)).Picture
Next I
```

basing the starting positions on the row offset passed as its parameter, *RowOffset*. It also reprints the row numbers, starting with the appropriate number:

```
For I = 1 To 6
    LabelNumber(I).Caption = Str$(RowOffset + I)
Next I
```

Finally, if the scroll bar is not at its maximum position, *ScrollIt* sets the *Scrolled* flag to TRUE, which prevents the player from dragging dice. (If the scroll bar is not at its maximum position, the current row is hidden; the player must scroll it back into view before making the next move.)

Enhancing the Game

Here are a few suggestions for enhancing the Deduce program.

- Make the game more difficult by permitting the same number to appear more than once in the sequence. This would increase the number of possible arrangements from 720 to 46,656 (6 raised to the 6th power).

- Use tiles or other graphic elements rather than dice.
- Allow the player to vary the game by changing the number of items to choose from and the number of items in a sequence. For example, the player might choose from eight dice (or other objects) and place five items in a sequence.

CHAPTER FIVE

WORD SQUARES

In the game Word Squares, the player arranges a collection of letters to form words that can be read in both the horizontal and vertical directions. The code for Word Squares demonstrates a new method for animating a graphical object, in which a picture box is moved within the form in response to mouse movements. In learning this technique, you will also discover a variety of ways to control the mouse pointer by using Windows API functions.

About Word Squares

A "word square" consists of equal-length words that can be read in both the vertical (top-to-bottom) and horizontal (left-to-right) directions. For example, here is a word square consisting of three-letter words:

```
A   C   E

C   A   N

E   N   D
```

and here is a word square consisting of four-letter words:

```
A   T   O   M

T   O   M   E

O   M   E   N

M   E   N   D
```

Word squares were a popular amusement in England in the 1800s. In one kind of puzzle, the player would start with a single word and would then try to complete the word square, using any letters that formed valid words. Here is an example of such a puzzle:

```
A   T   O   M

T   _   _   _

O   _   _   _

M   _   _   _
```

In another kind of puzzle, akin to the modern crossword, the player would ponder definitions or riddles provided for each word and would attempt to derive the word square designed by the puzzlemaker. Here is an example of such a puzzle:

```
An indivisible particle    _ _ _ _

A scholarly book           _ _ _ _

A sign of a future event   _ _ _ _

To repair                  _ _ _ _
```

Creating word squares with three-letter words is easy. As the number of letters increases, however, the difficulty increases greatly. Making word squares of eight or more letters might require choosing uncommon words. Creating a word square of ten or more letters is an extremely difficult task and might be impossible using valid English words.

Playing Word Squares

In the Word Squares game presented in this chapter, all the individual letters are given to you. Your task is to arrange them so that they form a valid word square. When you run Word Squares (WS.EXE), the program starts a game, displaying an "empty" three-letter word square and nine letters below it, as shown in Figure 5-1.

To play the game, simply drag each letter from the area at the bottom of the form, and drop it on one of the empty squares within the grid at the top. You can change a move you have already made by dragging a letter from one square to another or to a position outside the grid. You can also freely rearrange the letters in the area outside the grid. Figure 5-2 shows Word Squares after a player has dropped three letters on the grid.

Figure 5-1.
Opening of a Word Squares game, using three-letter words.

Figure 5-2.
A Word Squares game underway.

As soon as you correctly guess the word square, the program displays a congratulatory message and ends the game. To begin a new game, choose one of the seven Game commands from the Game menu (Game 1 through Game 7). Each command creates a different game. When you open the Game menu, you see a check mark beside the game that was played previously.

> ### TIP
>
> If you choose a command from the Game menu before com-
> pleting a game, the current game will be terminated and a new
> one started. To rescramble the letters for the game you are
> currently playing, simply choose the same command used to
> start the game from the Game menu (the checked command).

You can change the size of the word square by choosing a command from the Options menu. The *3 × 3* command, which is in effect
when you start the program, selects a three-letter word square; the *4 × 4*
command selects a four-letter word square. For both these commands,
the program provides 7 games—14 games in all.. When you choose either of the commands from the Options menu, the program begins a
new game (Game 1), terminating any game already in progress.

Note: For each game, the program begins with a given word square
and scrambles the letters it contains. You might be able to arrange these
letters into a valid word square *other* than the one used as the basis for
the game. The program, however, will not acknowledge your achievement.

Strategy and Hints

The easiest way to become acquainted with Word Squares is to begin
playing using three-letter word squares; you can then graduate to four-
letter words.

One rule of thumb might help you narrow the possible arrangements: If a letter occurs an odd number of times, at least one of these
letters must be placed along the diagonal between the upper left corner
and the lower right corner of the word square. For example, if three *T*s
are available, at least one *T* will end up on the diagonal. You might therefore begin by arranging the letters into pairs, working in the area at the
bottom of the window. The letters left over can be separated from the
rest; these letters must be placed along the diagonal.

Figure 5-3 shows Game 1 after a player has sorted the letters. In this
game, the three odd letters at the left must fill the squares along the
diagonal. The next step might be to guess the word in the top row and

in the first column, which must begin with one of the odd letters, and then use letters from the pairs to fill in the remaining squares.

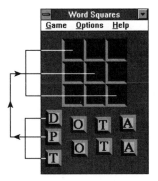

Figure 5-3.
Beginning a game by sorting the letters.

Coding Word Squares

The source code for the Word Squares program is contained in the files listed in the following table.

File	Purpose
GLOBALWS.BAS	Contains global type definitions
WS.FRM	Defines the main form, FormMain, and the controls it contains
WSABOUT.FRM	Defines the ABOUT form, FormAbout, and the controls it contains
WS.MAK	Contains the Word Squares project file

You can load all these files into Visual Basic by choosing the Open Project command from the File menu and specifying the file WS.MAK at the prompt.

Figures 5-4 through 5-9 beginning on the following page present the form designs, properties, menu commands, and source code for the Word Squares program.

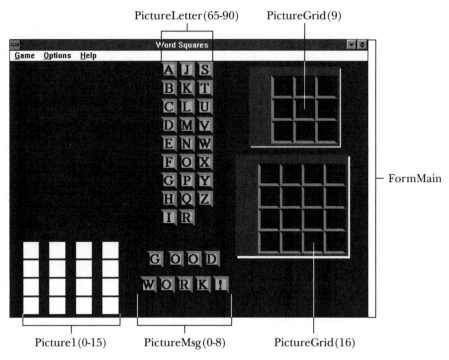

PictureLetter (65-90)   PictureGrid (9)

FormMain

Picture1 (0-15)   PictureMsg (0-8)   PictureGrid (16)

Figure 5-4.
WS.FRM at design time. (The form shown here has been maximized to show all the controls it contains. At runtime, it is explicitly sized to reveal only the visible objects.)

Object Name	Object Type	Property	Setting
FormMain	Form	BackColor	&H00808000& [dark cyan]
		BorderStyle	1 - Fixed Single
		Caption	Word Squares
		FormName	FormMain
		Grid Height	4 [pixels]
		Grid Width	4 [pixels]
		Height	3375 [twips]
		Icon	(Icon) [WS.ICO]
		Left	180 [twips]

Figure 5-5.   *(continued)*
WS.FRM form and control properties.

Figure 5-5 *continued*

Object Name	Object Type	Property	Setting
		MaxButton	False
		ScaleMode	3 - Pixel
		Top	390 [twips]
Picture1	Array of picture boxes	BorderStyle	0 - None
		Height	29 [pixels]
		Index	0 - 15
		Left	[varies]
		ScaleMode	3 - Pixel
		Top	[varies]
		Width	29 [pixels]
PictureGrid	Array of picture boxes	BorderStyle	0 - None
		CtlName	PictureGrid
		Height	[varies]
		Index	9 and 16
		Left	[varies]
		Picture	(Bitmap) PictureGrid(9): WS2.BMP PictureGrid(16): WS3.BMP
		Top	[varies]
		Visible	False
		Width	[varies]
PictureLetter	Array of picture boxes	BorderStyle	0 - None
		CtlName	PictureLetter
		Height	29 [pixels]
		Index	65 - 90
		Left	[varies]
		Picture	(Bitmap) [from WS1.BMP]
		Top	[varies]
		Visible	False
		Width	29 [pixels]

(continued)

Figure 5-5 *continued*

Object Name	Object Type	Property	Setting
PictureMsg	Array of picture boxes	BorderStyle	0 - None
		CtlName	PictureMsg
		Height	29 [pixels]
		Index	0 - 8
		Left	[varies]
		Picture	(Bitmap) [from WS1.BMP]
		Top	[varies]
		Visible	False
		Width	29 [pixels]

Indentation/Caption	Control Name	Other Features
&Game	MenuGame	
....Game &1	MenuInitGame	Index = 0 Checked
....Game &2	MenuInitGame	Index = 1
....Game &3	MenuInitGame	Index = 2
....Game &4	MenuInitGame	Index = 3
....Game &5	MenuInitGame	Index = 4
....Game &6	MenuInitGame	Index = 5
....Game &7	MenuInitGame	Index = 6
....-	MenuSep1	
....E&xit	MenuExit	
&Options	MenuOptions	
....&3 x 3	Menu3x3	Checked
....&4 x 4	Menu4x4	
&Help	MenuHelp	
....&Index	MenuIndex	Accelerator = F1
....&How to Play	MenuHowTo	
....&Commands	MenuCommands	

Figure 5-6. *(continued)*

WS.FRM menu design.

Figure 5-6 *continued*

Indentation/Caption	Control Name	Other Features
....&Using Help	MenuUsingHelp	
....-	MenuSep2	
....&About Word Squares...	MenuAbout	

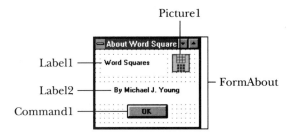

Figure 5-7.
WSABOUT.FRM at design time.

Object Name	Object Type	Property	Setting
Command1	Command button	Caption	OK
		Default	True
		Height	375 [twips]
		Left	840 [twips]
		Top	1440 [twips]
		Width	1095 [twips]
FormAbout	Form	BorderStyle	3 - Fixed Double
		Caption	About Word Squares
		FormName	FormAbout
		Grid Height	120 [twips]
		Grid Width	120 [twips]
		Height	2445 [twips]
		Left	1140 [twips]

Figure 5-8. *(continued)*
WSABOUT.FRM form and control properties.

Figure 5-8 *continued*

Object Name	Object Type	Property	Setting
		MaxButton	False
		MinButton	False
		Top	1440 [twips]
		Width	2880 [twips]
Label1	Label	Caption	Word Squares
		Height	375 [twips]
		Left	240 [twips]
		Top	240 [twips]
		Width	1575 [twips]
Label2	Label	Alignment	2 - Center
		Caption	By Michael J. Young
		Height	375 [twips]
		Left	0 [twips]
		Top	960 [twips]
		Width	2745 [twips]
Picture1	Picture box	AutoSize	True
		BorderStyle	0 - None
		Height	480 [twips]
		Left	2040 [twips]
		Picture	(Icon) [WS.ICO]
		Top	120 [twips]
		Width	480 [twips]

GLOBALWS.BAS code

```
Type APIPOINT
    X As Integer
    Y As Integer
End Type

Type RECT
    Left As Integer
```

Figure 5-9.   *(continued)*

Source code for the Word Squares program. (Notice that long program lines are wrapped to the next line and indented one space.)

Figure 5-9 *continued*

```
    Top As Integer
    Right As Integer
    Bottom As Integer
End Type

Type SQUARE
    X1 As Integer
    Y1 As Integer
    X2 As Integer
    Y2 As Integer
    Index As Integer
End Type
```

WS.FRM code

```
'Help Section:
'Help file:
Const HELP_FILE = "WS.HLP"
'WinHelp wCommand values:
Const HELP_CONTEXT = &H1
Const HELP_HELPONHELP = &H4
Const HELP_INDEX = &H3
Const HELP_QUIT = &H2
'WinHelp dwData values (help topics):
Const HELP_HOWTOPLAY = 10&
Const HELP_COMMANDS = 20&
'Windows help API:
Declare Sub WinHelp Lib "USER" (ByVal hWnd As Integer, ByVal
 lpHelpFile As String, ByVal wCommand As Integer,
 ByVal dwData As Long)

Dim FourByWords(6) As String
Dim GameOver As Integer
Dim MoveIdx As Integer
Dim NumSquares As Integer    '9 or 16
Dim Solution As String
Dim SquareTable(15) As SQUARE
Dim ThreeByWords(6) As String
Dim XOffset As Integer
Dim YOffset As Integer

Const WS_CAPTION = &HC00000
Const WS_THICKFRAME = &H40000
```

(continued)

Figure 5-9 *continued*

```
Declare Sub AdjustWindowRect Lib "USER" (lpRect As RECT, ByVal
 dwStyle&, ByVal bMenu%)

Declare Sub ClientToScreen Lib "USER" (ByVal hWnd As Integer,
 Pt As APIPOINT)
Declare Sub ClipCursor Lib "USER" (Rec As Any)

Const LOGPIXELSX = 88
Const LOGPIXELSY = 90
Declare Function GetDeviceCaps Lib "GDI" (ByVal hDC%, ByVal
 Index%) As Integer

Declare Sub ReleaseCapture Lib "USER" ()
Declare Sub SetCapture Lib "USER" (ByVal hWnd As Integer)
Declare Sub ShowCursor Lib "USER" (ByVal ShowIt As Integer)

Function GameSolved () As Integer
    Dim I As Integer

    GameSolved = 0
    For I = 0 To NumSquares - 1
        If SquareTable(I).Index = -1 Then Exit Function
        If Picture1(SquareTable(I).Index).Tag <> Mid$(Solution,
 I + 1, 1) Then Exit Function
    Next I
    GameSolved = -1
End Function

Sub InitNewGame (GameIdx As Integer)
    Dim I As Integer, J As Integer
    Dim Idx As Integer
    Static Table(15) As Integer
    Dim Upper As Integer

    For I = 0 To 8
        PictureMsg(I).Visible = 0
    Next I
    If NumSquares = 9 Then
        Picture1(0).Move 32, 136
        Picture1(1).Move 80, 136
        Picture1(2).Move 128, 136
        Picture1(3).Move 32, 168
        Picture1(4).Move 80, 168
        Picture1(5).Move 128, 168
```

(continued)

Figure 5-9 *continued*

```
        Picture1(6).Move 32, 200
        Picture1(7).Move 80, 200
        Picture1(8).Move 128, 200
        Solution = ThreeByWords(GameIdx)
    Else
        Picture1(0).Move 28, 176
        Picture1(1).Move 76, 176
        Picture1(2).Move 124, 176
        Picture1(3).Move 28, 208
        Picture1(4).Move 76, 208
        Picture1(5).Move 124, 208
        Picture1(6).Move 28, 240
        Picture1(7).Move 76, 240
        Picture1(8).Move 124, 240
        Picture1(9).Move 28, 272
        Picture1(10).Move 76, 272
        Picture1(11).Move 124, 272
        Picture1(12).Move 172, 176
        Picture1(13).Move 172, 208
        Picture1(14).Move 172, 240
        Picture1(15).Move 172, 272
        Solution = FourByWords(GameIdx)
    End If
    For I = 0 To NumSquares - 1
        Table(I) = Asc(Mid$(Solution, I + 1, 1))
    Next I
    Upper = NumSquares - 1
    For I = 0 To NumSquares - 1
        Idx = Int((Upper + 1) * Rnd)
        Picture1(I).Picture = PictureLetter(Table(Idx)).Picture
        Picture1(I).Tag = Chr$(Table(Idx))
        For J = Idx To Upper - 1
            Table(J) = Table(J + 1)
        Next J
        Upper = Upper - 1
    Next I
    For I = 0 To 6
        If I = GameIdx Then
            MenuInitGame(I).Checked = -1
        Else
            MenuInitGame(I).Checked = 0
        End If
    Next I
    For I = 0 To NumSquares - 1
```

(continued)

Figure 5-9 *continued*

```
            SquareTable(I).Index = -1
        Next I
        GameOver = 0
    End Sub

    Sub InitNewGrid (Squares As Integer)
        Dim ClientBottom As Integer
        Dim ClientRight As Integer
        Dim I As Integer
        Dim Rec As RECT

        If Squares = 9 Then
            ClientRight = 191
            ClientBottom = 255
            FormMain.Picture = PictureGrid(9).Picture
            PictureMsg(0).Move 32, 152
            PictureMsg(1).Move 64, 152
            PictureMsg(2).Move 96, 152
            PictureMsg(3).Move 128, 152
            PictureMsg(4).Move 16, 192
            PictureMsg(5).Move 48, 192
            PictureMsg(6).Move 80, 192
            PictureMsg(7).Move 112, 192
            PictureMsg(8).Move 144, 192
            For I = 9 To 15
                Picture1(I).Visible = 0
            Next I
            Menu3x3.Checked = -1
            Menu4x4.Checked = 0
        Else
            ClientRight = 231
            ClientBottom = 319
            FormMain.Picture = PictureGrid(16).Picture
            PictureMsg(0).Move 52, 192
            PictureMsg(1).Move 84, 192
            PictureMsg(2).Move 116, 192
            PictureMsg(3).Move 148, 192
            PictureMsg(4).Move 36, 236
            PictureMsg(5).Move 68, 236
            PictureMsg(6).Move 100, 236
            PictureMsg(7).Move 132, 236
            PictureMsg(8).Move 164, 236
            For I = 9 To 15
                Picture1(I).Visible = -1
```

(continued)

Figure 5-9 *continued*

```
        Next I
        Menu3x3.Checked = 0
        Menu4x4.Checked = -1
    End If

    Rec.Left = 0
    Rec.Top = 0
    Rec.Right = ClientRight
    Rec.Bottom = ClientBottom
    AdjustWindowRect Rec, WS_CAPTION, -1
    FormMain.Width = (Rec.Right - Rec.Left + 1) * (1440 /
 GetDeviceCaps(hDC, LOGPIXELSX))
    FormMain.Height = (Rec.Bottom - Rec.Top + 1) * (1440 /
 GetDeviceCaps(hDC, LOGPIXELSY))

    NumSquares = Squares
    InitNewGame 0
End Sub

Function SquareHit (X As Single, Y As Single) As Integer
    Dim I As Integer

    For I = 0 To NumSquares - 1
        If X >= SquareTable(I).X1 And X <= SquareTable(I).X2 Then
            If Y >= SquareTable(I).Y1 And Y <= SquareTable(I).Y2
 Then
                SquareHit = I
                Exit Function
            End If
        End If
    Next I
    SquareHit = -1
End Function

Sub Form_Load ()
    Dim I As Integer

    For I = 0 To 15
        Picture1(I).Width = 29: Picture1(I).Height = 29
    Next I
    For I = 0 To 8
        PictureMsg(I).Width = 29: PictureMsg(I).Height = 29
    Next I
    SquareTable(0).X1 = 37: SquareTable(0).Y1 = 13:      '
```

(continued)

Figure 5-9 *continued*

```
SquareTable(0).X2 = 75: SquareTable(0).Y2 = 51
   SquareTable(1).X1 = 76: SquareTable(1).Y1 = 13:
SquareTable(1).X2 = 114: SquareTable(1).Y2 = 51
   SquareTable(2).X1 = 115: SquareTable(2).Y1 = 13:
SquareTable(2).X2 = 153: SquareTable(2).Y2 = 51
   SquareTable(3).X1 = 37: SquareTable(3).Y1 = 52:
SquareTable(3).X2 = 75: SquareTable(3).Y2 = 90
   SquareTable(4).X1 = 76: SquareTable(4).Y1 = 52:
SquareTable(4).X2 = 114: SquareTable(4).Y2 = 90
   SquareTable(5).X1 = 115: SquareTable(5).Y1 = 52:
SquareTable(5).X2 = 153: SquareTable(5).Y2 = 90
   SquareTable(6).X1 = 37: SquareTable(6).Y1 = 91:
SquareTable(6).X2 = 75: SquareTable(6).Y2 = 129
   SquareTable(7).X1 = 76: SquareTable(7).Y1 = 91:
SquareTable(7).X2 = 114: SquareTable(7).Y2 = 129
   SquareTable(8).X1 = 115: SquareTable(8).Y1 = 91:
SquareTable(8).X2 = 153: SquareTable(8).Y2 = 129
   SquareTable(9).X1 = 37: SquareTable(9).Y1 = 130:
SquareTable(9).X2 = 75: SquareTable(9).Y2 = 168
   SquareTable(10).X1 = 76: SquareTable(10).Y1 = 130:
SquareTable(10).X2 = 114: SquareTable(10).Y2 = 168
   SquareTable(11).X1 = 115: SquareTable(11).Y1 = 130:
SquareTable(11).X2 = 153: SquareTable(11).Y2 = 168
   SquareTable(12).X1 = 154: SquareTable(12).Y1 = 13:
SquareTable(12).X2 = 192: SquareTable(12).Y2 = 51
   SquareTable(13).X1 = 154: SquareTable(13).Y1 = 52:
SquareTable(13).X2 = 192: SquareTable(13).Y2 = 90
   SquareTable(14).X1 = 154: SquareTable(14).Y1 = 91:
SquareTable(14).X2 = 192: SquareTable(14).Y2 = 129
   SquareTable(15).X1 = 154: SquareTable(15).Y1 = 130:
SquareTable(15).X2 = 192: SquareTable(15).Y2 = 168
   ThreeByWords(0) = "PATADOTOT"
   ThreeByWords(1) = "ELFLEAFAD"
   ThreeByWords(2) = "CATACETEA"
   ThreeByWords(3) = "MADADODOT"
   ThreeByWords(4) = "BATATETEN"
   ThreeByWords(5) = "WINICENET"
   ThreeByWords(6) = "FANADONOD"
   FourByWords(0) = "CRERAVEVEWERWERE"
   FourByWords(1) = "DARAMEREAENDENDS"
   FourByWords(2) = "SPIPACICENESNEST"
   FourByWords(3) = "LANARENEAEAREARS"
   FourByWords(4) = "GNANAMAMETENTENT"
   FourByWords(5) = "BIRIDEREADADDADA"
   FourByWords(6) = "STOTOMOMEPENPENT"
```

(continued)

Figure 5-9 *continued*

```
    MoveIdx = -1
    Randomize
    InitNewGrid 9
End Sub

Sub Form_MouseMove (Button As Integer, Shift As Integer,
 X As Single, Y As Single)
    If MoveIdx <> -1 Then
        Picture1(MoveIdx).Move X - XOffset, Y - YOffset
        Picture1(MoveIdx).Refresh
    End If
End Sub

Sub Form_MouseUp (Button As Integer, Shift As Integer,
 X As Single, Y As Single)
    Dim CodeSmallest As Integer '0=left,1=top,2=right,3=bottom
    Dim Hold As Integer
    Dim I As Integer
    Dim Smallest As Integer
    Dim SquareIdx As Integer
    Dim X1 As Integer, Y1 As Integer, X2 As Integer,
 Y2 As Integer

    If MoveIdx = -1 Then Exit Sub
    ShowCursor -1
    ReleaseCapture
    ClipCursor ByVal 0&
    SquareIdx = SquareHit(Picture1(MoveIdx).Left + 15,
Picture1(MoveIdx).Top + 15)
    If SquareIdx = -1 Then   'Letter NOT dropped on a square
        MoveIdx = -1
        Exit Sub
    End If
    If SquareTable(SquareIdx).Index = -1 Then 'Square is empty
        SquareTable(SquareIdx).Index = MoveIdx
        Picture1(MoveIdx).Move SquareTable(SquareIdx).X1 + 5,
SquareTable(SquareIdx).Y1 + 5
        If GameSolved() Then
            For I = 0 To 8
                PictureMsg(I).Visible = -1
            Next I
            Beep
            GameOver = -1
        End If
```

(continued)

Figure 5-9 *continued*

```
    Else  'Square contains a letter
        'left:
        Smallest = Picture1(MoveIdx).Left -
(SquareTable(SquareIdx).X1 - 20)
        CodeSmallest = 0
        'top:
        Hold = Picture1(MoveIdx).Top -
(SquareTable(SquareIdx).Y1 - 20)
        If Hold < Smallest Then
            Smallest = Hold
            CodeSmallest = 1
        End If
        'right:
        Hold = SquareTable(SquareIdx).X1 + 20 -
Picture1(MoveIdx).Left
        If Hold < Smallest Then
            Smallest = Hold
            CodeSmallest = 2
        End If
        'bottom:
        Hold = SquareTable(SquareIdx).Y1 + 20 -
Picture1(MoveIdx).Top
        If Hold < Smallest Then
            Smallest = Hold
            CodeSmallest = 3
        End If
        If Smallest > 0 Then
            Select Case CodeSmallest
                Case 0
                    Picture1(MoveIdx).Move
Picture1(MoveIdx).Left - Smallest
                Case 1
                    Picture1(MoveIdx).Move
Picture1(MoveIdx).Left, Picture1(MoveIdx).Top - Smallest
                Case 2
                    Picture1(MoveIdx).Move
Picture1(MoveIdx).Left + Smallest
                Case 3
                    Picture1(MoveIdx).Move
Picture1(MoveIdx).Left, Picture1(MoveIdx).Top + Smallest
            End Select
        End If
    End If
    MoveIdx = -1
End Sub
```

(continued)

Figure 5-9 *continued*

```
Sub Form_Unload (Cancel As Integer)
    WinHelp hWnd, HELP_FILE, HELP_QUIT, 0
End Sub

Sub Menu3x3_Click ()
    InitNewGrid 9
End Sub

Sub Menu4x4_Click ()
    InitNewGrid 16
End Sub

Sub MenuAbout_Click ()
    FormAbout.Show 1
End Sub

Sub MenuCommands_Click ()
    WinHelp hWnd, HELP_FILE, HELP_CONTEXT, HELP_COMMANDS
End Sub

Sub MenuExit_Click ()
    WinHelp hWnd, HELP_FILE, HELP_QUIT, 0
    End
End Sub

Sub MenuHowTo_Click ()
    WinHelp hWnd, HELP_FILE, HELP_CONTEXT, HELP_HOWTOPLAY
End Sub

Sub MenuIndex_Click ()
    WinHelp hWnd, HELP_FILE, HELP_INDEX, 0
End Sub

Sub MenuInitGame_Click (Index As Integer)
    InitNewGame Index
End Sub

Sub MenuUsingHelp_Click ()
    WinHelp hWnd, HELP_FILE, HELP_HELPONHELP, 0
End Sub

Sub Picture1_MouseDown (Index As Integer, Button As Integer,
 Shift As Integer, X As Single, Y As Single)
```

(continued)

Figure 5-9 *continued*

```
    Dim I As Integer
    Dim Pt As APIPOINT
    Dim Rec As RECT

    If GameOver Then Exit Sub
    For I = 0 To NumSquares - 1
        If SquareTable(I).Index = Index Then
            SquareTable(I).Index = -1
        End If
    Next I
    XOffset = X: YOffset = Y
    ShowCursor 0
    SetCapture hWnd
    Pt.X = 0
    Pt.Y = 0
    ClientToScreen hWnd, Pt
    Rec.Left = Pt.X
    Rec.Top = Pt.Y
    Pt.X = ScaleWidth
    Pt.Y = ScaleHeight
    ClientToScreen hWnd, Pt
    Rec.Right = Pt.X
    Rec.Bottom = Pt.Y
    ClipCursor Rec
    MoveIdx = Index
End Sub
```

WSABOUT.FRM code

```
Sub Command1_Click ()
    Unload FormAbout
End Sub
```

Programming Techniques

As with Peg Solitaire, discussed in Chapter 3, Word Squares is created by assigning a bitmap to the form to serve as the game background and by placing individual picture boxes on top of this bitmap to represent game objects (in this case, letters). At runtime, both the game background and the letters in the foreground are changed (as necessary) by assigning different bitmaps to their Picture properties.

Word Squares also demonstrates a new technique for animating graphical objects. Rather than using the Visual Basic drag-and-drop method, Word Squares actually moves the entire picture box containing the letter in response to mouse movements. This is accomplished by processing the following three events:

- *MouseDown.* If a MouseDown event occurs in one of the picture boxes containing a letter (indicating that the user wants to move the letter), the *Picture1_MouseDown* event procedure hides the mouse pointer and sets the *MoveIdx* flag to indicate that a move operation is in progress.

- *MouseMove.* If the *MoveIdx* flag indicates that a move is in progress, each time the *Form_MouseMove* event procedure is called it uses the Visual Basic *Move* method to move the picture box to the current mouse coordinates. As the picture box is moved, Windows saves and restores the image that lies underneath it.

- *MouseUp.* When the player releases the mouse button, generating a MouseUp event, the *Form_MouseUp* event procedure restores the mouse pointer, resets the *MoveIdx* flag to indicate that the move operation has ceased, and records the new position of the picture box if it is over an empty element of the grid.

Using this move-the-picture-box method for animating graphical objects has two important advantages over the drag-and-drop technique employed in the previous two games (Peg Solitaire and Deduce). First, the object retains all its colors as it is moved. (Recall that the drag-and-drop method displays the drag icon in black and white.) Second, the size of the object is not limited. (With the drag-and-drop method, the object is limited to the size of an icon, 32 bits by 32 bits.)

This animation method has an important disadvantage: A picture box is always rectangular. If the image you are moving is also rectangular (as in Word Squares) this does not present a problem; simply make the picture box the exact size needed to contain the image. The method also works if the image is nonrectangular (say, a ball) and the game background is a solid color; in this case, set the background color of the picture box to match the background color of the underlying form.

If, however, the image is nonrectangular and the background consists of a variety of colors (such as the peg in Peg Solitaire), then the background area of the picture box will overlay the game background; the moving image will thus have an unwanted rectangular aura. (Recall that with the drag-and-drop method, this problem was avoided by using the *Screen* color for the icon background.)

In Chapter 8, you will learn how to use Windows bit operations to move any kind of object over any kind of background.

Program Overview

Here is a summary of the main sequence of events in the Word Squares program.

- When the program starts, the *Form_Load* event procedure performs one-time initialization tasks and then calls *Init-NewGrid* to initialize a 3-by-3 game grid.

- When the player chooses one of the grid sizes from the Options menu, the *PictureGrid_Click* event procedure also calls *InitNewGrid* to initialize a game grid of the requested size.

- The *InitNewGrid* general procedure initializes the form for a particular grid size (3 by 3 or 4 by 4) and then calls *InitNew-Game* to initialize a new game (game 0).

- *InitNewGame* initializes the picture boxes and the data structures for a new game.

- When the player presses the mouse button while the mouse pointer is on a picture box containing a letter, the *Picture1-_MouseDown* event procedure starts a move operation so that the player can drag the letter to a new location.

- As the player moves the mouse pointer while holding down the mouse button, the *Form_MouseMove* event procedure moves the picture box containing the letter to each new location of the mouse pointer.

- When the player releases the mouse button, the *Form-_MouseUp* event procedure terminates the move operation, and, if the puzzle has been solved, it ends the game.

Initializing the Program

The initialization code in the *Form_Load* event procedure begins by explicitly assigning the desired size to all of the visible picture boxes. As you have seen in the previous chapters, this is part of the usual code for assuring device independence. (Later in the program, the form is sized and the picture boxes are positioned.)

The procedure then initializes the coordinate values in the array SquareTable, which contains information on each of the squares within the grid displayed at the top of the form. SquareTable is declared in the (declarations) section of WS.FRM as an array of SQUARE elements, indexed from 0 through 15:

```
Dim SquareTable(15) As SQUARE
```

SQUARE is a user-defined data type declared in GLOBALWS.BAS, as follows:

```
Type SQUARE
    X1 As Integer       'Horizontal coordinate of upper left corner
    Y1 As Integer       'Vertical coordinate of upper left corner
    X2 As Integer       'Horizontal coordinate of lower right corner
    Y2 As Integer       'Vertical coordinate of lower right corner
    Index As Integer    'Index of Picture1 element positioned on
                        'square
End Type
```

The *Index* values are initialized later in the program.

SquareTable contains 16 elements, so it can store information for either 9 squares (if the player has chosen three-letter word squares) or 16 squares (if the player has chosen four-letter word squares). Figure 5-10 shows the Word Squares grid and displays the index of the SquareTable element that stores the information for each square in this grid. Notice that the squares are not simply numbered row-by-row; the unusual numbering scheme was selected to make it easy to work with either 9 squares or 16 squares: With 9 squares, SquareTable indexes 0 through 8 are used; and with 16 squares, indexes 0 through 15 are used. Later in the chapter, you will see exactly how SquareTable is processed.

Figure 5-10.
Numbering of the Word Squares grid.

Next, *Form_Load* initializes the ThreeByWords and FourByWords string arrays, which store the correctly ordered letters for each of the different word squares used by the program. The order of the letters in the strings matches the numbering scheme shown in Figure 5-10 on the preceding page, to make it easy to compare the player's arrangement of letters (stored in SquareTable) with the correct arrangement (stored in an element of ThreeByWords or FourByWords).

Form_Load also calls the general procedure *InitNewGrid* to initialize the game display. This procedure is passed an integer indicating the total number of squares requested. *Form_Load* passes the value *9*, which is the appropriate number of squares for a three-letter word-square game:

```
InitNewGrid 9
```

Whenever the player chooses a command from the Options menu, the event procedure also calls *InitNewGrid*, passing either 9 (from the *Menu3x3_Click* procedure) or 16 (from the *Menu4x4_Click* procedure).

The *InitNewGrid* Procedure

To change the size of a word square used in the game, the *InitNewGrid* general procedure must set the game background, adjust the positions and visibility of the picture boxes, and adjust the overall size of the form to accommodate the new arrangement. To accomplish this, *InitNewGrid* performs the following steps:

- It sets the game background by assigning the appropriate picture to the main form. To create a 9-square grid, it assigns the picture stored in PictureGrid(9):

  ```
  Form1.Picture = PictureGrid(9).Picture
  ```

  To create a 16-square grid, it assigns the picture stored in PictureGrid(16).

- It moves the elements of PictureMsg so that the array is centered below the grid. This array contains the letters of the congratulatory message that are made visible when the player wins the game.

- If it is creating a 9-square grid, it makes the unnecessary members of Picture1 invisible (elements 9 through 15), and if it is creating a 16-square grid, it makes these elements visible. Picture1 is an array of picture boxes used to hold the letters that the player arranges during the game.

- It places a check mark next to the selected command on the Options menu.

- It adjusts the Width and Height properties of the form to accommodate the new grid size.

- It saves the current number of squares (contained in the parameter *Squares*) in the form-level variable *NumSquares*. This variable is used by other procedures in the program.

After performing these steps, *InitNewGrid* calls the *InitNewGame* general procedure to initialize a game using the new grid arrangement:

```
InitNewGame 0
```

The parameter indicates the number of the game chosen; the seven games are numbered 0 through 6.

InitNewGame is also called whenever the player chooses one of the Game commands (Game 1 through Game 7) from the Game menu. The commands for Game 1 through Game 7 belong to a control array, named MenuInitGame, and are indexed from 0 through 6. Whenever the player chooses one of these items, the *MenuInitGame_Click* event procedure is called and is passed the index of the specific menu item chosen:

```
Sub MenuInitGame_Click (Index As Integer)
    InitNewGame Index
End Sub
```

Because the games are numbered identically to the corresponding menu commands, *MenuInitGame_Click* simply passes its *Index* parameter to *InitNewGame* to start the appropriate game.

The *InitNewGame* Procedure

The *InitNewGame* general procedure initializes a new game by performing the following steps:

- It hides the congratulatory message displayed when the prior game (if any) was completed, by assigning FALSE to the Picture property of all members of the PictureMsg array.

- It moves each member of the Picture1 array to its initial position below the grid.

- It stores the solution to the requested game in the form-level string variable *Solution*.

- It copies a picture of each letter in the solution to a random element of the Picture1 array. The pictures are obtained from PictureLetter, which is an array of picture boxes indexed from 65 through 90. Each element of this array stores a bitmap portraying a letter of the alphabet, beginning with *A*; the index of each element thus equals the ANSI value of the character it portrays. The random elements of Picture1 are selected using the Visual Basic random-number generator. The method is the same as that used in Deduce, which is explained in Chapter 4 (in the section titled "Generating Random Sequences").

- It places a check mark next to the command for the current game so that when the Game menu is opened again, the player will know which game was played previously.

- It initializes the *Index* field of each element of SquareTable to the value -1; this value indicates that *no* letter is currently placed on top of the corresponding square.

- It sets the form-level variable *GameOver* to FALSE, which tells other parts of the program that a game is in progress.

F Y I

The bitmaps assigned to the members of the PictureLetter array and the PictureMsg array were all obtained from the file WS1.BMP (which contains images for all letters of the alphabet) by copying individual letters and pasting them into the appropriate array members.

Processing the MouseDown Event

After a new game has been initialized, the program waits until the player begins moving a letter by pressing a mouse button while the mouse pointer is over a member of Picture1. When this occurs, the *Picture1_MouseDown* event procedure receives control. This procedure initiates a move operation for the specific member of Picture1 under the mouse pointer.

If *GameOver* is TRUE, indicating that a game is not in progress, *Picture1_MouseDown* exits immediately. Otherwise it begins by updating SquareTable, as follows:

```
For I = 0 To NumSquares - 1
    If SquareTable(I).Index = Index Then
        SquareTable(I).Index = -1
    End If
Next I
```

If any element of SquareTable contains the index of the letter being moved (contained in the *Index* parameter), this routine assigns −1 to the Index field of this element to indicate that square is now empty.

Next, the procedure saves the *X* and *Y* offsets of the mouse pointer within the picture box, in the form-level variables *XOffset* and *YOffset*:

```
XOffset = X: YOffset = Y
```

These offsets are used by the *MouseMove* event procedure, explained in the next section. They are illustrated in Figure 5-11.

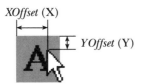

Figure 5-11.
The mouse pointer offsets within the picture box.

Picture1_MouseDown then "hides" the mouse pointer, so only the picture box will appear as the player moves the letter. (You do not need to hide the mouse pointer. However, if you leave it visible while the player moves the picture box, it flickers in an annoying way.) The mouse pointer is hidden by calling the Windows API function *ShowCursor*, described in Figure 5-12 on the following page, with a *0* (FALSE) parameter:

```
ShowCursor 0
```

Next, *Picture1_MouseDown* captures mouse events by calling the Windows API function *SetCapture* (described in Figure 5-13 on the following page) and passing the window handle:

```
SetCapture hWnd
```

Windows API Function: *ShowCursor*

Purpose Shows or hides the mouse pointer.

Declaration
```
Declare Sub ShowCursor Lib "USER" (ByVal ShowIt As Integer)
```

Parameter	Description
ShowIt	If this value is FALSE (0), the function hides the mouse pointer; if it is TRUE (–1), it shows the mouse pointer. (More accurately, it either decrements or increments an internal counter; the mouse pointer is visible when the counter >= 0.)

Figure 5-12.
The ShowCursor *Windows API function.*

After calling *SetCapture, all* mouse events are processed by the form. It is necessary to call *SetCapture* to "capture" the mouse so that the MouseMove events are processed by the main form, even while the picture is being moved over a picture box. (Normally, when the mouse pointer is over a picture box, the picture box, rather than the form, processes the MouseMove events.)

Windows API Function: *SetCapture*

Purpose Forces all future mouse events to be handled by the form specified by the *hWnd* parameter, regardless of the location of the mouse pointer.

Declaration
```
Declare Sub SetCapture Lib "USER" (ByVal hWnd As Integer)
```

Parameter	Description
hWnd	The hWnd property of the form that is to process mouse events

Comment See also *ReleaseCapture* under the "Declaration" heading in Figure 5-16 on page 127.

Figure 5-13.
The SetCapture *Windows API function.*

The *Picture1_MouseDown* event procedure also restricts the movement of the mouse pointer so that the player cannot move it outside the window. Moving the mouse pointer outside the window would cause the program to try to position the picture box outside the form, which would make the picture box disappear; if the player released the mouse button outside the form, the picture box would never reappear.

The mouse pointer is confined by calling the Windows API function *ClipCursor* (described in Figure 5-14 on the following page), passing it a structure containing the left, top, right, and bottom coordinates of the inside area of the form. The left and top coordinates are both *0*, the right coordinate is contained in the form's ScaleWidth property, and the bottom coordinate is contained in the ScaleHeight property. The only problem, however, is that you must pass *ClipCursor* the screen coordinates of the form's area—that is, the coordinates with respect to the upper left corner of the screen, *not* the form.

Fortunately, the Windows API supplies a function, *ClientToScreen* (described in Figure 5-15 on page 125), that converts the coordinates of a point from form coordinates to screen coordinates. The following code does the trick:

```
Pt.X = 0
Pt.Y = 0
ClientToScreen hWnd, Pt
Rec.Left = Pt.X
Rec.Top = Pt.Y
Pt.X = ScaleWidth
Pt.Y = ScaleHeight
ClientToScreen hWnd, Pt
Rec.Right = Pt.X
Rec.Bottom = Pt.Y
ClipCursor Rec
```

Pt is an APIPOINT type variable, and *Rec* is a RECT type variable. Both these types are defined in the global module (GLOBALWS.BAS); therefore, they match the structure types expected by the Windows API functions.

Windows API Function: *ClipCursor*

Purpose Confines the mouse pointer to the inside of the specified rectangle.

Declaration
```
Declare Sub ClipCursor Lib "USER" (Rect As Any)
```

Parameter	Description
Rect	A structure (passed by reference) giving the screen coordinates of the confining rectangle. The structure should have the following format:

```
Type RECT
    Left As Integer
    Top As Integer
    Right As Integer
    Bottom As Integer
End Type
```

If you pass *0* (by value):

```
ClipCursor ByVal 0&
```

the mouse pointer is free to move anywhere on the screen.

Figure 5-14.
The ClipCursor *Windows API function.*

Finally, the *Picture1_MouseDown* event procedure assigns to the form-level variable *MoveIdx* the index of the Picture1 element that is being moved:

```
MoveIdx = Index
```

As you will see, the other event procedures use *MoveIdx* to determine which picture box is being moved.

MoveIdx was initialized to the value *-1* (in the *Form_Load* event procedure), indicating that no picture box is being moved. After *MoveIdx* is set to the index of a picture box (the indexes range from 0 through 15), the event procedures described in the next section know that a move operation is in progress and which Picture1 element is being moved.

Windows API Function: *ClientToScreen*

Purpose Converts the coordinates of a point from form coordinates (relative to the origin of the form) to screen coordinates (relative to the upper left corner of the screen).

Declaration

```
Declare Sub ClientToScreen Lib "USER" (ByVal hWnd As
  Integer, Pt As APIPOINT)
```

Parameter	Description
hWnd	The hWnd property of the form.
Pt	A structure giving the coordinates of the point relative to the origin of the form identified by *hWnd*. The structure should have the following format:

```
Type APIPOINT
    X As Integer
    Y As Integer
End Type
```

ClientToScreen converts the coordinates by directly modifying the fields of this structure.

Figure 5-15.
The ClientToScreen *Windows API function.*

Processing the MouseMove Event

Because of the call to the *SetCapture* function, all MouseMove events that occur while the player moves a letter are processed by the form's event procedure, as follows:

```
Sub Form_MouseMove (Button As Integer, Shift As Integer, X As
  Single, Y As Single)
    If MoveIdx <> -1 Then
        Picture1(MoveIdx).Move X - XOffset, Y - YOffset
        Picture1(MoveIdx).Refresh
    End If
End Sub
```

If *MoveIdx* is equal to a value other than −*1*, indicating that a move operation is in progress, the procedure calls the *Move* method to reposition the picture box at the current mouse pointer coordinates (contained in the *X* and *Y* parameters). The *Move* method, however, places the upper left corner of the picture box at the position specified by the coordinates you pass to the method. If the user had positioned the mouse pointer somewhere *within* the picture box at the start of the move, the first MouseMove event would cause the picture box to abruptly jump below and to the right of the mouse pointer. To prevent this, the initial offsets of the mouse pointer within the picture box, saved in *XOffset* and *YOffset* (as explained in the previous section), are subtracted from the actual mouse pointer coordinates. (See Figure 5-11 on page 121.)

F Y I

To obtain the correct mouse pointer coordinates, the Scale-Mode properties of Picture1 and FormMain must have the same setting (so that the mouse pointer offsets are given in the same units). In Word Squares, they both have the *3 - Pixel* setting.

After placing the picture box at its new location, the procedure calls the *Refresh* method. This method causes Visual Basic to restore the original contents of the picture box—namely, the bitmap assigned to its Picture property. This call is necessary because the contents of the picture box can become corrupted as the picture box moves over another picture box.

Processing the MouseUp Event

When the player releases the mouse button after completing a move, the *Form_MouseUp* event procedure receives control. (Note: Because of the call to the *SetCapture* function, the MouseUp event is processed by the main form, even if the mouse pointer is over a picture box.)

If a move operation is not in progress, the *Form_MouseUp* procedure exits immediately:

```
If MoveIdx = -1 Then Exit Sub
```

Otherwise, it proceeds to complete the move operation. To do this, it first restores the mouse pointer to its normal state by calling three Windows API functions:

```
ShowCursor -1
ReleaseCapture
ClipCursor ByVal 0&
```

The functions *ShowCursor* and *ClipCursor* were explained in the section titled "Processing the MouseDown Event," earlier in this chapter. Passing TRUE to *ShowCursor* restores the visibility of the mouse pointer (see Figure 5-12 on page 122), and passing *0* (a NULL variable address) to *ClipCursor* allows the player to move the mouse pointer to any position on the screen (see Figure 5-14 on page 124). The call to *ReleaseCapture* (described in Figure 5-16) releases the mouse from the captured state initiated by the prior call to *SetCapture*.

Next, *Form_MouseUp* calls the function procedure *SquareHit*, which is declared in the (general) section of WS.FRM, to determine whether the picture box has been dropped within one of the squares in the grid. *SquareHit* is passed the coordinates of the approximate center of the picture box; it compares these coordinates with the coordinates of the squares within the grid, which are stored within *SquareTable*. If the coordinates fall within a square, *SquareHit* returns the number of the square; otherwise, *SquareHit* returns −1.

If the letter has *not* been dropped on a square (that is, *SquareHit* returned −1), then *Form_MouseUp* sets *MoveIdx* back to −1 to indicate that the move operation has ended, and immediately exits.

Windows API Function: *ReleaseCapture*

Purpose Frees the mouse from the captured state. After calling this function, mouse events are processed by the object under the mouse pointer.

Declaration
```
Declare Sub ReleaseCapture Lib "USER" ()
```

Comment See also *SetCapture* under the "Declaration" heading in Figure 5-13 on page 122.

Figure 5-16.
The ReleaseCapture *Windows API function.*

If, however, the letter has been dropped on a square, *Form_Mouse-Up* proceeds to check whether the square is currently empty—that is, whether *SquareTable(SquareIdx).Index = −1*. If the square is empty, *Form-_MouseUp* performs the following actions:

- It updates *SquareTable* to indicate the presence of the new letter:

  ```
  SquareTable(SquareIdx).Index = MoveIdx
  ```

- It centers the picture box within the square:

  ```
  Picture1(MoveIdx).Move SquareTable(SquareIdx).X1 + 5,
    SquareTable(SquareIdx).Y1 + 5
  ```

  This statement makes it appear as if the letter had fallen onto the center of the square.

- It calls the function procedure *GameSolved* to determine whether the player has correctly completed the word square. *GameSolved*, declared in the (general) section, checks each square in the grid; it returns TRUE only if all squares contain the correct letter. (The current letter in each square, if any, is stored in *SquareTable*; the correct letters are stored in the string *Solution*). If the game has been won, *Form_Mouse-Up* makes the "GOOD WORK!" message visible, beeps, and sets *GameOver* to TRUE to end the game.

If, however, the square is not empty, the *Form_MouseUp* procedure executes a routine to adjust the position of the picture box:

```
Else
    'left:
    Smallest = Picture1(MoveIdx).Left -
(SquareTable(SquareIdx).X1 - 20)
    CodeSmallest = 0
      .
      .
      .
    [other instructions]
      .
      .
      .
End If
```

128

This routine prevents the letter that is being dropped from obscuring the letter already located in the square. If the letter covers more than half of the square, it is moved toward the nearest edge of the square.

Before exiting, the *Form_MouseUp* procedure resets *MoveIdx* to *−1* to indicate that the move operation has terminated.

Enhancing the Game

Here are a few suggestions for enhancing the Word Squares program.

- Provide a Solution command on the Game menu, which would display the solution to the current puzzle.

- Provide an option for keeping track of the amount of time it takes the player to solve a given puzzle. You could use a Visual Basic timer control to monitor the elapsed time and periodically display the current time in a label control.

- Provide a wider variety of different word-square puzzles by storing the data for the word squares within disk files. You could provide several of these files (and add a File menu to the program), and players could open different files to access new sets of puzzles.

- Make the game more challenging by using larger word squares (five-letter squares and larger). Add the new sizes to the Options menu. Creating these larger word squares is also quite a challenge.

   If the game allows the player to choose from a wider variety of word-square sizes, you probably would not want to store each grid in a separate bitmap—because this would make the program quite large. Rather, you could build up grids of various size by combining individual picture boxes, each containing a copy of a bitmap depicting a single square. You could also use Visual Basic drawing statements to create the grid—a technique explained in the next chapter.

■ Recognize alternative valid word squares. Currently, the program checks the arrangement of letters against only a single solution (that is, the original word square used to generate the current game). You could also check the letters against one or more other solutions. You will, of course, have to discover these solutions. For example, Game 6 is based on the following word square:

W I N

I C E

N E T

You might also want to recognize the following equally valid arrangement of these same letters:

T I N

I C E

N E W

CHAPTER SIX

QUEENS

The objective of Queens is to arrange a set of queens on a game board so that no two queens occupy the same row, column, or diagonal.

The code for Queens introduces an important new technique for creating game graphics: Rather than using bitmaps and icons, the graphics are created at runtime by means of drawing statements. In this chapter, you will learn how to use the Visual Basic drawing methods and how to extend them using Windows API functions. You will also learn how to *scale* graphics as the player changes the game configuration or the size of the form.

About Queens

The Queens game is based on the traditional puzzle of trying to arrange eight queens on a standard 8-square-by-8-square chess board so that no queen can attack any other queen. According to the rules of chess, a queen can attack along any row, column, or diagonal. To solve the puzzle, therefore, the player must position the queens so that there is one queen only on every row and one queen only on every column, without any queens sharing a diagonal. Figure 6-1 shows a winning arrangement.

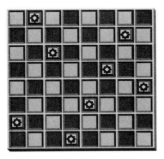

Figure 6-1.
A solution to the traditional eight-queens game.

The Queens game can be varied by using different numbers of queens. The number of squares on each side of the playing board should match the number of queens. For example, a six-queens game should be played on a 6-by-6 board because this is the minimum number of squares that can accommodate six queens placed in a winning arrangement.

A computer program can easily find all possible solutions to the Queens puzzle by using a technique known as *backtracking* (a method also used to solve mazes). The backtracking algorithm proceeds by placing queens one at a time (say, one in each row), checking the validity of each placement. This continues until either all the queens have been placed (in which case, a solution is recorded) or no more queens can be placed. If no more queens can be placed, it adjusts the placement of the previous queen and proceeds again from that point. This process continues until all possible arrangements have been tested.

I used a backtracking algorithm to calculate the total numbers of winning arrangements for various numbers of queens. The results are shown in the following table.

Number of Queens	Size of Board	Total Number of Solutions
4	4 by 4	2
5	5 by 5	10
6	6 by 6	4
7	7 by 7	40
8	8 by 8	92
9	9 by 9	352
10	10 by 10	724

Playing Queens

When you run Queens (QP.EXE), the program starts a game using four queens. The opening window is shown in Figure 6-2. To begin playing the game, simply drag each queen from the holder at the top of the window and drop it on a square within the playing board.

After you have placed a queen on the board, you are permitted to move it to another square or to return it to the holder. If you drop a queen outside the board or on top of another queen, the program immediately returns it to the holder.

Figure 6-2.
Queens at the beginning of a game.

Each time you place a queen on a square, the program checks the validity of your move. If one or more queens have already been placed within the same row, column, or diagonal, each of these queens is highlighted and the program beeps. You must then move the queen you just dropped either to another square on the board or back to the holder. The program does *not* allow you to leave this queen at the invalid position while you make other moves.

When you have successfully placed all the queens on the board, the program flashes the window and beeps, to celebrate your success.

To start a new game, choose one of the Queens commands (4 Queens through 10 Queens) from the Game menu. A new game begins that uses the indicated number of queens. The command starts a new game even if you have not yet solved the current game.

The objective of the game is to find as many solutions as possible for a given number of queens. Refer to the table on page 132 to learn the total number of solutions that are possible for the game you are playing.

Strategy and Hints

When playing Queens, keep in mind that only one queen can be placed in each row. Therefore, you might proceed row by row, placing a queen at the first valid position within each row. If you reach a row that does not have a valid position, you must go back to the previous row and move its queen to the next valid position; if there is no such position, you must go back another row. Then resume placing queens in the following rows.

If you continue this process, you will eventually arrive at all the solutions to the puzzle, because you are systematically testing every possible arrangement according to the same method used by the computer's backtracking algorithm described previously. The problem is that this process can take quite a long time. (Even a fast computer can take several minutes to find the solutions to the ten-queens puzzle.) Therefore, you might want to proceed in a more haphazard manner, observing the pattern of queens, trusting your intuition, and testing your luck.

Coding Queens

The source code for the Queens program is contained in the files listed in the following table.

File	Purpose
GLOBALQP.BAS	Contains global type definitions
QP.FRM	Defines the main form, FormMain, and the controls it contains
QPABOUT.FRM	Defines the ABOUT form, FormAbout, and the controls it contains
QP.MAK	Contains the Queens project file

You can load all these files into Visual Basic by choosing the Open Project command from the File menu and specifying the file QP.MAK at the prompt.

Figures 6-3 through 6-8 present the form designs, properties, menu commands, and source code for the Queens program.

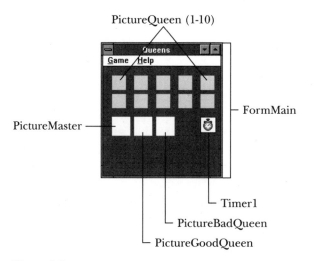

Figure 6-3.
QP.FRM at design time.

Object Name	Object Type	Property	Setting
FormMain	Form	AutoRedraw	True
		BackColor	&H00800000& [dark blue]
		Caption	Queens
		FillStyle	0 - Solid
		FormName	FormMain
		Grid Height	8 [pixels]
		Grid Width	8 [pixels]
		Height	3555 [twips]
		Icon	(Icon) [QP.ICO]
		Left	1035 [twips]
		ScaleMode	3 - Pixel
		Top	1140 [twips]
		Width	3300 [twips]
PictureBadQueen	Picture box	BorderStyle	0 - None
		CtlName	PictureBadQueen
		Height	33 [pixels]
		Left	96 [pixels]
		Top	88 [pixels]
		Visible	False
		Width	33 [pixels]
PictureGoodQueen	Picture box	BorderStyle	0 - None
		CtlName	PictureGoodQueen
		Height	33 [pixels]
		Left	56 [pixels]
		Top	88 [pixels]
		Visible	False
		Width	33 [pixels]
PictureMaster	Picture box	AutoRedraw	True
		BorderStyle	0 - None
		CtlName	PictureMaster
		FillStyle	0 - Solid
		Height	33 [pixels]

Figure 6-4.

QP.FRM form and control properties.

(continued)

Figure 6-4 *continued*

Object Name	Object Type	Property	Setting
		Left	16 [pixels]
		ScaleMode	3 - Pixel
		Top	33 [pixels]
		Visible	False
		Width	33 [pixels]
PictureQueen	Array of picture boxes	BackColor	&H00FFFF00& [cyan]
		BorderStyle	0 - None
		CtlName	PictureQueen
		Height	25 [pixels]
		Index	1 - 10
		Left	[varies]
		ScaleMode	3 - Pixel
		Top	[varies]
		Width	25 [pixels]
Timer1	Timer	Enabled	False
		Interval	250 [milliseconds]

Indentation/Caption	Control Name	Other Features
&Game	MenuGame	
....&4 Queens	MenuNQ	Index = 4 Checked
....&5 Queens	MenuNQ	Index = 5
....&6 Queens	MenuNQ	Index = 6
....&7 Queens	MenuNQ	Index = 7
....&8 Queens	MenuNQ	Index = 8
....&9 Queens	MenuNQ	Index = 9
....&10 Queens	MenuNQ	Index = 10
....-	MenuSep1	
....E&xit	MenuExit	
&Help	MenuHelp	

Figure 6-5.
QP.FRM menu design.

(continued)

Figure 6-5 *continued*

Indentation/Caption	Control Name	Other Features
....&Index	MenuIndex	Accelerator = F1
....&How to Play	MenuHowTo	
....&Commands	MenuCommands	
....&Using Help	MenuUsingHelp	
....-	MenuSep2	
....&About Queens...	MenuAbout	

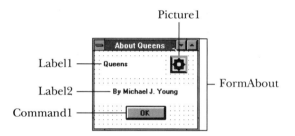

Figure 6-6.
QPABOUT.FRM at design time.

Object Name	Object Type	Property	Setting
Command1	Command button	Caption	OK
		Default	True
		Height	375 [twips]
		Left	840 [twips]
		Top	1440 [twips]
		Width	1095 [twips]
FormAbout	Form	BorderStyle	3 - Fixed Double
		Caption	About Queens
		FormName	FormAbout
		Grid Height	120 [twips]
		Grid Width	120 [twips]

Figure 6-7.
QPABOUT.FRM form and control properties.

(continued)

Figure 6-7 *continued*

Object Name	Object Type	Property	Setting
		Height	2445 [twips]
		Left	1140 [twips]
		MaxButton	False
		MinButton	False
		Top	1440 [twips]
		Width	2880 [twips]
Label1	Label	Caption	Queens
		Height	375 [twips]
		Left	240 [twips]
		Top	240 [twips]
		Width	1575 [twips]
Label2	Label	Alignment	2 - Center
		Caption	By Michael J. Young
		Height	375 [twips]
		Left	0 [twips]
		Top	960 [twips]
		Width	2745 [twips]
Picture1	Picture box	AutoSize	True
		BorderStyle	0 - None
		Height	480 [twips]
		Left	2040 [twips]
		Picture	(Icon) [QP.ICO]
		Top	120 [twips]
		Width	480 [twips]

GLOBALQP.BAS code

```
Type APIPOINT
    X As Integer
    Y As Integer
End Type
```

Figure 6-8.   *(continued)*

Source code for the Queens program. (Notice that long program lines are wrapped to the next line and indented one space.)

Figure 6-8 *continued*

```
Type RECT
    Left As Integer
    Top As Integer
    Right As Integer
    Bottom As Integer
End Type

Type SQUARE
    X1 As Integer
    Y1 As Integer
    X2 As Integer
    Y2 As Integer
    XPos As Integer
    YPos As Integer
    Index As Integer
End Type
```

QP.FRM code

```
'Help Section:
'Help file:
Const HELP_FILE = "QP.HLP"
'WinHelp wCommand values:
Const HELP_CONTEXT = &H1
Const HELP_HELPONHELP = &H4
Const HELP_INDEX = &H3
Const HELP_QUIT = &H2
'WinHelp dwData values (help topics):
Const HELP_HOWTOPLAY = 10&
Const HELP_COMMANDS = 20&
'Windows help API:
Declare Sub WinHelp Lib "USER" (ByVal hWnd As Integer, ByVal
 lpHelpFile As String, ByVal wCommand As Integer,
 ByVal dwData As Long)

Const WS_CAPTION = &HC00000
Const WS_THICKFRAME = &H40000
Declare Sub AdjustWindowRect Lib "USER" (lpRect As RECT,
 ByVal dwStyle&, ByVal bMenu%)
```

(continued)

Figure 6-8 *continued*

```
Declare Sub ClientToScreen Lib "USER" (ByVal hWnd As Integer,
  Pt As APIPOINT)
Declare Sub ClipCursor Lib "USER" (Rec As Any)

Const LOGPIXELSX = 88
Const LOGPIXELSY = 90
Declare Function GetDeviceCaps Lib "GDI" (ByVal hDC%,
  ByVal Index%) As Integer

Declare Sub InvertRect Lib "USER" (ByVal hDC As Integer,
  Rec As RECT)
Declare Sub Polygon Lib "GDI" (ByVal hDC As Integer,
  Points As APIPOINT, ByVal Count As Integer)
Declare Sub ReleaseCapture Lib "USER" ()
Declare Sub SetCapture Lib "USER" (ByVal hWnd As Integer)
Declare Sub ShowCursor Lib "USER" (ByVal ShowIt As Integer)

Dim BadQueen As Integer
Dim BadQueens(1 To 10) As Integer
Dim FormLoaded As Integer
Dim MoveIdx As Integer
Dim NewGame As Integer
Dim NumBadQueens As Integer
Dim NQ As Integer      'Number of Queens
Dim PointTable(5) As APIPOINT
Dim SF As Single       'Scaling Factor
Dim SquareTable(1 To 11, 1 To 10) As SQUARE
Dim XOffset As Integer
Dim YOffset As Integer

Sub CheckQueen (Row As Integer, Col As Integer)
    Dim I As Integer, J As Integer
    Dim Rec As RECT

    If Row = 1 Then Exit Sub
    For I = 2 To NQ + 1
        For J = 1 To NQ
            If (I <> Row Or J <> Col) And
SquareTable(I, J).Index <> 0 Then
                If I = Row Or J = Col Or
Abs(I - Row) = Abs(J - Col) Then
                    Beep
                    NumBadQueens = NumBadQueens + 1
```

(continued)

Figure 6-8 *continued*

```
                    BadQueens(NumBadQueens) =
  SquareTable(I, J).Index
                        BadQueen = SquareTable(Row, Col).Index
                        PictureQueen(BadQueens(NumBadQueens)
).Picture = PictureBadQueen.Picture
                    End If
                End If
            Next J
        Next I
End Sub

Sub DrawWindow ()
    Dim Col As Integer
    Dim I As Integer
    Dim Rec As RECT
    Dim Row As Integer
    Dim StartYellow As Integer
    Dim X1 As Single
    Dim Y1 As Single
    Dim Yellow As Integer

    Cls

    'Draw the borders of the playing board and queen holder:
    'Draw cyan background:
    FillColor = &HFFFF00
    Line (12 * SF, 12 * SF)-((14 + 29 * NQ) * SF - 1, 43 * SF
- 1), &HFFFF00, B
    Line (12 * SF, 53 * SF)-((14 + 29 * NQ) * SF - 1, (55 + 29
* NQ) * SF - 1), &HFFFF00, B

    'Draw light gray right edges:
    FillColor = &HC0C0C0
    ForeColor = &HC0C0C0
    PointTable(0).X = (14 + 29 * NQ) * SF
    PointTable(0).Y = 12 * SF
    PointTable(1).X = (18 + 29 * NQ) * SF - 1
    PointTable(1).Y = 15 * SF
    PointTable(2).X = (18 + 29 * NQ) * SF - 1
    PointTable(2).Y = 47 * SF - 1
    PointTable(3).X = (14 + 29 * NQ) * SF
    PointTable(3).Y = 47 * SF - 1
    Polygon hDC, PointTable(0), 4
```

(continued)

Figure 6-8 *continued*

```
PointTable(0).X = (14 + 29 * NQ) * SF
PointTable(0).Y = 53 * SF
PointTable(1).X = (18 + 29 * NQ) * SF - 1
PointTable(1).Y = 56 * SF
PointTable(2).X = (18 + 29 * NQ) * SF - 1
PointTable(2).Y = (59 + 29 * NQ) * SF - 1
PointTable(3).X = (14 + 29 * NQ) * SF
PointTable(3).Y = (59 + 29 * NQ) * SF - 1
Polygon hDC, PointTable(0), 4

'Draw dark gray bottom edges:
FillColor = &H808080
ForeColor = &H808080
PointTable(0).X = 12 * SF
PointTable(0).Y = 43 * SF
PointTable(1).X = (14 + 29 * NQ) * SF - 1
PointTable(1).Y = 43 * SF
PointTable(2).X = (17 + 29 * NQ) * SF - 1
PointTable(2).Y = 47 * SF - 1
PointTable(3).X = 15 * SF
PointTable(3).Y = 47 * SF - 1
Polygon hDC, PointTable(0), 4

PointTable(0).X = 12 * SF
PointTable(0).Y = (55 + 29 * NQ) * SF
PointTable(1).X = (14 + 29 * NQ) * SF - 1
PointTable(1).Y = (55 + 29 * NQ) * SF
PointTable(2).X = (17 + 29 * NQ) * SF - 1
PointTable(2).Y = (59 + 29 * NQ) * SF - 1
PointTable(3).X = 15 * SF
PointTable(3).Y = (59 + 29 * NQ) * SF - 1
Polygon hDC, PointTable(0), 4

'Draw the squares:
X1 = 14
Y1 = 14
For Row = 1 To NQ + 1
    Yellow = StartYellow
    StartYellow = StartYellow Xor -1
    For Col = 1 To NQ
        'Draw light gray slanted borders:
        FillColor = &HC0C0C0
        Line (X1 * SF, Y1 * SF)-((X1 + 27) * SF - 1, (Y1 +
27) * SF - 1), &HC0C0C0, B
```

(continued)

Figure 6-8 *continued*

```
            'Draw dark gray slanted borders:
            PointTable(0).X = (X1 + 1) * SF
            PointTable(0).Y = Y1 * SF
            PointTable(1).X = (X1 + 27) * SF - 1
            PointTable(1).Y = Y1 * SF
            PointTable(2).X = (X1 + 27) * SF - 1
            PointTable(2).Y = (Y1 + 26) * SF - 1
            PointTable(3).X = (X1 + 24) * SF
            PointTable(3).Y = (Y1 + 24) * SF - 1
            PointTable(4).X = (X1 + 24) * SF
            PointTable(4).Y = (Y1 + 3) * SF - 1
            PointTable(5).X = (X1 + 3) * SF
            PointTable(5).Y = (Y1 + 3) * SF - 1
            FillColor = &H808080
            ForeColor = &H808080
            Polygon hDC, PointTable(0), 6

            'Draw inner solid color:
            If Yellow Then
                FillColor = &HFFFF&
                Line ((X1 + 3) * SF, (Y1 + 3) * SF)-((X1 + 24)
      * SF - 1, (Y1 + 24) * SF - 1), &HFFFF&, B
            Else
                FillColor = &HFF&
                Line ((X1 + 3) * SF, (Y1 + 3) * SF)-((X1 + 24)
      * SF - 1, (Y1 + 24) * SF - 1), &HFF&, B
            End If
            Yellow = Yellow Xor -1

            'Initialize SquareTable:
            SquareTable(Row, Col).X1 = (X1 - 1) * SF
            SquareTable(Row, Col).Y1 = (Y1 - 1) * SF
            SquareTable(Row, Col).X2 = (X1 + 28) * SF - 1
            SquareTable(Row, Col).Y2 = (Y1 + 28) * SF - 1
            SquareTable(Row, Col).XPos = (X1 + 3) * SF
            SquareTable(Row, Col).YPos = (Y1 + 3) * SF
            If NewGame Then
                If Row = 1 Then
                    SquareTable(Row, Col).Index = Col
                Else
                    SquareTable(Row, Col).Index = 0
                End If
            End If
            X1 = X1 + 29
```

(continued)

Figure 6-8 *continued*

```
        Next Col
        X1 = 14
        If Row = 1 Then
            Y1 = 55
        Else
            Y1 = Y1 + 29
        End If
    Next Row

    'Draw master picture for queens:
    'Size master picture:
    PictureMaster.Width = 21 * SF
    PictureMaster.Height = 21 * SF

    'Draw light gray borders:
    PictureMaster.FillColor = &HC0C0C0
    PictureMaster.Line (0, 0)-(21 * SF - 1, 21 * SF - 1),
&HC0C0C0, B

    'Draw dark gray borders:
    PointTable(0).X = 0
    PointTable(0).Y = 0
    PointTable(1).X = 3 * SF - 1
    PointTable(1).Y = 2 * SF
    PointTable(2).X = 3 * SF - 1
    PointTable(2).Y = 18 * SF
    PointTable(3).X = 19 * SF - 1
    PointTable(3).Y = 18 * SF
    PointTable(4).X = 21 * SF - 1
    PointTable(4).Y = 21 * SF - 1
    PointTable(5).X = 0
    PointTable(5).Y = 21 * SF - 1
    PictureMaster.FillColor = &H808080
    PictureMaster.ForeColor = &H808080
    Polygon PictureMaster.hDC, PointTable(0), 6

    'Draw inner color:
    PictureMaster.FillColor = &HFFFF00
    PictureMaster.Line (3 * SF, 3 * SF)-(18 * SF - 1, 18 * SF
- 1), &HFFFF00, B

    'Draw inner boxes:
    PictureMaster.FillColor = &H0&
```

(continued)

Figure 6-8 *continued*

```
   PictureMaster.ForeColor = &H0&
   PictureMaster.Line (5 * SF, 5 * SF)-(16 * SF - 1, 16 * SF
- 1), &H0&, B
   PointTable(0).X = 3 * SF
   PointTable(0).Y = 10 * SF
   PointTable(1).X = 10 * SF
   PointTable(1).Y = 3 * SF
   PointTable(2).X = 18 * SF - 1
   PointTable(2).Y = 10 * SF
   PointTable(3).X = 10 * SF
   PointTable(3).Y = 18 * SF - 1
   Polygon PictureMaster.hDC, PointTable(0), 4

   'Draw central circle:
   PictureMaster.FillColor = &HFFFF00
   PictureMaster.Circle (10 * SF, 10 * SF), 2.5 * SF,
&HFFFF00

   'Store images in PictureGoodQueen & PictureBadQueen
pictures:
   PictureGoodQueen.Picture = PictureMaster.Image
   Rec.Left = 3 * SF
   Rec.Top = 3 * SF
   Rec.Right = 18 * SF
   Rec.Bottom = 18 * SF
   InvertRect PictureMaster.hDC, Rec
   PictureBadQueen.Picture = PictureMaster.Image

   'Initialize the queen picture boxes:
   For I = 1 To 10
       PictureQueen(I).Visible = 0
   Next I
   For Row = 1 To NQ + 1
       For Col = 1 To NQ
           If SquareTable(Row, Col).Index <> 0 Then
               I = SquareTable(Row, Col).Index
               PictureQueen(I).Left = SquareTable(Row,
Col).XPos
               PictureQueen(I).Top = SquareTable(Row,
Col).YPos
               PictureQueen(I).Width = 21 * SF
               PictureQueen(I).Height = 21 * SF
               PictureQueen(I).Picture =
```

(continued)

Figure 6-8 *continued*

```
PictureGoodQueen.Picture
                PictureQueen(I).Visible = -1
            End If
        Next Col
    Next Row
    For I = 1 To NumBadQueens
        PictureQueen(BadQueens(I)).Picture =
    PictureBadQueen.Picture
    Next I
End Sub

Function SquareHit (X As Single, Y As Single, Row As Integer,
 Col As Integer) As Integer
    Dim I As Integer, J As Integer

    For I = 1 To NQ + 1
        For J = 1 To NQ
            If X >= SquareTable(I, J).X1 And X <=
    SquareTable(I, J).X2 Then
                If Y >= SquareTable(I, J).Y1 And Y <=
    SquareTable(I, J).Y2 Then
                    SquareHit = -1
                    Row = I
                    Col = J
                    Exit Function
                End If
            End If
        Next J
    Next I
    SquareHit = 0
    Row = 0
    Col = 0
End Function

Sub Form_Load ()
    Dim HeightPix As Integer
    Dim Rec As RECT
    Dim WidthPix As Integer

    NQ = 4

    WidthPix = 30 + 29 * NQ
    HeightPix = 72 + 29 * NQ
    Rec.Left = 0
```

(continued)

Figure 6-8 *continued*

```
    Rec.Top = 0
    Rec.Right = WidthPix - 1
    Rec.Bottom = HeightPix - 1
    AdjustWindowRect Rec, WS_CAPTION Or WS_THICKFRAME, -1
    FormMain.Width = (Rec.Right - Rec.Left + 1) * (1440 /
GetDeviceCaps(hDC, LOGPIXELSX))
    FormMain.Height = (Rec.Bottom - Rec.Top + 1) * (1440 /
GetDeviceCaps(hDC, LOGPIXELSY))

    SF = 1
    NewGame = -1
    DrawWindow
    FormLoaded = -1
End Sub

Sub Form_MouseMove (Button As Integer, Shift As Integer,
 X As Single, Y As Single)
    If MoveIdx <> 0 Then
        PictureQueen(MoveIdx).Move X - XOffset, Y - YOffset
        PictureQueen(MoveIdx).Refresh
    End If
End Sub

Sub Form_MouseUp (Button As Integer, Shift As Integer,
 X As Single, Y As Single)
    Dim I As Integer
    Dim GoHome As Integer
    Dim Row As Integer, Col As Integer

    If MoveIdx = 0 Then Exit Sub
    ShowCursor -1
    ReleaseCapture
    ClipCursor ByVal 0&
    If SquareHit(PictureQueen(MoveIdx).Left + 10 * SF,
PictureQueen(MoveIdx).Top + 10 * SF, Row, Col) Then
        If SquareTable(Row, Col).Index <> 0 Then
            GoHome = -1
        Else
            PictureQueen(MoveIdx).Move SquareTable(Row,
Col).XPos, SquareTable(Row, Col).YPos
            SquareTable(Row, Col).Index = MoveIdx
            CheckQueen Row, Col
        End If
```

(continued)

Figure 6-8 *continued*

```
    Else
        GoHome = -1
    End If
    If GoHome Then
        For I = 1 To NQ
            If SquareTable(1, I).Index = 0 Then
                PictureQueen(MoveIdx).Move SquareTable(1,
  I).XPos, SquareTable(1, I).YPos
                SquareTable(1, I).Index = MoveIdx
                Exit For
            End If
        Next I
    End If
    MoveIdx = 0
    For I = 1 To NQ
        If SquareTable(1, I).Index <> 0 Then Exit Sub
    Next I
    If NumBadQueens = 0 Then Timer1.Enabled = -1
End Sub

Sub Form_Resize ()
    Dim HeightPix As Integer
    Dim HorizSF As Single
    Dim NewSF As Single
    Dim VertSF As Single
    Dim WidthPix As Integer

    If Not FormLoaded Then Exit Sub
    NewGame = 0
    WidthPix = 30 + 29 * NQ
    HeightPix = 71 + 29 * NQ
    HorizSF = ScaleWidth / WidthPix
    VertSF = ScaleHeight / HeightPix
    If HorizSF < VertSF Then
        NewSF = HorizSF
    Else
        NewSF = VertSF
    End If
    If NewSF = SF Then
        Exit Sub
    End If
    SF = NewSF
    MousePointer = 11
```

(continued)

Figure 6-8 *continued*

```
        DrawWindow
        MousePointer = 0
    End Sub

    Sub Form_Unload (Cancel As Integer)
        WinHelp hWnd, HELP_FILE, HELP_QUIT, 0
    End Sub

    Sub MenuAbout_Click ()
        FormAbout.Show 1
    End Sub

    Sub MenuCommands_Click ()
        WinHelp hWnd, HELP_FILE, HELP_CONTEXT, HELP_COMMANDS
    End Sub

    Sub MenuExit_Click ()
        WinHelp hWnd, HELP_FILE, HELP_QUIT, 0
        End
    End Sub

    Sub MenuHowTo_Click ()
        WinHelp hWnd, HELP_FILE, HELP_CONTEXT, HELP_HOWTOPLAY
    End Sub

    Sub MenuIndex_Click ()
        WinHelp hWnd, HELP_FILE, HELP_INDEX, 0
    End Sub

    Sub MenuNQ_Click (Index As Integer)
        Dim HeightPix As Integer
        Dim HorizSF As Single
        Dim VertSF As Single
        Dim WidthPix As Integer

        MenuNQ(NQ).Checked = 0
        MenuNQ(Index).Checked = -1
        NQ = Index
        NumBadQueens = 0
        NewGame = -1
        HeightPix = 71 + 29 * NQ
        WidthPix = 30 + 29 * NQ
        HorizSF = ScaleWidth / WidthPix
```

(continued)

Figure 6-8 *continued*

```
    VertSF = ScaleHeight / HeightPix
    If HorizSF < VertSF Then
        SF = HorizSF
    Else
        SF = VertSF
    End If
    MousePointer = 11
    DrawWindow
    MousePointer = 0
End Sub

Sub MenuUsingHelp_Click ()
    WinHelp hWnd, HELP_FILE, HELP_HELPONHELP, 0
End Sub

Sub PictureQueen_MouseDown (Index As Integer,
 Button As Integer, Shift As Integer, X As Single,
 Y As Single)
    Dim Col As Integer
    Dim I As Integer
    Dim Pt As APIPOINT
    Dim Rec As RECT
    Dim Row As Integer

    If NumBadQueens > 0 Then
        If Index <> BadQueen Then
            Exit Sub
        Else
            For I = 1 To NumBadQueens
                PictureQueen(BadQueens(I)).Picture =
PictureGoodQueen.Picture
            Next I
            NumBadQueens = 0
        End If
    End If
    For Row = 1 To NQ + 1
        For Col = 1 To NQ
            If SquareTable(Row, Col).Index = Index Then
                SquareTable(Row, Col).Index = 0
                Exit For
            End If
        Next Col
    Next Row
```

(continued)

Figure 6-8 *continued*

```
    XOffset = X: YOffset = Y
    ShowCursor 0
    SetCapture hWnd
    Pt.X = 0
    Pt.Y = 0
    ClientToScreen hWnd, Pt
    Rec.Left = Pt.X
    Rec.Top = Pt.Y
    Pt.X = ScaleWidth
    Pt.Y = ScaleHeight
    ClientToScreen hWnd, Pt
    Rec.Right = Pt.X
    Rec.Bottom = Pt.Y
    ClipCursor Rec
    MoveIdx = Index
End Sub

Sub Timer1_Timer ()
    Static Counter As Integer
    Dim Rec As RECT

    If Counter >= 4 Then
        Timer1.Enabled = 0
        Counter = 0
        Exit Sub
    End If
    Counter = Counter + 1
    Beep
    Rec.Left = 0
    Rec.Top = 0
    Rec.Right = ScaleWidth
    Rec.Bottom = ScaleHeight
    InvertRect hDC, Rec
    Refresh
End Sub
```

QPABOUT.FRM code

```
Sub Command1_Click ()
    Unload FormAbout
End Sub
```

Programming Techniques

The Queens program uses the same animation technique used in the Word Squares program presented in Chapter 5. Namely, it moves an entire picture box in response to movements of the mouse. This method is suitable for the Queens program because the object that moves is rectangular (a square representation of a chess queen).

As with the Deduce game, presented in Chapter 4, Queens uses a Visual Basic timer control to celebrate (Queens flashes the window rather than flashing a message) when the player solves the puzzle.

The Queens program introduces an entirely new method for creating the game graphics. The previous games have all used bitmaps or icons, generated in a separate program and added to the form or picture boxes at design time, to create the background and the game objects. Queens, however, generates all the game graphics using drawing statements at runtime. Consequently, the form at design time (shown in Figure 6-3 on page 134) bears little resemblance to the game at runtime (shown in Figure 6-2 on page 133). The drawing methods provided by Visual Basic are supplemented with drawing functions supplied by the Windows API.

The use of drawing statements rather than bitmaps renders the Queens program small and fast-loading. This method also allows Queens to easily *scale* the program graphics, without significant loss of precision, whenever the player changes the size of the form or chooses a different number of queens. Consequently, the main form for the Queens program is the first program presented in this book that includes a maximize button and sizable borders (permitting the player to change the size and proportions of the form). Using drawing statements also makes it easy to change the number of squares displayed by the program. (Recall that Word Squares had to store a separate bitmap for each square configuration.)

As the Queens game reveals, however, drawing statements can be tedious to code and difficult to modify. Using drawing statements is especially troublesome for creating complex graphics or creating images that cannot easily be broken down into separate geometric shapes.

Another complication in the use of drawing statements is the need to redraw the form or picture box whenever a portion of it has been obscured and then comes back into view—for example, when the player enlarges the form or removes an overlapping window. If you assign a bitmap or icon to a form or picture box, Visual Basic restores the image whenever necessary. If, however, you create an image using drawing statements, your program is normally responsible for redrawing the image. Visual Basic notifies the program whenever redrawing is needed by calling the *Paint* event procedure of the affected form or picture box. Handling this event requires extra coding; in addition, redrawing an entire image with drawing commands can be quite time-consuming and can result in a slow response to changes in the size or position of a window.

To eliminate the need to redraw the form, the Queens program assigns True to the AutoRedraw property of the main form. When this property is set to True (it is False by default), Visual Basic stores all graphics and text drawn in the form in an internal bitmap. Visual Basic then uses this bitmap to restore the graphics whenever necessary. As a result, the form is restored almost instantly (Windows bitmap operations are fast), and the program does not need to manually redraw it (in fact, the *Paint* event procedure is never called).

If the AutoRedraw feature seems too good to be true, be aware that enabling it consumes a large amount of memory at runtime. If a form has sizable borders—as does the Queens program—Visual Basic uses a bitmap large enough to store the entire screen. (This permits it to save graphics drawn beyond the borders of the form, and then display these graphics if the user enlarges the form.)

Program Overview

Here is a summary of the main sequence of events in the Queens program.

- When the program first starts running, the *Form_Load* event procedure initializes variables, assigns the form its initial size, sets the form-level flag *NewGame* to TRUE, and calls *DrawWindow*.

- When the player chooses a command from the Game menu to start a new game with a specific number of queens, the *MenuNQ_Click* event procedure calculates the required scaling factor, sets *NewGame* to TRUE, and calls *DrawWindow*.

- Whenever the player changes the size of the form, the *Form_Resize* event procedure calculates the required scaling factor, sets *NewGame* to FALSE, and calls *DrawWindow*.

- The *DrawWindow* general procedure draws the game board and the queens, using the current scaling factor to determine the image sizes. Also, if *NewGame* is TRUE, *DrawWindow* initializes a new game.

- When the player presses the mouse button while the mouse pointer is on a queen, the *PictureQueen_MouseDown* event procedure initiates a move operation.

- After a move operation has been started, the *Form_MouseMove* event procedure moves the picture box containing the queen to each new position of the mouse pointer.

- When the player releases the mouse button, the *Form_MouseUp* event procedure terminates the move operation. If the queen was dropped on a position other than an empty square, it is returned to an empty position in the queen holder. If the move is illegal, *Form_MouseUp* marks all other queens sharing the same row, column, or diagonal. If the puzzle has been solved, *Form_MouseUp* enables the timer; the timer event handler, *Timer1_Timer*, then flashes the form several times to announce the player's success.

Initializing the Program

The following event procedures perform important initialization tasks:

- *Form_Load*, which is called when Queens first starts running. Its purpose is to initialize the program and start a four-queens game.

- *MenuNQ_Click*, which receives control whenever the player chooses one of the Queens commands from the Game menu (4 Queens through 10 Queens). Its purpose is to start a new game; the number of queens depends on which command was chosen.

- *Form_Resize*, which is called whenever the player changes the size of the form. Its purpose is to scale the game graphics to fit the form's new size.

Each of these three procedures initializes variables and performs other preparatory tasks and then each calls the general procedure *DrawWindow*, which creates the program graphics.

The *Form_Load* Procedure

The *Form_Load* event procedure begins by assigning *4* to the form-level variable *NQ*, which stores the current number of queens.

The procedure then sets the initial size of the form:

```
WidthPix = 30 + 29 * NQ
HeightPix = 72 + 29 * NQ
Rec.Left = 0
Rec.Top = 0
Rec.Right = WidthPix - 1
Rec.Bottom = HeightPix - 1
AdjustWindowRect Rec, WS_CAPTION Or WS_THICKFRAME, -1
FormMain.Width = (Rec.Right - Rec.Left + 1) * (1440 /
  GetDeviceCaps(hDC, LOGPIXELSX))
FormMain.Height = (Rec.Bottom - Rec.Top + 1) * (1440 /
  GetDeviceCaps(hDC, LOGPIXELSY))
```

The form is made just large enough to contain the queen holder and the playing board. The width and the height of the *inside* of the form (in pixels) are stored in the variables *WidthPix* and *HeightPix*. These values depend on the initial number of queens, stored in *NQ*. The method used to convert the inside pixel coordinates of the form to outside twip coordinates is the same as that employed in most of the games in this book. (For an explanation, see the section "Coding for Device Independence" in Chapter 3.) Notice, however, that when calling *Adjust-WindowRect* (see Figure 3-13), the value WS_THICKFRAME must be included in the second parameter because—unlike the other programs in this book—the form has sizable borders (that is, the BorderStyle property is set to *2 - Sizable*).

Note: To learn how the specific constants (such as the 30 and 29) were obtained, see the section "The *DrawWindow* Procedure," later in the chapter.

Next, the *Form_Load* procedure initializes several form-level variables, as follows:

■ It assigns *1* to the variable *SF*, which stores the scaling factor. The scaling factor determines the size of the graphics drawn by the *DrawWindow* procedure. The value *1* results in full-size graphic images; values less than 1 produce reduced images, and values greater than 1 produce expanded images.

■ It sets the variable *NewGame* to TRUE. This variable signals *DrawWindow* that a new game is starting.

The *Form_Load* procedure then calls *DrawWindow* to create the program graphics. Before exiting, it sets the variable *FormLoaded* to TRUE. As you will see, this variable is used by *Form_Resize* to prevent scaling the graphics unnecessarily before the initialization has been completed.

The *MenuNQ_Click* Procedure

The Queens commands (4 Queens through 10 Queens) on the Game menu belong to the MenuNQ control array. Each item in this array is assigned an index that matches the number of queens in the caption; for example, the 4 Queens command is assigned the index *4*. As a result, whenever the player chooses one of these commands, the *MenuNQ_Click* event procedure receives control and the *Index* parameter equals the number of queens chosen for the new game:

```
Sub MenuNQ_Click (Index As Integer)
```

The menu procedure begins by removing the check from the previously chosen command and adding a check to the current command:

```
MenuNQ(NQ).Checked = 0    'NQ still stores the former
                          'number of queens.
MenuNQ(Index).Checked = -1
```

As with the *Form_Load* event procedure, *MenuNQ_Click* initializes a variety of form-level variables before calling *DrawWindow*, as follows:

■ It sets *NQ* to the new number of queens:

```
NQ = Index
```

■ It sets *NumBadQueens* to *0*. If the player places a queen at an invalid position, this variable is assigned the number of previously positioned queens that share the same row, column, or diagonal. At the beginning of a new game, it is *0*.

■ As with *Form_Load*, it sets *NewGame* to TRUE.

■ It assigns a new scaling factor to *SF*.

Rather than changing the size of the form to accommodate the new number of queens, the procedure adjusts the scaling factor, *SF*, so that the graphics will fit properly within the existing window size. The routine for calculating the scaling factor first determines the internal width and height required for full-size graphic images, given the current number of queens:

```
HeightPix = 71 + 29 * NQ
WidthPix = 30 + 29 * NQ
```

It then calculates the horizontal scaling factor by dividing the *actual* internal width of the form, contained in the form's ScaleWidth property, by the *required* width for full-size graphics:

```
HorizSF = ScaleWidth / WidthPix
```

It calculates the vertical scaling factor in the same manner:

```
VertSF = ScaleHeight / HeightPix
```

The *DrawWindow* procedure, however, uses only a *single* scaling factor (*SF*) that affects all horizontal and vertical measurements equally; changing the scaling factor thus affects the overall size of the graphics without changing its proportions. Accordingly, the procedure assigns the smaller of the two scaling factors to *SF*, to ensure that the image fits completely within the form:

```
If HorizSF < VertSF Then
    SF = HorizSF
Else
    SF = VertSF
End If
```

Finally, *MenuNQ_Click* calls *DrawWindow* to redraw the program graphics. Immediately before making the call, however, it assigns the hourglass icon to the mouse pointer to indicate that a lengthy operation is in progress. (Yes, *DrawWindow* is a little slow.) After the call, it restores the default mouse pointer:

```
MousePointer = 11
DrawWindow
MousePointer = 0
```

The *Form_Resize* Procedure

As you saw in the previous section, the graphics must be scaled whenever the number of queens changes and the form stays the same size. The graphics must also be scaled whenever the number of queens remains the same, but the player changes the size of the form. When this occurs, the *Form_Resize* event procedure receives control:

```
Sub Form_Resize ()
```

The procedure first tests the *FormLoaded* variable, and exits immediately if the variable is set to FALSE, indicating that the *Form_Load*

157

procedure has not yet exited (because the *FormLoaded* variable is not set to TRUE until the last statement of the *Form_Load* procedure):

```
If Not FormLoaded Then Exit Sub
```

This variable is used because *Form_Load* assigns new settings to the form's Width and Height properties. Each time the program changes one of these properties, Visual Basic calls the *Form_Resize* event procedure. Using the *FormLoaded* variable prevents *Form_Resize* from making two unnecessary calls to the lengthy *DrawWindow* procedure before *Form_Load* has completed initialization.

Next, *Form_Resize* sets *NewGame* to FALSE to signal *DrawWindow* to redraw the graphics without initializing a new game. The procedure then calculates the new scaling factor, using the same method as *MenuNQ_Click*, described in the previous section. The new scaling factor, however, is first assigned to the local variable *NewSF*. If the newly calculated scaling factor is equal to the previous scaling factor (still stored in *SF*), the procedure exits to avoid unnecessarily redrawing the graphics; otherwise, it assigns the new scaling factor to *SF* and lets *Draw-Window* do its job:

```
If NewSF = SF Then
    Exit Sub
End If
SF = NewSF
MousePointer = 11
DrawWindow
MousePointer = 0
```

If *Form_Resize* is called only when the form changes size, how can the new scaling factor be the same as the previous one? This can occur under the following two circumstances:

- The player has changed the width of the form without changing the height or vice versa.

- The player has minimized the form to an icon or has restored the form from an icon. In either case, *Form_Resize* is called, but the scaling factor does not change.

    Note: When a form is minimized to an icon, the Width and Height properties still store the dimensions of the non-minimized form. The Queens program does not need to redraw the form when it is restored from an icon because the AutoRedraw property is set to True. (Visual Basic thus *automatically* restores the graphics from the internal bitmap it maintains.)

The *DrawWindow* Procedure

The general procedure *DrawWindow* draws (or redraws) all the program graphics, sets the sizes and positions of the picture boxes containing the queens, and performs several other initialization tasks. *DrawWindow* bases the sizes and positions of all the images it draws, as well as the sizes and positions it assigns to the picture boxes, on the current number of queens (*NQ*) and the current scaling factor (*SF*).

DrawWindow begins by calling *Cls* to clear the entire form. It then performs the following main tasks:

- It draws the game background.

- It creates master drawings of the queen (PictureGood-Queen and PictureBadQueen).

- It initializes the picture boxes containing the individual queen images (the elements of PictureQueen).

Drawing the Game Background

The game background consists of the queen holder at the top of the form and the checkered playing board below. (See Figure 6-2 on page 133.) The drawings are composed of rectangles and other polygonal shapes of solid color.

DrawWindow uses Visual Basic's *Line* method to draw the rectangular areas. For example, the following statements draw the rectangular cyan background for the queen holder at the top of the form:

```
FillColor = &HFFFF00
Line (12 * SF, 12 * SF)-((14 + 29 * NQ) * SF - 1, (43 * SF) - 1),
  &HFFFF00, B
```

The first parameter passed to the *Line* method gives the coordinates of the upper left corner and lower right corner of the rectangle. The second parameter specifies the color of the border around the rectangle (*&HFFFF00*, for cyan), and the third coordinate is a *B*, causing the method to draw a rectangle rather than a simple line segment. Because the FillStyle property of the form was assigned the *0 - Solid* setting at design time, the rectangle is automatically filled with the color assigned to the form's FillColor property, which is also cyan. The result is a solid block of cyan color.

NQ appears as a factor in the horizontal (*X*) coordinate of the lower right corner of the rectangle because the width of the queen holder depends on the current number of queens. *NQ* appears in many of the coordinates passed to the drawing statements in *DrawWindow*, for similar reasons.

Notice also that all the coordinate expressions passed to drawing commands within the *DrawWindow* procedure contain constant numbers. For example, the first coordinate passed to the *Line* method contains the constant *12*:

```
12 * SF
```

These constants were derived using the following method:

1. The game graphics were first drawn in Paintbrush. (For an example, see Figure 6-9. The drawing shown is included on the companion disk, in the file QP.BMP.)

2. The Cursor Position command on Paintbrush's View menu was enabled so that Paintbrush would display the current coordinates of the mouse pointer (in pixels).

3. Each of the coordinates passed to a drawing statement was obtained by placing the mouse pointer on the point within the Paintbrush drawing and reading the coordinates displayed by Paintbrush.

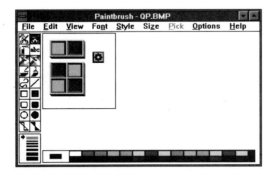

Figure 6-9.
The prototype graphics, drawn in Paintbrush.

F Y I

Because Paintbrush displays coordinates in pixels, the form's ScaleMode property is assigned the pixel setting *(3 - Pixel)*. This makes it possible to pass coordinates read from Paintbrush directly to the program drawing statements, simplifying the coding and making the drawings precise.

The current scaling factor, *SF*, appears in all the coordinate expressions passed to drawing statements in the *DrawWindow* procedure. As a result, the size of the entire game graphics can be changed simply by assigning a new value to *SF* and calling *DrawWindow* again. Before *Draw-Window* is first called, *SF* is set to *1*. If it is later set to 2, for example, and *DrawWindow* is called again, all the objects in the game will become twice as big.

You might be wondering why the term − *1* appears in many of the coordinate expressions. For example, in the call to the *Line* method shown above, the coordinate for the *top* of the rectangle is given as

```
12 * SF
```

while the coordinate for the *bottom* of the rectangle is

```
43 * SF - 1
```

The − *1* term is necessary to ensure that scaling works properly. It must be included in the ending coordinates of every object drawn—that is, in the right horizontal coordinate or the bottom vertical coordinate.

A simple example will show why the − *1* term is necessary, and will save a lengthy explanation. Figure 6-10 on the following page shows a block of pixels at the upper left corner of a form. Notice that pixels are numbered beginning with *0*. Suppose you want to draw a vertical line that begins 2 pixels from the top of the form and 1 pixel from the left side of the form and is 5 pixels long, as shown in the illustration. You might be inclined to specify the top vertical coordinate as

```
2 * SF
```

and the bottom vertical coordinate as simply

```
6 * SF
```

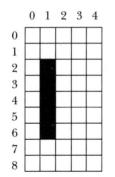

Figure 6-10.
Drawing a line.

If the scaling factor is 1, these coordinates yield the result you want. If the scaling factor is 2, you would want the line to begin 4 pixels from the top of the form and be 10 pixels long. The expression for the bottom coordinate, however, yields a line that is only 9 pixels long (and for greater scaling factors, the error would be magnified). To achieve the results you want, the bottom vertical coordinate must be specified as

```
7 * SF - 1
```

Note: Without using the − *1* term, objects would scale to the wrong size, and white gaps would appear between adjoining objects as the scaling factor is increased.

When you run Queens and change the size of the form, you will see that the graphics are drawn with acceptable accuracy at different scaling factors. Some loss of precision occurs when the scaling factor is not an integer because coordinates must be rounded to the nearest whole number of pixels.

The *DrawWindow* procedure also needs to draw filled areas that are *not* rectangular, such as the light gray border at the right of the queen holder and playing board. Visual Basic does not provide a method for drawing filled, nonrectangular polygons. (You could draw the border using separate calls to the *Line* method, but you would have no way to fill the area.) Fortunately, the Windows API comes to the rescue again, with the very useful *Polygon* function, described in Figure 6-11.

Windows API Function: *Polygon*

Purpose Draws a polygon.

Declaration
```
Declare Sub Polygon Lib "GDI" (ByVal hDC As Integer,
 Points As APIPOINT, ByVal Count As Integer)
```

Parameter	Description
hDC	The hDC property (device context handle) of the form or picture box.
Points	An array of structures that specify each vertex of the desired polygon. The member structures should have the following format:

```
Type APIPOINT
    X As Integer        'Horizontal coordinate
                        'of vertex
    Y As Integer        'Vertical coordinate
                        'of vertex
End Type
```

Count	The number of vertices specified by the Points array.

Comments You can control the drawing style and colors used by *Polygon* by assigning values to the form or picture box properties exactly as you do using a Visual Basic drawing method. For example, if you set the FillStyle property to *0* (solid), the polygon will be filled with the color currently assigned to the FillColor property.

Figure 6-11.
The Polygon *Windows API function.*

For example, the following code uses the *Polygon* function to create the bottom border of the queen holder (which has a parallelogram shape):

```
FillColor = &H808080
ForeColor = &H808080
PointTable(0).X = 12 * SF
PointTable(0).Y = 43 * SF
PointTable(1).X = (14 + 29 * NQ) * SF - 1
```

(continued)

continued

```
PointTable(1).Y = 43 * SF
PointTable(2).X = (17 + 29 * NQ) * SF - 1
PointTable(2).Y = 47 * SF - 1
PointTable(3).X = 15 * SF
PointTable(3).Y = 47 * SF - 1
Polygon hDC, PointTable(0), 4
```

First, the fill and border colors you want are assigned to the form's FillColor and ForeColor properties. (They are both set to dark gray, &*H808080*, to create a solid area.) The polygon is specified by assigning the coordinates of each vertex to an element of the PointTable array. The elements of this array have the user defined type APIPOINT, which is declared in the global module (GLOBALQP.BAS), as follows:

```
Type APIPOINT
    X As Integer    'Horizontal coordinate of vertex
    Y As Integer    'Vertical coordinate of vertex
End Type
```

Finally, the *Polygon* function is called, passing to it the address of the PointTable array and the number of vertices specified by this array.

DrawWindow draws the remainder of the game background using the methods that have been discussed. The procedure also initializes the array SquareTable. This array is used to store current information on each square within the queen holder and the playing board. It is declared in the (general) section of QP.FRM as a two-dimensional array, large enough to hold information for the maximum number of squares:

```
Dim SquareTable(1 To 11, 1 To 10) As SQUARE
```

The first dimension corresponds to the row of each square, and the second dimension corresponds to the column. Notice that the maximum number of rows is one greater than the maximum number of columns because of the queen holder at the top of the form. Each SQUARE element contains a number of fields, as follows:

```
Type SQUARE
    X1 As Integer
    Y1 As Integer
    X2 As Integer
    Y2 As Integer
    XPos As Integer
    YPos As Integer
    Index As Integer
End Type
```

These SQUARE element fields are explained in the following table.

SQUARE Fields	Meaning
X1, Y1	Coordinates of the upper left corner of the square within the form.
X2, Y2	Coordinates of the lower right corner of the square within the form.
XPos, YPos	Coordinates of a picture box placed within the square. When the player drops a PictureQueen picture box (containing an image of a queen) within the square, the picture box is assigned these coordinates so that it is centered in the square.
Index	The index of the PictureQueen element currently placed within the square. This field is assigned the value *0* if the square is empty.

Notice that the Index fields are initialized only if a new game has started (that is, *NewGame* is TRUE). Otherwise, the queens are left in their current positions.

Drawing the Queens

The images of the queens used to play the game need to be redrawn each time *DrawWindow* is called because the sizes of the images must be based on the current scaling factor.

The *DrawWindow* procedure begins by drawing a single master image of a queen within the invisible picture box PictureMaster using the techniques described in the previous section. In addition, it uses the *Circle* method to draw the central circle.

Next, *DrawWindow* copies the drawing of the queen to the picture box PictureGoodQueen by means of the statement

```
PictureGoodQueen.Picture = PictureMaster.Image
```

At design time, the AutoRedraw property of PictureMaster was set to True. Accordingly, Visual Basic stores all graphics drawn to this picture box within an internal bitmap. This bitmap can be copied to another picture box by assigning the Image property of the source picture box to the Picture property of the target picture box. PictureGood-Queen is used to store the image of a legally positioned queen; you will see how it is used as the game is played.

Next, *DrawWindow* creates a drawing for an illegally positioned queen. To do this, it first *inverts* the drawing contained in PictureMaster, using the Windows API function *InvertRect* (described in Figure 6-12):

```
Rec.Left = 3 * SF
Rec.Top = 3 * SF
Rec.Right = 18 * SF
Rec.Bottom = 18 * SF
InvertRect PictureMaster.hDC, Rec
```

This call inverts the central area of the queen image (the area inside the gray borders). Inverting changes all the colors within the specified rectangle.

Windows API Function: *InvertRect*

Purpose Inverts all colors within the specified rectangular area of a form or picture box.

Declaration
```
Declare Sub InvertRect Lib "USER" (ByVal hDC As Integer,
  Rec As RECT)
```

Parameter	Description
hDC	The hDC property (device context handle) of the form or picture box.
Rec	A structure giving the coordinates of the rectangular area to be inverted. It should have the following format:
	`Type RECT`
	`    Left As Integer`
	`    Top As Integer`
	`    Right As Integer`
	`    Bottom As Integer`
	`End Type`

Comment If you call this function twice for the same rectangular area, all colors are restored to their original values.

Figure 6-12.
The InvertRect *Windows API function.*

Note: The right and bottom coordinates passed to the *InvertRect* function do not contain the – *1* term discussed in the previous section. This is because the Windows graphics functions (unlike Visual Basic methods) *automatically* subtract 1 pixel from the right and bottom coordinates of the specified rectangle.

The inverted image is then copied to the invisible picture box PictureBadQueen, which is used to store the image of an illegally positioned queen:

```
PictureBadQueen.Picture = PictureMaster.Image
```

Initializing the Picture Boxes

Finally, the *DrawWindow* procedure initializes the elements of the PictureQueen array. The elements of this array contain the images of the queens that are visible at runtime and are moved by the player.

First, *DrawWindow* temporarily makes all the PictureQueen elements invisible. Next, it sets the position, size, and picture of each element used in the game, and then it makes the element visible. The elements are accessed by looping through the SquareTable array (described in the previous section), because this array stores the position of every queen currently used in the game.

All the picture boxes are initially assigned the image of a valid queen stored in PictureGoodQueen. The procedure then loops through the BadQueens array, which stores the indexes of any illegally positioned queens (you will see later how this array is maintained as the game is played), marking each illicit queen by assigning it the picture stored in PictureBadQueen.

Moving the Queens

The method for moving the queens is the same as that used for the letters in the Word Squares game, presented in Chapter 5. Namely, the entire picture box containing the image (in this case, an element of PictureQueen) is moved in response to movements of the mouse. As you will recall, this movement is accomplished by processing the following three events:

- MouseDown. The *PictureQueen_MouseDown* event procedure initiates the move operation and then updates SquareTable to indicate that the corresponding square no longer contains a picture box.

- MouseMove. If a move operation is in progress, the *Form-_MouseMove* event procedure moves the picture to the new coordinates of the mouse pointer.

- MouseUp. The *Form_MouseUp* event procedure terminates the move. Also, if the picture box is dropped on an empty square, it centers the picture in the square and updates SquareTable.

In addition to these general steps for managing a move operation (which are discussed in detail in Chapter 5), the *PictureQueen_MouseDown* and *Form_MouseUp* event procedures perform important actions that are specific to the logic of the Queens program.

The *PictureQueen_MouseDown* Procedure

If a queen has been dropped on an illegal position (that is, *NumBadQueens* > 0), the *PictureQueen_MouseDown* event procedure permits the player to move only the incorrectly placed queen. (Its index is stored in the form-level variable *BadQueen*.) If the player is moving the illicit queen, the other bad queens are *unmarked*—that is, the pictures of all queens in the same row, column, or diagonal are assigned the standard picture (PictureGoodQueen), replacing the inverted queen image (PictureBadQueen). The indexes of these queens are stored in the BadQueens array.

The *Form_MouseUp* Procedure

If the queen is dropped on an empty square (as reported by the *SquareHit* procedure), *Form_MouseUp* calls the *CheckQueen* general procedure to test the validity of the move. If the queen has been dropped anywhere else, *Form_MouseUp* places the picture box back on the leftmost empty square of the queen holder at the top of the form.

CheckQueen is declared in the (general) section of QP.FRM. It is passed the row and column of the square on which the player dropped the queen. It checks all the other queens that have been placed on the playing board. If it finds another element of PictureQueen occupying the same row, column, or diagonal (as indicated in SquareTable), *CheckQueen* beeps, adds the index of the picture box to the BadQueens array, increments *NumBadQueens*, and highlights the queen's picture box by assigning it the picture stored in PictureBadQueen. *CheckQueen* also assigns the index of the newly placed queen to the form-level variable *BadQueen*:

```
BadQueen = SquareTable(Row, Col).Index
```

As just explained, the *BadQueen* variable is used by the *PictureQueen-_MouseDown* event procedure.

Before exiting, *Form_MouseUp* checks to see whether the player has completed a solution. If all the queens have been removed from the holder, and if no queens have been illegally placed (*NumBadQueens* = 0), then a solution must have been completed. In this case, the procedure enables the Timer1 timer control. The code is as follows:

```
For I = 1 To NQ
    If SquareTable(1, I).Index <> 0 Then Exit Sub   'Check holder
Next I
If NumBadQueens = 0 Then Timer1.Enabled = -1
```

The *Timer1_Timer* event procedure then beeps repeatedly and inverts the entire form using the Windows API *InvertRect* function (described in Figure 6-12 on page 166). Notice that after calling *InvertRect*, the procedure calls Visual Basic's *Refresh* method to force the system to update the form display; otherwise, the inversions would have no visual effect. After calling *Refresh* four times, the procedure disables the timer, and the flashing stops.

Enhancing the Game

Here are a few suggestions for enhancing the Queens program.

- Provide a Solution command to display one or more of the solutions for the selected number of queens. To derive all the solutions, you can use a backtracking algorithm. For a complete discussion on using the backtracking method to solve the Queens puzzle, see Chapter 5 in *Combinatorial Algorithms* by Reingold et al. (Prentice Hall, 1977).

- Implement games using more than 10 queens. To increase the maximum number of queens, you will have to add additional elements to the PictureQueen picture box array, increase the dimensions of the SquareTable and BadQueens arrays, and modify the code that initializes these arrays. You could then add the additional commands to the Game menu.

- The program could maintain a count of the total number of unique solutions that the player has found for each number of queens. These scores could be stored in a disk file to preserve them between games. (See Chapter 11 for information on storing game information in the WIN.INI file.) The program could provide a command for displaying the player's current score for each number of queens, as well as the largest possible score (provided in the table on page 132).

- Keep track of the time that has elapsed since a new game was started. You could use a Visual Basic timer control to maintain a display of the total time elapsed. The objective of the game would be to find a solution in as short a time as possible or to find as many solutions as possible in a specified period of time.

FRACTAL PUZZLE
AND FRACTAL GENERATOR

Fractal Puzzle is a computer game based on the traditional sliding-tile puzzle. The traditional puzzle consists of a small square holding numbered tiles that you try to arrange in numeric order. In Fractal Puzzle, however, each tile contains a portion of a fractal pattern, and you try to arrange the tiles to form the complete image. Fractal Puzzle combines the visual challenge of a jigsaw puzzle with the mechanical challenge involved in moving the tiles to the correct positions.

The first part of this chapter presents the Fractal Puzzle program. You will learn some interesting facts about the traditional sliding-tile puzzle as well as how to play Fractal Puzzle. You will also learn how the game is coded. The code for this program introduces an important new programming technique: using the Windows API *BitBlt* function for transferring blocks of graphics precisely.

Although the Fractal Puzzle program displays fractal patterns, it does not actually create these patterns. The second part of this chapter presents a separate program for generating the fractal patterns used in the puzzle. This program not only shows how to calculate and plot fractal equations, but it also explains several new Visual Basic programming techniques, such as the use of the *PSet* and *QBColor* functions to draw colored points and the use of the *DoEvents* function to prevent the blocking of system events during a long process. Additionally, the program shows how to display a dialog box for collecting numeric data and how to copy bitmap data to the Windows Clipboard.

Fractal Puzzle

This portion of the chapter presents the Fractal Puzzle program.

About Fractal Puzzle

The traditional sliding-tile puzzle, which forms the basis for Fractal Puzzle, was invented in America toward the end of the nineteenth century. The original puzzle consisted of a small square frame containing fifteen numbered tiles and one open space. The game was played by scrambling the tiles and then attempting to rearrange them in numeric order. Tiles were moved by sliding them into the open space. Figure 7-1 shows the puzzle with the tiles in the proper order.

1	2	3	4
5	6	7	8
9	10	11	12
13	14	15	

Figure 7-1.
The traditional sliding-tile puzzle.

An interesting feature is that if only two of the tiles are swapped during the puzzle's construction, the resulting puzzle cannot be solved. For example, it would be impossible to solve a puzzle built as shown in Figure 7-2; in this puzzle, the tiles numbered 14 and 15 are reversed while all other tiles are in their proper positions.

1	2	3	4
5	6	7	8
9	10	11	12
13	15	14	

Figure 7-2.
A tile puzzle that cannot be solved.

If the puzzle is constructed correctly, it can, of course, be solved no matter how the tiles are scrambled. (One solution would be to reverse each of the movements made when scrambling the tiles.) However, when a computer version of the sliding-tile puzzle scrambles the tiles, its program must ensure that the resulting arrangement can be solved—because the computer is not subject to the mechanical constraints of sliding physical tiles. Later in the chapter, you will learn how the Fractal Puzzle program accomplishes this.

Playing Fractal Puzzle

When you run Fractal Puzzle (FP.EXE), a form appears containing 16 blank tiles. To begin playing, you must choose one of the four Puzzle commands (Puzzle 1, Puzzle 2, Puzzle 3, or Puzzle 4) from the Game menu. Each of these commands draws a different fractal pattern on the tiles. Figure 7-3 shows the form after you choose the Puzzle 1 command. (Figures 7-13 through 7-16, which appear later in the chapter, show all four patterns.)

Figure 7-3.
Fractal Puzzle after choosing Puzzle 1.

After you have chosen a Puzzle command and have observed the fractal pattern, choose the Scramble command from the Game menu. The program removes one of the tiles (the specific tile is selected randomly) and randomly rearranges the remaining 15 tiles. Figure 7-4 shows the form after you choose the Scramble command.

 — empty space

Figure 7-4.
Fractal Puzzle after scrambling Puzzle 1.

173

Note: You can choose the Scramble command more than once if you want to scramble the tiles more thoroughly. If, however, you choose Scramble after arranging the tiles, your work will be lost!

You can move any of the tiles that adjoin the empty space. To move one of these tiles into the empty space, simply click on it.

The object of the game is to continue moving tiles until you have formed the fractal pattern that was displayed before the tiles were scrambled. Remember, however, that one tile will be missing from the original pattern because a tile was removed when you first chose the Scramble command.

Note: In the traditional hand-held puzzle, the missing tile is always the one that is located at the lower right corner of the solved puzzle (as shown in Figure 7-1). In Fractal Puzzle, however, the missing tile can be at *any* position within the solved puzzle.

When you finally solve the puzzle, the program beeps and restores the missing tile, so you can again see the complete fractal pattern. You can now choose the Scramble command to play a new game using the same pattern, or you can choose another Puzzle command to play a game using a different pattern. When you open the Game menu, the Puzzle command you chose previously (if any) is checked.

If, while you are solving a puzzle, you give up and want to see the solution, you can simply choose the same Puzzle command that you chose to start the game (that is, the checked one).

Strategy and Hints

Before you scramble the tiles, study the fractal pattern for a while because you will not be able to refer to it after scrambling. Alternatively, you can press the Alt-PrintScreen key combination to copy the form to the Clipboard and then use the Windows Clipboard program to view the pattern while solving the puzzle. (This should not be construed as cheating; recall that while working on a jigsaw puzzle, you are always allowed to look at the picture on the lid.)

While you are moving the tiles, keep in mind that all the fractal patterns are symmetric; the part of the pattern that you have already completed can reveal the way to complete the part you are currently solving.

The following steps provide a systematic method for solving the puzzle efficiently. Refer to Figure 7-5 for the numbering of the tile positions and rows.

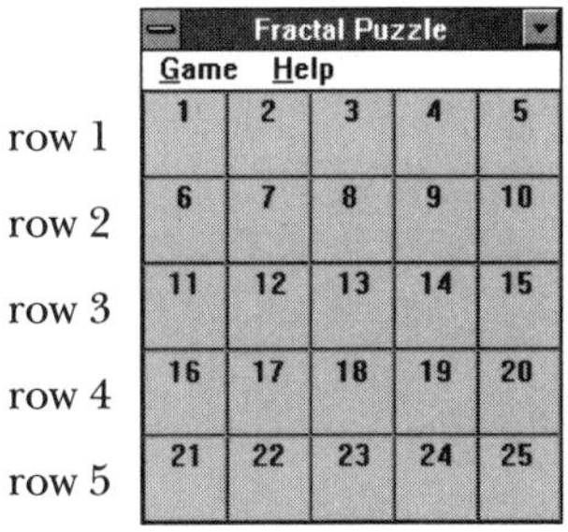

Figure 7-5.
The tile positions and rows.

1. Place the correct tiles in positions 1 through 4. In this step, you should proceed from left to right, and after you have positioned a tile correctly, you should not move it while positioning subsequent tiles.

2. Place the correct tile in position 5. To do this, you will have to temporarily move the tile in position 4.

3. Position the tiles in the second row, proceeding as in steps 1 and 2, without disturbing the tiles in the first row.

4. Continue using this procedure for the following rows, until you reach a position for which you cannot find a tile. (Recall that the missing tile occurs in a randomly chosen position.) You should then abandon the current row, begin positioning tiles in the last row, and proceed row by row back toward the missing tile (row 5, then row 4, and so on).

5. When you have completed all rows except two, proceed column by column rather than row by row, without disturbing tiles outside these last two rows. Start by placing the two tiles in the left column, and move right until you encounter the missing tile; then start from the right column and move left. When you reach the missing tile, the puzzle will be solved.

For example, consider a game in which the missing tile is at position 13. You would place tiles first in row 1 and then in row 2. When placing tiles in row 3, however, you would encounter the missing tile; you would therefore abandon this row and begin placing tiles in row 5. After completing row 5, only two rows would be left; you would therefore place tiles in positions 11 and 16, then 12 and 17, then 15 and 20, and finally 14 and 19. The puzzle would then be solved.

Coding Fractal Puzzle

The source code for the Fractal Puzzle program is contained in the files listed in the following table.

File	Purpose
GLOBALFP.BAS	Contains global type definitions
FP.FRM	Defines the main form, FormMain, and the controls it contains
FPABOUT.FRM	Defines the ABOUT form, FormAbout, and the controls it contains
FP.MAK	Contains the Fractal Puzzle project file

Figures 7-6 through 7-11 present the form designs, properties, menu commands, and source code for the Fractal Puzzle program.

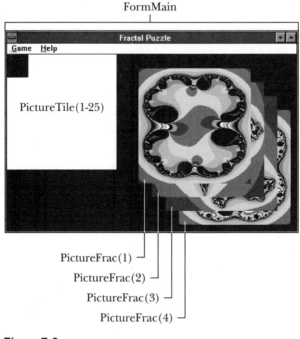

Figure 7-6.
FP.FRM at design time.

Object Name	Object Type	Property	Setting	
FormMain	Form	BackColor	&H00000000& [black]	
		BorderStyle	1 - Fixed Single	
		Caption	Fractal Puzzle	
		CtlName	FormMain	
		Grid height	8 [pixels]	
		Grid width	8 [pixels]	
		Height	5280 [twips]	
		Icon	(Icon) [FP.ICO]	
		Left	1035 [twips]	
		MaxButton	False	
		ScaleMode	3 - Pixel	
		Top	1140 [twips]	
		Width	7950 [twips]	
PictureFrac	Array of picture boxes	AutoRedraw	True	
		AutoSize	True	
		BorderStyle	0 - None	
		CtlName	PictureFrac	
		Height	200 [pixels]	
		Index	1 - 4	
		Left	[varies]	
		Picture	(Bitmap)	
			Index	*File*
			1	FRAC1.BMP
			2	FRAC2.BMP
			3	FRAC3.BMP
			4	FRAC4.BMP
		ScaleMode	3 - Pixel	
		Top	[varies]	
		Visible	False	
		Width	200 [pixels]	

Figure 7-7.   *(continued)*
FP.FRM form and control properties.

Figure 7-7 *continued*

Object Name	Object Type	Property	Setting
PictureTile	Array of picture boxes	AutoRedraw	True
		AutoSize	True
		BorderStyle	0 - None
		CtlName	PictureTile
		Height	40 [pixels]
		Index	1 - 25
		Left	[varies]
		Picture	PictureTile(1) only: (Bitmap) [TILE.BMP]
		ScaleMode	3 - Pixel
		Top	[varies]
		Width	40 [pixels]

Indentation/Caption	Control Name	Other Features
&Game	MenuGame	
....&Scramble	MenuScramble	Enabled = False
....-	MenuSep1	
....Puzzle &1	MenuPuzzle	Index = 1
....Puzzle &2	MenuPuzzle	Index = 2
....Puzzle &3	MenuPuzzle	Index = 3
....Puzzle &4	MenuPuzzle	Index = 4
....-	MenSep2	
....E&xit	MenuExit	
&Help	MenuHelp	
....&Index	MenuIndex	Accelerator = F1
....&How to Play	MenuHowTo	
....&Commands	MenuCommands	
....&Using Help	MenuUsingHelp	
....-	MenuSep3	
....&About Fractal Puzzle...	MenuAbout	

Figure 7-8.
FP.FRM menu design.

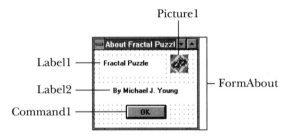

Figure 7-9.
FPABOUT.FRM at design time.

Object Name	Object Type	Property	Setting
Command1	Command button	Caption	OK
		Default	True
		Height	375 [twips]
		Left	840 [twips]
		Top	1440 [twips]
		Width	1095 [twips]
FormAbout	Form	BorderStyle	3 - Fixed Double
		Caption	About Fractal Puzzle
		FormName	FormAbout
		Grid Height	120 [twips]
		Grid Width	120 [twips]
		Height	2445 [twips]
		Left	1545 [twips]
		MaxButton	False
		MinButton	False
		Top	1920 [twips]
		Width	2880 [twips]
Label1	Label	Caption	Fractal Puzzle
		Height	375 [twips]
		Left	240 [twips]

Figure 7-10. *(continued)*
FPABOUT.FRM form and control properties.

Figure 7-10 *continued*

Object Name	Object Type	Property	Setting
		Top	240 [twips]
		Width	1575 [twips]
Label2	Label	Alignment	2 - Center
		Caption	By Michael J. Young
		Height	375 [twips]
		Left	0 [twips]
		Top	960 [twips]
		Width	2745 [twips]
Picture1	Picture box	AutoSize	True
		BorderStyle	0 - None
		Height	480 [twips]
		Left	2040 [twips]
		Picture	(Icon) [FP.ICO]
		Top	120 [twips]
		Width	480 [twips]

GLOBALFP.BAS code

```
Type POSITION
    X As Integer
    Y As Integer
    Idx As Integer
End Type

Type RECT
    Left As Integer
    Top As Integer
    Right As Integer
    Bottom As Integer
End Type
```

Figure 7-11. *(continued)*

Source code for the Fractal Puzzle program. (Notice that long program lines are wrapped to the next line and indented one space.)

Figure 7-11 *continued*

FP.FRM code

```
'Help Section:
'Help file:
Const HELP_FILE = "FP.HLP"
'WinHelp wCommand values:
Const HELP_CONTEXT = &H1
Const HELP_HELPONHELP = &H4
Const HELP_INDEX = &H3
Const HELP_QUIT = &H2
'WinHelp dwData values (help topics):
Const HELP_HOWTOPLAY = 10&
Const HELP_COMMANDS = 20&
'Windows help API:
Declare Sub WinHelp Lib "USER" (ByVal hWnd As Integer,
 ByVal lpHelpFile As String, ByVal wCommand As Integer,
 ByVal dwData As Long)

Const CLIENTBOTTOM = 200
Const CLIENTRIGHT = 199

Dim IdxHidden As Integer
Dim IdxOpen As Integer
Dim NumGame As Integer
Dim PosTable(1 To 25) As POSITION
Dim Scrambled As Integer

Const WS_CAPTION = &HC00000
Const WS_THICKFRAME = &H40000
Declare Sub AdjustWindowRect Lib "USER" (lpRect As RECT,
 ByVal dwStyle&, ByVal bMenu%)

Const SRCCOPY = &HCC0020      'dest = source
Declare Sub BitBlt Lib "GDI" (ByVal HDestDC%, ByVal X%,
 ByVal Y%, ByVal nWidth%, ByVal nHeight%, ByVal HSrcDC%,
 ByVal XSrc%, ByVal YSrc%, ByVal ROP&)

Const LOGPIXELSX = 88
Const LOGPIXELSY = 90
Declare Function GetDeviceCaps Lib "GDI" (ByVal hDC%,
 ByVal Index%) As Integer

Function GetPosIdx (Index As Integer)
    Dim I As Integer
```

(continued)

Figure 7-11 *continued*

```
    For I = 1 To 25
        If PosTable(I).Idx = Index Then
            GetPosIdx = I
            Exit Function
        End If
    Next I
    GetPosIdx = 0
End Function

Sub InitNewGame (Won As Integer)
    Dim I As Integer

    MenuScramble.Enabled = -1
    For I = 1 To 25
        PictureTile(I).Visible = 0
        If Won Then Beep
    Next I
    For I = 1 To 25
        PosTable(I).Idx = I
        PictureTile(I).Move PosTable(I).X, PosTable(I).Y
        BitBlt PictureTile(I).hDC, 1, 1, 38, 38,
 PictureFrac(NumGame).hDC, PosTable(I).X + 1, PosTable(I).Y
+ 1, SRCCOPY
        PictureTile(I).Visible = -1
        If Won Then Beep
    Next I
    IdxHidden = 0
    IdxOpen = 0
    Scrambled = 0
End Sub

Sub Form_Load ()
    Dim I As Integer
    Dim Rec As RECT

    'code for display device independence:
    Rec.Left = 0
    Rec.Top = 0
    Rec.Right = CLIENTRIGHT
    Rec.Bottom = CLIENTBOTTOM
    AdjustWindowRect Rec, WS_CAPTION, -1
    FormMain.Width = (Rec.Right - Rec.Left + 1) * (1440 /
```

(continued)

Figure 7-11 *continued*

```
GetDeviceCaps(hDC, LOGPIXELSX))
    FormMain.Height = (Rec.Bottom - Rec.Top + 1) * (1440 /
GetDeviceCaps(hDC, LOGPIXELSY))

    For I = 1 To 25
        PosTable(I).X = ((I - 1) Mod 5) * 40
        PosTable(I).Y = ((I - 1) \ 5) * 40
        PictureTile(I).Top = PosTable(I).X
        PictureTile(I).Left = PosTable(I).Y
        PictureTile(I).Picture = PictureTile(1).Picture
    Next I
End Sub

Sub Form_Unload (Cancel As Integer)
    WinHelp hWnd, HELP_FILE, HELP_QUIT, 0
End Sub

Sub MenuAbout_Click ()
    FormAbout.Show 1
End Sub

Sub MenuCommands_Click ()
    WinHelp hWnd, HELP_FILE, HELP_CONTEXT, HELP_COMMANDS
End Sub

Sub MenuExit_Click ()
    WinHelp hWnd, HELP_FILE, HELP_QUIT, 0
    End
End Sub

Sub MenuHowTo_Click ()
    WinHelp hWnd, HELP_FILE, HELP_CONTEXT, HELP_HOWTOPLAY
End Sub

Sub MenuIndex_Click ()
    WinHelp hWnd, HELP_FILE, HELP_INDEX, 0
End Sub

Sub MenuPuzzle_Click (Index As Integer)
    Dim I As Integer

    For I = 1 To 4
        If I = Index Then
            MenuPuzzle(I).Checked = -1
```

(continued)

Figure 7-11 *continued*

```
        Else
            MenuPuzzle(I).Checked = 0
        End If
    Next I
    NumGame = Index
    InitNewGame 0
End Sub

Sub MenuScramble_Click ()
    Dim I As Integer
    Dim IdxTile As Integer
    Dim RandNum As Integer

    If IdxOpen = 0 Then
        RandNum = Int(25 * Rnd + 1)        'random number 1 -> 25
        IdxHidden = RandNum
        PictureTile(IdxHidden).Visible = 0
        IdxOpen = RandNum
    End If
    For I = 1 To 500
        RandNum = Int(4 * Rnd + 1)         'random number 1 -> 4
        Select Case RandNum
            Case 1:     'left tile
                If IdxOpen Mod 5 = 1 Then
                    'in col 1; move right tile:
                    IdxTile = IdxOpen + 1
                Else
                    'move left tile:
                    IdxTile = IdxOpen - 1
                End If
            Case 2:     'upper tile
                If IdxOpen < 6 Then
                    'in row 1; move lower tile:
                    IdxTile = IdxOpen + 5
                Else
                    'move upper tile:
                    IdxTile = IdxOpen - 5
                End If
            Case 3:     'right tile
                If IdxOpen Mod 5 = 0 Then
                    'in col 5; move left tile:
                    IdxTile = IdxOpen - 1
```

(continued)

Figure 7-11 *continued*

```
                Else
                    'move right tile:
                    IdxTile = IdxOpen + 1
                End If
            Case 4:      'lower tile:
                If IdxOpen > 20 Then
                    'in row 5; move upper tile:
                    IdxTile = IdxOpen - 5
                Else
                    'move lower tile:
                    IdxTile = IdxOpen + 5
                End If
        End Select
        PictureTile(PosTable(IdxTile).Idx).Move
 PosTable(IdxOpen).X, PosTable(IdxOpen).Y
        PosTable(IdxOpen).Idx = PosTable(IdxTile).Idx
        PosTable(IdxTile).Idx = 0
        IdxOpen = IdxTile
    Next I
    Scrambled = -1
End Sub

Sub MenuUsingHelp_Click ()
    WinHelp hWnd, HELP_FILE, HELP_HELPONHELP, 0
End Sub

Sub PictureTile_MouseDown (Index As Integer, Button As Integer,
 Shift As Integer, X As Single, Y As Single)
    Dim IdxTile As Integer

    If Not Scrambled Then Exit Sub
    IdxTile = GetPosIdx(Index)
    If IdxOpen = IdxTile - 1 Or IdxOpen = IdxTile + 1 Or
 IdxOpen = IdxTile - 5 Or IdxOpen = IdxTile + 5 Then
        PictureTile(Index).Move PosTable(IdxOpen).X,
 PosTable(IdxOpen).Y
        PosTable(IdxOpen).Idx = PosTable(IdxTile).Idx
        PosTable(IdxTile).Idx = 0
        IdxOpen = IdxTile
    End If

    'test if game is won:
    For IdxTile = 1 To 25
        If IdxTile <> IdxOpen And PosTable(IdxTile).Idx <>
```

(continued)

185

Figure 7-11 *continued*

```
    IdxTile Then
                Exit Sub
            End If
        Next IdxTile

        'game won:
        InitNewGame -1
    End Sub
```

FPABOUT.FRM code

```
    Sub Command1_Click ()
        Unload FormAbout
    End Sub
```

Programming Techniques

The tiles in Fractal Puzzle are created using an array of 25 picture boxes (PictureTile1 through PictureTile25). Using a separate picture box for each tile makes it easy to determine the location of the mouse pointer when the player clicks a tile. (The *MouseDown* event procedure is passed the index of the picture box containing the pointer.) Assigning each tile its own picture box also makes it easy to move the tiles (by means of the *Move* method).

The gray borders around each tile are created by assigning a bitmap (TILE.BMP, created in Paintbrush) to the Picture property of each picture box.

The four fractal images are stored within invisible picture boxes (PictureFrac1 through PictureFrac4). These images were created using the Fractal Generator program (discussed in the second portion of this chapter), copied to the Clipboard, and then pasted into the PictureFrac picture boxes at design time.

When the player chooses a specific fractal image from the Game menu, the appropriate portion of the image is transferred into each of the PictureTile picture boxes (to the area inside the border), using the Windows API function *BitBlt*. *BitBlt* is a very powerful function that will be used in many of the games in the following chapters. As you have seen in previous games, you can transfer an entire bitmap from one picture box to another by simply assigning the Picture property of the source picture box to the Picture property of the target picture box. The advantage of using *BitBlt*, however, is that this function permits you to transfer *any rectangular portion* of the bitmap in the source picture box to *any position* within the target picture box. In later chapters, you will see that you can also achieve a wide variety of visual effects by specifying various bit operations when calling *BitBlt*.

Finally, the Fractal Puzzle program uses Visual Basic's random-number generator to scramble the tiles at the beginning of a game.

Program Overview

Here is a summary of the main sequence of events in the Fractal Puzzle program.

- When the program starts, the *Form_Load* event procedure performs the one-time initialization tasks, displaying 25 blank tiles within the form.

- When the player chooses one of the Puzzle commands from the Game menu, the *MenuPuzzle_Click* event procedure calls *InitNewGame* to initialize a new game, displaying the selected fractal pattern on top of the tiles.

- When the player chooses the Scramble command from the Game menu, the *MenuScramble_Click* event procedure hides one tile and randomly rearranges the remaining tiles.

- If the player presses the mouse button while the mouse pointer is over one of the tiles adjoining the open space, the *PictureTile_MouseDown* event procedure moves the tile into the open space. Also, if the puzzle has been solved, this procedure calls *InitNewGame* to reveal the hidden tile (so the player can see the entire pattern) and to initialize a new game.

Initializing the Program

The *Form_Load* procedure handles the initialization tasks that need to be performed once only, at the beginning of the program. *InitNewGame* performs the tasks required to initialize each new game.

The *Form_Load* Procedure

Form_Load begins by setting the width and height of the form so that the form will have the proper size regardless of the video mode (as explained in Chapter 3). The procedure then initializes the coordinate values stored in the PosTable array. This array stores information about each of the 25 tile positions within the form and is declared as follows:

```
Type POSITION
    X As Integer       'Horizontal coordinate of upper left
                       'corner of position.
    Y As Integer       'Vertical coordinate of upper left
                       'corner of position.
    Idx As Integer     'Index of the tile currently at the
                       'position (or 0 if no tile).
End Type

Dim PosTable(1 To 25) As POSITION
```

PosTable(1) stores information about the tile position in the upper left corner, PosTable(2) stores information about the tile in the next position to the right, and so on. (The indexes are given the numbers shown in Figure 7-5 on page 175.) The *X* and *Y* fields store the horizontal and vertical coordinates of the upper left corner of the tile position. The *Idx* field stores the index of the PictureTile element currently located at the position (which holds an image of a tile), or it stores the value 0 if the position is empty. (Recall that after the tiles are scrambled, the puzzle has one empty position.)

The *X* and *Y* values are assigned in the following loop:

```
For I = 1 To 25
    PosTable(I).X = ((I - 1) Mod 5) * 40
    PosTable(I).Y = ((I - 1) \ 5) * 40
    PictureTile(I).Top = PosTable(I).X
    PictureTile(I).Left = PosTable(I).Y
    PictureTile(I).Picture = PictureTile(1).Picture
Next I
```

After assigning the coordinates to PosTable, the loop assigns the initial positions of the PictureTile picture boxes. As explained in Chapter 3, if the program uses bitmaps, visible picture boxes must be explicitly positioned at runtime to assure video-mode independence.

The loop also copies the bitmap from the first tile to each of the other tiles. This bitmap depicts a blank tile with a border; it was created in Paintbrush, stored in the file TILE.BMP, and assigned to the first tile at design time.

The *Idx* fields of PosTable are assigned later in the program by the *InitNewGame* procedure.

The *InitNewGame* Procedure

The *InitNewGame* general procedure is called from two points within the Fractal Puzzle program.

First, when the player chooses one of the Puzzle commands from the Game menu, the *MenuPuzzle_Click* event procedure checks the selected command and removes the check mark from any previously checked command, sets the form-level variable *NumGame* to the number of the selected game, and calls *InitNewGame*:

```
For I = 1 To 4
    If I = Index Then
        MenuPuzzle(I).Checked = -1
    Else
        MenuPuzzle(I).Checked = 0
    End If
Next I
NumGame = Index
InitNewGame 0
```

The value assigned to *NumGame* tells *InitNewGame* which fractal pattern to use when drawing the image on the tiles.

Second, when the player solves the puzzle, the *PictureTile_MouseDown* procedure (described later in the chapter) also calls *InitNewGame*, so the hidden tile becomes visible again and the player sees the complete fractal pattern:

```
InitNewGame -1
```

Notice that *InitNewGame* is passed a single parameter, *Won*:

```
Sub InitNewGame (Won As Integer)
```

This parameter is assigned TRUE only when *InitNewGame* is called from *PictureTile_MouseDown*. When *Won* is set to TRUE, *InitNewGame* beeps repeatedly to signal that the puzzle has been solved.

InitNewGame begins by enabling the Scramble command on the Game menu:

```
MenuScramble.Enabled = -1
```

This command is disabled at design time and is enabled at runtime only after a puzzle has been selected.

The procedure then temporarily hides the tiles:

```
For I = 1 To 25
    PictureTile(I).Visible = 0
    If Won Then Beep
Next I
```

189

Each tile will be made visible again only after it has been properly positioned and assigned its graphic image. Temporarily hiding the tiles produces a less confusing visual display. Also, be aware that if the *Won* parameter passed to *InitNewGame* is TRUE, the procedure beeps as each tile is hidden.

InitNewGame next initializes each of the 25 tile positions:

```
For I = 1 To 25
    PosTable(I).Idx = I
    PictureTile(I).Move PosTable(I).X, PosTable(I).Y
    BitBlt PictureTile(I).hDC, 1, 1, 38, 38,
  PictureFrac(NumGame).hDC,PosTable(I).X + 1, PosTable(I).Y + 1,
    SRCCOPY PictureTile(I).Visible = -1
    If Won Then Beep
Next I
```

The For loop arranges the tiles by placing PictureTile elements 1 through 25 at positions 1 through 25 on the form. To do this, the loop assigns the appropriate indexes to the *Idx* fields of the PosTable array (which was explained previously), and it calls the *Move* method to move the picture boxes to these positions. The loop also calls *BitBlt* to copy the appropriate portion of the fractal image to each PictureTile element. At the end of each pass of the loop, the procedure makes the picture box visible, and, if the game has been won, it beeps.

In general, the *BitBlt* function (described in Figure 7-12) lets you transfer a rectangular block of graphics from any position to any other position. The source and target locations can be in the same picture box or form, in separate picture boxes or forms, or even in separate devices. (For example, you can transfer graphics from a form to a printer.)

Also, by assigning various values to the last *BitBlt* parameter (*ROP*), you can perform a wide variety of bit operations when transferring the graphics. Many of the games in later chapters use a variety of bit operations to achieve special visual effects.

In each call it makes to *BitBlt*, the *InitNewGame* procedure assigns *ROP* the value *SRCCOPY* to perform a simple copy operation:

```
BitBlt PictureTile(I).hDC, 1, 1, 38, 38,
 PictureFrac(NumGame).hDC, PosTable(I).X + 1, PosTable(I).Y + 1,
 SRCCOPY
```

The specified dimensions and starting positions cause *BitBlt* to transfer the graphics to the portion of the PictureTile picture box *inside the tile border* so that the border around each tile does not disappear.

Windows API Function: *BitBlt*

Purpose Transfers a rectangular block of graphics from one location to another.

Declaration
```
Declare Sub BitBlt Lib "GDI" (ByVal HDestDC%, ByVal X%,
 ByVal Y%, ByVal nWidth%, ByVal nHeight%, ByVal HSrcDC%,
 ByVal XSrc%, ByVal YSrc%, ByVal ROP&)
```

Parameter	Description
HDestDC%	hDC property of destination form, picture box, printer, or other object.
X%	Horizontal coordinate of upper left corner of destination rectangle.
Y%	Vertical coordinate of upper left corner of destination rectangle.
nWidth%	Width of destination and source rectangles.
nHeight%	Height of destination and source rectangles.
HSrcDC%	hDC property of source form, picture box, or other object.
XSrc%	Horizontal coordinate of upper left corner of source rectangle.
YScr%	Vertical coordinate of upper left corner of source rectangle.
ROP&	Code indicating how the bits from the source rectangle are to be combined with the existing bits in the destination rectangle. The following are some typical values:

ROP& value	*Effect*
&H00CC0020 (SRCCOPY)	destination = source
&H008800C6 (SRCAND)	destination = source AND destination
&H00EE0086 (SRCPAINT)	destination = source OR destination
&H00660046 (SRCINVERT)	destination = source XOR destination

Figure 7-12.
The BitBlt *Windows API function.*

F Y I

Because the picture boxes in the PictureFrac array are invisible at runtime, their AutoRedraw properties must be set to True, so that the graphics they contain will be permanently accessible for the *BitBlt* transfer. The AutoRedraw properties of the PictureTile elements are also set to True, as a convenience, so that these picture boxes do not have be redrawn if the picture box is overlaid or the form is minimized.

Finally, *InitNewGame* sets several form-level variables to *0*:

```
IdxHidden = 0
IdxOpen = 0
Scrambled = 0
```

These variables are used by other procedures and have meanings defined in the following table.

Variable	Meaning
IdxHidden	The PictureFrac index of the picture box element that the *MenuScramble_Click* event procedure hides to create the initial empty space.
IdxOpen	The PosTable index of the tile space that is currently empty. (In other words, it is the current position of the open space within the form.)
Scrambled	A variable that the *MenuScramble_Click* event procedure sets to TRUE when the tiles have been scrambled. Tiles cannot be moved until they have been scrambled and one tile has been removed.

Scrambling the Tiles

When the player chooses the Scramble command from the Game menu, the *MenuScramble_Click* event procedure receives control. This procedure begins by selecting a random tile to hide and updates *IdxHidden* and *IdxOpen* accordingly:

```
If IdxOpen = 0 Then
    RandNum = Int(25 * Rnd + 1)        'random number 1 -> 25
    IdxHidden = RandNum
    PictureTile(IdxHidden).Visible = 0
    IdxOpen = RandNum
End If
```

(Initially, *IdxHidden* and *IdxOpen* are equal; they will become unequal, however, after the tiles are scrambled.)

Next, the procedure scrambles the remaining 24 visible tiles by repeatedly moving tiles into the open space. The tile-moving routine is placed within the following loop so that the program makes 500 moves (resulting in a thorough scrambling of the tiles):

```
For I = 1 To 500
    'Move a randomly selected tile into the open space.
Next I
```

The tile-moving routine first obtains a random number in the range 1 through 4:

```
RandNum = Int(4 * Rnd + 1)
```

Assuming that the open space is surrounded by four tiles, the routine chooses a tile to move into the space according to the value of the random number in *RandNum*, as shown in the following table.

RandNum Value	Move This Tile into Open Space
1	Tile to the left of open space
2	Tile above open space
3	Tile to the right of open space
4	Tile below open space

If, however, the open space is along an edge and no tile exists in the chosen direction, the routine simply moves the tile that is on the opposite side of the open space.

The procedure *could* scramble tiles much more quickly by simply selecting a random location for each tile and then moving each tile directly to the selected location. One danger of this approach, however, is that the resulting arrangement of tiles might not be solvable; rather, it might be a scrambled version of the unsolvable puzzle described previously in the chapter (and shown in Figure 7-2 on page 172). The technique used in the procedure—namely, scrambling the tiles by making a series of valid moves—assures that the resulting arrangement can be solved and also creates an interesting visual effect.

Finally, *MenuScramble_Click* sets the variable *Scrambled* to TRUE to signal the *PictureTile_MouseDown* procedure (described next) that the tiles have been scrambled and the player is free to start moving tiles:

```
Scrambled = -1
```

Moving the Tiles

When the user presses the mouse button while the mouse pointer is over one of the tiles, control passes to the *PictureTile_MouseDown* event procedure:

```
Sub PictureTile_MouseDown (Index As Integer, Button As Integer,
  Shift As Integer, X As Single, Y As Single)
```

This procedure exits immediately if the tiles have not yet been scrambled:

```
If Not Scrambled Then Exit Sub
```

It then calls the general function *GetPosIdx* to obtain the PosTable index of the tile under the mouse pointer (the *Index* parameter contains the *PictureTile* index of the tile under the mouse pointer):

```
IdxTile = GetPosIdx(Index)
```

Next, if the tile under the mouse pointer is adjacent to the open space, the procedure calls the *Move* method to move the picture box displaying the tile into the empty space, and it updates PosTable and *Idx-Open* accordingly:

```
If IdxOpen = IdxTile - 1 Or IdxOpen = IdxTile + 1 Or IdxOpen =
  IdxTile - 5 Or IdxOpen = IdxTile + 5 Then
    PictureTile(Index).Move PosTable(IdxOpen).X,
  PosTable(IdxOpen).Y
    PosTable(IdxOpen).Idx = PosTable(IdxTile).Idx
    PosTable(IdxTile).Idx = 0    '0 means that the position does
                                 'NOT contain a tile.
    IdxOpen = IdxTile
End If
```

Finally, *PictureTile_MouseDown* tests whether the puzzle has been solved, and if so, it calls *InitNewGame,* assigning TRUE to the parameter *Won* to cause the procedure to produce a beep:

```
For IdxTile = 1 To 25
    If IdxTile <> IdxOpen And PosTable(IdxTile).Idx <> IdxTile
  Then
        Exit Sub     'A tile is out of place; therefore, the
                     'puzzle is not yet solved.
    End If
Next IdxTile

'All tiles are in the correct positions; therefore, the puzzle
'is solved.
InitNewGame -1
```

194

> **TIP**
>
> To create a file containing a bitmap of a fractal pattern, begin by drawing the pattern you want and saving it in the Windows Clipboard using the Fractal Generator program, which is presented in the remainder of the chapter. Paste the bitmap into Paintbrush, and while the image is still selected, choose the Copy To command from Paintbrush's Edit menu, and specify the filename you want to use. Using this technique, you can create any number of different fractal patterns, each one stored in a separate disk file.
>
> Use Visual Basic disk, directory, and file list controls to permit the player to select the file wanted at runtime. After the player selects a bitmap file, you have Visual Basic call its *LoadPicture* function to read this file into a picture box. You can then transfer the image to the tiles exactly as you do in the current version of the program.

Enhancing the Game

Here are two suggestions for enhancing the Fractal Puzzle program.

- Rather than always using 25 tiles, allow the player to choose a different number of tiles. For example, you might provide options for using 16 (4 by 4) tiles or 36 (6 by 6) tiles. You could use Visual Basic's *Load* method to add new elements to the PictureTile array, thus accommodating additional tiles at runtime, and you could use the *Unload* method to reduce the number of elements.

- The puzzle currently displays only one of the four fractal patterns built into the program. You could provide a much greater choice of patterns by storing the patterns in disk files and allowing the player to choose any of these files at runtime.

Fractal Generator

The Fractal Generator program is used to create the fractal patterns displayed by Fractal Puzzle.

About the Fractal Patterns

The type of fractal patterns created by the Fractal Generator program (and displayed in the Fractal Puzzle program) are known as "Julia sets" (named after the French mathematician, Gaston Julia, 1893–1978). Julia sets are based on the repeated function

$$Z_n = Z_{n-1}^2 + C$$

in which both Z and C are complex numbers—that is, numbers consisting of a real component and an imaginary component.

To plot a specific Julia set, C is assigned a fixed value. The behavior of the function is then entirely dependent on the first function value, Z_0. When plotting the function, the horizontal coordinate of each point (X) represents the real component of Z_0, and the vertical coordinate of each point (Y) represents the imaginary component of Z_0. The color assigned each point (X, Y) is based on the behavior of the corresponding function: If the values of the function do *not* approach infinity, the point is left black (the background color); if the values *do* approach infinity, the point is assigned a color indicating how rapidly they approach infinity. (A change in color indicates only a change in how rapidly the function approaches infinity; the specific colors have no inherent significance. Rather, you can freely alter the colors to produce different visual effects.)

As you will see, the computer operations required to plot each point are quite simple (although time consuming), and the result is a fantastic set of curves, which bear a remarkable similarity to shapes found in nature.

The Fractal Generator program allows you to create a wide variety of fractal patterns by adjusting the parameters used to plot the Julia set. First, you can set the real and imaginary parts of C. Assigning various values to C creates different Julia sets. (As you might expect, Julia sets with similar C values are similar in appearance.)

Second, you can set the ranges of X values (*XMin* and *XMax*) and Y values (*YMin* and *YMax*) that the program plots. Increasing the ranges of X and Y values causes the program to plot a larger portion of the Julia set, effectively "zooming out" on the pattern. If you keep increasing the ranges, you will reach a point where no additional detail will be displayed; rather, you will simply reveal a larger area of uniform color surrounding the pattern. If the absolute values of *XMin* and *XMax* are equal (for example, if they are assigned *−1* and *+1*), and the absolute values of *YMin* and *YMax* are equal, the pattern will be perfectly symmetric around the point in the center of the drawing (like the symmetry of the letter S).

Finally, you can set the maximum value of n in the repeated equation (*NMax*). In other words, you can adjust the number of times the program calculates the function when determining whether the values approach infinity. Assigning larger values to *NMax* tends to add detail and reduce the black areas within the pattern. (With a greater number of calculations, the values of the function are more likely to drift toward infinity, causing the corresponding point to be assigned a nonblack color.) Increasing *NMax* also increases the time required to draw the pattern.

The following table gives the values of the parameters used to calculate the fractal patterns displayed by the Fractal Generator program; it also gives the number of the figure that illustrates the pattern. (See Figures 7-13 through 7-16.) You can use these values as the starting points for generating your own fractal patterns; if you simply choose numbers at random, many of the resulting patterns might not be interesting.

Puzzle No.	Refer to Figure	CR*	CI**	XMin	XMax	YMin	YMax	NMax
1	7-13	0.28	-0.0035	-0.9	0.9	-1.2	1.2	24
2	7-14	-1.03	-0.26	-1.65	1.65	-0.8	0.8	32
3	7-15	0.14	0.65	-1.2	1.2	-1.2	1.2	32
4	7-16	0.27	-0.0035	-0.9	0.9	-1.15	1.15	48

* Real part of C
** Imaginary part of C

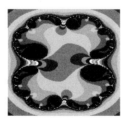

Figure 7-13.
The fractal pattern used in Puzzle 1.

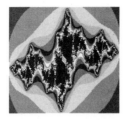

Figure 7-14.
The fractal pattern used in Puzzle 2.

Figure 7-15.
The fractal pattern used in Puzzle 3.

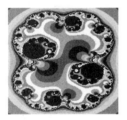

Figure 7-16.
The fractal pattern used in Puzzle 4.

Using the Fractal Generator

When you run the Fractal Generator program (FRACTAL.EXE), you will see a form containing a black rectangle. All program actions are performed by choosing commands from the Fractal menu. These commands are listed in the following table.

Command	Action
Preview	Quickly draws a small image of the fractal pattern in the upper left corner of the black rectangle, using the current parameters. (The image has the same size as an icon: 32 pixels by 32 pixels.) When you use this command to experiment with new parameters, you can preview the pattern without taking the time to create the full-size image.
Draw	Draws the full-size fractal pattern, which fills the entire black rectangle, using the current parameters. While the pattern is being drawn, this command changes to Quit Draw; choose the Quit Draw command if you want to stop generating the image. (It can take quite a while to draw some of the fractal patterns.)
Save To Clipboard	After a full-sized fractal pattern is generated, this command copies the image to the Windows Clipboard (as a bitmap). If you want, you can paste the image into Paintbrush, which lets you edit the image, print it, or save it in a file. You can also paste the image directly into a Visual Basic form or picture box.
Parameters	Changes the parameters used to generate the fractal pattern. The parameters were explained in the previous section. If you do not set the parameters, the program uses a default setting, which generates the fractal pattern shown in Figure 7-15.
Exit	Terminates the program.

Coding the Fractal Generator

The source code for the Fractal Generator program is contained in the files listed in the following table.

File	Purpose
GLOBALFR.BAS	Contains global variable and type definitions
FRACTAL.FRM	Defines the main form, FormMain, and the controls it contains
FRPARAM.FRM	Defines the Julia Set Parameters form, FormParam, and the controls it contains
FRACTAL.MAK	Contains the Fractal Generator project file

Figures 7-17 through 7-22 beginning on the following page present the information on the form designs, properties, menu commands, and source code for the Fractal Generator program.

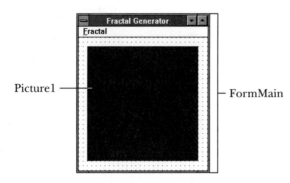

Picture1 —

— FormMain

Figure 7-17.
FRACTAL.FRM at design time.

Object Name	Object Type	Property	Setting
FormMain	Form	BorderStyle	1 - Fixed Single
		Caption	Fractal Generator
		FormName	FormMain
		Grid Height	8 [pixels]
		Grid Width	8 [pixels]
		Height	4185 [twips]
		Icon	(Icon) [FRACTAL.ICO]
		Left	1035 [twips]
		MaxButton	False
		ScaleMode	3 - Pixel
		Top	1140 [twips]
		Width	3615 [twips]
Picture1	Picture box	AutoRedraw	True
		BackColor	&H00000000& [black]
		BorderStyle	0 - None
		Height	200 [pixels]
		Left	16 [pixels]
		ScaleMode	3 - Pixel
		Top	16 [pixels]
		Width	200 [pixels]

Figure 7-18.
FRACTAL.FRM form and control properties.

Indentation/Caption	Control Name	Other Features
&Fractal	MenuFractal	
....&Preview	MenuPreview	
....&Draw	MenuDraw	
....&Save to Clipboard	MenuSave	Enabled = False
....Pa&rameters...	MenuParm	
....-	MenuSep	
....E&xit	MenuExit	

Figure 7-19.
FRACTAL.FRM menu design.

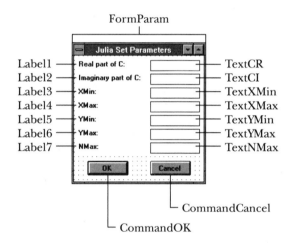

Figure 7-20.
FRPARAM.FRM at design time.

Object Name	Object Type	Property	Setting
CommandCancel	Command button	Cancel	True
		Caption	Cancel
		CtlName	CommandCancel

Figure 7-21. *(continued)*
FRPARAM.FRM form and control properties.

Figure 7-21 *continued*

Object Name	Object Type	Property	Setting
		Height	375 [twips]
		Left	2040 [twips]
		TabIndex	9
		Top	2760 [twips]
		Width	1095 [twips]
CommandOK	Command button	Caption	OK
		CtlName	CommandOK
		Default	True
		Height	375 [twips]
		Left	360 [twips]
		TabIndex	8
		Top	2760 [twips]
		Width	1095 [twips]
FormParam	Form	BorderStyle	3 - Fixed Double
		Caption	Julia Set Parameters
		FormName	FormParam
		Grid Width	120 [twips]
		Grid Height	120 [twips]
		Height	3705 [twips]
		Left	1860 [twips]
		MaxButton	False
		MinButton	False
		Top	2205 [twips]
		Width	3600 [twips]
Label1	Label	Caption	Real part of C:
		Height	255 [twips]
		Left	120 [twips]
		Top	120 [twips]
		Width	1815 [twips]
Label2	Label	Caption	Imaginary part of C:
		Height	255 [twips]
		Left	120 [twips]

(continued)

Figure 7-21 *continued*

Object Name	Object Type	Property	Setting
		Top	480 [twips]
		Width	1815 [twips]
Label3	Label	Caption	XMin:
		Height	255 [twips]
		Left	120 [twips]
		Top	840 [twips]
		Width	1815 [twips]
Label4	Label	Caption	XMax:
		Height	255 [twips]
		Left	120 [twips]
		Top	1200 [twips]
		Width	1815 [twips]
Label5	Label	Caption	YMin:
		Height	255 [twips]
		Left	120 [twips]
		Top	1560 [twips]
		Width	1815 [twips]
Label6	Label	Caption	YMax:
		Height	255 [twips]
		Left	120 [twips]
		Top	1920 [twips]
		Width	1815 [twips]
Label7	Label	Caption	NMax:
		Height	255 [twips]
		Left	120 [twips]
		Top	2280 [twips]
		Width	1815 [twips]
TextCl	Text box	CtlName	TextCl
		Height	285 [twips]
		Left	2040 [twips]
		TabIndex	2
		Top	480 [twips]
		Width	1335 [twips]

(continued)

Figure 7-21 *continued*

Object Name	Object Type	Property	Setting
TextCR	Text box	CtlName	TextCR
		Height	285 [twips]
		Left	2040 [twips]
		TabIndex	1
		Top	120 [twips]
		Width	1335 [twips]
TextNMax	Text box	CtlName	TextNMax
		Height	285 [twips]
		Left	2040 [twips]
		TabIndex	7
		Top	2280 [twips]
		Width	1335 [twips]
TextXMax	Text box	CtlName	TextXMax
		Height	285 [twips]
		Left	2040 [twips]
		TabIndex	4
		Top	1200 [twips]
		Width	1335 [twips]
TextXMin	Text box	CtlName	TextXMin
		Height	285 [twips]
		Left	2040 [twips]
		TabIndex	3
		Top	840 [twips]
		Width	1335 [twips]
TextYMax	Text box	CtlName	TextYMax
		Height	285 [twips]
		Left	2040 [twips]
		TabIndex	6
		Top	1920 [twips]
		Width	1335 [twips]
TextYMin	Text box	CtlName	TextYMin
		Height	285 [twips]

(continued)

Figure 7-21 *continued*

Object Name	Object Type	Property	Setting
		Left	2040 [twips]
		TabIndex	5
		Top	1560 [twips]
		Width	1335 [twips]

GLOBALFR.BAS code

```
Global CI As Single
Global CR As Single
Global NMax As Integer
Global XMax As Single
Global XMin As Single
Global YMax As Single
Global YMin As Single
```

DFRACTAL.FRM code

```
Dim Drawing As Integer
Dim QuitNow As Integer

Sub DrawFrac (Create As Integer)
    Dim Col As Integer
    Dim ColMax As Integer
    Dim ColorVal As Integer
    Dim DX As Single
    Dim DY As Single
    Dim Row As Integer
    Dim RowMax As Integer
    Dim X As Single
    Dim XSqr As Single
    Dim Y As Single
    Dim YSqr As Single
```

Figure 7-22.   *(continued)*

Source code for the Fractal Generator program. (Notice that long lines are wrapped to the next line and indented one space.)

Figure 7-22 *continued*

```
    If Create Then
        ColMax = Picture1.Width - 1
        RowMax = Picture1.Height - 1
    Else
        ColMax = 31
        RowMax = 31     End If
    Picture1.Cls
    DX = (XMax - XMin) / ColMax
    DY = (YMax - YMin) / RowMax
    For Col = 0 To ColMax
        For Row = 0 To RowMax
            X = XMin + Col * DX
            Y = YMax - Row * DY
            XSqr = 0
            YSqr = 0
            ColorVal = 0
            Do While ColorVal < NMax And XSqr + YSqr < 4
                ColorVal = ColorVal + 1
                XSqr = X * X
                YSqr = Y * Y
                Y = 2 * X * Y + CI
                X = XSqr - YSqr + CR
            Loop
            If ColorVal < NMax Then
                Picture1.PSet (Col, Row), QBColor(ColorVal
  Mod 15 + 1)
            End If
        Next Row
        Picture1.Refresh
        Dummy = DoEvents()
        If QuitNow Then
            QuitNow = 0
            Exit Sub
        End If
    Next Col
End Sub

Sub Form_Load ()
    CR = .14
    CI = .65
    XMin = -1.2
    XMax = 1.2
    YMin = -1.2
    YMax = 1.2
    NMax = 32
End Sub
```

(continued)

Figure 7-22 *continued*

```
Sub Form_Unload (Cancel As Integer)
    End
End Sub

Sub MenuDraw_Click ()
    If Drawing Then
        QuitNow = -1
    Else
        Drawing = -1
        MenuDraw.Caption = "&Quit draw"
        MenuPreview.Enabled = 0
        MenuSave.Enabled = 0
        MenuParm.Enabled = 0
        DrawFrac -1
        Drawing = 0
        MenuDraw.Caption = "&Draw"
        MenuPreview.Enabled = -1
        MenuSave.Enabled = -1
        MenuParm.Enabled = -1
    End If
End Sub

Sub MenuExit_Click ()
    End
End Sub

Sub MenuParm_Click ()
    FormParam.Show 1
End Sub

Sub MenuPreview_Click ()
    MenuDraw.Enabled = 0
    MenuPreview.Enabled = 0
    MenuSave.Enabled = 0
    MenuParm.Enabled = 0
    DrawFrac 0
    MenuDraw.Enabled = -1
    MenuPreview.Enabled = -1
    MenuParm.Enabled = -1
End Sub

Sub MenuSave_Click ()
    Clipboard.SetData Picture1.Image, 2
End Sub
```

(continued)

Figure 7-22 *continued*

FRPARAM.FRM code

```
Sub CommandOK_Click ()
    CR = Val(TextCR.Text)
    CI = Val(TextCI.Text)
    XMin = Val(TextXMin.Text)
    XMax = Val(TextXMax.Text)
    YMin = Val(TextYMin.Text)
    YMax = Val(TextYMax.Text)
    NMax = Val(TextNMax.Text)
    Unload FormParam
End Sub

Sub CommandCancel_Click ()
    Unload FormParam
End Sub

Sub Form_Load ()
    TextCR.Text = Str$(CR)
    TextCI.Text = Str$(CI)
    TextXMin.Text = Str$(XMin)
    TextXMax.Text = Str$(XMax)
    TextYMin.Text = Str$(YMin)
    TextYMax.Text = Str$(YMax)
    TextNMax.Text = Str$(NMax)
End Sub
```

Drawing the Fractal Pattern

The general procedure *DrawFrac* draws the fractal image within the Picture1 picture box, which is centered within the form. *DrawFrac* is called by the *MenuPreview_Click* event procedure when the user chooses the Preview command:

```
DrawFrac 0
```

DrawFrac is also called by the *MenuDraw_Click* event procedure when the user chooses the Draw command:

```
DrawFrac -1
```

DrawFrac receives a single parameter, *Create*:

```
Sub DrawFrac (Create As Integer)
```

Setting this parameter to TRUE causes *DrawFrac* to draw a full-sized fractal pattern; setting it to FALSE causes *DrawFrac* to draw a small preview image.

DrawFrac begins by setting the variables *ColMax* and *RowMax*, which contain the coordinates of the lower right corner of the image, according to the value of *Create*:

```
If Create Then
    ColMax = Picture1.Width - 1        'Image fills entire
                                       'picture box.
    RowMax = Picture1.Height - 1
Else
    ColMax = 31                        'Small preview image in upper
                                       'left corner of picture box.
    RowMax = 31
End If
```

(Note: The ScaleMode property of Picture1 was set to *3 - Pixel*. Accordingly, all measurements are in pixels.)

DrawFrac then calls the *Cls* method to erase any former image drawn in the picture box:

```
Picture1.Cls
```

The procedure next assigns values to the variables *DX* and *DY*:

```
DX = (XMax - XMin) / ColMax
DY = (YMax - YMin) / RowMax
```

XMin, *XMax*, *YMin*, and *YMax* are global variables. (Later, you will see how they are set.) As explained previously (in the section "About the Fractal Patterns"), they contain the ranges of *X* and *Y* values that will be plotted. *DX* stores the amount *X* changes with each row of pixels in the picture box, and *DY* stores the amount *Y* changes with each column of pixels.

The procedure then draws each point within the image area, proceeding column by column, by placing the point drawing routine within the following loops:

```
For Col = 0 To ColMax
    For Row = 0 To RowMax

        'Draw point at Row, Col.

    Next Row

    'After each row, refresh display and permit user to quit.

Next Col
```

The routine for drawing the point at *Row* and *Col* begins by initializing several variables:

```
X = XMin + Col * DX
Y = YMax - Row * DY
XSqr = 0
YSqr = 0
ColorVal = 0
```

X contains the real part of Z_0 and *Y* contains the imaginary part of Z_0. As you saw before, Z_0 is the starting value of the repeated function

$$Z_n = Z_{n-1}^2 + C$$

XSqr and *YSqr* are used to store the squares of *X* and *Y*, and *ColorVal* is a counter used to calculate the color that is to be plotted at *Row* and *Col*.

The point drawing routine then enters a loop for testing whether the values of the function approach infinity:

```
Do While ColorVal < NMax And XSqr + YSqr < 4
    ColorVal = ColorVal + 1
    XSqr = X * X
    YSqr = Y * Y
    Y = 2 * X * Y + CI
    X = XSqr - YSqr + CR
Loop
```

Each pass of the loop calculates the real (*X*) and imaginary (*Y*) parts of the next value of the function, which are based on the previous values of *X* and *Y*, according to the following formulas:

$$Y_{n+1} = 2X_nY_n + CI$$
$$X_{n+1} = X_n^2 - Y_n^2 + CR$$

CI and *CR* are global variables holding the real and imaginary parts of the *C* in the repeated function. (Later, you will see how they are assigned values.) Note: These formulas follow the rules of complex-number arithmetic.

How does this loop test whether the values of the function approach infinity? The loop makes use of a theorem, which states that if the value of the function ever exceeds 2, the values of the function will eventually become infinite. The variable *NMax* contains the maximum number of loop repetitions that will be performed. If the value of the function exceeds 2 before *NMax* calculations have been completed, the loop exits immediately. (Actually, because the loop has already calculated the square of the value of the function, the loop exit condition tests whether the *square of the value* exceeds *the square of 2*, eliminating an unnecessary square-root operation.)

If, however, the value of the function never exceeds 2, the loop does not exit until the number of calculations performed (which is stored in ColorVal) exceeds *NMax*.

A technical note: In this discussion, the expression *value of the function* actually refers to the *absolute value* of the function Z, because Z is a complex number. The *absolute value* of a complex number is equal to the square root of the sum of the squares of the real and imaginary parts.

After the *Do While* loop exits, if *ColorVal* is less than *NMax*, the function value must have exceeded 2, and the values of the function must approach infinity. Therefore, the point at *Row* and *Col* is assigned a color indicating how fast the values of the function approach infinity; that is, the point is drawn using a color that is based on the number of times the loop was repeated before the function exceeded 2:

```
If ColorVal < NMax Then
    Picture1.PSet (Col, Row), QBColor(ColorVal Mod 15 + 1)
End If
```

Notice that *ColorVal* is converted to a number between *1* and *15* using the modulus operator. This number is then passed to the *QBColor* function, which returns the Visual Basic color value for one of the pure (that is, nondithered) Windows colors. This color value is then passed to the *PSet* method, which draws the point within the picture box.

If, however, *ColorVal* is greater than or equal to *NMax* after the *Do While* loop has exited, then the function never exceeded 2, and the routine assumes that the values of the function do *not* approach infinity. In this case, the routine does not plot a point; rather, the point remains black, which is the background color assigned to the picture box.

What about functions that might have exceeded 2 if the loop had been allowed to continue longer? A rule of thumb states that almost all functions that are going to exceed 2 will do so within 1000 calculations. Setting *NMax* to values much smaller than 1000 (such as 32) will fail to plot some of the points but will cause the image to be drawn much more quickly, and the resulting patterns can be quite detailed and attractive (even if not totally accurate).

After plotting each column, the *DrawFrac* procedure calls the *Refresh* method to make the newly drawn points visible. Thus, the pattern gradually reveals itself to the player, column by column.

Allowing the User to Interrupt the Process Plotting a fractal pattern can take a long time—perhaps up to 30 minutes, depending on the computer. Normally, during this entire time the system is unable to process other events. (Because Windows is a nonpreemptive multitasking system, the program must normally return from the current event handler before other events can be processed.) Thus, the user would have no way to signal the program to quit drawing the fractal, because keyboard or mouse events could not be processed.

To avoid blocking other events and to permit the user to abort the drawing process, the *DrawFrac* procedure executes the following statements after plotting each column:

```
Dummy = DoEvents()
If QuitNow Then
    QuitNow = 0
    Exit Sub
End If
```

Calling Visual Basic's *DoEvents* function allows the system to process any other pending events. Most importantly, if the player has chosen the Draw command (which is changed to Quit Draw while *DrawFrac* is active), the system can call the event handler for this event, *MenuDraw_Click*. *MenuDraw_Click* then sets the *QuitNow* variable to TRUE, which, as you can see in the code above, causes *DrawFrac* to exit as soon as it regains control following the call to *DoEvents*.

Also, *MenuDraw_Click* disables (as does the *MenuPreview_Click* event procedure) the other commands while *DrawFrac* is active. Disabling these commands prevents the player from choosing another command while the fractal is being drawn. (Remember that commands *can* be processed while *DrawFrac* is active because of the call to *DoEvents*.) For

F Y I

If you look at the code for the *MenuDraw_Click* procedure, you can see that while *DrawFrac* is active, *MenuDraw_Click* changes the Draw command to Quit Draw and sets the *Drawing* variable to TRUE. If the player then chooses the Quit Draw command during the drawing process, the *Drawing* variable will be TRUE, and *MenuDraw_Click* will merely set QuitDraw to TRUE and exit.

example, the user might choose the Parameters command and alter the fractal parameters while a fractal is being drawn (with the possible results being difficult to imagine!).

T I P

Although calling *DoEvents* from within *DrawFrac* allows the system to process other events, the program is still unable to terminate while *DrawFrac* is active. To allow the user to exit the program during this time, you must include the *End* statement in the *Form_Unload* event procedure.

Setting the Parameters

When the program first starts running, the *Form_Load* event procedure for FormMain initializes the parameters that define the fractal pattern:

```
CR = .14
CI = .65
XMin = -1.2
XMax = 1.2
YMin = -1.2
YMax = 1.2
NMax = 32
```

The variables are declared within the global module. These initial values create the fractal shown in Figure 7-15 (on page 198).

When the user chooses the Parameters command to change the parameters, the *MenuParm_Click* event procedure displays the FormParam form:

```
FormParam.Show 1
```

Note: The *1* parameter value causes the form to be modal, as is the case with the About dialog boxes displayed by each of the games in this book. (See Chapter 2 for a discussion of displaying dialog boxes.)

The *Form_Load* procedure for the FormParam form displays the value of each parameter within a separate text box control, using the *Str$* function to convert the numeric value to a string that can be assigned to the box's Text property:

```
TextCR.Text = Str$(CR)
TextCI.Text = Str$(CI)
TextXMin.Text = Str$(XMin)
```

(continued)

continued

```
TextXMax.Text = Str$(XMax)
TextYMin.Text = Str$(YMin)
TextYMax.Text = Str$(YMax)
TextNMax.Text = Str$(NMax)
```

The user can now freely alter the contents of any of the text boxes. If the user clicks the OK button, the *CommandOK_Click* event procedure converts the current text within each text box back to a numeric value (by using the *Val* function) and then calls *Unload* to remove the form:

```
CR = Val(TextCR.Text)
CI = Val(TextCI.Text)
XMin = Val(TextXMin.Text)
XMax = Val(TextXMax.Text)
YMin = Val(TextYMin.Text)
YMax = Val(TextYMax.Text)
NMax = Val(TextNMax.Text)
Unload FormParam
```

If, however, the user clicks the Cancel button, the *CommandCancel-_Click* event procedure merely calls *Unload* to remove the form without reassigning the numeric variables.

Saving the Pattern to the Clipboard

After a full-sized fractal pattern has been drawn, the *MenuDraw_Click* procedure enables the Save To Clipboard command. If the user then chooses this command, the *MenuSave_Click* event procedure copies the graphics to the Windows Clipboard by means of the following statement:

```
Clipboard.SetData Picture1.Image, 2
```

The first parameter, *Picture1.Image*, specifies the source of the data to be placed on the Clipboard. Because the AutoRedraw property of Picture1 is set to True, its Image property is a handle to a bitmap containing the current contents of the picture box. The second parameter specifies the data format; the value 2 indicates that the data is stored as a bitmap.

PART III

STRATEGIC
BOARD GAMES

TIC TAC TOE

In this three-dimensional version of Tic Tac Toe, you play against the computer. The game is a bit more interesting than the one-dimensional version and is typically completed very quickly.

The code for Tic Tac Toe uses many of the techniques you have seen in previous games and introduces several new ones. First, the program demonstrates a technique for quickly drawing images without altering the game background, using the Windows API *BitBlt* function. Also, because the computer acts as one of the players, the program contains an algorithm for choosing optimal game moves. Additionally, the program includes a routine for hit-testing within nonrectangular areas—that is, for determining whether the player has clicked within one of the diamond-shaped playing positions.

Playing Tic Tac Toe

When you run Tic Tac Toe (TT.EXE), the program starts a game. You can start a new game at any time, even before the current one is completed, by choosing the New Game command from the Game menu.

In this version of Tic Tac Toe, the computer's pieces are red Xs, and your pieces are yellow Os. The program randomly selects the player who makes the first move. If the computer is selected as the player to move first, you will see a red X already drawn within a square in the playing area, and it will be your turn to move. If you are selected as the player to move first, all the squares will be empty, and you will have to make the first move. Figure 8-1 on the following page shows Tic Tac Toe at the beginning of a game in which the computer has made the first move.

To make a move, simply position the mouse pointer within the target empty square, and press either mouse button. A yellow O will immediately appear in that square.

The winner of the game is the first player to position three pieces in a row. This row can be within a single level, or it can pass vertically or diagonally through all three levels. Figure 8-2 on the following page shows three winning rows within a single level, and Figure 8-3 on the following page shows three winning rows that pass through all levels.

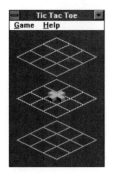

Figure 8-1.
A Tic Tac Toe game in which the computer has made the first move.

Figure 8-2.
Three winning rows within a single level.

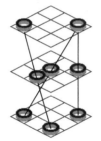

Figure 8-3.
Three winning rows passing through all levels.

As soon as either player arranges three pieces in a row, the program beeps, flashes the three pieces, and terminates the game. You can then start a new game by choosing the New Game command from the Game menu.

Strategy and Hints

You should choose your move according to the following guidelines, which are arranged in the order of priority; in other words, go to the next guideline only if the current one does not apply.

- If possible, position your piece so that it completes a row. You will then win immediately.

- If your opponent has placed two pieces in a row and if the third position in this row is empty, place your piece in that third position to prevent your opponent from winning on the next move. (If your opponent can complete more than one row on the next move, you have in effect already lost the game.)

- If possible, place your piece so that you will have more than one way to complete a row on your next move. Figure 8-4 shows how you would apply this guideline on a single level. (In an actual game, you have to consider all three levels.) The number in each empty square indicates the number of ways you could complete a row on the *next* move if you put a piece on the square on the *current* move. You should, of course, place your piece on one of the squares labeled *2*.

Figure 8-4.
Number of possible ways to complete a row
as a result of the next move.

These guidelines are the same ones that the program uses to calculate the computer's move.

Coding Tic Tac Toe

The source code for the Tic Tac Toe program is contained in the files listed in the following table.

File	Purpose
GLOBALTT.BAS	Contains global type definitions
TT.FRM	Defines the main form, FormMain, and the controls it contains
TTABOUT.FRM	Defines the ABOUT form, FormAbout, and the controls it contains
TT.MAK	Contains the Tic Tac Toe project file

Figures 8-5 through 8-10 present the form designs, properties, commands, and source code for the Tic Tac Toe program.

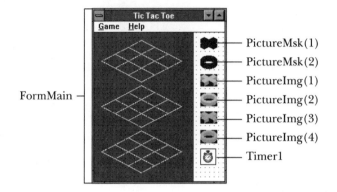

Figure 8-5.
TT.FRM at design time.

Object Name	Object Type	Property	Setting
FormMain	Form	AutoRedraw	True
		BorderStyle	1 - Fixed Single
		Caption	Tic Tac Toe
		FormName	FormMain
		Height	4530 [twips]
		Icon	(Icon) [TT.ICO]
		Left	1035 [twips]
		MaxButton	False
		Picture	(Bitmap) [TT.BMP]
		ScaleMode	3 - Pixel
		Top	1140 [twips]
		Width	3645 [twips]
PictureImg	Array of picture boxes	AutoRedraw	True
		AutoSize	True
		BorderStyle	0 - None

Figure 8-6. *(continued)*
TT.FRM form and control properties.

Figure 8-6 *continued*

Object Name	Object Type	Property	Setting	
		CtlName	PictureImg	
		Height	21 [pixels]	
		Index	1 - 4	
		Left	192 [pixels]	
		Picture	(Bitmap)	
			Index	*File*
			1	REDXIMG.BMP
			2	YELOIMG.BMP
			3	GRNXIMG.BMP
			4	GRNOIMG.BMP
		Top	[varies]	
		Visible	False	
		Width	30 [pixels]	
PictureMsk	Array of picture boxes	AutoRedraw	True	
		AutoSize	True	
		BorderStyle	0 - None	
		CtlName	PictureMsk	
		Height	21 [pixels]	
		Index	1 - 2	
		Left	192 [pixels]	
		Picture	(Bitmap)	
			Index	*File*
			1	XMSK.BMP
			2	OMSK.BMP
		Top	[varies]	
		Visible	False	
		Width	30 [pixels]	
Timer1		Enabled	False	
		Interval	250 [milli-seconds]	

Indentation/Caption	Control Name	Other Features
&Game	MenuGame	
....&New Game	MenuNew	
....-	MenuSep1	
....E&xit	MenuExit	
&Help	MenuHelp	
....&Index	MenuIndex	Accelerator = F1
....&How to Play	MenuHowTo	
....&Commands	MenuCommands	
....&Using Help	MenuUsingHelp	
....-	MenuSep2	
....&About Tic Tac Toe...	MenuAbout	

Figure 8-7.
TT.FRM menu design.

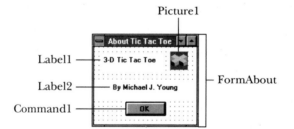

Figure 8-8.
TTABOUT.FRM at design time.

Object Name	Object Type	Property	Setting
Command1	Command button	Caption	OK
		Default	True
		Height	375 [twips]
		Left	840 [twips]

Figure 8-9.
TTABOUT.FRM form and control properties.

(continued)

222

Figure 8-9 *continued*

Object Name	Object Type	Property	Setting
		Top	1440 [twips]
		Width	1095 [twips]
FormAbout	Form	BorderStyle	3 - Fixed Double
		Caption	About Tic Tac Toe
		FormName	FormAbout
		Grid Height	120 [twips]
		Grid Width	120 [twips]
		Height	2445 [twips]
		Left	1140 [twips]
		MaxButton	False
		MinButton	False
		Top	1440 [twips]
		Width	2880 [twips]
Label1	Label	Caption	3-D Tic Tac Toe
		Height	375 [twips]
		Left	240 [twips]
		Top	240 [twips]
		Width	1575 [twips]
Label2	Label	Alignment	2 - Center
		Caption	By Michael J. Young
		Height	375 [twips]
		Left	0 [twips]
		Top	960 [twips]
		Width	2745 [twips]
Picture1	Picture box	AutoSize	True
		BorderStyle	0 - None
		Height	480 [twips]
		Left	2040 [twips]
		Picture	(Icon) [TT.ICO]
		Top	120 [twips]
		Width	480 [twips]

GLOBALTT.BAS code

```
Type RECT
    Left As Integer
    Top As Integer
    Right As Integer
    Bottom As Integer
End Type

Type WINPIECE
    Level As Integer
    Row As Integer
    Col As Integer
End Type
```

TT.FRM code

```
'Help Section:
'Help file:
Const HELP_FILE = "TT.HLP"
'WinHelp wCommand values:
Const HELP_CONTEXT = &H1
Const HELP_HELPONHELP = &H4
Const HELP_INDEX = &H3
Const HELP_QUIT = &H2
'WinHelp dwData values (help topics):
Const HELP_HOWTOPLAY = 10&
Const HELP_COMMANDS = 20&
'Windows help API:
Declare Sub WinHelp Lib "USER" (ByVal hWnd As Integer,
 ByVal lpHelpFile As String, ByVal wCommand As Integer,
 ByVal dwData As Long)
Const CLIENTBOTTOM = 255
Const CLIENTRIGHT = 171

Const OFFOX = 9        'Offsets for displaying pieces:
Const OFFOY = -2
Const OFFXX = 9
Const OFFXY = -1
```

Figure 8-10.   *(continued)*

*Source code for the Tic Tac Toe program. (Notice that long program lines
are wrapped to the next line and indented one space.)*

Figure 8-10 *continued*

```
                         'Codes for PieceTable:
Const NONE = -1          'no piece
Const OUT = 0            'array element is out of bounds
Const REDX = 1           'red X
Const YELO = 2           'yellow O
Const GRNX = 3           'green X
Const GRNO = 4           'green O


Dim CoordTable(1 To 3, 1 To 3, 1 To 3) As RECT
Dim GameOver As Integer
Dim PieceTable(0 To 4, 0 To 4, 0 To 4) As Integer
Dim Winner As Integer
Dim WinPieceList(1 To 3) As WINPIECE


Const WS_CAPTION = &HC00000
Const WS_THICKFRAME = &H40000
Declare Sub AdjustWindowRect Lib "USER" (lpRect As RECT,
 ByVal dwStyle&, ByVal bMenu%)


Const SRCAND = &H8800C6      'dest = source AND dest
Const SRCCOPY = &HCC0020     'dest = source
Const SRCINVERT = &H660046   'dest = source XOR dest
Declare Sub BitBlt Lib "GDI" (ByVal HDestDC%, ByVal X%,
 ByVal Y%, ByVal nWidth%, ByVal nHeight%, ByVal HSrcDC%,
 ByVal XSrc%, ByVal YSrc%, ByVal ROP&)


Const LOGPIXELSX = 88
Const LOGPIXELSY = 90
Declare Function GetDeviceCaps Lib "GDI" (ByVal hDC%,
 ByVal Index%) As Integer


Sub DrawPieces ()
    Dim Col As Integer
    Dim Level As Integer
    Dim Row As Integer

    Cls
    For Level = 1 To 3
        For Row = 1 To 3
            For Col = 1 To 3
                If PieceTable(Level, Row, Col) <> NONE Then
                    BitBlt hDC, CoordTable(Level, Row, Col).Left
 + OFFOX, CoordTable(Level, Row, Col).Top + OFFOY, 30, 23,
```

(continued)

225

Figure 8-10 *continued*

```
PictureMsk(2 - PieceTable(Level, Row, Col) Mod 2).hDC, 0, 0,
SRCAND
                    BitBlt hDC, CoordTable(Level, Row, Col).Left
+ OFFOX, CoordTable(Level, Row, Col).Top + OFFOY, 30, 23,
PictureImg(PieceTable(Level, Row, Col)).hDC, 0, 0, SRCINVERT
                End If
            Next Col
        Next Row
    Next Level
End Sub

Function GameWon (Piece As Integer)
    Dim Col As Integer
    Dim Level As Integer
    Dim Row As Integer

    GameWon = -1

    'test for 3-in-a-row on horizontal level:
    For Level = 1 To 3
        WinPieceList(1).Level = Level: WinPieceList(2).Level =
Level: WinPieceList(3).Level = Level

        'from 1, 1:
        If PieceTable(Level, 1, 1) = Piece Then
            WinPieceList(1).Row = 1: WinPieceList(1).Col = 1
            If PieceTable(Level, 2, 1) = Piece Then
                WinPieceList(2).Row = 2: WinPieceList(2).Col
= 1
                If PieceTable(Level, 3, 1) = Piece Then
                    WinPieceList(3).Row = 3: WinPieceList(3).Col
= 1
                    Exit Function
                End If
            End If
            If PieceTable(Level, 2, 2) = Piece Then
                WinPieceList(2).Row = 2: WinPieceList(2).Col = 2
                If PieceTable(Level, 3, 3) = Piece Then
                    WinPieceList(3).Row = 3: WinPieceList(3).Col
= 3
                    Exit Function
                End If
            End If
```

(continued)

Figure 8-10 *continued*

```
                If PieceTable(Level, 1, 2) = Piece Then
                    WinPieceList(2).Row = 1: WinPieceList(2).Col = 2
                    If PieceTable(Level, 1, 3) = Piece Then
                        WinPieceList(3).Row = 1: WinPieceList(3).Col
= 3

                        Exit Function
                    End If
                End If
            End If

            'from 1, 2:
            If PieceTable(Level, 1, 2) = Piece Then
                WinPieceList(1).Row = 1: WinPieceList(1).Col = 2
                If PieceTable(Level, 2, 2) = Piece Then
                    WinPieceList(2).Row = 2: WinPieceList(2).Col = 2
                    If PieceTable(Level, 3, 2) = Piece Then
                        WinPieceList(3).Row = 3: WinPieceList(3).Col
= 2

                        Exit Function
                    End If
                End If
            End If

            'from 1, 3:
            If PieceTable(Level, 1, 3) = Piece Then
                WinPieceList(1).Row = 1: WinPieceList(1).Col = 3
                If PieceTable(Level, 2, 2) = Piece Then
                    WinPieceList(2).Row = 2: WinPieceList(2).Col = 2
                    If PieceTable(Level, 3, 1) = Piece Then
                        WinPieceList(3).Row = 3: WinPieceList(3).Col
= 1

                        Exit Function
                    End If
                End If
                If PieceTable(Level, 2, 3) = Piece Then
                    WinPieceList(2).Row = 2: WinPieceList(2).Col = 3
                    If PieceTable(Level, 3, 3) = Piece Then
                        WinPieceList(3).Row = 3: WinPieceList(3).Col
= 3

                        Exit Function
                    End If
                End If
            End If
```

(continued)

Figure 8-10 *continued*

```
        'from 2, 1:
        If PieceTable(Level, 2, 1) = Piece Then
            WinPieceList(1).Row = 2: WinPieceList(1).Col = 1
            If PieceTable(Level, 2, 2) = Piece Then
                WinPieceList(2).Row = 2: WinPieceList(2).Col = 2
                If PieceTable(Level, 2, 3) = Piece Then
                    WinPieceList(3).Row = 2: WinPieceList(3).Col
= 3
                    Exit Function
                End If
            End If
        End If

        'from 3, 1:
        If PieceTable(Level, 3, 1) = Piece Then
            WinPieceList(1).Row = 3: WinPieceList(1).Col = 1
            If PieceTable(Level, 3, 2) = Piece Then
                WinPieceList(2).Row = 3: WinPieceList(2).Col = 2
                If PieceTable(Level, 3, 3) = Piece Then
                    WinPieceList(3).Row = 3: WinPieceList(3).Col
= 3
                    Exit Function
                End If
            End If
        End If
    Next Level

    'test for 3-in-a-row on vertical level:
    WinPieceList(1).Level = 1: WinPieceList(2).Level = 2:
WinPieceList(3).Level = 3
    For Row = 1 To 3
        For Col = 1 To 3
            If PieceTable(1, Row, Col) = Piece Then
                WinPieceList(1).Row = Row
                WinPieceList(1).Col = Col

                'straight down:
                If PieceTable(2, Row, Col) = Piece Then
                    If PieceTable(3, Row, Col) = Piece Then
                        WinPieceList(2).Row = Row:
WinPieceList(2).Col = Col
                        WinPieceList(3).Row = Row:
WinPieceList(3).Col = Col
```

(continued)

Figure 8-10 *continued*

```
                              Exit Function
                      End If
              End If

              'west:
              If Col = 3 Then
                      If PieceTable(2, Row, Col - 1) = Piece Then
                              If PieceTable(3, Row, Col - 2) = Piece
Then
                                      WinPieceList(2).Row = Row:
WinPieceList(2).Col = Col - 1
                                      WinPieceList(3).Row = Row:
WinPieceList(3).Col = Col - 2
                                      Exit Function
                              End If
                      End If
              End If

              'east:
              If Col = 1 Then
                      If PieceTable(2, Row, Col + 1) = Piece Then
                              If PieceTable(3, Row, Col + 2) = Piece
Then
                                      WinPieceList(2).Row = Row:
WinPieceList(2).Col = Col + 1
                                      WinPieceList(3).Row = Row:
WinPieceList(3).Col = Col + 2
                                      Exit Function
                              End If
                      End If
              End If

              'north:
              If Row = 3 Then
                      If PieceTable(2, Row - 1, Col) = Piece Then
                              If PieceTable(3, Row - 2, Col) = Piece
Then
                                      WinPieceList(2).Row = Row - 1:
WinPieceList(2).Col = Col
                                      WinPieceList(3).Row = Row - 2:
WinPieceList(3).Col = Col
                                      Exit Function
                              End If
```

(continued)

Figure 8-10 *continued*

```
                    End If
            End If

            'south:
            If Row = 1 Then
                If PieceTable(2, Row + 1, Col) = Piece Then
                    If PieceTable(3, Row + 2, Col) = Piece
Then
                        WinPieceList(2).Row = Row + 1:
WinPieceList(2).Col = Col
                        WinPieceList(3).Row = Row + 2:
WinPieceList(3).Col = Col
                        Exit Function
                    End If
                End If
            End If

            'north west:
            If Row = 3 And Col = 3 Then
                If PieceTable(2, Row - 1, Col - 1) = Piece
Then
                    If PieceTable(3, Row - 2, Col - 2) =
Piece Then
                        WinPieceList(2).Row = Row - 1:
WinPieceList(2).Col = Col - 1
                        WinPieceList(3).Row = Row - 2:
WinPieceList(3).Col = Col - 2
                        Exit Function
                    End If
                End If
            End If

            'north east:
            If Row = 3 And Col = 1 Then
                If PieceTable(2, Row - 1, Col + 1) = Piece
Then
                    If PieceTable(3, Row - 2, Col + 2) =
Piece Then
                        WinPieceList(2).Row = Row - 1:
WinPieceList(2).Col = Col + 1
                        WinPieceList(3).Row = Row - 2:
WinPieceList(3).Col = Col + 2
```

(continued)

Figure 8-10 *continued*

```
                        Exit Function
                End If
            End If
        End If

        'south east:
        If Row = 1 And Col = 1 Then
            If PieceTable(2, Row + 1, Col + 1) = Piece
Then
                If PieceTable(3, Row + 2, Col + 2) =
Piece Then
                    WinPieceList(2).Row = Row + 1:
WinPieceList(2).Col = Col + 1
                    WinPieceList(3).Row = Row + 2:
WinPieceList(3).Col = Col + 2
                    Exit Function
                End If
            End If
        End If

        'south west:
        If Row = 1 And Col = 3 Then
            If PieceTable(2, Row + 1, Col - 1) = Piece
Then
                If PieceTable(3, Row + 2, Col - 2) =
Piece Then
                    WinPieceList(2).Row = Row + 1:
WinPieceList(2).Col = Col - 1
                    WinPieceList(3).Row = Row + 2:
WinPieceList(3).Col = Col - 2
                    Exit Function
                End If
            End If
        End If
    End If
    Next Col
  Next Row

  GameWon = 0

End Function
```

(continued)

Figure 8-10 *continued*

```
Sub InitNewGame ()
    Dim Col As Integer
    Dim Level As Integer
    Dim Row As Integer

    Timer1.Enabled = 0
    Cls
    GameOver = 0
    For Level = 1 To 3
        For Row = 1 To 3
            For Col = 1 To 3
                PieceTable(Level, Row, Col) = NONE
            Next Col
        Next Row
    Next Level
    If Int(2 * Rnd) Then
        PieceTable(2, 2, 2) = REDX
        DrawPieces
    End If
End Sub

Function InSquare (X As Single, Y As Single, L As Integer,
 T As Integer, R As Integer, B As Integer)
    Dim XOff As Integer
    Dim YOff As Integer

    InSquare = 0
    If X < L Or X > R Or Y < T Or Y > B Then Exit Function
    YOff = T + 12 - Y
    If X <= L + 23 Then
        XOff = X - L
    Else
        XOff = R - X
    End If
    If YOff > XOff / 2 Or YOff < -XOff / 2 Then Exit Function
    InSquare = -1
End Function

Sub RedMove ()
    Dim BlockC As Integer          'column of blocking position
    Dim BlockL As Integer          'level of blocking position
    Dim BlockR As Integer          'row of blocking position
    Dim C As Integer               'column
    Dim DC As Integer              'delta column
```

(continued)

Figure 8-10 *continued*

```
    Dim DL As Integer                'delta level
    Dim DR As Integer                'delta row
    Dim L As Integer                 'level
    Dim MaxC As Integer              'column for max moves
    Dim MaxL As Integer              'level for max moves
    Dim MaxMoveCount As Integer 'max num moves
    Dim MaxR As Integer              'row for max moves
    Dim MoveCount As Integer         'num moves for a position
    Dim R As Integer                 'row


    For L = 1 To 3
        For R = 1 To 3
            For C = 1 To 3
                If PieceTable(L, R, C) = NONE Then
                    MoveCount = 0
                    For DL = -1 To 1
                        For DR = -1 To 1
                            For DC = -1 To 1
                                If DL Or DR Or DC Then

                                    'check complete triplet:
                                    If PieceTable(L + DL, R +
DR, C + DC) = REDX Then
                                        If PieceTable(L + 2 *
DL, R + 2 * DR, C + 2 * DC) = REDX Then
                                            PieceTable(L, R,
C) = REDX

                                            Exit Sub
                                        End If
                                        If PieceTable(L - DL,
R - DR, C - DC) = REDX Then
                                            PieceTable(L, R,
C) = REDX

                                            Exit Sub
                                        End If
                                    End If

                                    'check blocking of yellow
pieces:
                                    If PieceTable(L + DL, R +
DR, C + DC) = YELO Then
                                        If PieceTable(L + 2 *
DL, R + 2 * DR, C + 2 * DC) = YELO Then
```

(continued)

Figure 8-10 *continued*

```
                                                 BlockL = L: BlockR
= R: BlockC = C
                                              ElseIf PieceTable(L -
DL, R - DR, C - DC) = YELO Then
                                                 BlockL = L: BlockR
= R: BlockC = C
                                              End If
                                           End If

                                           'check for move:
                                           If PieceTable(L + DL, R +
DR, C + DC) = REDX Then
                                              If PieceTable(L + 2 *
DL, R + 2 * DR, C + 2 * DC) = NONE Then
                                                 MoveCount =
MoveCount + 1
                                              ElseIf PieceTable(L -
DL, R - DR, C - DC) = NONE Then
                                                 MoveCount =
MoveCount + 1
                                              End If
                                           ElseIf PieceTable(L + DL,
R + DR, C + DC) = NONE Then
                                              If PieceTable(L + 2 *
DL, R + 2 * DR, C + 2 * DC) = REDX Then
                                                 MoveCount =
MoveCount + 1
                                              End If
                                           End If

                                     End If
                                  Next DC
                               Next DR
                            Next DL

                            If MoveCount >= MaxMoveCount Then
                               MaxMoveCount = MoveCount
                               MaxL = L: MaxR = R: MaxC = C
                            End If

                      End If
                 Next C
            Next R
       Next L
```

(continued)

Figure 8-10 *continued*

```
    If BlockL > 0 Then
        PieceTable(BlockL, BlockR, BlockC) = REDX
    Else
        PieceTable(MaxL, MaxR, MaxC) = REDX
    End If

End Sub

Function SquareHit (X As Single, Y As Single,
  Level As Integer, Row As Integer, Col As Integer)
    Dim C As Integer
    Dim L As Integer
    Dim R As Integer


    For L = 1 To 3
        For R = 1 To 3
            For C = 1 To 3
                If InSquare(X, Y, CoordTable(L, R, C).Left,
  CoordTable(L, R, C).Top, CoordTable(L, R, C).Right,
  CoordTable(L, R, C).Bottom) Then
                    Level = L
                    Row = R
                    Col = C
                    SquareHit = -1
                    Exit Function
                End If
            Next C
        Next R
    Next L
    SquareHit = 0
End Function

Sub Form_Load ()
    Dim Level As Integer
    Dim Rec As RECT
    Dim YOffset As Integer

    'code for display device independence:
    Rec.Left = 0
    Rec.Top = 0
    Rec.Right = CLIENTRIGHT
    Rec.Bottom = CLIENTBOTTOM
    AdjustWindowRect Rec, WS_CAPTION, -1
```

(continued)

Figure 8-10 *continued*

```
    FormMain.Width = (Rec.Right - Rec.Left + 1) * (1440 /
GetDeviceCaps(hDC, LOGPIXELSX))
    FormMain.Height = (Rec.Bottom - Rec.Top + 1) * (1440 /
GetDeviceCaps(hDC, LOGPIXELSY))

    For Level = 1 To 3
        CoordTable(Level, 1, 1).Left = 62: CoordTable(Level,
1, 1).Top = YOffset + 13
        CoordTable(Level, 1, 1).Right = 109: CoordTable(Level,
1, 1).Bottom = YOffset + 37
        CoordTable(Level, 1, 2).Left = 86: CoordTable(Level,
1, 2).Top = YOffset + 25
        CoordTable(Level, 1, 2).Right = 133: CoordTable(Level,
1, 2).Bottom = YOffset + 49
        CoordTable(Level, 1, 3).Left = 110: CoordTable(Level,
1, 3).Top = YOffset + 37
        CoordTable(Level, 1, 3).Right = 157: CoordTable(Level,
1, 3).Bottom = YOffset + 61
        CoordTable(Level, 2, 1).Left = 38: CoordTable(Level,
2, 1).Top = YOffset + 25
        CoordTable(Level, 2, 1).Right = 85: CoordTable(Level,
2, 1).Bottom = YOffset + 49
        CoordTable(Level, 2, 2).Left = 62: CoordTable(Level,
2, 2).Top = YOffset + 37
        CoordTable(Level, 2, 2).Right = 109: CoordTable(Level,
2, 2).Bottom = YOffset + 61
        CoordTable(Level, 2, 3).Left = 86: CoordTable(Level,
2, 3).Top = YOffset + 49
        CoordTable(Level, 2, 3).Right = 133: CoordTable(Level,
2, 3).Bottom = YOffset + 73
        CoordTable(Level, 3, 1).Left = 14: CoordTable(Level,
3, 1).Top = YOffset + 37
        CoordTable(Level, 3, 1).Right = 61: CoordTable(Level,
3, 1).Bottom = YOffset + 61
        CoordTable(Level, 3, 2).Left = 38: CoordTable(Level,
3, 2).Top = YOffset + 49
        CoordTable(Level, 3, 2).Right = 85: CoordTable(Level,
3, 2).Bottom = YOffset + 73
        CoordTable(Level, 3, 3).Left = 62: CoordTable(Level,
3, 3).Top = YOffset + 61
        CoordTable(Level, 3, 3).Right = 109: CoordTable(Level,
3, 3).Bottom = YOffset + 85
```

(continued)

Figure 8-10 *continued*

```
        YOffset = YOffset + 78
    Next Level
    Randomize
    InitNewGame
End Sub

Sub Form_MouseDown (Button As Integer, Shift As Integer,
 X As Single, Y As Single)
    Dim Col As Integer
    Dim Level As Integer
    Dim Row As Integer

    If GameOver Then Exit Sub
    If Not SquareHit(X, Y, Level, Row, Col) Then Exit Sub
    If PieceTable(Level, Row, Col) <> NONE Then Exit Sub
    PieceTable(Level, Row, Col) = YELO
    DrawPieces
    If GameWon(YELO) Then
        Beep: Beep: Beep
        Winner = YELO
        Timer1.Enabled = -1
        GameOver = -1
        Exit Sub
    End If
    RedMove
    DrawPieces
    If GameWon(REDX) Then
        Beep: Beep: Beep
        Winner = REDX
        Timer1.Enabled = -1
        GameOver = -1
        Exit Sub
    End If
End Sub

Sub Form_Unload (Cancel As Integer)
    WinHelp hWnd, HELP_FILE, HELP_QUIT, 0
End Sub

Sub MenuAbout_Click ()
    FormAbout.Show 1
End Sub
```

(continued)

237

Figure 8-10 *continued*

```
Sub MenuCommands_Click ()
    WinHelp hWnd, HELP_FILE, HELP_CONTEXT, HELP_COMMANDS
End Sub

Sub MenuExit_Click ()
    WinHelp hWnd, HELP_FILE, HELP_QUIT, 0
    End
End Sub

Sub MenuHowTo_Click ()
    WinHelp hWnd, HELP_FILE, HELP_CONTEXT, HELP_HOWTOPLAY
End Sub

Sub MenuIndex_Click ()
    WinHelp hWnd, HELP_FILE, HELP_INDEX, 0
End Sub

Sub MenuNew_Click ()
    InitNewGame
End Sub

Sub MenuUsingHelp_Click ()
    WinHelp hWnd, HELP_FILE, HELP_HELPONHELP, 0
End Sub

Sub Timer1_Timer ()
    Static Flag As Integer
    Dim I As Integer
    Dim NumImage As Integer

    If Flag Then
        NumImage = Winner
    Else
        NumImage = Winner + 2
    End If
    Flag = Flag Xor -1

    For I = 1 To 3
        PieceTable(WinPieceList(I).Level, WinPieceList(I).Row,
 WinPieceList(I).Col) = NumImage
    Next I
    DrawPieces
End Sub
```

(continued)

Figure 8-10 *continued*

TTABOUT.FRM code

```
Sub Command1_Click ()
    Unload FormAbout
End Sub
```

Programming Techniques

As in most of the other games, the program background consists of a single bitmap. This bitmap was created in Paintbrush, saved in a file (TT.BMP), and then assigned to the main form's Picture property.

Tic Tac Toe introduces a new technique for drawing the playing pieces. Previous games (Peg Solitaire, Deduce, and Word Squares) stored the image of each playing piece within a separate picture box (using a bitmap, an icon, or drawing commands). In contrast, Tic Tac Toe draws the playing pieces directly on top of the background bitmap in the main form; the playing pieces are *not* contained within individual picture boxes. In the program description that follows, you will learn the rationale for this approach. You will also learn how the pieces are quickly drawn without disturbing the background graphics, using bit operations provided by the Windows API *BitBlt* function (which was introduced in Chapter 7).

Note: Throughout the remainder of the chapter, the term "player" refers to the human user of the program, and the term "computer" refers to the computer-generated opponent.

Tic Tac Toe is the first game in this book in which the computer serves as one of the players. The program includes a procedure (*RedMove*) for determining the computer's best move. This procedure exhaustively tests all empty squares, calculating the relative benefit of moving to each square. In the next two games (Ludo and Ringo), you will see additional examples of evaluating game moves.

The program also demonstrates a technique for hit-testing within nonrectangular areas. In two previous games (Word Squares and Queens), the playing squares were rectangular, and it was simple to determine whether the mouse coordinates were within a given rectangle. In Tic Tac Toe, however, the playing "squares" are drawn as diamonds. The *SquareHit* and *InSquare* procedures (described later) contain routines for calculating which square, if any, contains the mouse pointer when the user presses a mouse button.

Finally, the program employs Visual Basic's random-number generator for determining whether the player or the computer makes the first move, and it uses a Visual Basic timer control to flash the winning pieces at the end of a game.

Program Overview

Here is a summary of the main sequence of events in the Tic Tac Toe program.

- The *Form_Load* event procedure performs one-time initialization tasks and calls *InitNewGame* to start a game.

- Whenever the player chooses the New Game command from the Game menu, the *MenuNew_Click* event procedure also calls *InitNewGame*.

- The *InitNewGame* general procedure disables the timer, performs initialization tasks to prepare for a new game, and chooses randomly whether the player or the computer moves first. If the computer is selected, the procedure places one of the computer's pieces at an initial location.

- When the player clicks an empty square, the *Form_Mouse-Down* event procedure places one of the player's pieces within the square and then calls *RedMove* to move the computer's piece. If either the player or the computer completes a winning triplet (see note below), the procedure terminates the game by setting *GameOver* to TRUE and enables the timer.

  Note: Throughout the programming discussion, a winning arrangement of pieces is called a "triplet" (rather than a "row") to distinguish it from one of the rows of playing squares. (The playing squares are arranged in levels, rows, and columns.)

- On each timer event, the *Timer1_Timer* event procedure changes the color of the three winning pieces, causing these pieces to flash.

Initializing the Program

As in the other games, the *Form_Load* procedure performs one-time initialization tasks, and the *InitNewGame* procedure performs the initialization tasks required for each new game.

The *Form_Load* Procedure

Following the standard statements for sizing the form, the *Form_Load* procedure initializes the form-level array CoordTable. This array is declared as follows:

```
Dim CoordTable(1 To 3, 1 To 3, 1 To 3) As RECT
```

RECT is a user-defined type you have seen in many of the games; it is defined as follows in the global module:

```
Type RECT
    Left As Integer
    Top As Integer
    Right As Integer
    Bottom As Integer
End Type
```

Each element of CoordTable stores the coordinates of the rectangle bounding one of the playing squares, which are drawn as diamonds. (See Figure 8-11.)

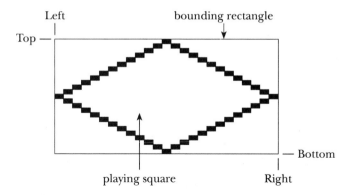

Figure 8-11.
A playing square is defined by the coordinates of its bounding rectangle, which are stored in the CoordTable array.

The first dimension of CoordTable indicates the level of the playing square, the second dimension indicates its row, and the third dimension indicates its column. For example, *CoordTable (1, 2, 3)* stores the coordinates for the square on the first level, in the second row, and in the third column. The levels, rows, and columns of the playing squares are labeled in Figure 8-12 on the following page.

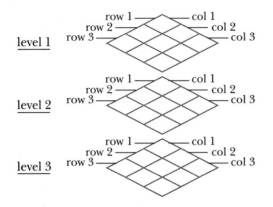

Figure 8-12.
The levels, rows, and columns of the playing squares.

The *InitNewGame* Procedure

The *InitNewGame* general procedure is called by the *Form_Load* procedure when the program is first run, and it is called by the *MenuNew-_Click* procedure whenever the player chooses the New Game command from the Game menu.

InitNewGame begins by disabling the timer. This step is necessary because at the end of every game the timer is enabled and the timer procedure begins flashing the winning pieces. At the start of a new game, the timer is disabled to stop the flashing (in case a previous game has been played).

InitNewGame then calls *Cls* to erase all playing pieces drawn on the form during the previous game (if any), and it assigns FALSE to the variable *GameOver* to signal other portions of the program that a game is under way.

F Y I

Coordinate values can be obtained by loading the background bitmap (TT.BMP) into Paintbrush, choosing the Cursor Position command from Paintbrush's View menu, placing the cursor on each required position, and reading the coordinates. As you will see, the coordinates stored in CoordTable are used both for determining when the user has clicked a particular square and for drawing the playing pieces within the squares.

InitNewGame now initializes the three-dimensional array PieceTable:

```
For Level = 1 To 3
    For Row = 1 To 3
        For Col = 1 To 3
            PieceTable(Level, Row, Col) = NONE
        Next Col
    Next Row
Next Level
```

PieceTable stores the current contents of each playing square. As with CoordTable, the first dimension indicates the level of the square, the second dimension indicates the row, and the third dimension indicates the column. (See Figure 8-12 to review how the levels, rows, and columns are numbered.) The possible values that can be assigned to an element of CoordTable are listed in the following table.

Symbolic Constant	Value	Meaning
NONE	−1	Square is empty
OUT	0	Array element does not correspond to a playing square (explained in the "FYI" box on page 249)
REDX	1	Square contains a red X (one of the computer's pieces)
YELO	2	Square contains a yellow O (one of the player's pieces)
GRNX	3	Square contains a green X (a flashing computer's piece at the end of the game)
GRNO	4	Square contains a green O (a flashing player's piece at the end of the game)

Later in the chapter, you will see how PieceTable is declared and how it is used throughout the game.

Finally, *InitNewGame* determines whether the computer or the player moves first:

```
If Int(2 * Rnd) Then
    PieceTable(2, 2, 2) = REDX
    DrawPieces
End If
```

The expression *Int(2 * Rnd)* randomly returns a value of either 0 or 1. If it returns a value of 1, the computer moves first. In this case, the procedure places one of the computer's pieces at the center of the grid—that is, at level 2, row 2, column 2—by assigning the value REDX to *PieceTable(2, 2, 2)*. The procedure then calls *DrawPieces* to draw the piece at this position. (The *DrawPieces* general procedure is explained in the section "Drawing the Pieces," later in this chapter.) The piece is placed at the center of the grid, because this position has a strategic advantage—namely, winning triplets can be formed from this position in all directions. (Thirteen of the possible winning triplets include this position, which is a greater number than for any other position.)

If the random expression returns a value of 0, the player moves first. In this case, the procedure leaves all the squares empty.

Moving the Pieces:
The *Form_MouseDown* Procedure

After a game has been initiated and the computer has made its first move (if it has been selected to start), the program waits for the player to make a move. The player moves by pressing the mouse button while the mouse pointer is on an empty square, causing the *Form_MouseDown* event procedure to receive control.

Form_MouseDown begins by testing *GameOver* and proceeds only if this variable is set to FALSE, indicating that a game is in progress:

```
If GameOver Then Exit Sub
```

Form_MouseDown then performs the following main steps:

1. It moves the player's piece.

2. It draws all the pieces.

3. It tests to see whether a winning triplet has been completed, and, if so, it terminates the game.

4. It moves the computer's piece.

5. It draws all the pieces again.

6. It tests again to see whether a winning triplet has been completed, and, if so, it terminates the game.

These steps are discussed individually in the following sections; steps 2 and 5 are discussed in a single section, as are steps 3 and 6.

Moving the Player's Piece

Before moving the player's piece, *Form_MouseDown* calls the general procedure *SquareHit* (described in the next section), passing it the current coordinates of the mouse pointer to determine which playing square, if any, currently contains the mouse pointer:

```
If Not SquareHit(X, Y, Level, Row, Col) Then Exit Sub
```

If the mouse pointer is *not* contained in a square, *SquareHit* returns FALSE and *Form_MouseDown* exits without taking any further action. If the mouse pointer *is* contained in a square, *SquareHit* returns TRUE and assigns the level, row, and column of that square to the procedure-level variables *Level*, *Row*, and *Col* that are passed as parameters. In this case, *Form_MouseDown* then checks whether the "hit" square is empty:

```
If PieceTable(Level, Row, Col) <> NONE Then Exit Sub
```

If the square already contains a piece, *Form_MouseDown* exits; otherwise, it positions the player's piece within the hit square by assigning the value YELO to the corresponding element of PieceTable:

```
PieceTable(Level, Row, Col) = YELO
```

Hit-Testing: The *SquareHit* Procedure

The *SquareHit* general procedure loops through all 27 squares in the playing area. For each square, *SquareHit* calls the general procedure *InSquare*, passing it the current coordinates of the mouse pointer and the coordinates of the square:

```
If InSquare(X, Y, CoordTable(L, R, C).Left, CoordTable(L,
R, C).Top, CoordTable(L, R, C).Right, CoordTable(L, R, C).Bottom)
Then

    'assign L, R, C to Level, Row, Col
    'return TRUE and exit
```

InSquare performs the actual hit-testing. If the mouse pointer coordinates fall within the square, *InSquare* returns TRUE. In this case, *SquareHit* assigns the indexes of the square (*L*, *R*, and *C*) to the parameters *Level*, *Row*, and *Col*, and exits immediately, returning the value TRUE. If the mouse pointer coordinates do not fall within the square, *InSquare* returns FALSE, and *SquareHit* proceeds to check the next square. If *SquareHit* loops through all 27 squares without finding a hit, it exits and returns FALSE.

The *InSquare* procedure is not trivial. Recall that to create a three-dimensional look, a playing square is actually drawn as a diamond, and each element of CoordTable stores the coordinates of the rectangle that bounds the diamond. (See Figure 8-11 on page 241.) *InSquare*, therefore, cannot simply compare the coordinates of the mouse pointer with the coordinates in CoordTable. Rather, it proceeds as follows:

1. It sets the return value to FALSE:

   ```
   InSquare = 0
   ```

2. If the mouse pointer coordinates (X, Y) are not within the bounding rectangle (L, T, R, B), it exits immediately (returning FALSE):

   ```
   If X < L Or X > R Or Y < T Or Y > B Then Exit Function
   ```

   Otherwise, it moves on to step 3.

3. It calculates the vertical offset $(YOff)$ of the mouse pointer from the center of the bounding rectangle:

   ```
   YOff = T + 12 - Y
   ```

4. It calculates the horizontal offset $(XOff)$ of the mouse pointer from the left edge of the bounding rectangle (if X falls to the left of the center of the rectangle) or from the right edge of the bounding rectangle (if X falls to the right of the center):

   ```
   If X <= L + 23 Then
       XOff = X - L
   Else
       XOff = R - X
   End If
   ```

5. If the vertical offset $(YOff)$ extends beyond one of the lines that define the diamond, it exits (returning FALSE):

   ```
   If YOff > XOff / 2 Or YOff < -XOff / 2 Then Exit Function
   ```

   This expression works because at all points along either of the upper two playing square lines, *YOff* equals *XOff* / 2, and at all points along either of the lower two playing square lines, *YOff* equals -*XOff* / 2. (The slope of the line is either $\frac{1}{2}$ or $-\frac{1}{2}$. Also, the lines pass through the "origin" of *XOff* and *YOff*—that is, through the point where both these values are *0*.)

6. If the above tests have been passed, *InSquare* returns TRUE:

```
InSquare = -1
```

Figure 8-13 shows the values used to perform the hit test when the mouse pointer is within the upper left quadrant of the playing square—that is, *XOff* is less than *L + 23*, and *YOff* is positive.

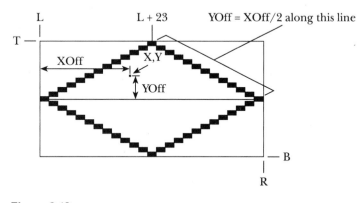

Figure 8-13.
Hit-testing within a playing square.

Moving the Computer's Piece

The *Form_MouseDown* event procedure calls the general procedure *Red-Move* to make the next move for the computer. *RedMove* examines each of the 27 squares and places one of the computer's pieces on the empty square that represents the best move. The procedure moves the piece by assigning the value REDX to the selected element of PieceTable; it does not, however, redraw the pieces or test whether a winning triplet has been formed. (*Form_MouseDown* performs these two steps after *RedMove* returns; these steps are explained in later sections.)

RedMove evaluates every empty square by placing the square-evaluation routine within the following nested loops and *If* statement:

```
For L = 1 To 3
    For R = 1 To 3
        For C = 1 To 3
            If PieceTable(L, R, C) = NONE Then     'square is empty
```

(continued)

247

continued

```
                    'square-evaluation routine:
                    'evaluate square at level L, row R, and column C

              End If
          Next C
      Next R
Next L
```

The square-evaluation routine begins by setting the variable *Move-Count* to *0*:

```
MoveCount = 0
```

As you will see, this variable is used to count the number of possible ways that a winning triplet could be completed on the next move if the piece were placed on the square being evaluated.

Next, the square-evaluation routine examines the immediately neighboring squares, moving in every possible direction from the square under evaluation. To test every possible direction, the square-evaluation routine places the direction-testing routine within the following nested loops and *If* statement:

```
For DL = -1 To 1
    For DR = -1 To 1
        For DC = -1 To 1
            If DL Or DR Or DC Then

                    'direction-testing routine:
                    'test the direction that results from combining
                    'DL, DR, and DC with L, R, and C

            End If
        Next DC
    Next DR
Next DL
```

To reach a neighboring square in a given direction you must change the level by −1, 0, or 1; change the row by −1, 0, or 1; and change the column by −1, 0, or 1. In these loops *DL*, *DR*, and *DC* represent the change in the level, row, and column. Nesting the loops generates all 27 possible combinations of these change values, and the *If* statement eliminates the one invalid combination (in which *DL*, *DR*, and *DC* are all the value 0, which would not access a neighboring square).

F Y I

Actually, only the square in the very center of the grid has immediate neighbors in all 26 directions. The other squares have neighbors in only some of the possible directions. Therefore, it might seem necessary to include a large number of boundary tests; each test would ensure that the square under evaluation has a neighboring square in a particular direction before testing in that direction: For example, if the square is in the first column, the routine would not attempt to examine the square to its left.

Rather than including boundary tests, however, the array containing the information about the contents of each square, PieceTable, is declared so that it has additional elements on all sides of the actual squares:

```
Dim PieceTable(0 To 4, 0 To 4, 0 To 4) As Integer
```

The additional elements (that is, elements with indexes of 0 or 4) have the value *0*, which signals all the direction tests that no playing piece is located at the corresponding position.

Although this technique causes the routine to perform a large number of futile comparisons, it also eliminates many tests for boundary conditions and thus greatly simplifies the code.

The direction-testing routine, deeply nested inside all these loops and *If* statements, consists of the following steps:

1. It tests whether placing a piece on the square being examined would complete a winning triplet in the direction being tested. If a triplet would be formed, the routine places a piece on the current square and exits the procedure immediately—because the computer has won the game, and no further tests are necessary:

```
'check complete triplet:
If PieceTable(L + DL, R + DR, C + DC) = REDX Then
    If PieceTable(L + 2 * DL, R + 2 * DR, C + 2 *
```

(continued)

continued

```
    DC) = REDX Then
            PieceTable(L, R, C) = REDX
            Exit Sub
        End If
        If PieceTable(L - DL, R - DR, C - DC) = REDX Then
            PieceTable(L, R, C) = REDX
            Exit Sub
        End If
    End If
End If
```

2. It tests whether placing a piece in the current square would
   block the player from completing a triplet in the tested direction on the player's next move. If a block would result,
   the routine saves the level, row, and column of the current
   square in the variables *BlockL*, *BlockR*, and *BlockC*; however, it
   does not exit from the procedure, because the routine must
   continue to test additional squares for the condition described in step 1. (Winning the game immediately is more
   important—that is, a better strategy—than blocking the
   opponent.)

```
'check blocking of yellow pieces:
If PieceTable(L + DL, R + DR, C + DC) = YELO Then
    If PieceTable(L + 2 * DL, R + 2 * DR, C + 2 *
DC) = YELO Then
        BlockL = L: BlockR = R: BlockC = C
    ElseIf PieceTable(L - DL, R - DR, C - DC) = YELO Then
        BlockL = L: BlockR = R: BlockC = C
    End If
End If
```

3. The routine tests to see whether placing a piece in the current square would allow the computer to form a complete
   triplet in the tested direction on the computer's next move.
   If so, it increments *MoveCount*, which stores the total number
   of complete triplets that could be formed on the next move
   if a piece is placed on the current square:

```
'check for move:
If PieceTable(L + DL, R + DR, C + DC) = REDX Then
    If PieceTable(L + 2 * DL, R + 2 * DR, C + 2 *
DC) = NONE Then
        MoveCount = MoveCount + 1
```

(continued)

continued

```
      ElseIf PieceTable(L - DL, R - DR, C - DC) = NONE Then
         MoveCount = MoveCount + 1
      End If
   ElseIf PieceTable(L + DL, R + DR, C + DC) = NONE Then
      If PieceTable(L + 2 * DL, R + 2 * DR, C + 2 *
   DC) = REDX Then
         MoveCount = MoveCount + 1
      End If
   End If
```

After testing all possible directions from a given square, the routine examines the resulting value of *MoveCount*. If this value equals or exceeds the highest value obtained from all previous square evaluations, the routine saves it in *MaxMoveCount* and saves the level, row, and column of the current square in *MaxL*, *MaxR*, and *MaxC*:

```
If MoveCount >= MaxMoveCount Then
    MaxMoveCount = MoveCount
    MaxL = L: MaxR = R: MaxC = C
End If
```

Finally, after testing all the squares in the playing area, if a square was found that would block the player from forming a complete triplet, the computer's piece is placed on that square. If, however, none of the squares would result in blocking the player, the piece is placed on the square that would provide the greatest number of ways to form a complete triplet on the computer's next move:

```
If BlockL > 0 Then
    PieceTable(BlockL, BlockR, BlockC) = REDX
Else
    PieceTable(MaxL, MaxR, MaxC) = REDX
End If
```

Drawing the Pieces

When placing a piece within a square, *Form_MouseDown* calls the general procedure *DrawPieces* to redraw the pieces. Because the individual pieces overlap, the program cannot simply draw a single new piece; rather, it calls *DrawPieces*, which erases the current pieces and then redraws all the pieces (including the new one) in the proper order.

Form_MouseDown calls *DrawPieces* immediately after assigning the player's piece to PieceTable and then again immediately after assigning the computer's piece to PieceTable. It calls *DrawPieces* twice so that the two new pieces do not appear at the same instant. The player's piece appears immediately after the player presses a mouse button, and the computer's piece appears after a slight delay (the time required to calculate the computer's move). The result simulates a real-life game.

As explained previously, the *InitNewGame* procedure also calls *DrawPieces* to draw the computer's first piece if the computer moves first. Also, the *Timer1_Timer* event procedure, discussed later in this chapter, calls *DrawPieces* repeatedly to flash the winning triplet.

The Drawing Technique

The basic drawing technique used by the *DrawPieces* procedure is also used in many of the games presented in the following chapters. (Later in this chapter, *DrawPieces* itself is discussed in detail.)

Previous games drew each playing piece by simply assigning a bitmap or icon to a picture box and then locating the picture box at the position wanted within the form. The Tic Tac Toe program, however, cannot use a picture box to display a playing piece, because a piece is nonrectangular and the surrounding picture box would obscure portions of the background graphics within the form, as well as portions of other playing pieces. (A picture box is always rectangular. If the playing piece is nonrectangular, the picture box will extend beyond the image of the piece, giving the piece an unwanted rectangular "aura" and possibly covering important details within the underlying graphics.)

Therefore, rather than using picture boxes to display each playing piece, the *DrawPieces* procedure calls the *BitBlt* function (described in Chapter 7, in Figure 7-12) to transfer a drawing of the piece from a hidden picture box directly to the location wanted within the form.

Note: *DrawPieces* could draw the playing pieces—without disturbing the surrounding graphics—using Visual Basic drawing statements. This method, however, would be more complex to code, and its execution would be too slow. (Remember that *DrawPieces* always draws all the pieces, and therefore the drawing routine must be called repeatedly.)

F Y I

The Fractal Puzzle game (Chapter 7) used *BitBlt* to copy rectangular blocks of graphics by setting the last parameter (*ROP*) to the value SRCCOPY. Employing a simple copy operation to draw the playing pieces in Tic Tac Toe, however, would cause the same problem caused by using a picture box.

To transfer the image of the playing piece *without* disturbing the existing graphics surrounding the image at the target location, *DrawPieces* calls *BitBlt* twice. The first call transfers a "mask" drawing using the AND operator, and the second call transfers an "image" drawing using the XOR operator. Here are the specific steps that *DrawPieces* takes to draw one of the computer's pieces (a red X):

1. The mask drawing of the X is stored in the picture box PictureMsk(1). In this drawing, the X is completely black (all bits in this area are *0*), and the background is completely white (all bits in this area are *1*).

2. The image drawing of the X is stored in the picture box PictureImg(1). In this drawing, the X is displayed in its actual colors (red, light gray, and dark gray), and the background is completely black (all bits in this area are *0*).

   Note: The source picture boxes for the *BitBlt* transfer are invisible at runtime. Therefore, as mentioned in Chapter 7, the AutoRedraw properties of these picture boxes must be set to True so that the graphics assigned to them will be available for the transfer.

3. The mask drawing is transferred from the picture box to the appropriate position within the form by calling *BitBlt*, assigning the *ROP* parameter the value SRCAND. This *ROP* operator causes *BitBlt* to combine the bits in the source picture box with the bits in the form using the logical AND operator. The resulting image of the X on the form is entirely black, but the existing background is left unaltered.

4. The image drawing is transferred from the picture box to the same position within the form used by the mask drawing by calling *BitBlt* again, this time assigning *ROP* the value SRCINVERT. This value causes *BitBlt* to combine the bits in the source picture box with the bits in the form, using the logical XOR operator. The resulting image of the X on the form is identical to the drawing in the source picture box (which has the wanted colors). The background, however, is again left unaltered.

The overall result of these steps is that the X itself is drawn on the playing board, without disturbing the existing graphics surrounding the X at the target location within the form. These steps are shown in Figure

8-14. *DrawPieces* uses the same technique to draw the other types of pieces (the green X, the red O, and the green O).

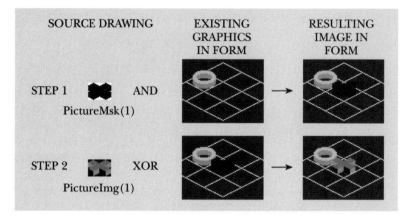

Figure 8-14.
Drawing one of the computer's pieces within a playing square.

F Y I

Windows uses the same drawing method just described when it displays an icon or a mouse pointer. (Icons and mouse pointers are often nonrectangular and must be drawn on top of existing graphics, as is done with the Tic Tac Toe playing pieces.)

The *DrawPieces* Procedure

DrawPieces first calls *Cls* to erase all current pieces from the playing area; it then proceeds to draw each of the pieces indicated by PieceTable, one at a time. Because a given piece partially overlaps any adjoining piece immediately above or to the left, *DrawPieces* draws the pieces row by row, starting at the top of the form and moving to the bottom.

The following *BitBlt* calls are used to transfer the mask bitmap and the image bitmap:

```
If PieceTable(Level, Row, Col) <> NONE Then
    BitBlt hDC, CoordTable(Level, Row, Col).Left + OFFOX,
CoordTable(Level, Row, Col).Top + OFFOY, 30, 23, PictureMsk(2
 - PieceTable(Level, Row, Col) Mod 2).hDC, 0, 0, SRCAND
    BitBlt hDC, CoordTable(Level, Row, Col).Left + OFFOX,
```

(continued)

continued

```
CoordTable(Level, Row, Col).Top + OFFOY, 30, 23,
PictureImg(PieceTable(Level, Row, Col)).hDC, 0, 0, SRCINVERT
End If
```

The coordinates for drawing the pieces are obtained directly from the CoordTable array. The mask bitmaps are stored in the PictureMsk picture-box array, and the image bitmaps are stored in the PictureImg picture-box array. Conveniently, the value in PieceTable—*REDX (= 1)*, *YELO (= 2)*, *GRNX (= 3)*, or *GRNO (= 4)*—is the same as the index of the PictureImg element containing the bitmap for the piece. However, because there are only two mask bitmaps, the value in PieceTable must be converted to either 1 or 2, using the following expression:

```
2 - PieceTable(Level, Row, Col) Mod 2
```

If the value in PieceTable is *REDX (= 1)* or *GRNX (= 3)*, this expression yields the value *1*, which is the index for the X mask bitmap in the PictureMsk array. If the value in PieceTable is *YELO (= 2)* or *GRNO (= 4)*, this expression yields the value *2*, which is the index for the O mask bitmap.

Testing for a Winning Triplet and Ending the Game

Immediately after moving the player's piece and redrawing the pieces, *Form_MouseDown* calls the general procedure *GameWon* to determine whether a complete triplet has just been formed, which would mean that the player has won the game. If a complete triplet exists, *GameWon* returns TRUE, and *Form_MouseDown* terminates the game:

```
If GameWon(YELO) Then
    Beep: Beep: Beep
    Winner = YELO
    Timer1.Enabled = -1
    GameOver = -1
    Exit Sub
End If
```

GameWon will be described next. Notice that to terminate the game, *Form_MouseDown* assigns TRUE to the variable *GameOver* to signal other parts of the program that a game is no longer in progress, and it enables the timer to begin flashing the winning pieces. It also assigns the code for the winner, YELO, to the variable *Winner*, which is used by the timer event handler, *Timer1_Timer* (described shortly).

Immediately after moving the computer's piece and redrawing the pieces, *Form_MouseDown* calls *GameWon* again, this time to test whether the computer has completed a triplet, terminating the game if a complete triplet exists:

```
If GameWon(REDX) Then
    Beep: Beep: Beep
    Winner = REDX
    Timer1.Enabled = -1
    GameOver = -1
    Exit Sub
End If
```

The *GameWon* Procedure

GameWon is passed a parameter indicating the type of piece, YELO or REDX, it is to check. If the procedure finds a triplet of the indicated type, it returns TRUE; otherwise, it returns FALSE.

GameWon first checks for horizontal triplets within a single level and then checks for vertical or diagonal triplets that pass through all three levels. If the procedure discovers a triplet, it exits immediately, returning the value TRUE. (The return value was initialized to TRUE at the beginning of the function.)

The test for horizontal triplets is placed inside the following loop so that all three levels are checked:

```
For Level = 1 To 3

    'check all possible triplets within Level

Next Level
```

Within a given level, it systematically tests all possible triplets.

To test for vertical or diagonal triplets passing through all three levels, *GameWon* examines each square within level one:

```
For Row = 1 To 3
    For Col = 1 To 3

    'check each possible triplet originating from Row, Col
    'in level 1 and passing through the other two levels

    Next Col
Next Row
```

When testing a particular square, the procedure examines all possible triplets that originate in that square and pass through the other two levels.

If *GameWon* discovers a complete triplet, it saves the indexes of all three pieces contained in this triplet in the form-level array WinPiece-List. This array is declared as follows:

```
Type WINPIECE
    Level As Integer
    Row As Integer
    Col As Integer
End Type
Dim WinPieceList(1 To 3) As WINPIECE
```

WinPieceList is used by the timer event procedure to flash the winning pieces.

The *Timer1_Timer* Procedure

After a game has been won, the timer is enabled and the *Timer1_Timer* event procedure begins receiving control every 250 milliseconds (which is the value assigned to the timer's Interval property at design time).

The timer procedure begins with the following code:

```
If Flag Then
    NumImage = Winner
Else
    NumImage = Winner + 2
End If
Flag = Flag Xor -1
```

These statements assign *NumImage* the appropriate value for the playing pieces within the winning triplet. The first time the timer procedure is called, and subsequently every other time it is called, it assigns the value for the normal image of the piece, which *Form_MouseDown* saved in the variable *Winner*. On alternate procedure calls, the procedure assigns *NumImage* the value for the *green* version of the image. For example, if the player wins, *NumImage* is alternately assigned *YELO (= 2)* and *GRNO (= 4)*. (*Flag* is a procedure-level "Static" variable—that is, it is local to the procedure but its value is retained between procedure calls.)

Next, *Timer1_Timer* assigns the code in *NumImage* to the members of PieceTable corresponding to the winning pieces. (Recall that *Game-Won* saves the indexes for these pieces in WinPieceList.) The procedure then calls *DrawPieces* to draw the pieces using the new color:

```
For I = 1 To 3
    PieceTable(WinPieceList(I).Level, WinPieceList(I).Row,
 WinPieceList(I).Col) = NumImage
Next I
DrawPieces
```

Enhancing the Game

You might want to enhance Tic Tac Toe by increasing the number of squares from 27 (3 by 3 by 3) to 64 (4 by 4 by 4). Playing a 4-by-4-by-4 game would be more challenging and less predictable. It would also be more challenging to code. Obviously, you would have to edit the background bitmap (TT.BMP) and increase the dimensions of the data structures to accommodate the greater number of squares. The most difficult part of the conversion would be modifying the routine for calculating the computer's move (the *RedMove* procedure).

CHAPTER NINE

LUDO

The traditional ludo race game is played on a board. In this computer version of the classic game, you play against the computer.

The Ludo program demonstrates an advanced animation technique that lets you move an irregular, full-color object over any type of background. Also, as in the Tic Tac Toe game presented in Chapter 8, the computer serves as one of the players; accordingly, the program demonstrates another method for calculating optimal game moves.

About Ludo

Ludo had its beginnings in ancient India. An entire family of race games originated in India, possibly more than several thousand years ago, later spreading to many areas of the world. All these games use a distinctive cross-shaped playing area. One such game, pachisi, is still played in India. ("Parcheesi" is the familiar trademarked name of a board game based on pachisi.) Ludo, which is similar to pachisi, became popular in England near the end of the nineteenth century. In the British Navy, ludo was known as uckers and was played as a gambling game.

Traditionally, ludo is for two, three, or four players. Each player has four pieces, which are initially positioned on a home base. The players take turns throwing a die and then moving a piece the number of squares indicated by the roll of the die. The players move their pieces in a clockwise direction, trying to move all the way around the board and then toward the finish at the center. The winner is the first player to get all four pieces into the center square. As in an actual race, typically the game continues until all players' pieces are in the center square.

Playing Ludo

The version of Ludo presented in this chapter is for two players: you and the computer. The winner is the first player to get all four pieces into the center square.

When you run Ludo (LD.EXE), the program starts a new game. You can later begin a new game, even before completing the current one, by choosing the New Game command from the Game menu. You play using the yellow pieces; initially, all four of your pieces are on your home base, which is in the upper left corner of the board. The computer plays using the red pieces, which are initially positioned on the computer's home base in the lower right corner of the board. Figure 9-1 shows the opening of a Ludo game.

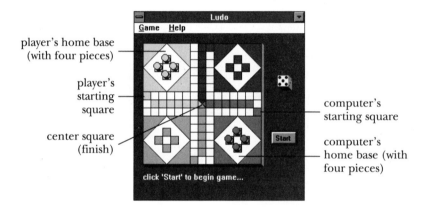

Figure 9-1.
Ludo at the beginning of a game.

At the beginning of a game, each player rolls the die to determine who takes the first turn. To proceed, click the Start button to signal the computer to roll the die. Next, click the Roll button to roll the die for yourself. The player rolling the highest number makes the first move; if both players roll the same number, you repeat this procedure.

If the computer rolls the higher number, a game window similar to the one shown in Figure 9-2 appears. In this case, simply click the OK button, and the computer will make its first move. If you roll the higher number, a window similar to the one shown in Figure 9-3 appears, and you will make the first move.

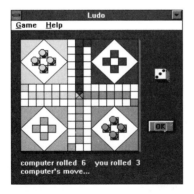

Figure 9-2.
A game in which the computer has won the right to take the first turn.

Figure 9-3.
A game in which the player has won the right to take the first turn.

When it is your turn to make a move in Ludo, click the Roll button to roll the die, and proceed according to the following rules:

- You can either move one of your pieces (if a move is possible), or you can click the Pass button to skip your turn without making a move. (If no move is possible, you must click Pass.) If you click Pass, the computer again takes a turn.

- If a piece is located on your home base, you can move the piece only when you have rolled a 6. If you roll a 6, you must move the piece to the yellow starting square. (See Figure 9-1 to review the locations of the home base and the starting square.)

- If a piece is *not* on your home base, you can move the piece forward the number of squares indicated by the roll of the die. For example, if you roll a *3*, you can move the piece three squares forward. Your pieces must follow the course shown in Figure 9-4. The computer's pieces must follow the course shown in Figure 9-5.

Figure 9-4.
The course of the player's pieces.

Figure 9-5.
The course of the computer's pieces.

- You *cannot* move a piece onto a square that is already occupied by one of your own pieces.

- You *can* move a piece onto a square already occupied by one of the computer's pieces. In this case, the computer's piece is restored (sent back) to its home base. (The same can happen to you if the computer moves one of its pieces onto a square occupied by one of your pieces!)

- To move a piece onto the center square, you must roll a number that is the exact number of squares between the piece and the center square. If you roll a greater number, you are not permitted to move the piece "beyond" the center. For example, consider a piece that is three squares away from the center square. If you roll *1*, *2*, or *3*, you can move the piece (a 3 permitting you to move it onto the center); if you roll a number larger than three, however, you cannot move the piece.

■ Whenever you roll a *6*, you can take another turn. You can then move either the same piece or another piece. You can continue making moves—without giving the computer a turn—as long as you continue to roll *6*.

■ You cannot drop a piece onto an invalid position. If you try to do so, the piece is restored to the position it occupied before you moved it.

■ After you have moved a piece onto a valid square, click OK (or, alternatively, press Enter) to allow the computer to take its next turn. Note: After dropping a piece onto a valid square, you cannot change your move.

After you click Pass to skip your move or make a valid move and click OK, the computer makes its next move. When the computer has completed its move, the message *your move…* appears at the bottom of the window. You can now make your next move according to the rules.

When a piece is moved onto the center square, it is removed from the game. When either you have or the computer has moved all four pieces onto this square, the game is over and an announcement of the outcome is displayed at the bottom of the window. If you want to start a new game, choose the New Game command from the Game menu.

Strategy and Hints

Playing Ludo involves both luck and strategy. Luck plays an important role; no amount of strategy can substitute for rolling a series of sixes! The following guidelines, however, can help you make the most of each move. (As you will see, the computer follows a similar set of guidelines when calculating its own moves.) These guidelines are listed roughly in order of priority.

■ If you roll a *6*, always move any piece still on the home base, provided that the starting square is available. This will help you avoid stranding a piece on the home base while waiting to roll a *6*.

- If one of your pieces is on the starting square, move it to make this square available to receive a piece still waiting on the home base.

- If a piece is on one of the last six squares, do the following: If you roll the exact value needed to place it on the center square, move the piece. If you roll a smaller number, do not move the piece. (Moving it would not increase your chances of placing it on the finish; move one of your other pieces instead.) If you roll a number greater than the exact value needed, you cannot move the piece. (Move one of your other pieces instead.)

- If possible, move a piece onto a square occupied by one of the computer's pieces, thereby sending the computer's piece back to its home base. If such a move is not possible, try to move a piece to a position six or fewer squares behind one of the computer's pieces so that you can later send it home if you roll the right number.

- Conversely, avoid leaving a piece six or fewer squares *ahead* of a computer's piece, because the computer also tries to send your pieces back to your home base.

- Favor a move that places a piece on one of the last six squares. You can then move the piece to the finish as soon as you roll the appropriate number. In the meantime, the piece is immune from capture (as you can see in Figures 9-4 and 9-5) because one player cannot move onto the last six squares of the other player's course.

Coding Ludo

The source code for the Ludo program is contained in the files listed in the following table.

File	Purpose
GLOBALLD.BAS	Contains global type definitions
LD.FRM	Defines the main form, FormMain, and the controls it contains
LDABOUT.FRM	Defines the ABOUT form, FormAbout, and the controls it contains
LD.MAK	Contains the Ludo project file

Figures 9-6 through 9-11 present the form designs, properties, menu commands, and source code for the Ludo program.

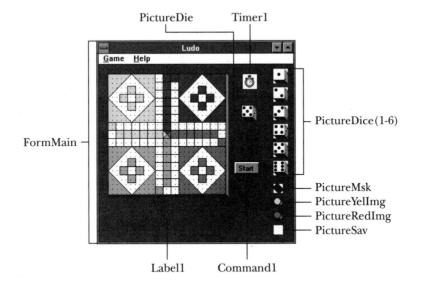

Figure 9-6.
LD.FRM at design time.

Object Name	Object Type	Property	Setting
Command1	Command button	BackColor	&H00008080& [dark yellow]
		Caption	Start
		Default	True
		Height	25 [pixels]
		Left	240 [pixels]
		Top	168 [pixels]
		Width	49 [pixels]
FormMain	Form	AutoRedraw	True
		BackColor	&H00008080& [dark yellow]

Figure 9-7. *(continued)*
LD.FRM form and control properties. (Notice that Ludo uses the dice icons from Deduce; the icon files are therefore located in the DD subdirectory of the directory in which you installed the companion disk.)

Figure 9-7 *continued*

Object Name	Object Type	Property	Setting
		BorderStyle	1 - Fixed Single
		Caption	Ludo
		FormName	FormMain
		Grid Height	8 [pixels]
		Grid Width	8 [pixels]
		Height	5310 [twips]
		Icon	(Icon) [LD.ICO]
		Left	1035 [twips]
		MaxButton	False
		Picture	(Bitmap) [LD.BMP]
		ScaleMode	3 - Pixel
		Top	1170
		Width	5325
Label1	Label	BackColor	&H00008080 [dark yellow]
		BorderStyle	0 - None
		Caption	[blank]
		FontName	System
		FontSize	9.75
		ForeColor	&H00FFFFFF& [white]
		Height	33 [pixels]
		Left	16 [pixels]
		Top	240 [pixels]
		Width	289 [pixels]
PictureDice	Array of picture boxes	BorderStyle	0 - None
		CtlName	PictureDice
		Height	25 [pixels]
		Index	1 - 6
		Left	312 [pixels]

(continued)

Figure 9-7 *continued*

Object Name	Object Type	Property	Setting	
		Picture	(Icon)	
			Index	*Icon*
			1	DD1D.ICO
			2	DD2D.ICO
			3	DD3D.ICO
			4	DD4D.ICO
			5	DD5D.ICO
			6	DD6D.ICO
		Top	[varies]	
		Visible	False	
		Width	25 [pixels]	
PictureDie	Picture box	AutoSize	True	
		BackColor	&H00008080& [dark yellow]	
		BorderStyle	0 - None	
		CtlName	PictureDie	
		Height	32 [pixels]	
		Left	256 [pixels]	
		Picture	(Icon) [DD5D.ICO]	
		Top	72 [pixels]	
		Width	32 [pixels]	
PictureMsk	Picture box	AutoRedraw	True	
		AutoSize	True	
		BorderStyle	0 - None	
		CtlName	PictureMsk	
		Height	16 [pixels]	
		Left	312 [pixels]	
		Picture	(Bitmap) [MSK.BMP]	
		Top	208 [pixels]	
		Visible	False	
		Width	16 [pixels]	

(continued)

Figure 9-7 *continued*

Object Name	Object Type	Property	Setting
PictureRedImg	Picture box	AutoRedraw	True
		AutoSize	True
		BorderStyle	0 - None
		CtlName	PictureRedImg
		Height	16 [pixels]
		Left	312 [pixels]
		Picture	(Bitmap) [REDIMG.BMP]
		Top	256 [pixels]
		Visible	False
		Width	16 [pixels]
PictureSav	Picture box	AutoRedraw	True
		BorderStyle	0 - None
		CtlName	PictureSav
		Height	16 [pixels]
		Left	312 [pixels]
		Top	280 [pixels]
		Visible	False
		Width	16 [pixels]
PictureYelImg	Picture box	AutoRedraw	True
		AutoSize	True
		BorderStyle	0 - None
		CtlName	PictureYelImg
		Height	16 [pixels]
		Left	312 [pixels]
		Picture	(Bitmap) [YELIMG.BMP]
		Top	232 [pixels]
		Visible	False
		Width	16 [pixels]
Timer1	Timer	Enabled	False
		Interval	500 [milliseconds]

Indentation/Caption	Control Name	Other Features
&Game	MenuGame	
....&New Game	MenuNew	
....-	MenuSep1	
....E&xit	MenuExit	
&Help	MenuHelp	
....&Index	MenuIndex	Accelerator = F1
....&How to Play	MenuHowTo	
....&Commands	MenuCommands	
....&Using Help	MenuUsingHelp	
....-	MenuSep2	
....&About Ludo...	MenuAbout	

Figure 9-8.
LD.FRM menu design.

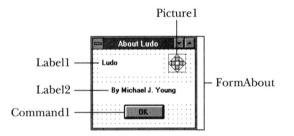

Figure 9-9.
LDABOUT.FRM at design time.

Object Name	Object Type	Property	Setting
Command1	Command button	Caption	OK
		Default	True
		Height	375 [twips]
		Left	840 [twips]

Figure 9-10.
LDABOUT.FRM form and control properties.

(continued)

Figure 9-10 *continued*

Object Name	Object Type	Property	Setting
		Top	1440 [twips]
		Width	1095 [twips]
FormAbout	Form	BorderStyle	3 - Fixed Double
		Caption	About Ludo
		FormName	FormAbout
		Grid Height	120 [twips]
		Grid Width	120 [twips]
		Height	2445 [twips]
		Left	1140 [twips]
		MaxButton	False
		MinButton	False
		Top	1440 [twips]
		Width	2880 [twips]
Label1	Label	Caption	Ludo
		Height	375 [twips]
		Left	240 [twips]
		Top	240 [twips]
		Width	1575 [twips]
Label2	Label	Alignment	2 - Center
		Caption	By Michael J. Young
		Height	375 [twips]
		Left	0 [twips]
		Top	960 [twips]
		Width	2745 [twips]
Picture1	Picture box	AutoSize	True
		BorderStyle	0 - None
		Height	480 [twips]
		Left	2040 [twips]
		Picture	(Icon) [LD.ICO]
		Top	120 [twips]
		Width	480 [twips]

GLOBALLD.BAS code

```
Type PIECE
    IdxMover As Integer
    IdxSquare As Integer
End Type

Type APIPOINT
    X As Integer
    Y As Integer
End Type

Type RECT
    Left As Integer
    Top As Integer
    Right As Integer
    Bottom As Integer
End Type
```

LD.FRM code

```
'Help Section:
'Help file:
Const HELP_FILE = "LD.HLP"
'WinHelp wCommand values:
Const HELP_CONTEXT = &H1
Const HELP_HELPONHELP = &H4
Const HELP_INDEX = &H3
Const HELP_QUIT = &H2
'WinHelp dwData values (help topics):
Const HELP_HOWTOPLAY = 10&
Const HELP_COMMANDS = 20&
'Windows help API:
Declare Sub WinHelp Lib "USER" (ByVal hWnd As Integer,
 ByVal lpHelp_File As String, ByVal wCommand As Integer,
 ByVal dwData As Long)

Const CLIENTBOTTOM = 287      'coordinates of LR corner of inside
                             'of form
Const CLIENTRIGHT = 304
Const OFFX = 16              'offsets of game board within form
Const OFFY = 16
```

Figure 9-11.   *(continued)*

*Source code for the Ludo program. (Notice that long program lines are
wrapped to the next line and indented one space.)*

Figure 9-11 *continued*

```
Const EMPTY = 0                    'codes for game mover:
Const PLAYER = 1
Const COMPUTER = 2
Const START = 0                    'values for variable State:
Const FIRSTROLL = 1
Const ROLL = 2
Const OK = 4
Const COMPMOVE = 5
Const GAMEOVER = 6

Dim MoveOrigin As Integer
Dim NumPieces As Integer
Dim Pieces(1 To 8) As PIECE
Dim PlayScore As Integer
Dim PrevX As Integer
Dim PrevY As Integer
Dim Squares(1 To 2, 1 To 67) As APIPOINT
Dim State As Integer
Dim XOffset As Integer
Dim YOffset As Integer

Const WS_CAPTION = &HC00000
Const WS_THICKFRAME = &H40000
Declare Sub AdjustWindowRect Lib "USER" (lpRect As RECT,
 ByVal dwStyle&, ByVal bMenu%)

Const SRCAND = &H8800C6      'dest = source AND dest
Const SRCCOPY = &HCC0020     'dest = source
Const SRCINVERT = &H660046   'dest = source XOR dest
Declare Sub BitBlt Lib "GDI" (ByVal HDestDC%, ByVal X%,
 ByVal Y%, ByVal nWidth%, ByVal nHeight%, ByVal HSrcDC%,
 ByVal XSrc%, ByVal YSrc%, ByVal ROP&)

Const LOGPIXELSX = 88
Const LOGPIXELSY = 90
Declare Function GetDeviceCaps Lib "GDI" (ByVal hDC%,
 ByVal Index%) As Integer

Declare Sub ClientToScreen Lib "USER" (ByVal hWnd As Integer,
 Pt As APIPOINT)
Declare Sub ClipCursor Lib "USER" (Rec As Any)
Declare Sub ReleaseCapture Lib "USER" ()
Declare Sub SetCapture Lib "USER" (ByVal hWnd As Integer)
Declare Sub ShowCursor Lib "USER" (ByVal ShowIt As Integer)
```

(continued)

Figure 9-11 *continued*

```
Sub AddPiece (IdxMover As Integer, IdxSquare As Integer)
    Dim I As Integer
    Dim IdxLower As Integer
    Dim X1 As Integer, Y1 As Integer
    Dim X2 As Integer, Y2 As Integer

    X1 = Squares(IdxMover, IdxSquare).X
    Y1 = Squares(IdxMover, IdxSquare).Y
    IdxLower = NumPieces + 1
    For I = 1 To NumPieces
        X2 = Squares(Pieces(I).IdxMover, Pieces(I).IdxSquare).X
        Y2 = Squares(Pieces(I).IdxMover, Pieces(I).IdxSquare).Y
        If Y2 > Y1 Or Y2 = Y1 And X2 > X1 Then
            IdxLower = I
            Exit For
        End If
    Next I
    For I = NumPieces To IdxLower Step -1
        Pieces(I + 1) = Pieces(I)
    Next I
    Pieces(IdxLower).IdxMover = IdxMover
    Pieces(IdxLower).IdxSquare = IdxSquare
    NumPieces = NumPieces + 1
End Sub

Sub ComputerMove ()
    Dim HighIdx As Integer
    Dim HighValue As Integer
    Dim I As Integer
    Dim IdxPiece As Integer
    Dim Score As Integer
    Dim TargetSquare As Integer
    Dim Value As Integer

    Score = RollIt()

    For I = 1 To NumPieces
        If Pieces(I).IdxMover = PLAYER Then       'player's piece
            Value = 0
        ElseIf Pieces(I).IdxSquare < 5 Then       'on home base
            If Score = 6 And InSquare(5, 33, IdxPiece) <>
COMPUTER Then
                Value = 30
```

(continued)

Figure 9-11 *continued*

```
            Else
                Value = 0
            End If
        ElseIf Pieces(I).IdxSquare > 60 Then      'on final
                                                  'stretch
            If Pieces(I).IdxSquare + Score = 67 Then
                Value = 25
            Else
                Value = 0
            End If
        Else                                      'on normal
                                                  'square
            If InSquare(Pieces(I).IdxSquare + Score,
MapSquareIdx(Pieces(I).IdxSquare + Score), IdxPiece) <>
COMPUTER Then
                If Pieces(I).IdxSquare = 5 Then
                    Value = 20
                ElseIf InSquare(Pieces(I).IdxSquare + Score,
MapSquareIdx(Pieces(I).IdxSquare + Score), IdxPiece) =
PLAYER Then
                    Value = 15
                ElseIf Pieces(I).IdxSquare + Score > 60 Then
                    Value = 10
                Else
                    Value = 5
                End If
            Else      'no move possible
                Value = 0
            End If
        End If
        If Value > HighValue Then
            HighValue = Value
            HighIdx = I
        End If
    Next I

    If Score = 6 Then
        Label1.Caption = "computer moves again..."
        Command1.Caption = "OK"
        State = COMPMOVE
    Else
        Label1.Caption = "your move..."
        Command1.Caption = "Roll"
        State = ROLL
    End If
```

(continued)

Figure 9-11 *continued*

```
    If HighValue = 0 Then Exit Sub                    .

    If Pieces(HighIdx).IdxSquare < 5 Then
        TargetSquare = 5
    Else
        TargetSquare = Pieces(HighIdx).IdxSquare + Score
    End If

    For I = HighIdx To NumPieces - 1
        Pieces(I) = Pieces(I + 1)
    Next I
    NumPieces = NumPieces - 1

    If InSquare(TargetSquare, MapSquareIdx(TargetSquare),
IdxPiece) = PLAYER Then
        For I = IdxPiece To NumPieces - 1
            Pieces(I) = Pieces(I + 1)
        Next I
        NumPieces = NumPieces - 1
        For I = 1 To 4
            If InSquare(0, I, IdxPiece) = EMPTY Then
                AddPiece PLAYER, I
                Exit For
            End If
        Next I
    End If

    If TargetSquare = 67 Then
        Beep: Beep: Beep: Beep: Beep: Beep
        If PiecesLeft(COMPUTER) = 0 Then
            Label1.Caption = "computer won!"
            Command1.Visible = 0
            State = GAMEOVER
            Timer1.Enabled = -1
        End If
    Else
        AddPiece COMPUTER, TargetSquare
    End If
    Cls
    DrawPieces
End Sub
Sub DrawPieces ()
    For I = 1 To NumPieces
```

(continued)

Figure 9-11 *continued*

```
            If Pieces(I).IdxMover = COMPUTER Then
                    BitBlt hDC, Squares(COMPUTER, Pieces(I).IdxSquare).X
        - 3, Squares(COMPUTER, Pieces(I).IdxSquare).Y - 3, 16, 16,
        PictureMsk.hDC, 0, 0, SRCAND
                    BitBlt hDC, Squares(COMPUTER, Pieces(I).IdxSquare).X
        - 3, Squares(COMPUTER, Pieces(I).IdxSquare).Y - 3, 16, 16,
        PictureRedImg.hDC, 0, 0, SRCINVERT
                ElseIf Pieces(I).IdxMover = PLAYER Then
                    BitBlt hDC, Squares(PLAYER, Pieces(I).IdxSquare).X
        - 3, Squares(PLAYER, Pieces(I).IdxSquare).Y - 3, 16, 16,
        PictureMsk.hDC, 0, 0, SRCAND
                    BitBlt hDC, Squares(PLAYER, Pieces(I).IdxSquare).X
        - 3, Squares(PLAYER, Pieces(I).IdxSquare).Y - 3, 16, 16,
        PictureYelImg.hDC, 0, 0, SRCINVERT
            End If
        Next I
End Sub

Sub InitNewGame ()
    For I = 1 To 4
        Pieces(I).IdxMover = COMPUTER
        Pieces(I + 4).IdxMover = PLAYER
        Pieces(I).IdxSquare = I
        Pieces(I + 4).IdxSquare = I
    Next I
    NumPieces = 8
    Cls
    DrawPieces
    Command1.Caption = "Start"
    Command1.Visible = -1
    Label1.Caption = "click 'Start' to begin game..."
    State = START
End Sub

Function InSquare (IdxComp As Integer, IdxPlay As Integer,
  IdxPiece As Integer) As Integer
    Dim I As Integer

    InSquare = EMPTY
    IdxPiece = 0
    For I = 1 To NumPieces
        If Pieces(I).IdxMover = COMPUTER And
  Pieces(I).IdxSquare = IdxComp Then
            InSquare = COMPUTER
```

(continued)

Figure 9-11 *continued*

```
              IdxPiece = I
              Exit For
         End If
         If Pieces(I).IdxMover = PLAYER And Pieces(I).IdxSquare
 = IdxPlay Then
              InSquare = PLAYER
              IdxPiece = I
              Exit For
         End If
    Next I
End Function

Function MapSquareIdx (IdxIn As Integer)
    If IdxIn < 5 Then
        MapSquareIdx = 0
    ElseIf IdxIn < 33 Then
        MapSquareIdx = IdxIn + 28
    ElseIf IdxIn < 61 Then
        MapSquareIdx = IdxIn - 28
    Else
        MapSquareIdx = 0
    End If
End Function

Sub Pause (Interval As Single)    'Interval = length of pause
                                  'in seconds
    Dim StartTime As Single

    StartTime = Timer
    Do While Timer < StartTime + Interval
    Loop
End Sub

Function PieceHit (X As Single, Y As Single, XOffset As Integer,
 YOffset As Integer)
    Dim I As Integer

    For I = 1 To NumPieces
        If Pieces(I).IdxMover = PLAYER And X >= Squares(PLAYER,
 Pieces(I).IdxSquare).X - 3 And X <= Squares(PLAYER,
 Pieces(I).IdxSquare).X + 12 Then
            If Y >= Squares(PLAYER, Pieces(I).IdxSquare).Y - 3
 And Y <= Squares(PLAYER, Pieces(I).IdxSquare).Y + 12 Then
                XOffset = X - (Squares(PLAYER,
```

(continued)

Figure 9-11 *continued*

```
    Pieces(I).IdxSquare).X - 3)
                YOffset = Y - (Squares(PLAYER,
    Pieces(I).IdxSquare).Y - 3)
                PieceHit = I
                Exit Function
            End If
        End If
    Next I
    PieceHit = 0
End Function

Function PiecesLeft (Code As Integer) As Integer
    Dim Count As Integer
    Dim I As Integer

    For I = 1 To NumPieces
        If Pieces(I).IdxMover = Code Then Count = Count + 1
    Next I
    PiecesLeft = Count
End Function

Function RollIt ()
    Dim I As Integer
    Dim Value As Integer

    For I = 1 To 8
        Value = Int(6 * Rnd + 1)
        PictureDie.Picture = PictureDice(Value).Picture
        Beep
        Pause .05
    Next I
    RollIt = Value
End Function

Function SquareHit (X As Single, Y As Single, Idx As Integer) As
  Integer
    Dim XCoord As Integer
    Dim YCoord As Integer

    XCoord = X - XOffset + 8
    YCoord = Y - YOffset + 8
    SquareHit = 0
    If XCoord >= Squares(PLAYER, Idx).X And XCoord <=
Squares(PLAYER, Idx).X + 12 Then
        If YCoord >= Squares(PLAYER, Idx).Y And YCoord <=
```

(continued)

Figure 9-11 *continued*

```
    Squares(PLAYER, Idx).Y + 12 Then
            SquareHit = -1
        End If
    End If
End Function

Sub Command1_Click ()
    Static CompScore As Integer
    Dim I As Integer
    Dim Message As String
    Dim Score As Integer

    Select Case State
        Case COMPMOVE
            ComputerMove
        Case FIRSTROLL
            Score = RollIt()
            Message = "computer rolled " + Str$(CompScore)
+ "    you rolled " + Str$(Score) + Chr$(13) + Chr$(10)
            If Score = CompScore Then
                Message = Message + "start again..."
                Command1.Caption = "Start"
                State = START
            ElseIf Score > CompScore Then
                Message = Message + "your move..."
                State = ROLL
            Else
                Message = Message + "computer's move..."
                Command1.Caption = "OK"
                State = COMPMOVE
            End If
            Label1.Caption = Message
        Case OK      'player clicked "Pass" button
            If PlayScore = 6 Then
                Label1.Caption = "your move again..."
                Command1.Caption = "Roll"
                State = ROLL
            Else
                ComputerMove
            End If
        Case ROLL
            PlayScore = RollIt()
            Message = "move piece or click 'Pass'..."
            Label1.Caption = Message
```

(continued)

Figure 9-11 *continued*

```
            Command1.Caption = "Pass"
            State = OK
        Case START
            CompScore = RollIt()
            Message = "computer rolled " + Str$(CompScore)
            Label1.Caption = Message
            Command1.Caption = "Roll"
            State = FIRSTROLL
    End Select
End Sub


Sub Form_Load ()
    Dim Rec As RECT

    'code for display device independence:
    Rec.Left = 0
    Rec.Top = 0
    Rec.Right = CLIENTRIGHT
    Rec.Bottom = CLIENTBOTTOM
    AdjustWindowRect Rec, WS_CAPTION, -1
    FormMain.Width = (Rec.Right - Rec.Left + 1) * (1440 /
GetDeviceCaps(hDC, LOGPIXELSX))
    FormMain.Height = (Rec.Bottom - Rec.Top + 1) * (1440 /
GetDeviceCaps(hDC, LOGPIXELSY))
    FormMain.Left = 20 * (1440 /
GetDeviceCaps(hDC, LOGPIXELSX))
    FormMain.Top = 20 * (1440 /
GetDeviceCaps(hDC, LOGPIXELSY))
    PictureDie.Left = 256: PictureDie.Top = 72
    Command1.Left = 243: Command1.Top = 168
    Command1.Width = 49: Command1.Height = 25
    Label1.Left = 16: Label1.Top = 240
    Label1.Width = 286: Label1.Height = 33
    PictureSav.Width = 16: PictureSav.Height = 16

    'initialize Squares array:
    Squares(COMPUTER, 1).X = 162 + OFFX:
Squares(COMPUTER, 1).Y = 148 + OFFY
    Squares(COMPUTER, 2).X = 148 + OFFX:
Squares(COMPUTER, 2).Y = 162 + OFFY
    Squares(COMPUTER, 3).X = 176 + OFFX:
Squares(COMPUTER, 3).Y = 162 + OFFY
    Squares(COMPUTER, 4).X = 162 + OFFX:
Squares(COMPUTER, 4).Y = 176 + OFFY
```

(continued)

Figure 9-11 *continued*

```
     Squares(COMPUTER, 5).X = 197 + OFFX:
Squares(COMPUTER, 5).Y = 113 + OFFY
     Squares(COMPUTER, 6).X = 183 + OFFX:
Squares(COMPUTER, 6).Y = 113 + OFFY
     Squares(COMPUTER, 7).X = 169 + OFFX:
Squares(COMPUTER, 7).Y = 113 + OFFY
     Squares(COMPUTER, 8).X = 155 + OFFX:
Squares(COMPUTER, 8).Y = 113 + OFFY
     Squares(COMPUTER, 9).X = 141 + OFFX:
Squares(COMPUTER, 9).Y = 113 + OFFY
     Squares(COMPUTER, 10).X = 127 + OFFX:
Squares(COMPUTER, 10).Y = 113 + OFFY
     Squares(COMPUTER, 11).X = 113 + OFFX:
Squares(COMPUTER, 11).Y = 113 + OFFY
     Squares(COMPUTER, 12).X = 113 + OFFX:
Squares(COMPUTER, 12).Y = 127 + OFFY
     Squares(COMPUTER, 13).X = 113 + OFFX:
Squares(COMPUTER, 13).Y = 141 + OFFY
     Squares(COMPUTER, 14).X = 113 + OFFX:
Squares(COMPUTER, 14).Y = 155 + OFFY
     Squares(COMPUTER, 15).X = 113 + OFFX:
Squares(COMPUTER, 15).Y = 169 + OFFY
     Squares(COMPUTER, 16).X = 113 + OFFX:
Squares(COMPUTER, 16).Y = 183 + OFFY
     Squares(COMPUTER, 17).X = 113 + OFFX:
Squares(COMPUTER, 17).Y = 197 + OFFY
     Squares(COMPUTER, 18).X = 99 + OFFX:
Squares(COMPUTER, 18).Y = 197 + OFFY
     Squares(COMPUTER, 19).X = 85 + OFFX:
Squares(COMPUTER, 19).Y = 197 + OFFY
     Squares(COMPUTER, 20).X = 85 + OFFX:
Squares(COMPUTER, 20).Y = 183 + OFFY
     Squares(COMPUTER, 21).X = 85 + OFFX:
Squares(COMPUTER, 21).Y = 169 + OFFY
     Squares(COMPUTER, 22).X = 85 + OFFX:
Squares(COMPUTER, 22).Y = 155 + OFFY
     Squares(COMPUTER, 23).X = 85 + OFFX:
Squares(COMPUTER, 23).Y = 141 + OFFY
     Squares(COMPUTER, 24).X = 85 + OFFX:
Squares(COMPUTER, 24).Y = 127 + OFFY
     Squares(COMPUTER, 25).X = 85 + OFFX:
Squares(COMPUTER, 25).Y = 113 + OFFY
     Squares(COMPUTER, 26).X = 71 + OFFX:
Squares(COMPUTER, 26).Y = 113 + OFFY
```

(continued)

Figure 9-11 *continued*

```
     Squares(COMPUTER, 27).X = 57 + OFFX:
Squares(COMPUTER, 27).Y = 113 + OFFY
     Squares(COMPUTER, 28).X = 43 + OFFX:
Squares(COMPUTER, 28).Y = 113 + OFFY
     Squares(COMPUTER, 29).X = 29 + OFFX:
Squares(COMPUTER, 29).Y = 113 + OFFY
     Squares(COMPUTER, 30).X = 15 + OFFX:
Squares(COMPUTER, 30).Y = 113 + OFFY
     Squares(COMPUTER, 31).X = 1 + OFFX:
Squares(COMPUTER, 31).Y = 113 + OFFY
     Squares(COMPUTER, 32).X = 1 + OFFX:
Squares(COMPUTER, 32).Y = 99 + OFFY
     Squares(COMPUTER, 33).X = 1 + OFFX:
Squares(COMPUTER, 33).Y = 85 + OFFY
     Squares(COMPUTER, 34).X = 15 + OFFX:
Squares(COMPUTER, 34).Y = 85 + OFFY
     Squares(COMPUTER, 35).X = 29 + OFFX:
Squares(COMPUTER, 35).Y = 85 + OFFY
     Squares(COMPUTER, 36).X = 43 + OFFX:
Squares(COMPUTER, 36).Y = 85 + OFFY
     Squares(COMPUTER, 37).X = 57 + OFFX:
Squares(COMPUTER, 37).Y = 85 + OFFY
     Squares(COMPUTER, 38).X = 71 + OFFX:
Squares(COMPUTER, 38).Y = 85 + OFFY
     Squares(COMPUTER, 39).X = 85 + OFFX:
Squares(COMPUTER, 39).Y = 85 + OFFY
     Squares(COMPUTER, 40).X = 85 + OFFX:
Squares(COMPUTER, 40).Y = 71 + OFFY
     Squares(COMPUTER, 41).X = 85 + OFFX:
Squares(COMPUTER, 41).Y = 57 + OFFY
     Squares(COMPUTER, 42).X = 85 + OFFX:
Squares(COMPUTER, 42).Y = 43 + OFFY
     Squares(COMPUTER, 43).X = 85 + OFFX:
Squares(COMPUTER, 43).Y = 29 + OFFY
     Squares(COMPUTER, 44).X = 85 + OFFX:
Squares(COMPUTER, 44).Y = 15 + OFFY
     Squares(COMPUTER, 45).X = 85 + OFFX:
Squares(COMPUTER, 45).Y = 1 + OFFY
     Squares(COMPUTER, 46).X = 99 + OFFX:
Squares(COMPUTER, 46).Y = 1 + OFFY
     Squares(COMPUTER, 47).X = 113 + OFFX:
Squares(COMPUTER, 47).Y = 1 + OFFY
     Squares(COMPUTER, 48).X = 113 + OFFX:
Squares(COMPUTER, 48).Y = 15 + OFFY
```

(continued)

Figure 9-11 *continued*

```
    Squares(COMPUTER, 49).X = 113 + OFFX:
Squares(COMPUTER, 49).Y = 29 + OFFY
    Squares(COMPUTER, 50).X = 113 + OFFX:
Squares(COMPUTER, 50).Y = 43 + OFFY
    Squares(COMPUTER, 51).X = 113 + OFFX:
Squares(COMPUTER, 51).Y = 57 + OFFY
    Squares(COMPUTER, 52).X = 113 + OFFX:
Squares(COMPUTER, 52).Y = 71 + OFFY
    Squares(COMPUTER, 53).X = 113 + OFFX:
Squares(COMPUTER, 53).Y = 85 + OFFY
    Squares(COMPUTER, 54).X = 127 + OFFX:
Squares(COMPUTER, 54).Y = 85 + OFFY
    Squares(COMPUTER, 55).X = 141 + OFFX:
Squares(COMPUTER, 55).Y = 85 + OFFY
    Squares(COMPUTER, 56).X = 155 + OFFX:
Squares(COMPUTER, 56).Y = 85 + OFFY
    Squares(COMPUTER, 57).X = 169 + OFFX:
Squares(COMPUTER, 57).Y = 85 + OFFY
    Squares(COMPUTER, 58).X = 183 + OFFX:
Squares(COMPUTER, 58).Y = 85 + OFFY
    Squares(COMPUTER, 59).X = 197 + OFFX:
Squares(COMPUTER, 59).Y = 85 + OFFY
    Squares(COMPUTER, 60).X = 197 + OFFX:
Squares(COMPUTER, 60).Y = 99 + OFFY
    Squares(COMPUTER, 61).X = 183 + OFFX:
Squares(COMPUTER, 61).Y = 99 + OFFY
    Squares(COMPUTER, 62).X = 169 + OFFX:
Squares(COMPUTER, 62).Y = 99 + OFFY
    Squares(COMPUTER, 63).X = 155 + OFFX:
Squares(COMPUTER, 63).Y = 99 + OFFY
    Squares(COMPUTER, 64).X = 141 + OFFX:
Squares(COMPUTER, 64).Y = 99 + OFFY
    Squares(COMPUTER, 65).X = 127 + OFFX:
Squares(COMPUTER, 65).Y = 99 + OFFY
    Squares(COMPUTER, 66).X = 113 + OFFX:
Squares(COMPUTER, 66).Y = 99 + OFFY
    Squares(COMPUTER, 67).X = 99 + OFFX:
Squares(COMPUTER, 67).Y = 99 + OFFY

    Squares(PLAYER, 1).X = 36 + OFFX:
Squares(PLAYER, 1).Y = 22 + OFFY
    Squares(PLAYER, 2).X = 22 + OFFX:
Squares(PLAYER, 2).Y = 36 + OFFY
```

(continued)

Figure 9-11 *continued*

```
    Squares(PLAYER, 3).X = 50 + OFFX:
Squares(PLAYER, 3).Y = 36 + OFFY
    Squares(PLAYER, 4).X = 36 + OFFX:
Squares(PLAYER, 4).Y = 50 + OFFY
    Squares(PLAYER, 5).X = 1 + OFFX:
Squares(PLAYER, 5).Y = 85 + OFFY
    Squares(PLAYER, 6).X = 15 + OFFX:
Squares(PLAYER, 6).Y = 85 + OFFY
    Squares(PLAYER, 7).X = 29 + OFFX:
Squares(PLAYER, 7).Y = 85 + OFFY
    Squares(PLAYER, 8).X = 43 + OFFX:
Squares(PLAYER, 8).Y = 85 + OFFY
    Squares(PLAYER, 9).X = 57 + OFFX:
Squares(PLAYER, 9).Y = 85 + OFFY
    Squares(PLAYER, 10).X = 71 + OFFX:
Squares(PLAYER, 10).Y = 85 + OFFY
    Squares(PLAYER, 11).X = 85 + OFFX:
Squares(PLAYER, 11).Y = 85 + OFFY
    Squares(PLAYER, 12).X = 85 + OFFX:
Squares(PLAYER, 12).Y = 71 + OFFY
    Squares(PLAYER, 13).X = 85 + OFFX:
Squares(PLAYER, 13).Y = 57 + OFFY
    Squares(PLAYER, 14).X = 85 + OFFX:
Squares(PLAYER, 14).Y = 43 + OFFY
    Squares(PLAYER, 15).X = 85 + OFFX:
Squares(PLAYER, 15).Y = 29 + OFFY
    Squares(PLAYER, 16).X = 85 + OFFX:
Squares(PLAYER, 16).Y = 15 + OFFY
    Squares(PLAYER, 17).X = 85 + OFFX:
Squares(PLAYER, 17).Y = 1 + OFFY
    Squares(PLAYER, 18).X = 99 + OFFX:
Squares(PLAYER, 18).Y = 1 + OFFY
    Squares(PLAYER, 19).X = 113 + OFFX:
Squares(PLAYER, 19).Y = 1 + OFFY
    Squares(PLAYER, 20).X = 113 + OFFX:
Squares(PLAYER, 20).Y = 15 + OFFY
    Squares(PLAYER, 21).X = 113 + OFFX:
Squares(PLAYER, 21).Y = 29 + OFFY
    Squares(PLAYER, 22).X = 113 + OFFX:
Squares(PLAYER, 22).Y = 43 + OFFY
    Squares(PLAYER, 23).X = 113 + OFFX:
Squares(PLAYER, 23).Y = 57 + OFFY
    Squares(PLAYER, 24).X = 113 + OFFX:
Squares(PLAYER, 24).Y = 71 + OFFY
```

(continued)

Figure 9-11 *continued*

```
    Squares(PLAYER, 25).X = 113 + OFFX:
Squares(PLAYER, 25).Y = 85 + OFFY
    Squares(PLAYER, 26).X = 127 + OFFX:
Squares(PLAYER, 26).Y = 85 + OFFY
    Squares(PLAYER, 27).X = 141 + OFFX:
Squares(PLAYER, 27).Y = 85 + OFFY
    Squares(PLAYER, 28).X = 155 + OFFX:
Squares(PLAYER, 28).Y = 85 + OFFY
    Squares(PLAYER, 29).X = 169 + OFFX:
Squares(PLAYER, 29).Y = 85 + OFFY
    Squares(PLAYER, 30).X = 183 + OFFX:
Squares(PLAYER, 30).Y = 85 + OFFY
    Squares(PLAYER, 31).X = 197 + OFFX:
Squares(PLAYER, 31).Y = 85 + OFFY
    Squares(PLAYER, 32).X = 197 + OFFX:
Squares(PLAYER, 32).Y = 99 + OFFY
    Squares(PLAYER, 33).X = 197 + OFFX:
Squares(PLAYER, 33).Y = 113 + OFFY
    Squares(PLAYER, 34).X = 183 + OFFX:
Squares(PLAYER, 34).Y = 113 + OFFY
    Squares(PLAYER, 35).X = 169 + OFFX:
Squares(PLAYER, 35).Y = 113 + OFFY
    Squares(PLAYER, 36).X = 155 + OFFX:
Squares(PLAYER, 36).Y = 113 + OFFY
    Squares(PLAYER, 37).X = 141 + OFFX:
Squares(PLAYER, 37).Y = 113 + OFFY
    Squares(PLAYER, 38).X = 127 + OFFX:
Squares(PLAYER, 38).Y = 113 + OFFY
    Squares(PLAYER, 39).X = 113 + OFFX:
Squares(PLAYER, 39).Y = 113 + OFFY
    Squares(PLAYER, 40).X = 113 + OFFX:
Squares(PLAYER, 40).Y = 127 + OFFY
    Squares(PLAYER, 41).X = 113 + OFFX:
Squares(PLAYER, 41).Y = 141 + OFFY
    Squares(PLAYER, 42).X = 113 + OFFX:
Squares(PLAYER, 42).Y = 155 + OFFY
    Squares(PLAYER, 43).X = 113 + OFFX:
Squares(PLAYER, 43).Y = 169 + OFFY
    Squares(PLAYER, 44).X = 113 + OFFX:
Squares(PLAYER, 44).Y = 183 + OFFY
    Squares(PLAYER, 45).X = 113 + OFFX:
Squares(PLAYER, 45).Y = 197 + OFFY
    Squares(PLAYER, 46).X = 99 + OFFX:
Squares(PLAYER, 46).Y = 197 + OFFY
```

(continued)

Figure 9-11 *continued*

```
   Squares(PLAYER, 47).X = 85 + OFFX:
Squares(PLAYER, 47).Y = 197 + OFFY
   Squares(PLAYER, 48).X = 85 + OFFX:
Squares(PLAYER, 48).Y = 183 + OFFY
   Squares(PLAYER, 49).X = 85 + OFFX:
Squares(PLAYER, 49).Y = 169 + OFFY
   Squares(PLAYER, 50).X = 85 + OFFX:
Squares(PLAYER, 50).Y = 155 + OFFY
   Squares(PLAYER, 51).X = 85 + OFFX:
Squares(PLAYER, 51).Y = 141 + OFFY
   Squares(PLAYER, 52).X = 85 + OFFX:
Squares(PLAYER, 52).Y = 127 + OFFY
   Squares(PLAYER, 53).X = 85 + OFFX:
Squares(PLAYER, 53).Y = 113 + OFFY
   Squares(PLAYER, 54).X = 71 + OFFX:
Squares(PLAYER, 54).Y = 113 + OFFY
   Squares(PLAYER, 55).X = 57 + OFFX:
Squares(PLAYER, 55).Y = 113 + OFFY
   Squares(PLAYER, 56).X = 43 + OFFX:
Squares(PLAYER, 56).Y = 113 + OFFY
   Squares(PLAYER, 57).X = 29 + OFFX:
Squares(PLAYER, 57).Y = 113 + OFFY
   Squares(PLAYER, 58).X = 15 + OFFX:
Squares(PLAYER, 58).Y = 113 + OFFY
   Squares(PLAYER, 59).X = 1 + OFFX:
Squares(PLAYER, 59).Y = 113 + OFFY
   Squares(PLAYER, 60).X = 1 + OFFX:
Squares(PLAYER, 60).Y = 99 + OFFY
   Squares(PLAYER, 61).X = 15 + OFFX:
Squares(PLAYER, 61).Y = 99 + OFFY
   Squares(PLAYER, 62).X = 29 + OFFX:
Squares(PLAYER, 62).Y = 99 + OFFY
   Squares(PLAYER, 63).X = 43 + OFFX:
Squares(PLAYER, 63).Y = 99 + OFFY
   Squares(PLAYER, 64).X = 57 + OFFX:
Squares(PLAYER, 64).Y = 99 + OFFY
   Squares(PLAYER, 65).X = 71 + OFFX:
Squares(PLAYER, 65).Y = 99 + OFFY
   Squares(PLAYER, 66).X = 85 + OFFX:
Squares(PLAYER, 66).Y = 99 + OFFY
   Squares(PLAYER, 67).X = 99 + OFFX:
Squares(PLAYER, 67).Y = 99 + OFFY
```

(continued)

Figure 9-11 *continued*

```
     Randomize
     InitNewGame
End Sub

Sub Form_MouseDown (Button As Integer, Shift As Integer,
  X As Single, Y As Single)
    Dim I As Integer
    Dim Idx As Integer
    Dim Pt As APIPOINT
    Dim Rec As RECT

    If State <> OK Then Exit Sub
    Idx = PieceHit(X, Y, XOffset, YOffset)
    If Idx = 0 Then Exit Sub

    'control pointer:
    ShowCursor 0
    SetCapture hWnd
    Pt.X = 0
    Pt.Y = 0
    ClientToScreen hWnd, Pt
    Rec.Left = Pt.X
    Rec.Top = Pt.Y
    Pt.X = 232
    Pt.Y = 232
    ClientToScreen hWnd, Pt
    Rec.Right = Pt.X
    Rec.Bottom = Pt.Y
    ClipCursor Rec

    'initialize move variables:
    MoveOrigin = Pieces(Idx).IdxSquare
    PrevX = Squares(PLAYER, MoveOrigin).X - 3
    PrevY = Squares(PLAYER, MoveOrigin).Y - 3

    'initialize PictureSav picture box:
    Cls
    Pieces(Idx).IdxMover = EMPTY
    DrawPieces
    BitBlt PictureSav.hDC, 0, 0, 16, 16, hDC, PrevX, PrevY,
SRCCOPY
    Pieces(Idx).IdxMover = PLAYER
    DrawPieces
    For I = Idx To NumPieces - 1
        Pieces(I) = Pieces(I + 1)
```

(continued)

Figure 9-11 *continued*

```
    Next I
    NumPieces = NumPieces - 1
End Sub

Sub Form_MouseMove (Button As Integer, Shift As Integer,
 X As Single, Y As Single)
    If MoveOrigin = 0 Then Exit Sub
    BitBlt hDC, PrevX, PrevY, 16, 16, PictureSav.hDC, 0, 0,
SRCCOPY
    PrevX = X - XOffset
    PrevY = Y - YOffset
    BitBlt PictureSav.hDC, 0, 0, 16, 16, hDC, PrevX, PrevY,
SRCCOPY
    BitBlt hDC, PrevX, PrevY, 16, 16, PictureMsk.hDC, 0, 0,
SRCAND
    BitBlt hDC, PrevX, PrevY, 16, 16, PictureYelImg.hDC, 0, 0,
SRCINVERT
    Refresh
End Sub

Sub Form_MouseUp (Button As Integer, Shift As Integer,
 X As Single, Y As Single)
    Dim I As Integer
    Dim IdxPiece As Integer
    Dim TargetSquare As Integer

    If MoveOrigin = 0 Then Exit Sub
    ShowCursor -1
    ReleaseCapture
    ClipCursor ByVal 0&

    If MoveOrigin < 5 Then
        If PlayScore <> 6 Or Not SquareHit(X, Y, 5) Then
            TargetSquare = MoveOrigin
        ElseIf InSquare(33, 5, IdxPiece) = PLAYER Then
            TargetSquare = MoveOrigin
        Else
            TargetSquare = 5
        End If
    ElseIf MoveOrigin + PlayScore > 67 Then
        TargetSquare = MoveOrigin
    ElseIf Not SquareHit(X, Y, MoveOrigin + PlayScore) Then
        TargetSquare = MoveOrigin
    ElseIf InSquare(MapSquareIdx(MoveOrigin + PlayScore),
```

(continued)

Figure 9-11 *continued*

```
MoveOrigin + PlayScore, IdxPiece) = PLAYER Then
        TargetSquare = MoveOrigin
    Else
        TargetSquare = MoveOrigin + PlayScore
    End If

    If InSquare(MapSquareIdx(TargetSquare), TargetSquare,
IdxPiece) = COMPUTER Then
        For I = IdxPiece To NumPieces - 1
            Pieces(I) = Pieces(I + 1)
        Next I
        NumPieces = NumPieces - 1
        For I = 1 To 4
            If InSquare(I, 0, IdxPiece) = EMPTY Then
                AddPiece COMPUTER, I
                Exit For
            End If
        Next I
    End If

    If TargetSquare = 67 Then
        Beep: Beep: Beep: Beep: Beep: Beep
        If PiecesLeft(PLAYER) = 0 Then
            Label1.Caption = "You won!"
            Command1.Visible = 0
            State = GAMEOVER
            Timer1.Enabled = -1
        End If
    Else
        AddPiece PLAYER, TargetSquare
    End If
    Cls
    DrawPieces

    If TargetSquare = MoveOrigin Then
        Beep
    ElseIf State <> GAMEOVER Then
        If PlayScore = 6 Then
            Label1.Caption = "your move again..."
            Command1.Caption = "Roll"
            State = ROLL
        Else
            Label1.Caption = "computer's move..."
            Command1.Caption = "OK"
```

(continued)

Figure 9-11 *continued*

```
            State = COMPMOVE
        End If
    End If

    MoveOrigin = 0
End Sub

Sub Form_Unload (Cancel As Integer)
    WinHelp hWnd, HELP_FILE, HELP_QUIT, 0
End Sub

Sub MenuAbout_Click ()
    FormAbout.Show 1
End Sub

Sub MenuCommands_Click ()
    WinHelp hWnd, HELP_FILE, HELP_CONTEXT,
 HELP_COMMANDS
End Sub

Sub MenuExit_Click ()
    WinHelp hWnd, HELP_FILE, HELP_QUIT, 0
    End
End Sub

Sub MenuHowTo_Click ()
    WinHelp hWnd, HELP_FILE, HELP_CONTEXT,
 HELP_HOWTOPLAY
End Sub

Sub MenuIndex_Click ()
    WinHelp hWnd, HELP_FILE, HELP_INDEX, 0
End Sub

Sub MenuNew_Click ()
    InitNewGame
End Sub

Sub MenuUsingHelp_Click ()
    WinHelp hWnd, HELP_FILE, HELP_HELPONHELP, 0
End Sub

Sub Timer1_Timer ()
    Static Count As Integer
```

(continued)

Figure 9-11 *continued*

```
    If Count > 3 Then
        Timer1.Enabled = 0
        Count = 0
        Exit Sub
    End If
    Beep: Beep: Beep: Beep: Beep: Beep
    If Count Mod 2 Then
        Label1.Visible = -1
    Else
        Label1.Visible = 0
    End If
    Count = Count + 1
End Sub
```

LDABOUT.FRM code

```
Sub Command1_Click ()
    Unload FormAbout
End Sub
```

Programming Techniques

As with many of the games presented in this book, Ludo uses a bitmap for the game background. As usual, this bitmap was created in Paintbrush, saved in a file, and then assigned to the main form's Picture property.

Ludo introduces a versatile new technique for moving a playing piece in response to movements of the mouse, permitting the player to drag the piece from one square to another. This animation technique employs the Windows API *BitBlt* function to draw the piece at each new location of the mouse pointer. The technique creates the drawing at each position by first transferring a mask drawing (using an AND operation) and then an image drawing (using an XOR operation). This is the same method that was used in the Tic Tac Toe game (Chapter 8). Each time the piece is redrawn, Ludo uses two additional *BitBlt* calls to save and restore the existing graphics underneath the image. These additional calls to *BitBlt* specify a copy operation (the *ROP* parameter is set to SRCCOPY) to copy the existing graphics to or from a picture box used for temporary storage.

The animation technique used in Ludo is the most advanced one presented in this book, and it also provides the greatest flexibility. The technique lets you move a full-color nonrectangular object over any type of background, without disturbing this background. The following table provides an overview of the animation techniques that are presented in this book.

Summary of Animation Techniques

Technique	Where Used: Game (Chapter)	Move Nonrec-tangular Object?	Move Over Heterogeneous Background?	Object in Full Color?
Visual Basic drag-and-drop	Peg Solitaire (3) and Deduce (4)	Yes	Yes	No
Move picture box using *Move* method	Word Squares (5), Queens (6), and Grid War (12)	No (unless background is single color and objects do not nest)	Yes	Yes
AND/XOR *BitBlt*	TriPack (11)	Yes	No	Yes
AND/ XOR/COPY *BitBlt*	Ludo (9), Ringo (10), and Boule (13)	Yes	Yes	Yes

In Ludo, as in the Tic Tac Toe game, the computer serves as one of the players. As you will see, when moving the computer's piece, the program follows a simple set of rules for evaluating each possible move. As you become an experienced player, you might want to enhance these rules to make the computer a more challenging opponent.

Note: Throughout the following discussion, the term "player" refers to the human user of the program, and the term "computer" refers to the computer-generated opponent.

Program Overview

Here is a summary of the sequence of events in the Ludo program.

■ When the program begins running, the *Form_Load* event procedure performs the one-time initialization tasks and calls *InitNewGame* to start a game.

- Whenever the player chooses the New Game command from the Game menu, the *MenuNew_Click* event procedure also calls *InitNewGame* to start a new game.

- *InitNewGame* takes care of the initialization tasks required for each new game, including enabling the command button and setting its caption to Start.

- Whenever the player clicks the command button (Command1), the *Command1_Click* event procedure performs the game's next action (rolling the die, calling *ComputerMove* to move the computer's piece, or permitting the player to make a move).

- The general procedure *ComputerMove* calculates the best move for the computer and moves a piece. Also, if the computer has won, *ComputerMove* terminates the game.

- If the player presses the mouse button while the mouse pointer is on a yellow piece, the *Form_MouseDown* event procedure initiates a move operation, provided that the player is permitted to move.

- During a move operation, the *Form_MouseMove* event procedure draws the player's piece at each new location of the mouse pointer, erasing the piece from its prior location.

- When the player releases the mouse button, the *Form_MouseUp* event procedure terminates the move operation. If the piece is dropped at an invalid location, it is returned to its origin. Also, if the player has won, *Form_MouseUp* terminates the game.

Initializing the Program

The program initialization tasks are performed by the *Form_Load* and *InitNewGame* procedures.

The *Form_Load* Procedure

As usual, the *Form_Load* event procedure handles all the one-time initialization tasks that are required when the program is first loaded.

One of its tasks is to initialize the Squares array, which is defined as follows:

```
Dim Squares(1 To 2, 1 To 67) As APIPOINT
```

APIPOINT is a user-defined type, defined in GLOBALLD.FRM as follows:

```
Type APIPOINT
    X As Integer   'Horizontal coordinate of upper left corner
                   'of square
    Y As Integer   'Vertical coordinate of upper left corner
                   'of square
End Type
```

The Squares array holds the coordinates of the upper left corner of each square on the playing board that is used in the game. The first row of this array, Squares (1,...), holds the coordinates of the 67 squares used by the player, and the second row, Squares(2,...), holds the coordinates of the 67 squares used by the computer.

F Y I

I derived the coordinates of the Squares array by loading the bitmap used for the main form (LD.BMP) into Paintbrush, choosing the Cursor Position command from the View menu, and placing the mouse pointer on the appropriate points and reading the coordinates displayed by Paintbrush.

The squares in each portion of the array are arranged in the order of the circuit followed by the pieces. For example, the coordinates of the player's starting square are stored in Squares(1, 5), and the coordinates of the next square to the right are stored in Squares(1, 6). This arrangement makes it easy to calculate game moves. Figure 9-12 shows the indexes for each square. In this figure, the top number displayed in each square is the index to the player's portion of the array, Square(1, ...), and the bottom number is the index to the computer's portion, Squares(2, ...). Notice that some squares have only a single index, so the opponent cannot move onto those squares.

For convenience in accessing the Squares array, the program defines the symbolic constants *PLAYER (= 1)* and *COMPUTER (= 2)*.

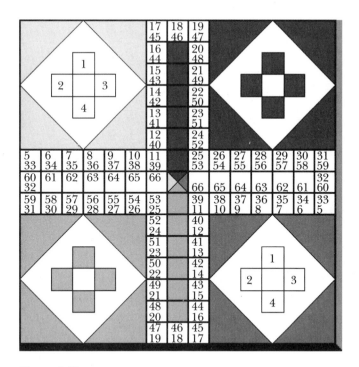

Figure 9-12.
The indexes to the Squares array for each playing square. (The center square is 67.)

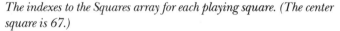

F Y I

As you can see in Figure 9-12, most of the squares have two indexes. The program sometimes needs to convert from one index to the other. This is accomplished by means of the general procedure *MapSquareIdx*; if one index for a given square is passed to this procedure, it returns the other index.

The *InitNewGame* Procedure

Before exiting, *Form_Load* calls the general procedure *InitNewGame* to start a new game. Whenever the user chooses the New Game command from the Game menu, the *MenuNew_Click* procedure also calls *Init-NewGame*.

InitNewGame performs the initialization tasks that are required to start a new game. Among these tasks is the initialization of another important array, Pieces. The Pieces array stores current information on each of the playing pieces and is defined as follows:

```
Dim Pieces(1 To 8) As PIECE
```

PIECE is a user-defined type, having the following format:

```
Type PIECE
    IdxMover As Integer
    IdxSquare As Integer
End Type
```

The *IdxMover* field indicates whether the piece belongs to the player or the computer; it is set either to *PLAYER (= 1)* or *COMPUTER (= 2)*. The *IdxSquare* field contains the index of the square currently holding the piece.

Note: If the piece belongs to the player, the index in *IdxSquare* refers to the player's row of Squares—that is, Squares(PLAYER, ...); if the piece belongs to the computer, the index refers to the computer's row of Squares—that is, Squares(COMPUTER, ...).

InitNewGame initializes Pieces so that each piece is placed within the appropriate home base (as shown in Figure 9-1). *InitNewGame* also assigns *8* to the *NumPieces* variable, which holds the number of pieces currently on the board. During the game, the number of pieces can decrease because pieces are removed as soon as they reach the center square.

Before terminating, *InitNewGame* calls the procedure *DrawPieces* to draw the playing pieces at their initial locations on the board.

Drawing the Pieces

Whenever the playing pieces need to be drawn or redrawn, the program calls the general procedure *DrawPieces*. Specifically, this procedure is called whenever a new game is started (by *InitNewGame*) or whenever a piece is removed from or added to a square on the playing board (by the *ComputerMove*, *Form_MouseDown*, or *Form_MouseUp* procedures).

DrawPieces draws all the playing pieces currently stored in the Pieces array. For each element of Pieces, the procedure draws the type of piece (COMPUTER or PLAYER) indicated by the *IdxMover* field, within the square indicated by the *IdxSquare* field.

As occurs in the Tic Tac Toe program, the Ludo program redraws *all* the pieces, even if only a single piece has been moved, because the pieces overlap and must therefore be drawn in a specific order. Ludo starts drawing the leftmost piece in the highest row and proceeds drawing pieces row by row toward the bottom of the board. (A given piece may overlap the piece immediately above it or to its immediate left.)

F Y I

The program maintains the elements of the Pieces array in the order in which the corresponding pieces should be drawn on the board. Therefore, *DrawPieces* can simply loop through this array, drawing the pieces in the same order in which they occur in the array. (Each time the program places a piece at a new position on the board, it calls the *AddPiece* procedure, which inserts an entry for the piece into the appropriate position within the array.)

DrawPieces draws the pieces within the main form, directly on top of the bitmap depicting the playing board. As in Tic Tac Toe (Chapter 8), the procedure draws each piece by calling the *BitBlt* function (described in Figure 7-12 on page 191) twice, first to transfer a mask drawing and then to transfer an image drawing. For example, *DrawPieces* makes the following calls to *BitBlt* to draw one of the computer's pieces:

```
BitBlt hDC, Squares(COMPUTER, Pieces(I).IdxSquare).X - 3,
  Squares(COMPUTER, Pieces(I).IdxSquare).Y - 3, 16, 16,
  PictureMsk.hDC, 0, 0, SRCAND
BitBlt hDC, Squares(COMPUTER, Pieces(I).IdxSquare).X - 3,
  Squares(COMPUTER, Pieces(I).IdxSquare).Y - 3, 16, 16,
  PictureRedImg.hDC, 0, 0, SRCINVERT
```

The mask drawing for either the computer's piece or the player's piece is stored in the PictureMsk picture box. The image drawing for the computer's piece is stored in PictureRedImg, and the image drawing for the player's piece is stored in PictureYelImg. The -3 terms make the upper left corner of the piece appear 3 pixels above and to the left of the playing square. (For an explanation of this drawing method, see Chapter 8, the section titled "The Drawing Technique.")

F Y I

Immediately before each call to *DrawImages*, the program calls Visual Basic's *Cls* method to erase the previous pieces from the board.

Responding to the Command Button

After a new game has been initialized by *InitNewGame*, the basic flow of program control is as follows: When ready for the next step, the player clicks the Command1 command button, and the *Command1_Click* event procedure receives control. This procedure then performs the appropriate action based on the current value of the form-level variable *State*. After completing this action, the procedure resets *Start* to a value indicating the action that is to be performed the next time the player clicks the button. If necessary, the procedure also changes the caption on the command button to indicate the next action. This basic cycle continues until the game has been won or the player chooses the New Game menu command while a game is in progress.

> **F Y I**
>
> To make the program more readable, each of the *State* values is defined as a symbolic constant in the (declarations) section.

The *Command1_Click* procedure thus serves as the main program dispatcher. The following table indicates the actions it performs for each value of the *State* variable. Remember that whenever a new game is started, the *InitNewGame* procedure initializes *State* to the value START.

Value of *State*	Action Initiated by *Command1_Click*
START	Computer rolls die to determine who gets first turn; computer's score is saved; *State* is set to FIRSTROLL.
FIRSTROLL	Player rolls die to determine who gets first turn; if player's score is smaller than computer's score, *State* is set to COMPMOVE; if player's score is larger than computer's score, *State* is set to ROLL; if scores are equal, *State* is reset to START.
COMPMOVE	*ComputerMove* procedure is called, which rolls die and moves computer's piece; if score is 6, it sets *State* to COMPMOVE; if score is less than 6, it sets *State* to ROLL; if computer has won the game, it sets *State* to GAMEOVER and hides the command button.

(continued)

continued

Value of *State*	Action Initiated by *Command1_Click*
ROLL	Player rolls die for next move; score is saved in the form-level variable *PlayScore*; *State* is initially set to OK; *State* remains set to OK if player clicks the Pass button; however, if player makes a valid move, *PictureBoard-_DragDrop* procedure sets *State* to ROLL if score is 6, to COMPMOVE if score is less than 6, or to GAMEOVER if the player has won the game.
OK	If player's score is 6, sets *State* to ROLL; otherwise, calls *ComputerMove* procedure (described above, for the COMPMOVE routine).

When the game has been won, *State* is set to the value GAMEOVER and the command button is made invisible until the player chooses the New Game command. The *InitNewGame* procedure then makes the button visible again and sets the value of *State* to START.

Rolling the Die

Whenever the program needs to roll the die, it calls the function *RollIt*. This function simulates the roll of a die by successively displaying eight die faces within the PictureDie picture box. The images of the die faces are stored within the PictureDice picture box array (invisible at runtime) and are randomly selected using the Visual Basic random-number generator. (See the section titled "Generating Random Sequences" in Chapter 4). *RollIt* returns the value of the final face displayed; this number is used as the value of the roll.

To make the simulation more realistic, *RollIt* pauses for 0.05 seconds after displaying each face, by calling the general procedure *Pause*:

```
Pause .05
```

Pause uses Visual Basic's *Timer* function, which returns the time (in seconds) that has elapsed since midnight. *Pause* contains a loop that repeatedly checks *Timer* until the amount of time specified by the parameter has elapsed.

Note: While the *Pause* procedure is running, other applications cannot process events, and the player cannot activate other windows or perform other tasks. Since the Ludo program specifies a pause of only 0.05 seconds, this does not present a problem.

T I P

To make the *Pause* procedure suitable for creating longer delays, you could insert a call to Visual Basic's *DoEvents* function into the delay loop. Calling *DoEvents* allows the system to process any pending events, thus preventing the procedure from blocking other processes. Keep in mind, however, that if *DoEvents* is called from within an event procedure, the event procedure might be called again while the procedure is already active; your code must be able to handle such recursive calls. See the section titled "Allowing the User to Interrupt the Process" in Chapter 7 for more information on this topic and for an example of the use of *DoEvents*.

Moving the Computer's Piece

As you saw, *Command1_Click* calls the general procedure *ComputerMove* to handle the computer's move. *ComputerMove* begins by calling *RollIt* to roll the die. The procedure must then determine whether a move is possible, and if more than one move is possible, it must attempt to choose the best one. *ComputerMove* does this by assigning a numeric value to each of the computer's pieces, indicating whether the piece can be moved, and if so, the relative benefit of moving it. Because the locations of all the current playing pieces are stored in the Pieces array, the procedure loops through this array and assigns a value to each piece according to the rules listed in the following table.

Type of Move	Value Assigned to Move
The piece is on the home base and can be moved to the starting square.	30
The piece is on one of the last six squares and can be moved directly to the center square (the finish).	25
The piece is on the starting square and can be moved off this square.	20
The piece can be moved onto a square occupied by one of the player's pieces (thereby sending that piece back to its home base).	15

(continued)

300

continued

Type of Move	Value Assigned to Move
The piece is not on one of the last six squares but can be moved onto one of these squares.	10
None of the above situations exist, but the piece can be moved.	5
The piece cannot be moved, the piece is on one of the last six squares and cannot be moved to the finish, or the piece belongs to the player.	0

The *ComputerMove* procedure then moves the piece having the highest value, provided that this value is greater than 0. To move the piece, it does the following:

1. It removes the piece from its current position in the Squares array, as follows:

```
For I = HighIdx To NumPieces - 1
    Pieces(I) = Pieces(I + 1)
Next I
NumPieces = NumPieces - 1
```

(*HighIdx* is the index of the piece having the highest value.)

2. It moves the piece to its new position within Squares by calling the general procedure *AddPiece*:

```
AddPiece COMPUTER, TargetSquare
```

3. If one of the player's pieces is in the target square, the procedure moves that piece back to its home square, using the method employed in steps 1 and 2, above.

4. It redraws all the pieces in Squares by calling *Cls* and *DrawPieces*:

```
Cls
DrawPieces
```

5. If the computer has won the game (that is, none of its pieces are left in Squares), rather than performing step 4, the procedure terminates the game by setting *State* to GAMEOVER and enables the timer. The timer routine then beeps and flashes the winning message.

Moving the Player's Piece

After taking a turn and rolling the die, the player is permitted to move a piece on the board. As usual, the player begins a move by pressing the mouse button while the mouse pointer is over one of the player's pieces. The move operation is then processed by the following three event procedures:

1. The *Form_MouseDown* procedure initiates the move operation.

2. The *Form_MouseMove* procedure redraws the image of the piece at each new location of the mouse pointer.

3. The *Form_MouseUp* procedure terminates the move operation.

During a move operation, the normal mouse pointer is hidden, and an image of the piece appears in its place. Also, the mouse pointer is confined to the portion of the form surrounding the playing board. The method used for managing the mouse pointer is the same as that used when moving picture boxes in the Word Squares and Queens games. (See Chapter 5 for a complete explanation.) The primary difference in the method used by Ludo is that the *MouseMove* procedure redraws the image in each new mouse pointer location rather than simply moving a picture box.

The *Form_MouseDown* Procedure

The *Form_MouseDown* event procedure receives control whenever the player presses the mouse button while the mouse pointer is over the form. This procedure exits immediately if *State* is not currently set to *OK*; as explained previously, the value *OK* indicates that the player has just finished rolling the die and is therefore permitted to move a piece.

If a move is allowed, the procedure calls the general function *PieceHit* to determine whether the mouse pointer is on one of the player's pieces:

```
Idx = PieceHit(X, Y, XOffset, YOffset)
```

If the mouse pointer is within the area occupied by one of the player's pieces, *PieceHit* returns the index of the piece within the Pieces array. In this case, the procedure also assigns to the *XOffset* and *YOffset* parameters the horizontal and vertical offsets of the mouse pointer from the upper left corner of the piece. These variables are later used by the *Form_MouseMove* procedure so that it can properly position the image of the piece and by the *SquareHit* function so that it can derive the position of the piece from the position of the mouse pointer.

If the mouse pointer is *not* over one of the player's pieces, *SquareHit* returns a value of *0*. In this case, *Form_MouseMove* exits immediately:

```
If Idx = 0 Then Exit Sub
```

If the mouse pointer is located over a piece, *Form_MouseDown* proceeds to initiate a move operation. To do this, it first executes a series of statements to control the mouse pointer. These statements use Windows API functions and are the same as those employed in the Word Squares and Queens games. (These statements are fully explained in Chapter 5.) Here is a review of the main *Form_MouseDown* steps:

1. It calls *ShowCursor* to hide the mouse pointer.
2. It calls *SetCapture* to ensure that the main form processes all mouse events.
3. It calls *ClipCursor* to confine the mouse pointer to the area of the form surrounding the playing board.

Previous games have used *ClipCursor* to confine the mouse pointer to the *entire* area within the form. Ludo, however, confines the mouse pointer to a *portion* of the form—specifically, the area surrounding the playing board. This is done because a small problem would occur if the piece were moved into an area occupied by one of the visible controls (the picture box, label, or command button): The moving piece is drawn within the form itself; a visible control, however, always *covers* the underlying graphics belonging to the form. Consequently, if the piece were moved into an area of the form occupied by a control, the piece would become partially or completely invisible, giving the impression that it is sliding underneath the control. (In contrast, an object that is moved by means of the Visual Basic drag-and-drop facility always appears on *top* of a control.)

Form_MouseDown next sets the value of the *MoveOrigin* variable:

```
MoveOrigin = Pieces(Idx).IdxSquare
```

MoveOrigin stores the index (to the Squares array) of the square containing the piece at the beginning of the move. This variable is used by the other procedures that manage the move, and it serves a double purpose. First, if *MoveOrigin* is set to a value other than 0, the *Form-_MouseMove* and *Form_MouseUp* event procedures know that a move operation is in progress. (At the end of the move, *Form_MouseUp* sets *MoveOrigin* back to *0*.) Second, if the piece is dropped on an invalid location, *MoveOrigin* supplies the index of the square to which the piece must be returned.

Next, *Form_MouseDown* initializes the variables *PrevX* and *PrevY* with the current location of the piece:

```
PrevX = Squares(PLAYER, MoveOrigin).X - 3
PrevY = Squares(PLAYER, MoveOrigin).Y - 3
```

These variables tell the *Form_MouseMove* procedure the previous location of the piece so that the procedure can erase the piece from that location before it draws the piece at its new location. The -3 terms are required because the upper left corner of the piece is to be drawn 3 pixels above and to the left of the playing square.

Form_MouseDown then issues a series of statements to initialize the graphics stored in the PictureSav picture box:

```
'Remove the piece from the board:
Cls
Pieces(Idx).IdxMover = EMPTY    'Prevents DrawPieces from
                                'drawing the piece.
DrawPieces

'Save the image of the blank square:
BitBlt PictureSav.hDC, 0, 0, 16, 16, hDC, PrevX, PrevY, SRCCOPY

'Replace the piece:
Pieces(Idx).IdxMover = PLAYER
DrawPieces
```

By means of these statements, *Form_MouseDown* temporarily removes the piece from its square on the playing board and then saves the image of the blank square in *PictureSav*. (When the player begins moving the mouse, *Form_MouseMove* will use *PictureSav* to erase the piece from its initial location.) *Form_MouseDown* then replaces the piece within the square that it originally occupied, to prevent the piece from disappearing when the player first presses the mouse button.

Finally, *Form_MouseDown* removes the piece from the Pieces array:

```
For I = Idx To NumPieces - 1
    Pieces(I) = Pieces(I + 1)
Next I
NumPieces = NumPieces - 1
```

When the piece is later dropped, it will be reinserted into the proper position within Squares.

The *Form_MouseMove* Procedure

As the player moves the mouse, certain MouseMove events occur. On each event, the *Form_MouseMove* procedure redraws the image at the new location of the mouse pointer.

If a move operation is in progress (that is, *MoveOrigin <> 0*), *Form-_MouseMove* redraws the image by following these steps:

1. It erases the image of the piece at the previous location by calling *BitBlt* to restore the graphics that were saved in *PictureSav:*

```
BitBlt hDC, PrevX, PrevY, 16, 16, PictureSav.hDC, 0, 0,
  SRCCOPY
```

2. It sets *PrevX* and *PrevY* to the new location of the piece:

```
PrevX = X - XOffset
PrevY = Y - YOffset
```

Notice that rather than placing the upper left corner of the piece at the exact location of the mouse pointer (*X, Y*), the initial offsets of the pointer from the upper left corner of the piece (*XOffset* and *YOffset*) are subtracted, preventing the piece from jumping abruptly on the first MouseMove event.

3. It saves the underlying graphics at the new location of the piece (so that the graphics can be restored when the piece moves on to the next location):

```
BitBlt PictureSav.hDC, 0, 0, 16, 16, hDC, PrevX,
  PrevY, SRCCOPY
```

4. It draws the piece at its new location using *BitBlt* to transfer the mask drawing and then the image drawing:

```
BitBlt hDC, PrevX, PrevY, 16, 16, PictureMsk.hDC,
  0, 0, SRCAND
BitBlt hDC, PrevX, PrevY, 16, 16, PictureYelImg.hDC,
  0, 0, SRCINVERT
```

5. It calls *Refresh* to make visible the results of the bit transfers.
    Note: If the AutoRedraw property of a form or picture box is set to True, you must call the *Refresh* method to make visible the results of a *BitBlt* call. If, however, the procedure

calling *BitBlt* also makes one or more calls to standard Visual Basic drawing methods, calling *Refresh* is unnecessary because, in this case, Visual Basic will automatically refresh the graphics.

The *Form_MouseUp* Procedure

When the player finally releases the mouse button to deposit the piece in its new location, the *Form_MouseUp* event procedure receives control. If *MoveOrigin* is *0*, indicating that a move operation is not in progress, the procedure exits immediately. Otherwise, the procedure begins by calling the *ShowCursor, ReleaseCapture,* and *ClipCursor* Windows API functions to release control of the mouse pointer. (These function calls are discussed in Chapter 5, in the section titled "Processing the MouseUp Event.")

Form_MouseUp then tests whether the piece has been dropped on a valid square. If it has, the procedure moves the piece to that square; otherwise, the procedure returns the piece to the square from which it originated (stored in the variable *MoveOrigin*). As with the *ComputerMove* procedure, described previously, the procedure positions the piece in the new location by calling *AddPiece* and redraws the squares by calling *Cls* and *DrawPieces*. If the target square contains one of the computer's pieces, that piece is sent back to the computer's home base. Also, if none of the player's pieces are left, the procedure terminates the game and displays the winning message.

Notice that *Form_MouseUp* resets the *State* variable (as explained previously) only if the player has made a valid move. Otherwise, the procedure leaves *State* set to OK, which lets the player try again to move the piece correctly.

Finally, *Form_MouseUp* resets *MoveOrigin* to *0* to indicate that the move operation has ended.

Enhancing the Game

Here are a few suggestions for enhancing the Ludo program.

- Increase the total number of players to 4. Allow from 0 through 4 players to participate, and have the computer supply any missing players. For example, if one human player participated, the computer would serve as the other three players. If no human players participated, the game would be played by four computer-generated players, and you could sit back and watch (perhaps placing bets on the outcome!).

■ Increase the computer's skill level. The rules that the computer uses to select its moves (in the procedure *Computer-Move*) are quite simple. You could refine these rules or create additional ones. For example, the computer could study the positions of the player's pieces; it could then attempt to position a piece *behind* an opponent's piece whenever possible, to increase its chances of sending the piece back to the home base. Similarly, the computer could avoid placing a piece six squares or less in front of an opponent's piece.

■ Allow the player to save the current game. Some games take quite a while to complete. You could let the player save the state of the current game in a disk file so that this game could be resumed the next time the player runs the program. (The method for saving information in the WIN.INI file is discussed in Chapter 11.)

■ Flash the pieces of the player who wins the roll of the die and the right to move first.

CHAPTER TEN

RINGO

Ringo is a game of tactics that originated in Germany. One player is the attacker, who tries to capture the "fortress" at the center of the circular playing board. The other player is the defender, who tries to seize all of the attacker's pieces before the fortress can be taken. In the computer version of the game presented in this chapter, you play as the defender and the computer plays as the attacker.

The source code for Ringo demonstrates how to create device-independent graphics using Visual Basic drawing statements in conjunction with the twip scale mode. As in previous games, Ringo uses the Windows API *BitBlt* function to animate and draw the playing pieces. Ringo also demonstrates methods for calculating optimal game moves and for hit-testing within nonrectangular areas (that is, for determining whether the mouse pointer is within one of the playing areas).

Playing Ringo

When you run Ringo (RG.EXE), the program starts a game. Your playing pieces are yellow; initially, you have four pieces arranged around the fortress, which is the black area in the center of the playing board. The computer's pieces are red; initially, the computer has seven pieces arranged around the outside of the playing board. Figure 10-1 on the following page shows Ringo at the beginning of a game.

During the game, you and the computer take turns making moves. The computer (the "attacker") attempts to move its pieces into the fortress; if the computer manages to place two pieces within the fortress, it wins the game. If you (the "defender") manage to eliminate all but one of the computer's pieces before it can move two pieces into the fortress, you win the game.

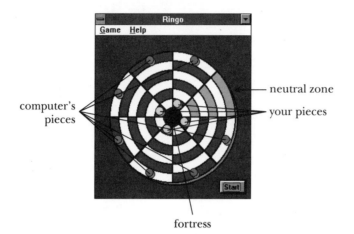

computer's pieces

neutral zone

your pieces

fortress

Figure 10-1.
Ringo at the beginning of a game.

To begin playing, click the Start button. The computer makes the first move. (According to the traditional rules for Ringo, the attacker always moves first.) Thereafter, the computer moves as soon as you have completed your move (or have clicked the Pass button to skip your turn). The computer moves according to the following rules:

- The computer can *move* a piece into the adjoining space toward the center of the board or to either side of the piece, provided that the target space is empty. (See Figure 10-2.)

- The computer can *jump* one of its pieces over one of your pieces and into an empty space on the other side. Your piece must be in an adjoining space toward the center of the board or on either side of the computer's piece. If the computer jumps over one of your pieces, that piece is removed from the board. (See Figure 10-2.)

- The computer, however, cannot jump over one of your pieces if your piece is in the "neutral zone." The neutral zone is the sector of the playing area that contains green and white areas, the sector just above the three-o'clock position. (See Figure 10-1.) The opposite is also true: You cannot jump over a computer piece that is in the neutral zone.

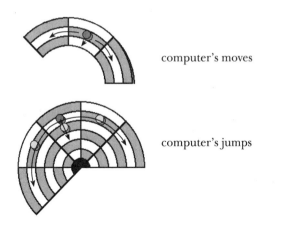

computer's moves

computer's jumps

Figure 10-2.
The computer's moves and jumps.

After the computer makes its first move, it is your turn to move a piece. To move one of your pieces, use the mouse to drag your piece from its current position to a new position, observing the following rules:

- You can *move* a piece into any of the four adjoining spaces (toward the center of the board, away from the center, or on either side), provided that the target space is empty. (See Figure 10-3 on the following page.)

- You cannot move a piece into the fortress.

- You can *jump* a piece over one of the computer's pieces in an adjoining space (in any direction) and into an empty space on the other side. The computer's piece will be removed from the board. (See Figure 10-3.)

- You can also jump a piece over one of the computer's pieces that is located within the fortress. Your piece must be within a space adjoining the fortress, and the space on the opposite side of the fortress must be empty. (See Figure 10-3.)

- You cannot, however, jump over one of the computer's pieces if it is located within the neutral zone.

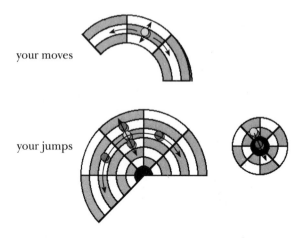

your moves

your jumps

Figure 10-3.
Your moves and jumps.

Note: If you attempt an invalid move, the computer will beep and then return your piece to its original position.

You are not required to make a move. If you choose not to move, simply click the Pass button to skip your turn. After you complete a valid move or click the Pass button, the computer makes its next move. You and the computer will continue to alternate turns throughout the remainder of the game.

Note: If you drop a piece on a valid position, you cannot undo your move because the computer makes its next move immediately. If, while dragging a piece around the board, you forget which space the piece came from, you can easily return it to its original location by dropping it outside the board.

The game continues until either the computer wins by placing two pieces within the fortress or you win by removing all but one of the computer's pieces. You can then start a new game by choosing the New Game command from the Game menu. (As usual, if you choose this command before completing a game, the current game ends and a new game starts.)

Strategy and Hints

The following guidelines, the first defensive and the second offensive, will help you win more games.

- Your greatest disadvantage is that you begin a game with fewer pieces than the computer. Accordingly, be very careful not to let the computer capture any of your pieces. Look before you drop, and avoid intentionally sacrificing a piece. If you lose a piece near the beginning or middle of a game, you will be at a great disadvantage. Losing a piece near the conclusion of a game, however, might be unavoidable.

- Your greatest advantage is that you can move or jump in one of four directions, while the computer can move in one of only three directions. Capitalize on this advantage by attempting to move your pieces around and *behind* the computer's pieces. After you have placed a piece immediately behind an enemy piece, you might be able to jump it without the risk that it will jump you. To move a piece behind the enemy lines, go through the neutral zone whenever possible, where the piece is immune from attack while in transit.

Coding Ringo

The source code for the Ringo program is contained in the files listed in the following table.

File	Purpose
GLOBALRG.BAS	Contains global type definitions
RG.FRM	Defines the main form, FormMain, and the controls it contains
RGABOUT.FRM	Defines the ABOUT form, FormAbout, and the controls it contains
RG.MAK	Contains the Ringo project file

Figures 10-4 through 10-9 beginning on the following page present the form designs, properties, menu commands, and source code for the Ringo program.

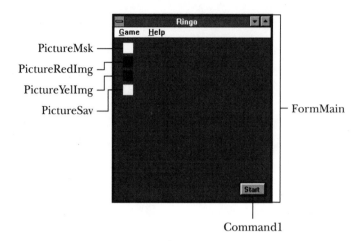

PictureMsk

PictureRedImg

PictureYelImg

PictureSav

FormMain

Command1

Figure 10-4.
RG.FRM at design time.

Object Name	Object Type	Property	Setting
Command1	Command button	BackColor	&H00008080& [dark yellow]
		Caption	Start
		Default	True
		Height	375 [twips]
		Left	3360 [twips]
		Top	3720 [twips]
		Width	735 [twips]
FormMain	Form	AutoRedraw	True
		BackColor	&H00008080& [dark yellow]
		BorderStyle	1 - Fixed Single
		Caption	Ringo
		FormName	FormMain
		Grid Height	120 [twips]
		Grid Width	120 [twips]
		Height	4890 [twips]

Figure 10-5.   *(continued)*
RG.FRM form and control properties.

314

Figure 10-5 *continued*

Object Name	Object Type	Property	Setting
		Icon	(Icon) [RG.ICO]
		Left	1035 [twips]
		MaxButton	False
		Top	1140 [twips]
		Width	4320 [twips]
PictureMsk	Picture box	AutoRedraw	True
		BackColor	&H00FFFFFF& [white]
		BorderStyle	0 - None
		CtlName	PictureMsk
		FillStyle	0 - Solid
		Height	270 [twips]
		Left	240 [twips]
		Top	120 [twips]
		Visible	False
		Width	270 [twips]
PictureRedImg	Picture box	AutoRedraw	True
		BackColor	&H00000000& [black]
		BorderStyle	0 - None
		CtlName	PictureRedImg
		FillStyle	0 - Solid
		Height	270 [twips]
		Left	240 [twips]
		Top	480 [twips]
		Visible	False
		Width	270 [twips]
PictureSav	Picture box	AutoRedraw	True
		BorderStyle	0 - None
		CtlName	PictureSav
		FillStyle	0 - Solid
		Height	270 [twips]
		Left	240 [twips]

(continued)

Figure 10-5 *continued*

Object Name	Object Type	Property	Setting
		Top	1200 [twips]
		Visible	False
		Width	270 [twips]
PictureYelImg	Picture box	AutoRedraw	True
		BackColor	&H00000000& [black]
		BorderStyle	0 - None
		CtlName	PictureYelImg
		FillStyle	0 - Solid
		Height	270 [twips]
		Left	240 [twips]
		Top	840 [twips]
		Visible	False
		Width	270 [twips]

Indentation/Caption	Control Name	Other Features
&Game	MenuGame	
....&New Game	MenuNew	
....-	MenuSep1	
....E&xit	MenuExit	
&Help	MenuHelp	
....&Index	MenuIndex	Accelerator = F1
....&How to Play	MenuHowTo	
....&Commands	MenuCommands	
....&Using Help	MenuUsingHelp	
....-	MenuSep2	
....&About Ringo...	MenuAbout	

Figure 10-6.
RG.FRM menu design.

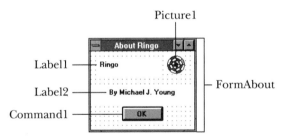

Figure 10-7.

RGABOUT.FRM at design time.

Object Name	Object Type	Property	Setting
Command1	Command button	Caption	OK
		Default	True
		Height	375 [twips]
		Left	840 [twips]
		Top	1440 [twips]
		Width	1095 [twips]
FormAbout	Form	BorderStyle	3 - Fixed Double
		Caption	About Ringo
		FormName	FormAbout
		Grid Height	120 [twips]
		Grid Width	120 [twips]
		Height	2445 [twips]
		Left	1605 [twips]
		MaxButton	False
		MinButton	False
		Top	2085 [twips]
		Width	2880 [twips]
Label1	Label	Caption	Ringo
		Height	375 [twips]
		Left	240 [twips]

Figure 10-8. *(continued)*

RGABOUT.FRM form and control properties.

Figure 10-8 *continued*

Object Name	Object Type	Property	Setting
		Top	240 [twips]
		Width	1575 [twips]
Label2	Label	Alignment	2 - Center
		Caption	By Michael J. Young
		Height	375 [twips]
		Left	0 [twips]
		Top	960 [twips]
		Width	2745 [twips]
Picture1	Picture box	AutoSize	True
		BorderStyle	0 - None
		Height	480 [twips]
		Left	2040 [twips]
		Picture	(Icon) [RG.ICO]
		Top	120 [twips]
		Width	480 [twips]

GLOBALRG.BAS code

```
Type APIPOINT
    X As Integer
    Y As Integer
End Type

Type MOVETYPE
    Ring As Integer
    Sect As Integer
    Direct As Integer
    Score As Integer
End Type
```

Figure 10-9.   *(continued)*

Source code for the Ringo program. (Notice that long program lines are wrapped to the next line and indented one space.)

Figure 10-9 *continued*

```
Type POSITION
    Piece As Integer
    X As Integer
    Y As Integer
End Type

Type RECT
    Left As Integer
    Top As Integer
    Right As Integer
    Bottom As Integer
End Type
```

RG.FRM code

```
'Help Section:
'Help file:
Const HELP_FILE = "RG.HLP"
'WinHelp wCommand values:
Const HELP_CONTEXT = &H1
Const HELP_HELPONHELP = &H4
Const HELP_INDEX = &H3
Const HELP_QUIT = &H2
'WinHelp dwData values (help topics):
Const HELP_HOWTOPLAY = 10&
Const HELP_COMMANDS = 20&
'Windows help API:
Declare Sub WinHelp Lib "USER" (ByVal hWnd As Integer,
 ByVal lpHelpFile As String, ByVal wCommand As Integer,
 ByVal dwData As Long)

'constants for drawing:
Const PI = 3.14159265
Const RADIUS = 1700
Const XCENT = 2100
Const YCENT = 2100

'constants for "Piece" field of PosTable:
Const NONE = 0
Const RED = 1
Const YEL = 2
```

(continued)

Figure 10-9 *continued*

```
'constants for size of picture boxes:
Const HEIGHTPIC = 270
Const WIDTHPIC = 270

'constants for direction of move ("Direct" field of MOVETYPE):
Const CCW = 0
Const CCWJMP = 1
Const CW = 2
Const CWJMP = 3
Const IN = 4
Const INJMP = 5

'constants for CompMove return values:
Const PLAY = 0
Const REDWIN = 1
Const YELWIN = 2


Dim GameOver As Integer
Dim MoveRing As Integer
Dim MoveSect As Integer
Dim NumRedPieces As Integer
Dim NumYelPieces As Integer
Dim PicHPix As Integer   'Picture Height in Pixels (for BitBlt)
Dim PicWPix As Integer   'Picture Width in Pixels (for BitBlt)
Dim PosTable(1 To 7, 1 To 8) As POSITION
Dim PrevXPix As Integer
Dim PrevYPix As Integer
Dim XOffset As Integer
Dim XPPT As Single        'X Pixels Per Twip
Dim YOffset As Integer
Dim YPPT As Single        'Y Pixels Per Twip


Const SRCAND = &H8800C6        'dest = source AND dest
Const SRCCOPY = &HCC0020       'dest = source
Const SRCINVERT = &H660046     'dest = source XOR dest
Declare Sub BitBlt Lib "GDI" (ByVal HDestDC%, ByVal X%,
  ByVal Y%, ByVal nWidth%, ByVal nHeight%, ByVal HSrcDC%,
  ByVal XSrc%, ByVal YSrc%, ByVal ROP&)


Const LOGPIXELSX = 88
Const LOGPIXELSY = 90
Declare Function GetDeviceCaps Lib "GDI" (ByVal hDC%,
  ByVal Index%) As Integer
```

(continued)

Figure 10-9 *continued*

```
Declare Sub ClientToScreen Lib "USER" (ByVal hWnd As Integer,
 Pt As APIPOINT)
Declare Sub ClipCursor Lib "USER" (Rec As Any)
Declare Sub ReleaseCapture Lib "USER" ()
Declare Sub SetCapture Lib "USER" (ByVal hWnd As Integer)
Declare Sub ShowCursor Lib "USER" (ByVal ShowIt As Integer)

Function AreaHit (X As Single, Y As Single, Ring As Integer,
 Sect As Integer)
    Dim DX As Integer    'Cartesian change in X
    Dim DXS As Single    'DX squared
    Dim DY As Integer    'Cartesian change in Y
    Dim DYS As Single    'DY squared
    Dim Rad As Integer   'radius

    DX = X - XCENT
    DY = YCENT - Y

    'find ring:
    DXS = DX: DXS = DXS * DXS
    DYS = DY: DYS = DYS * DYS
    Rad = Sqr(DXS + DYS)
    Ring = Rad \ (RADIUS / 7)
    Ring = 7 - Ring
    If Ring < 1 Then
        AreaHit = 0
        Exit Function
    End If
    If Ring = 7 Then
        Sect = 1
        AreaHit = -1
        Exit Function
    End If

    'find sector:
    If DX >= 0 And DY >= 0 Then       'quadrant 1: upper right
        If DX = 0 Then DX = 1
        If Atn(DY / DX) >= PI / 4 Then
            Sect = 2
        Else
            Sect = 1
        End If
```

(continued)

Figure 10-9 *continued*

```
      ElseIf DX < 0 And DY >= 0 Then   'quadrant 2: upper left
          If Atn(-DY / DX) >= PI / 4 Then
              Sect = 3
          Else
              Sect = 4
          End If
      ElseIf DX < 0 And DY < 0 Then    'quadrant 3: lower left
          If Atn(DY / DX) >= PI / 4 Then
              Sect = 6
          Else
              Sect = 5
          End If
      Else                             'quadrant 4: lower right
          If DX = 0 Then DX = 1
          If Atn(-DY / DX) > PI / 4 Then
              Sect = 7
          Else
              Sect = 8
          End If
      End If
      AreaHit = -1
End Function

Function CompMove ()
    Dim BestMove As MOVETYPE
    Dim Ring As Integer
    Dim Score As Integer
    Dim Sect As Integer
    Dim Targ1 As Integer
    Dim Targ2 As Integer

    If NumRedPieces < 2 Then
        CompMove = YELWIN
        Exit Function
    End If

    For Ring = 1 To 6
        For Sect = 1 To 8
            If PosTable(Ring, Sect).Piece = RED Then

                'IN:
                'move 2nd piece into fortress:
                If Ring = 6 And PosTable(7, 1).Piece = RED
```

(continued)

Figure 10-9 *continued*

```
Then
                    PosTable(Ring, Sect).Piece = NONE
                    CompMove = REDWIN
                    Exit Function
            End If

            'jump 2nd piece into fortress:
            If Sect <> 1 And Ring = 5 And PosTable(6,
 Sect).Piece = YEL And PosTable(7, 1).Piece = RED Then
                    PosTable(Ring, Sect).Piece = NONE
                    PosTable(6, Sect).Piece = NONE
                    NumYelPieces = NumYelPieces - 1
                    CompMove = REDWIN
                    Exit Function
            End If

            'jump 1st piece into fortress:
            If Sect <> 1 And Ring = 5 And PosTable(6,
 Sect).Piece = YEL And PosTable(7, 1).Piece = NONE Then
                    PosTable(6, Sect).Piece = NONE
                    If PosSafe(7, 1) Then
                        Score = 20
                    Else
                        Score = 10
                    End If
                    PosTable(6, Sect).Piece = YEL
                    If Score > BestMove.Score Then
                        BestMove.Ring = Ring
                        BestMove.Sect = Sect
                        BestMove.Direct = INJMP
                        BestMove.Score = Score
                    End If
            End If

            'jump, not into fortress:
            If Sect <> 1 And Ring < 5 Then
                    If PosTable(Ring + 1, Sect).Piece = YEL
 And PosTable(Ring + 2, Sect).Piece = NONE Then
                        PosTable(Ring + 1, Sect).Piece = NONE
                        If PosSafe(Ring + 2, Sect) Then
                            Score = 19
                        Else
                            Score = 9
```

(continued)

Figure 10-9 *continued*

```
                        End If
                        PosTable(Ring + 1, Sect).Piece = YEL
                    End If
                    If Score > BestMove.Score Then
                        BestMove.Ring = Ring
                        BestMove.Sect = Sect
                        BestMove.Direct = INJMP
                        BestMove.Score = Score
                    End If
                End If

                'move 1st piece into fortress:
                If Ring = 6 And PosTable(7, 1).Piece = NONE
Then
                    PosTable(Ring, Sect).Piece = NONE
                    If PosSafe(7, 1) Then
                        Score = 18
                    Else
                        Score = 8
                    End If
                    PosTable(Ring, Sect).Piece = RED
                    If Score > BestMove.Score Then
                        BestMove.Ring = Ring
                        BestMove.Sect = Sect
                        BestMove.Direct = IN
                        BestMove.Score = Score
                    End If
                End If

                'move in:
                If PosTable(Ring + 1, Sect).Piece = NONE Then
                    PosTable(Ring, Sect).Piece = NONE
                    If PosSafe(Ring + 1, Sect) Then
                        Score = 17
                    Else
                        Score = 7
                    End If
                    PosTable(Ring, Sect).Piece = RED
                    If Score > BestMove.Score Then
                        BestMove.Ring = Ring
                        BestMove.Sect = Sect
                        BestMove.Direct = IN
                        BestMove.Score = Score
```

(continued)

Figure 10-9 *continued*

```
                    End If
            End If

            'CW:
            If Sect = 1 Then
                Targ1 = 8
                Targ2 = 7
            ElseIf Sect = 2 Then
                Targ1 = 1
                Targ2 = 8
            Else
                Targ1 = Sect - 1
                Targ2 = Sect - 2
            End If

            'jump:
            If Sect <> 2 And PosTable(Ring, Targ1).Piece
  = YEL And PosTable(Ring, Targ2).Piece = NONE Then
                PosTable(Ring, Targ1).Piece = NONE
                If PosSafe(Ring, Targ2) Then
                    Score = 19
                Else
                    Score = 9
                End If
                PosTable(Ring, Targ1).Piece = YEL
                If Score > BestMove.Score Then
                    BestMove.Ring = Ring
                    BestMove.Sect = Sect
                    BestMove.Direct = CWJMP
                    BestMove.Score = Score
                End If
            End If

            'move sideways:
            If PosTable(Ring, Targ1).Piece = NONE Then
                PosTable(Ring, Sect).Piece = NONE
                If PosSafe(Ring, Targ1) Then
                    Score = 16
                Else
                    Score = 6
                End If
                PosTable(Ring, Sect).Piece = RED
```

(continued)

Figure 10-9 *continued*

```
                          If Score > BestMove.Score Then
                              BestMove.Ring = Ring
                              BestMove.Sect = Sect
                              BestMove.Direct = CW
                              BestMove.Score = Score
                          End If
                      End If

                      'CCW:
                      If Sect = 8 Then
                          Targ1 = 1
                          Targ2 = 2
                      ElseIf Sect = 7 Then
                          Targ1 = 8
                          Targ2 = 1
                      Else
                          Targ1 = Sect + 1
                          Targ2 = Sect + 2
                      End If

                      'jump:
                      If Sect <> 8 And PosTable(Ring, Targ1).Piece
= YEL And PosTable(Ring, Targ2).Piece = NONE Then
                          PosTable(Ring, Targ1).Piece = NONE
                          If PosSafe(Ring, Targ2) Then
                              Score = 19
                          Else
                              Score = 9
                          End If
                          PosTable(Ring, Targ1).Piece = YEL
                          If Score > BestMove.Score Then
                              BestMove.Ring = Ring
                              BestMove.Sect = Sect
                              BestMove.Direct = CCWJMP
                              BestMove.Score = Score
                          End If
                      End If

                      'move sideways:
                      If PosTable(Ring, Targ1).Piece = NONE Then
                          PosTable(Ring, Sect).Piece = NONE
                          If PosSafe(Ring, Targ1) Then
                              Score = 16
```

(continued)

Figure 10-9 *continued*

```
                            Else
                                Score = 6
                            End If
                            PosTable(Ring, Sect).Piece = RED
                            If Score > BestMove.Score Then
                                BestMove.Ring = Ring
                                BestMove.Sect = Sect
                                BestMove.Direct = CCW
                                BestMove.Score = Score
                            End If
                        End If
                    End If
                Next Sect
            Next Ring

            If BestMove.Score = 0 Then        'exit if no move possible
                CompMove = YELWIN
                Exit Function
            End If

            PosTable(BestMove.Ring, BestMove.Sect).Piece = NONE
            Select Case BestMove.Direct
                Case CCW
                    If BestMove.Sect = 8 Then
                        PosTable(BestMove.Ring, 1).Piece = RED
                    Else
                        PosTable(BestMove.Ring, BestMove.Sect
+ 1).Piece = RED
                    End If
                Case CCWJMP
                    PosTable(BestMove.Ring, BestMove.Sect + 1).Piece
= NONE
                    If BestMove.Sect = 7 Then
                        PosTable(BestMove.Ring, 1).Piece = RED
                    Else
                        PosTable(BestMove.Ring, BestMove.Sect
+ 2).Piece = RED
                    End If
                    NumYelPieces = NumYelPieces - 1
                Case CW
                    If BestMove.Sect = 1 Then
                        PosTable(BestMove.Ring, 8).Piece = RED
                    Else
```

(continued)

Figure 10-9 *continued*

```
                    PosTable(BestMove.Ring, BestMove.Sect
 - 1).Piece = RED
            End If
        Case CWJMP
            If BestMove.Sect = 1 Then
                PosTable(BestMove.Ring, 8).Piece = NONE
                PosTable(BestMove.Ring, 7).Piece = RED
            Else
                PosTable(BestMove.Ring, BestMove.Sect
 - 1).Piece = NONE
                PosTable(BestMove.Ring, BestMove.Sect
 - 2).Piece = RED
            End If
            NumYelPieces = NumYelPieces - 1
        Case IN
            If BestMove.Ring = 6 Then
                PosTable(BestMove.Ring + 1, 1).Piece = RED
            Else
                PosTable(BestMove.Ring + 1, BestMove.Sect)
.Piece = RED
            End If
        Case INJMP
            PosTable(BestMove.Ring + 1, BestMove.Sect).Piece
 = NONE
            If BestMove.Ring = 5 Then
                PosTable(BestMove.Ring + 2, 1).Piece = RED
            Else
                PosTable(BestMove.Ring + 2,
 BestMove.Sect).Piece = RED
            End If
            NumYelPieces = NumYelPieces - 1
    End Select
    If NumYelPieces = 0 Then
        CompMove = REDWIN
    Else
        CompMove = PLAY
    End If
End Function

Sub DrawImages ()
    Dim Dark As Integer
    Dim Green As Integer
    Dim Rad As Single
    Dim Theta As Single
```

(continued)

Figure 10-9 *continued*

```
'draw game board:

'gray shadow circle:
DrawWidth = 2
DrawStyle = 0
FillStyle = 0
FillColor = &HC0C0C0
Circle (XCENT + 60, YCENT + 60), RADIUS


'colored sectors and concentric circles:
For Rad = RADIUS To 2 * RADIUS / 7 - 10 Step -RADIUS / 7
    Dark = Dark Xor -1
    Green = 1
    DrawStyle = 5
    FillStyle = 0
    For Theta = PI / 4 To 2 * PI Step PI / 4
        If Dark Then
            If Green Then
                FillColor = &HFF00&      'green
            Else
                FillColor = &HFF0000     'blue
            End If
        Else
            FillColor = &HFFFFFF
        End If
        Dark = Dark Xor -1
        Green = 0
        Circle (XCENT, YCENT), Rad, , -(Theta - PI / 4),
-Theta
    Next Theta
    DrawStyle = 0
    FillStyle = 1
    Circle (XCENT, YCENT), Rad
Next Rad

'central black circle:
DrawStyle = 0
FillStyle = 0
FillColor = 0
Circle (XCENT, YCENT), RADIUS / 7

'radial lines:
For Theta = 0 To 7.1 * PI / 4 Step PI / 4
```

(continued)

Figure 10-9 *continued*

```
        Line (XCENT, YCENT)-Step(RADIUS * Cos(Theta), -
    RADIUS * Sin(Theta))
    Next Theta

    'save game board drawing in permanent bitmap:
    Picture = Image

    'draw pieces:
    PictureMsk.FillColor = &H0&
    PictureMsk.Circle (150, 150), 105
    PictureMsk.Circle (105, 105), 105

    PictureRedImg.FillColor = &HC0C0C0
    PictureRedImg.Circle (150, 150), 105
    PictureRedImg.FillColor = &HFF&
    PictureRedImg.Circle (105, 105), 105

    PictureYelImg.FillColor = &HC0C0C0
    PictureYelImg.Circle (150, 150), 105
    PictureYelImg.FillColor = &HFFFF&
    PictureYelImg.Circle (105, 105), 105
End Sub

Sub DrawPieces ()
    Dim Ring As Integer
    Dim Sect As Integer
    Dim StartRing As Integer
    Dim StepVal As Integer
    Dim StopRing As Integer

    For Sect = 1 To 8
        Select Case Sect
            Case 1
                StartRing = 7
                StopRing = 1
                StepVal = -1
            Case 2, 7, 8
                StartRing = 6
                StopRing = 1
                StepVal = -1
            Case 3, 4, 5, 6
                StartRing = 1
                StopRing = 6
                StepVal = 1
```

(continued)

Figure 10-9 *continued*

```
        End Select
        For Ring = StartRing To StopRing Step StepVal
            If PosTable(Ring, Sect).Piece = RED Then
                BitBlt hDC, PosTable(Ring, Sect).X * XPPT,
PosTable(Ring, Sect).Y * YPPT, PicWPix, PicHPix,
PictureMsk.hDC, 0, 0, SRCAND
                BitBlt hDC, PosTable(Ring, Sect).X * XPPT,
PosTable(Ring, Sect).Y * YPPT, PicWPix, PicHPix,
PictureRedImg.hDC, 0, 0, SRCINVERT
            ElseIf PosTable(Ring, Sect).Piece = YEL Then
                BitBlt hDC, PosTable(Ring, Sect).X * XPPT,
PosTable(Ring, Sect).Y * YPPT, PicWPix, PicHPix,
PictureMsk.hDC, 0, 0, SRCAND
                BitBlt hDC, PosTable(Ring, Sect).X * XPPT,
PosTable(Ring, Sect).Y * YPPT, PicWPix, PicHPix,
PictureYelImg.hDC, 0, 0, SRCINVERT
            End If
        Next Ring
    Next Sect
End Sub

Sub EndGame (Winner As Integer)
    Dim Message As String

    Beep: Beep: Beep: Beep: Beep: Beep
    Message = "Game Over" + Chr$(13) + Chr$(10)
    If Winner = REDWIN Then
        Message = Message + "The computer won!"
    Else
        Message = Message + "You won!"
    End If
    MsgBox Message, 0, "Ringo"
    Command1.Enabled = 0
    GameOver = -1
End Sub

Sub InitNewGame ()
    Dim Ring As Integer
    Dim Sect As Integer

    Cls             'erase pieces from previous game

    'place pieces at initial positions:
    For Ring = 1 To 7
```

(continued)

Figure 10-9 *continued*

```
            For Sect = 1 To 8
                PosTable(Ring, Sect).Piece = NONE
            Next Sect
        Next Ring
        For Sect = 2 To 8
            PosTable(1, Sect).Piece = RED
        Next Sect
        For Sect = 2 To 8 Step 2
            PosTable(6, Sect).Piece = YEL
        Next Sect
        DrawPieces

        NumRedPieces = 7
        NumYelPieces = 4
        Command1.Enabled = -1
        Command1.Caption = "Start"
        GameOver = -1
End Sub

Sub Pause (Interval As Single)
    Dim StartTime As Single

    StartTime = Timer
    Do While Timer < StartTime + Interval
        Loop
End Sub

Function PosHit (X As Single, Y As Single, Ring As Integer,
 Sect As Integer, XOffset As Integer, YOffset As Integer)
    Dim R As Integer
    Dim S As Integer

    For R = 1 To 7
        For S = 1 To 8
            If X >= PosTable(R, S).X And X <= PosTable(R, S).X
+ WIDTHPIC Then
                If Y >= PosTable(R, S).Y And Y <=
PosTable(R, S).Y + HEIGHTPIC Then
                    Ring = R
                    Sect = S
                    XOffset = X - PosTable(R, S).X
                    YOffset = Y - PosTable(R, S).Y
                    PosHit = -1
                    Exit Function
```

(continued)

Figure 10-9 *continued*

```
                End If
            End If
            If R = 7 Then Exit For
        Next S
    Next R
    PosHit = 0
End Function

Function PosSafe (Ring As Integer, Sect As Integer)
    Dim S As Integer
    Dim Source As Integer
    Dim Target As Integer

    If Ring < 7 And Sect = 1 Then    'safe in neutral zone
        PosSafe = -1
        Exit Function
    End If

    PosSafe = 0

    'attack in ring 7
    If Ring = 7 Then
        For S = 1 To 4
            If PosTable(6, S).Piece = YEL And PosTable(6,
S + 4).Piece = NONE Then
                Exit Function
            End If
        Next S
        For S = 5 To 8
            If PosTable(6, S).Piece = YEL And PosTable(6,
S - 4).Piece = NONE Then
                Exit Function
            End If
        Next S
        PosSafe = -1
        Exit Function
    End If

    'attack from CW direction:
    If Sect = 8 Then
        Source = 7
        Target = 1
```

(continued)

Figure 10-9 *continued*

```
    Else
        Source = Sect - 1
        Target = Sect + 1
    End If
    If PosTable(Ring, Source).Piece = YEL And PosTable(Ring,
Target).Piece = NONE Then
        Exit Function
    End If

    'attack from CCW direction:
    If Sect = 8 Then
        Source = 1
        Target = 7
    Else
        Source = Sect + 1
        Target = Sect - 1
    End If
    If PosTable(Ring, Source).Piece = YEL And PosTable(Ring,
Target).Piece = NONE Then
        Exit Function
    End If

    'attack from outside:
    If Ring > 1 And Ring < 6 Then
        If PosTable(Ring - 1, Sect).Piece = YEL And
PosTable(Ring + 1, Sect).Piece = NONE Then
            Exit Function
        End If
    End If

    'attack from inside:
    If Ring > 1 And Ring < 6 Then
        If PosTable(Ring + 1, Sect).Piece = YEL And
PosTable(Ring - 1, Sect).Piece = NONE Then
            Exit Function
        End If
    End If

    PosSafe = -1
End Function

Sub Command1_Click ()
    Dim Result As Integer
```

(continued)

Figure 10-9 *continued*

```
    If Command1.Caption = "Start" Then
        Command1.Caption = "Pass"
        GameOver = 0
    End If
    Pause (.25)
    Result = CompMove()
    Cls
    DrawPieces
    Refresh
    If Result <> PLAY Then EndGame (Result)
End Sub

Sub Form_Load ()
    Dim Rad As Single
    Dim Ring As Integer
    Dim Sect As Integer
    Dim Theta As Single

    XPPT = GetDeviceCaps(hDC, LOGPIXELSX) / 1440
    YPPT = GetDeviceCaps(hDC, LOGPIXELSY) / 1440
    PicWPix = WIDTHPIC * XPPT
    PicHPix = HEIGHTPIC * YPPT

    Ring = 1
    For Rad = RADIUS - RADIUS / 14 To RADIUS / 7 Step
-RADIUS / 7
        Sector = 1
        For Theta = PI / 8 To 2 * PI Step PI / 4
            PosTable(Ring, Sector).X = XCENT + Rad *
Cos(Theta) - WIDTHPIC / 2
            PosTable(Ring, Sector).Y = YCENT - Rad *
Sin(Theta) - HEIGHTPIC / 2
            Sector = Sector + 1
        Next Theta
        Ring = Ring + 1
    Next Rad
    PosTable(7, 1).X = XCENT - WIDTHPIC / 2
    PosTable(7, 1).Y = YCENT - HEIGHTPIC / 2

    DrawImages
    InitNewGame
End Sub
```

(continued)

Figure 10-9 *continued*

```
Sub Form_MouseDown (Button As Integer, Shift As Integer,
 X As Single, Y As Single)
    Dim Pt As APIPOINT
    Dim Rec As RECT
    Dim Ring As Integer
    Dim Sect As Integer

    If GameOver Then Exit Sub
    If Not PosHit(X, Y, Ring, Sect, XOffset, YOffset) Then
Exit Sub
    If PosTable(Ring, Sect).Piece <> YEL Then Exit Sub

    'control pointer:
    ShowCursor 0
    SetCapture hWnd
    Pt.X = 0
    Pt.Y = 0
    ClientToScreen hWnd, Pt
    Rec.Left = Pt.X
    Rec.Top = Pt.Y
    Pt.X = ScaleWidth * XPPT
    Pt.Y = ScaleHeight * YPPT
    ClientToScreen hWnd, Pt
    Rec.Right = Pt.X
    Rec.Bottom = Pt.Y
    ClipCursor Rec

    'initialize move variables:
    MoveRing = Ring
    MoveSect = Sect
    PrevXPix = PosTable(Ring, Sect).X * XPPT
    PrevYPix = PosTable(Ring, Sect).Y * YPPT

    'initialize PictureSav picture box:
    Cls
    PosTable(Ring, Sect).Piece = NONE
    DrawPieces
    BitBlt PictureSav.hDC, 0, 0, PicWPix, PicHPix, hDC,
 PrevXPix, PrevYPix, SRCCOPY
    PosTable(Ring, Sect).Piece = YEL
    DrawPieces
    PosTable(Ring, Sect).Piece = NONE
End Sub
```

(continued)

Figure 10-9 *continued*

```
Sub Form_MouseMove (Button As Integer, Shift As Integer,
 X As Single, Y As Single)
    If MoveRing = 0 Then Exit Sub
    BitBlt hDC, PrevXPix, PrevYPix, PicWPix, PicHPix,
PictureSav.hDC, 0, 0, SRCCOPY
    PrevXPix = (X - XOffset) * XPPT
    PrevYPix = (Y - YOffset) * YPPT
    BitBlt PictureSav.hDC, 0, 0, PicWPix, PicHPix, hDC,
PrevXPix, PrevYPix, SRCCOPY
    BitBlt hDC, PrevXPix, PrevYPix, PicWPix, PicHPix,
PictureMsk.hDC, 0, 0, SRCAND
    BitBlt hDC, PrevXPix, PrevYPix, PicWPix, PicHPix,
PictureYelImg.hDC, 0, 0, SRCINVERT
    Refresh
End Sub

Sub Form_MouseUp (Button As Integer, Shift As Integer,
 X As Single, Y As Single)
    Dim GoodMove As Integer
    Dim Result As Integer
    Dim Ring As Integer
    Dim Sect As Integer

    If MoveRing = 0 Then Exit Sub
    ShowCursor -1
    ReleaseCapture
    ClipCursor ByVal 0&
    GoodMove = AreaHit(X - XOffset + WIDTHPIC / 2,
Y - YOffset + HEIGHTPIC / 2, Ring, Sect)
    If GoodMove Then
        If PosTable(Ring, Sect).Piece <> NONE Or Ring = 7 Then
            GoodMove = 0
        End If
    End If
    If GoodMove Then
        GoodMove = 0      'false unless one of following
                          'conditions is true

        'move/jump in or out:
        If Sect = MoveSect Then

            'move:
            If (Ring = MoveRing + 1 Or Ring = MoveRing - 1)
Then GoodMove = -1
```

(continued)

Figure 10-9 *continued*

```
            'jump in:
            If Sect <> 1 And Ring = MoveRing + 2 Then
                If PosTable(Ring - 1, Sect).Piece = RED Then
                    GoodMove = -1
                    PosTable(Ring - 1, Sect).Piece = NONE
                    NumRedPieces = NumRedPieces - 1
                End If
            End If

            'jump out:
            If Sect <> 1 And Ring = MoveRing - 2 Then
                If PosTable(Ring + 1, Sect).Piece = RED Then
                    GoodMove = -1
                    PosTable(Ring + 1, Sect).Piece = NONE
                    NumRedPieces = NumRedPieces - 1
                End If
            End If

        'move/jump sideways or across fortress:
        ElseIf Ring = MoveRing Then

            'move:
            If Sect = MoveSect + 1 Or Sect = MoveSect - 1 Then
GoodMove = -1

            'move across sector 1 to 8 boundary:
            If Sect = 1 And MoveSect = 8 Or Sect = 8 And
MoveSect = 1 Then GoodMove = -1

            'jump counterclockwise:
            If Sect = MoveSect + 2 Or Sect = 1 And
MoveSect = 7 Then
                If PosTable(Ring, MoveSect + 1).Piece = RED
Then
                    GoodMove = -1
                    PosTable(Ring, MoveSect + 1).Piece = NONE
                    NumRedPieces = NumRedPieces - 1
                End If
            End If

            'jump clockwise:
            If Sect = MoveSect - 2 Or Sect = 7 And
```

(continued)

Figure 10-9 *continued*

```
MoveSect = 1 Then
                If PosTable(Ring, Sect + 1).Piece = RED Then
                    GoodMove = -1
                    PosTable(Ring, Sect + 1).Piece = NONE
                    NumRedPieces = NumRedPieces - 1
                End If
            End If

            'test special jump across fortress:
            If Ring = 6 And MoveRing = 6 And PosTable(7,
1).Piece = RED Then
                If Sect = MoveSect + 4 Or Sect = MoveSect - 4
Then
                    GoodMove = -1
                    PosTable(7, 1).Piece = NONE
                    NumRedPieces = NumRedPieces - 1
                End If
            End If
        End If
    End If

    If GoodMove Then
        PosTable(Ring, Sect).Piece = YEL
        Cls
        DrawPieces
        Refresh
        Pause (.25)
        Result = CompMove()
        Cls
        DrawPieces
        Refresh
        If Result <> PLAY Then EndGame (Result)
    Else
        Beep
        PosTable(MoveRing, MoveSect).Piece = YEL
        Cls
        DrawPieces
        Refresh
    End If
    MoveRing = 0
End Sub
```

(continued)

Figure 10-9 *continued*

```
Sub Form_Unload (Cancel As Integer)
    WinHelp hWnd, HELP_FILE, HELP_QUIT, 0
End Sub

Sub MenuAbout_Click ()
    FormAbout.Show 1
End Sub

Sub MenuCommands_Click ()
    WinHelp hWnd, HELP_FILE, HELP_CONTEXT, HELP_COMMANDS
End Sub

Sub MenuExit_Click ()
    WinHelp hWnd, HELP_FILE, HELP_QUIT, 0
    End
End Sub

Sub MenuHowTo_Click ()
    WinHelp hWnd, HELP_FILE, HELP_CONTEXT, HelpHowToPlay
End Sub

Sub MenuIndex_Click ()
    WinHelp hWnd, HELP_FILE, HELP_INDEX, 0
End Sub

Sub MenuNew_Click ()
    InitNewGame
End Sub

Sub MenuUsingHelp_Click ()
    WinHelp hWnd, HELP_FILE, HELP_HELPONHELP, 0
End Sub
```

RGABOUT.FRM code

```
Sub Command1_Click ()
    Unload FormAbout
End Sub
```

Programming Techniques

As with the Queens game (Chapter 6), the Ringo background graphics are created using Visual Basic drawing methods and properties at runtime. This technique is suitable because the background is relatively simple and is easily divided into separate geometric shapes. (It consists entirely of lines and circles.)

As is not the case in any of the other games, however, Ringo uses the "twip" scale mode—that is, the ScaleMode property of the form is assigned the default *1 - Twip* setting. One reason for using this mode is that both the playing board and the playing pieces are supposed to be round. Using drawing statements in conjunction with the twip mode creates device-independent images—that is, circles remain circular even if the video mode changes, say, from EGA to VGA. (In contrast, the Queens program used the pixel mode rather than the twip mode because the images were not round and pixel-perfect precision was required.)

The Ringo playing pieces are drawn on the playing board and are animated using the Windows API *BitBlt* function exactly as it was used in the Ludo game (Chapter 9). However, rather than creating the mask and image bitmaps in another program, they are drawn within picture boxes at runtime, using the same techniques used to draw the background graphics—namely, Visual Basic drawing methods under the twip scale mode. Thus, the pieces fit properly on the playing board and maintain their round shape regardless of the video mode.

Note: In the remainder of the chapter, the term "player" refers to the human user of the program, and the term "computer" refers to the computer-generated opponent.

While the player drags a playing piece, the mouse pointer is controlled using the same set of Windows API functions employed by the Ludo program.

As does the Tic Tac Toe game (Chapter 8), Ringo contains a routine for hit-testing within nonrectangular playing areas—that is, for determining whether the mouse pointer is within one of the areas on which pieces are positioned during the game. In Ringo, each playing area is a portion of a sector of a circle. (See Figure 10-1 on page 310.) The hit-testing routine uses two Visual Basic math functions to perform the test—specifically, *Sqr*, for obtaining the square root, and *Atn*, for deriving the arc tangent of a ratio.

In Ringo, as in the other games in this part of the book (Tic Tac Toe and Ludo), the computer serves as one of the players. Accordingly, the program includes a routine (in the *CompMove* and *PosSafe* functions) for choosing the best move. This routine uses the same general approach seen in the other games but is adapted to meet the special requirements of the Ringo program.

Program Overview

Here is a summary of the sequence of events in the Ringo program.

- When the program starts, the *Form_Load* procedure performs one-time initialization tasks and calls *InitNewGame* to start a new game.

- Whenever the player chooses the New Game command from the Game menu, the *MenuNew_Click* event procedure calls *InitNewGame* to start a new game.

- The *InitNewGame* procedure performs the initialization tasks required for each new game, including enabling the command button and setting its caption to Start. As is not the case in most of the other games, *InitNewGame* sets the *Game-Over* variable to TRUE so that the player cannot move a piece before clicking the command button to start the game.

- When the user clicks the command button (labeled Start) to start the game, the *Command1_Click* procedure makes the computer's first move. It also changes the button caption to Pass, and sets *GameOver* to FALSE so that the player can move a piece.

- If the player presses the mouse button when the mouse pointer is over one of the player's pieces, the *Form_Mouse-Down* event procedure initiates a move operation, provided that *GameOver* is set to FALSE.

- After a move operation has begun, the *Form_MouseMove* event procedure redraws the piece in each new location as the mouse is moved.

- When the player releases the mouse button, the *Form-_MouseUp* event procedure stops the move operation. If the piece has been dropped on a valid position, the procedure moves the piece to the new location and then generates the computer's next move. If the piece has been dropped on an invalid position, the procedure returns the piece to its original position on the board.

- If, rather than moving a piece, the player clicks the command button (now labeled Pass), the *Command1_Click* procedure generates the computer's next move.

Initializing the Program

The *Form_Load* procedure performs all the one-time initialization tasks when the program starts, and the *InitNewGame* procedure handles the initialization tasks required for each new game.

The *Form_Load* Procedure

The *Form_Load* procedure begins by assigning values to the form-level variables *XPPT* and *YPPT*:

```
XPPT = GetDeviceCaps(hDC, LOGPIXELSX) / 1440
YPPT = GetDeviceCaps(hDC, LOGPIXELSY) / 1440
```

The *XPPT* variable stores the number of pixels per twip in the horizontal direction, and the *YPPT* variable stores the number of pixels per twip in the vertical direction. As you will see later, these variables are used for converting measurements in twips to equivalent measurements in pixels when calling Windows API functions—specifically, *ClipCursor* and *BitBlt*. The Windows API function *GetDeviceCaps* (described in Chapter 3) returns the number of pixels per inch in a particular direction; dividing this value by the number of twips per inch (1440) yields the number of pixels per twip. The values of *XPPT* and *YPPT* must be obtained at runtime because they depend on the particular video mode that is active when the program runs.

Note: See Chapter 3, the section titled "Coding for Device Independence," for a discussion of twip and pixel measurements and scale modes.

F Y I

All program variables that store measurements are in twips, except those variables containing *Pix* in their names, which store measurements in pixels.

Next, *Form_Load* assigns values to the form-level variables *PicWPix* and *PicHPix*:

```
PicWPix = WIDTHPIC * XPPT
PicHPix = HEIGHTPIC * YPPT
```

These variables store the width and height, in pixels, of the picture boxes used to draw the playing pieces. WIDTHPIC and HEIGHTPIC are symbolic constants that store the width and height of the picture boxes in twips; these values are easily converted to pixels using the *XPPT* and *YPPT* conversion factors. The pixel dimensions of the picture boxes are needed for calling *BitBlt*; they are calculated and stored once—at the beginning of the program—so they do not have to be calculated repeatedly for each of the many calls to *BitBlt*.

Note: In the remainder of the chapter, the term "area" refers to one of the curved areas on the playing board (which are numbered in Figure 10-10). The term "position" refers to the location of a playing piece *on* an area.

Form_Load next initializes the PosTable array. This array stores information on each of the areas on the playing board and is declared as follows:

```
Type POSITION
    Piece As Integer
    X As Integer
    Y As Integer
End Type
```

```
Dim PosTable(1 To 7, 1 To 8) As POSITION
```

The first dimension of PosTable corresponds to the playing board *ring* containing the area, and the second dimension corresponds to the *sector*. For example, *PosTable (3, 2)* stores information about the area within sector 2 of ring 3. Figure 10-10 shows how the areas on the playing board are numbered.

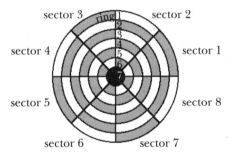

Figure 10-10.
Numbering of the areas on the playing board.

The *Piece* field of each PosTable element stores the current contents of the area. The *Piece* field can be assigned one of the values listed in the following table.

Symbolic Constant	Value	Meaning
NONE	0	Area is empty
RED	1	Area contains computer's piece
YEL	2	Area contains player's piece

The *Piece* fields are assigned values later in the program (in the *InitNewGame* procedure).

The *X* and *Y* fields of each PosTable element store the horizontal and vertical coordinates of the upper left corner of the actual position of a playing piece within the area. As you will see later, regardless of where the player drops the piece within the area, the program *centers* the piece by placing it at the coordinates provided by the corresponding *X* and *Y* fields.

F Y I

Ring 7, in the center of the board, is not divided into sectors. The information for the single position in the center of the board is stored in *PosTable(7, 1)*. The program does not use *PosTable(7, 2)* through *PosTable(7, 8)*.

Form_Load assigns the appropriate coordinate values to each of the *X* and *Y* fields, using Visual Basic's *Sin* and *Cos* functions. The following statements calculate the coordinates of the upper left corner of the position of a piece within ring *Ring* and sector *Sector*:

```
PosTable(Ring, Sector).X = XCENT + Rad * Cos(Theta) - WIDTHPIC
  / 2
PosTable(Ring, Sector).Y = YCENT - Rad * Sin(Theta) - HEIGHTPIC
  / 2
```

XCENT and YCENT are symbolic constants that store the coordinates of the center of the playing board. *Rad* is the radius of the ring containing the position, and *Theta* is the angle of the sector containing the position. These statements are contained within nested loops in which *Sector*, *Ring*, *Rad*, and *Theta* vary appropriately to calculate the coordinates of all positions on the playing board (except the position in the center of the board, which is calculated separately). Figure 10-11 shows the calculation of one of the positions.

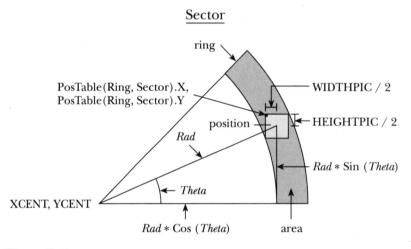

Figure 10-11.
Calculating the position of a playing piece.

Note: See Chapter 13, the section titled "Simulating the Throw," for more information on using the *Sin* and *Cos* functions to calculate points on a circle.

Finally, *Form_Load* calls *DrawImages* to create the images for the playing board and playing pieces, and it calls *InitNewGame* to start a game. These procedures are described in the following sections.

The *DrawImages* Procedure

Rather than using bitmaps created in another program (such as Paintbrush), the Ringo program creates its own graphics at runtime by using Visual Basic drawing methods. The program performs this task within the *DrawImages* procedure. *DrawImages* first draws the playing board, using the *Circle* and *Line* methods. The procedure draws the elements of the playing board by taking the following steps:

1. It draws the gray, semicircular shadow area along the lower right edge of the playing board.

2. It draws each of the red, white, and green areas, as well as the concentric circles.

3. It draws the central, black area (the fortress).

4. It draws the radial lines.

After drawing the playing board, *DrawImages* assigns the form's Image property to its Picture property:

```
Picture = Image
```

This statement causes Visual Basic to store within a permanent bitmap all the graphics that have been drawn on the form. Because the form's AutoRedraw property is set to True, the Image property identifies a bitmap that contains all graphics drawn on the form at runtime. Assigning Image to the Picture property causes Visual Basic to copy these graphics to a permanent bitmap that is *not* affected by subsequent drawing commands. Calling the *Cls* method removes any graphics drawn *after* creating the permanent bitmap but preserves the permanent bitmap. Thus, after the program has drawn the playing pieces on the form, it can erase all these pieces and restore the original playing board simply by calling *Cls*, without needing to redraw the board.

Finally, *DrawImages* draws the playing pieces within the picture boxes that will later be used to draw the pieces on the playing board by means of the *BitBlt* function. The procedure first draws a mask for the playing pieces within the PictureMsk picture box. The procedure then draws the image of the computer's piece within PictureRedImg and draws the image of the player's piece within PictureYelImg. The masks and images within these picture boxes are used in the same manner as those employed by the Ludo game (Chapter 9). The Ludo program, however, used masks and images created with Paintbrush at design time, rather than masks and images drawn at runtime.

The *InitNewGame* Procedure

The *InitNewGame* procedure begins by calling the *Cls* method to erase the playing pieces drawn on the board during the previous game. (When starting the first game, this step is unnecessary but harmless.)

InitNewGame then positions the initial playing pieces on the board by assigning the appropriate values to the *Piece* fields of the PosTable array (described earlier) and by calling the *DrawPieces* procedure (explained in the next section) to actually draw the pieces on the board.

Next, the procedure assigns to *NumRedPieces* the initial number of computer pieces and assigns to *NumYelPieces* the initial number of player pieces:

```
NumRedPieces = 7
NumYelPieces = 4
```

Then the procedure enables the command button (which is disabled at the end of each game) and sets its caption to Start:

```
Command1.Enabled = -1
Command1.Caption = "Start"
```

The caption is set to Pass after a game has started.

Finally, as is not the case in most of the other games, the *InitNewGame* procedure sets the *GameOver* variable to TRUE; consequently, the *Form_MouseDown* procedure (explained later) will not allow the player to move a piece. When the player clicks the Start button, however, the *Command1_Click* procedure sets *GameOver* to FALSE and moves the computer's piece. As a result, the computer is always allowed to move first. *Command1_Click* also changes the caption of the command button to Pass; this button subsequently permits the player to skip a turn.

The *DrawPieces* Procedure

The *DrawPieces* procedure draws all the pieces currently positioned on the playing board, at the locations given by the PosTable array. *DrawPieces* is called by *InitNewGame* at the beginning of a new game and subsequently whenever a piece is removed or repositioned on the board. As do the Tic Tac Toe and Ludo programs, the Ringo program redraws all the pieces, even if only a single piece has been moved, because the pieces overlap and must therefore be drawn in a specific order.

DrawPieces draws all the current pieces by looping through each of the sectors and rings of the playing board:

```
For Sect = 1 To 8
    Select Case Sect
        Case 1
            StartRing = 7
            StopRing = 1
            StepVal = -1
        Case 2, 7, 8
            StartRing = 6
            StopRing = 1
            StepVal = -1
        Case 3, 4, 5, 6
            StartRing = 1
            StopRing = 6
            StepVal = 1
    End Select
    For Ring = StartRing To StopRing Step StepVal

        'Draw piece, if any, at 'Ring' and 'Sector'.

    Next Ring
Next Sect
```

The *Select* statement at the beginning of the outer loop assigns the starting, stopping, and step values for the inner loop so that:

- Pieces are drawn from left to right, to assure that they overlap properly.

- The procedure draws a piece within ring 7 only when the sector value is *1*. Remember that ring 7 is not divided into sectors, and the single position within this ring is defined in *PosTable(7, 1)*.

You might want to refer back to Figure 10-10 on page 345 to review the numbering of the rings and sectors.

As in the other board games, *DrawPieces* draws each piece by calling *BitBlt* twice, first to transfer a mask and then to transfer an image. Note, however, that all position and size values passed to *BitBlt* must be in pixels. The previous games automatically passed pixel values because their programs used the pixel scale mode. Ringo, however, uses the twip mode and must therefore convert to pixel values the measurements it passes to *BitBlt*. The conversion is accomplished using the variables *XPPT*, *YPPT*, *PicWPix*, and *PicHPix*, which were assigned in *Form_Load* and were described previously. For example, the following call transfers the mask:

```
BitBlt hDC, PosTable(Ring, Sect).X * XPPT, PosTable(Ring,
  Sect).Y * YPPT, PicWPix, PicHPix, PictureMsk.hDC, 0, 0, SRCAND
```

F Y I

Although Windows API functions are affected by the settings of many Visual Basic properties (such as *DrawStyle* and *Fill-Color*), they are not affected by the *ScaleMode* setting. Rather, the API functions use the pixel scale mode regardless of the current setting of the ScaleMode property of the form or picture box. (To change the scale mode used by the API, you would have to call additional API functions.)

Moving the Player's Piece

Ringo moves the player's pieces using the same technique employed in the Ludo program (Chapter 9). Using this technique, a full-color image of the piece is repeatedly redrawn using several *BitBlt* calls, and the mouse pointer is controlled by using a series of calls to Windows API functions. This section briefly reviews the main steps and describes any unique features of the Ringo program. (For a detailed explanation of the techniques, see Chapter 9, the section "Moving the Player's Piece.")

As is the case in Ludo, the move operation is handled by the *Form-_MouseDown*, *Form_MouseMove*, and *Form_MouseUp* event procedures.

The *Form_MouseDown* Procedure

When the player presses a mouse button, *Form_MouseDown* receives control. This procedure calls the general function *PosHit* to determine whether the mouse pointer is on one of the playing-piece positions.

PosHit simply loops through PosTable, comparing the mouse pointer coordinates it is passed with the coordinates contained in the *X* and *Y* fields of each PosTable element. If the coordinates fall within one of the positions, *PosHit* assigns the ring and sector of the piece to the *Ring* and *Sect* parameters and assigns the horizontal and vertical offsets of the mouse pointer from the upper left corner of the position to the *XOffset* and *YOffset* parameters; the function then returns TRUE. If the coordinates fall outside all the positions, *PosHit* returns FALSE.

If *PosHit* returns TRUE, before proceeding *Form_MouseDown* ensures that the hit position contains one of the player's pieces:

```
If PosTable(Ring, Sect).Piece <> YEL Then Exit Sub
```

Form_MouseDown then makes the following series of calls to control the mouse pointer during the move operation:

1. It calls *ShowCursor* to hide the mouse pointer.

2. It calls *SetCapture* to direct all mouse events to the main form.

3. It calls *ClipCursor* to keep the mouse pointer within the form.

As is not the case in the Ludo program, the coordinates passed to *ClipCursor* in Ringo must be converted to pixels using the *XPPT* and *YPPT* factors, as explained earlier in this chapter (in the section titled "The *DrawPieces* Procedure").

Form_MouseDown then initializes several variables used during the move:

```
MoveRing = Ring
MoveSect = Sect
PrevXPix = PosTable(Ring, Sect).X * XPPT
PrevYPix = PosTable(Ring, Sect).Y * YPPT
```

MoveRing and *MoveSect* store the ring and sector of the piece at the beginning of the move. (If the player drops the piece on an invalid position, the piece will be returned to this ring and sector.) *PrevXPix* and *PrevYPix* store the previous coordinates of the piece in pixels; the *Form-_MouseMove* event procedure uses these values to erase the piece from this position before drawing it at the new location of the mouse pointer.

Finally, *Form_MouseDown* makes a series of calls to initialize the graphics stored in the PictureSav picture box, which the *Form_Mouse-Move* event procedure uses to erase the piece from its previous location.

The *Form_MouseMove* Procedure

As the player moves the mouse pointer within the form, the *Form-_MouseMove* event procedure receives control at each new mouse pointer position. The procedure begins by checking *MoveRing* to see whether a piece is currently being moved:

```
If MoveRing = 0 Then Exit Sub
```

This test is based on the fact that *MoveRing* has a nonzero value only while a piece is being moved. *MoveRing* thus serves a double purpose: It stores the original ring of the piece, and it serves as a flag indicating that a move is in progress.

Form_MouseMove then makes a series of calls to *BitBlt* to erase the piece from its former location and to draw it at the new location of the mouse pointer. (See Chapter 9 for an explanation of these calls.) The only unique feature of the *BitBlt* calls in Ringo is that all measurements (as already mentioned) are converted to pixels.

The *Form_MouseUp* Procedure

As with *Form_MouseMove*, the *Form_MouseUp* event procedure begins by checking *MoveRing* to see whether a piece is currently being moved. It then makes a series of calls to Windows API functions to restore the mouse pointer:

```
ShowCursor -1          'Make pointer visible.
ReleaseCapture         'Release capture of mouse events.
ClipCursor ByVal 0&    'Allow pointer to move anywhere on screen.
```

Form_MouseUp then tests whether the mouse pointer is currently within an area on the playing board where the piece can be dropped legally. The procedure performs three tests in steps, as follows:

1. It calls the function *AreaHit* (described in the next section):

   ```
   GoodMove = AreaHit(X - XOffset + WIDTHPIC / 2,
   Y - YOffset + HEIGHTPIC / 2, Ring, Sect)
   ```

   If the coordinates passed to *AreaHit* are within one of the areas on the playing board, the function assigns the ring and sector of the "hit" area to the *Ring* and *Sect* parameters and returns TRUE. If the coordinates are not within a valid area, the function returns FALSE.

2. If the mouse pointer is in a valid area, *Form_MouseUp* tests whether the area is currently empty and is in a ring other than ring 7:

   ```
   If GoodMove Then
       If PosTable(Ring, Sect).Piece <> NONE Or Ring
   = 7 Then
           GoodMove = 0
       End If
   End If
   ```

Note: The player can move a piece only into an empty square and is not allowed to move a piece into the fortress at ring 7.

3. If both of the above tests are passed, *GoodMove* will be TRUE. In this case, *Form_MouseUp* proceeds to conduct a test to determine whether placing the piece within the new area would constitute a legal move or jump:

```
If GoodMove Then

    'Test for a legal move or jump.
    'If test is passed, set 'GoodMove' to TRUE.

End If
```

The test is based on the rules for making a valid move that were listed near the beginning of this chapter (in the section titled "Playing Ringo").

If all three of these tests are passed, *Form_MouseUp* places the piece within the new location and proceeds to move the computer's piece:

```
If GoodMove Then
    PosTable(Ring, Sect).Piece = YEL
    Cls
    DrawPieces
    Refresh

    'Move computer's piece.

End If
```

If, however, one or more of the tests has failed, the procedure returns the piece to its original location at the beginning of the move:

```
Else
    Beep
    PosTable(MoveRing, MoveSect).Piece = YEL
    Cls
    DrawPieces
    Refresh
End If
```

Finally, *Form_MouseUp* sets *MoveRing* to *0* to signal other parts of the program that a move is no longer in progress:

```
MoveRing = 0
```

Hit-Testing: The *AreaHit* Function

The *AreaHit* function tests whether the point specified by the *X* and *Y* parameters is within one of the areas on the playing board.

AreaHit begins by determining whether the point is within one of the rings of the playing board. To do this, it first calculates the horizontal (*DX*) and vertical (*DY*) distances of the point from the center of the playing board:

```
DX = X - XCENT
DY = YCENT - Y
```

If the point is above the center, *DY* is positive, and if the point is to the right of the center, *DX* is positive. (This conforms to the Cartesian coordinate system.)

The function then uses the Pythagorean theorem to calculate the length of the line between the center of the playing board and the point—that is, the radius of the point. The result is stored in *Rad*:

```
DXS = DX: DXS = DXS * DXS
DYS = DY: DYS = DYS * DYS
Rad = Sqr(DXS + DYS)
```

Next, the function uses the radius of the point to calculate the number of the ring containing the point:

```
Ring = Rad \ (RADIUS / 7)
Ring = 7 - Ring
```

RADIUS is a symbolic constant storing the radius of the playing board. The thickness of each ring is *RADIUS / 7*, because the board has seven rings.

If the number of the ring is less than 1, the point is off the board, and the function exits, returning a value of FALSE:

```
If Ring < 1 Then
    AreaHit = 0
    Exit Function
End If
```

F Y I

The expression for calculating the radius uses the temporary *Single* type variables, *DXS* and *DYS*, to prevent a calculation overflow, which would occur if the expression attempted to square the integer values *DX* and *DY*.

If the point is in ring 7, the function exits immediately and returns TRUE, because it does not need to determine the sector of the ring (given that ring 7 is not divided into sectors):

```
If Ring = 7 Then
    Sect = 1
    AreaHit = -1
    Exit Function
End If
```

If the point is located in a ring other than 7, *AreaHit* proceeds to calculate the number of the sector containing the point. To find the sector, the routine first determines which of the four quadrants of the board contain the point (upper right, upper left, lower left, or lower right). This test is based on the signs of *DX* and *DY*. For example, if *DX* and *DY* are both positive, the point is in the upper right quadrant:

```
If DX >= 0 And DY >= 0 Then

    'Point is in upper right quadrant.
```

Because each quadrant contains two sectors, the routine must calculate the specific sector. This is done by comparing the angle of the point with the angle of the division between the sectors (which equals *PI / 4*). The angle of the point (that is, the angle between the radius to the point and a horizontal line) is calculated by calling Visual Basic's *Atn* (arc tangent) function to convert the tangent of the angle (*DY / DX*) to the angle itself. For example, if the point is within the upper right quadrant, the sector is determined as follows:

```
If DX = 0 Then DX = 1
If Atn(DY / DX) >= PI / 4 Then
    Sect = 2
Else
    Sect = 1
End If
```

The purpose of the first statement is to avoid division by 0 in case *DX* has a value of *0*. This calculation is shown in Figure 10-12 on the following page. After determining the number of the sector, *AreaHit* returns TRUE.

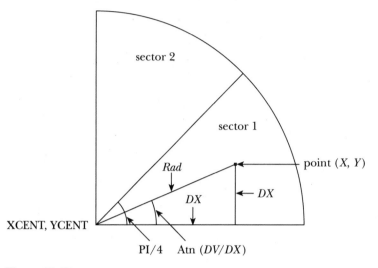

Figure 10-12.
Calculating the sector containing a point in the upper right quadrant of the playing board.

Moving the Computer's Piece

The Ringo program moves the computer's piece at two different points in the code: If the player has made a valid move, the *Form_ MouseUp* procedure moves one of the computer's pieces. If the player clicks the Pass button to skip a turn (or clicks the Start button at the beginning of a game), the *Command1_Click* procedure moves one of the computer's pieces. The routine for moving the computer's piece is the same at both points in the program and consists of the following steps:

1. The routine calls the general function procedure *Pause* to create a 0.25 millisecond pause:

   ```
   Pause (.25)
   ```

   The *Pause* procedure is described in Chapter 9, in the section titled "Rolling the Die." The brief pause after the player has made a move (or clicked the Pass button) simulates an actual game; the pause also makes it easier for the player to observe the computer's move.

2. The routine calls the general function procedure *CompMove*, which calculates the best move for the computer, and implements this move by updating PosTable; it does not, however, redraw the board to show the move. *CompMove* also returns one of the codes listed in the following table:

CompMove Return Code	Meaning
REDWIN	Computer won the game
YELWIN	Player won the game
PLAY	No winner—game is to continue

The return value is stored in *Result*:

```
Result = CompMove()
```

The inner workings of *CompMove* are described in the next section.

3. The routine redraws the playing pieces:

```
Cls
DrawPieces
Refresh
```

4. If either the computer or the player has won the game, the routine calls the general procedure *EndGame* to terminate the game:

```
If Result <> PLAY Then EndGame (Result)
```

EndGame beeps, displays a message to announce the winner (by means of the parameter passed to *EndGame* that indicates the winner), disables the command button, and sets *GameOver* to TRUE.

The *CompMove* Procedure

The *CompMove* general function procedure calculates the best move for the computer by using the same general technique presented in Chapters 8 and 9. *CompMove* examines each possible move, assigning each move a score based on its relative benefit, and then implements the move having the highest score. *CompMove* is also responsible for determining whether either of the participants has won the game.

CompMove begins by checking the current number of pieces belonging to the computer. If the computer has fewer than two pieces, it cannot win the game, and the function therefore immediately returns the code *YELWIN*:

```
If NumRedPieces < 2 Then
    CompMove = YELWIN
    Exit Function
End If
```

CompMove then examines all possible moves for each of the computer's pieces on the playing board. To access each of the computer's pieces, the function places the routine for examining moves inside the following nested loops and *If* statement:

```
For Ring = 1 To 6
    For Sect = 1 To 8
        If PosTable(Ring, Sect).Piece = RED Then

        'Assign a score to each possible move for this piece.
        'If any score is larger than the largest previous score,
        'Save a record of the move.

        End If
    Next Sect
Next Ring
```

To examine all possible moves for a given piece, the function first looks for all possible moves or jumps toward the center of the board, then looks for all possible moves or jumps in the clockwise direction, and finally looks for all possible moves or jumps in the counterclockwise direction. It assigns each type of move one of the unique scores listed in the following table.

Type of Move	Score
Move or jump second piece into fortress	No score assigned
Jump first piece into fortress	20
Any other jump	19
Move first piece into fortress	18
Any other type of move toward center	17
Any move in sideways direction	16

Note: The term "move" refers to moving a piece into an empty adjoining space. The term "jump" means jumping a piece over one of the player's pieces, thereby removing that piece from the board.

If a second piece can be moved into the fortress, the game can be won immediately. No score is needed for this type of move because if the move is possible, the routine implements the move and exits immediately, returning the value *REDWIN*.

The scores in this table assume that after making the move, the piece moved cannot be immediately jumped by one of the player's pieces. When assigning the score, the routine calls the general function procedure *PosSafe*. If the target location is immune from attack, *PosSafe* returns TRUE; in this case, the routine assigns the score given in the table. If, however, the piece in the target location could be jumped immediately, *PosSafe* returns FALSE, and the routine subtracts 10 from the score given in the table. As a result, the scores for safe moves are all higher than the scores for unsafe moves.

If the routine discovers that a given type of move is possible, and if the score for that move is greater than the largest previous score, the routine saves a complete record of the move in the *BestMove* variable. *BestMove* has the type MOVETYPE, which is defined in the global module, as follows:

```
Type MOVETYPE
     Ring As Integer      'Ring of piece to be moved.
     Sect As Integer      'Sector of piece to be moved.
     Direct As Integer    'Direction and type of move.
     Score As Integer     'The move's score.
End Type
```

The *Direct* field of *BestMove* stores one of the codes listed in the following table, indicating the direction and type of the move.

Direct Field Code	Meaning
CCW	Move in counterclockwise direction
CCWJMP	Jump in counterclockwise direction
CW	Move in clockwise direction
CWJMP	Jump in clockwise direction
IN	Move toward center of board
INJMP	Jump toward center of board

For example, the routine in the following source code determines whether the piece can be moved into the adjoining square toward the center of the board. If the move is possible, the routine assigns the appropriate score, and if this score is larger than the largest previous score, the routine saves a record of the move in *BestMove*:

```
If PosTable(Ring + 1, Sect).Piece = NONE Then
    PosTable(Ring, Sect).Piece = NONE
    If PosSafe(Ring + 1, Sect) Then
        Score = 17
    Else
        Score = 7
    End If
    PosTable(Ring, Sect).Piece = RED
    If Score > BestMove.Score Then
        BestMove.Ring = Ring
        BestMove.Sect = Sect
        BestMove.Direct = IN
        BestMove.Score = Score
    End If
End If
```

When the routine has finished examining all possible moves for all pieces, *BestMove* contains a record of the best of these moves. *CompMove* then implements this move, updating the appropriate elements of Pos-Table. Which elements need to be updated depends on the type of move or jump. Thus, the routine for implementing the change branches according to the value of the *Direct* field of *BestMove*:

```
Select Case BestMove.Direct

    'Update PosTable fields according to the type of move or jump.

End Select
```

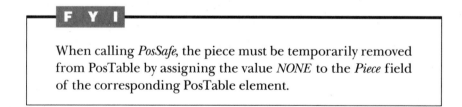

F Y I

When calling *PosSafe*, the piece must be temporarily removed from PosTable by assigning the value *NONE* to the *Piece* field of the corresponding PosTable element.

Enhancing the Game

Here are a few suggestions for enhancing the Ringo program.

- Increase the computer's skill level by improving the routine that evaluates its moves (*CompMove*). Currently, the computer moves toward the fortress and avoids the immediate capture of its pieces. You might add some tests so that the computer also seeks out and jumps its opponent's pieces and moves its pieces through the neutral zone whenever possible (to avoid capture).

- Make the computer less predictable. Currently, the computer's moves are somewhat predictable; for example, it always chooses the first move within a set of equally favorable moves. Instead, you might want to randomly select a move from a set of equally favorable moves, using Visual Basic's random-number generator.

- According to the traditional rules for Ringo, the attacker cannot place more pieces within the neutral zone than the total number of pieces currently possessed by the defender. You might want to implement this rule.

PART IV

ACTION AND GAMBLING GAMES

CHAPTER ELEVEN

TRIPACK

TriPack challenges your reflexes and tests your sense of spatial relationships. In TriPack, you race against time to arrange groups of falling
triangles. The object of the game is to pack the triangles as tightly as
possible, forming connections between the two sides of the playing
area. The code for TriPack demonstrates a method for moving game
pieces automatically in response to periodic timer events. You will also
learn how to process keystrokes using a low-level keyboard handler and
how to save game information in a private section of the Windows initialization file (WIN.INI).

Playing TriPack

When you run the TriPack program (TP.EXE), choose the New Game
command from the Game menu to start a game. As soon as you choose
this command, a block of triangles will appear at the top of the playing
area and begin falling, slowly but inexorably, toward the bottom. Figure
11-1 shows TriPack at the beginning of a game.

Figure 11-1.
TriPack at the beginning of a game.

As soon as the first block of triangles hits bottom, another block
appears at the top of the playing area and begins its descent toward the

bottom. This process is repeated until the triangles are stacked to the top of the window.

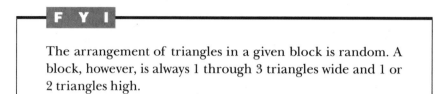

The arrangement of triangles in a given block is random. A block, however, is always 1 through 3 triangles wide and 1 or 2 triangles high.

You can use the following keys on the numeric keypad to manipulate a falling block of triangles before it reaches the bottom of the window or lands on top of another block:

- Left arrow (4): Moves the block to the left.

- Right arrow (6): Moves the block to the right.

- Up arrow (8): Flips the block in the vertical direction. (That is, it converts the block to its mirror image along the horizontal axis.)

- Center key (5): Flips the block in the horizontal direction.

- Down arrow (2): Causes the block to fall more rapidly straight down. (Note: After you press this key, you can no longer use any of the keys to manipulate the falling block.)

These keys are illustrated in Figure 11-2.

Figure 11-2.
The keys for manipulating a falling block of triangles.

Whenever a block of triangles forms a continuous horizontal connection—that is, when the "baselines" of the triangles form a horizontal line—between the two sides of the playing area, both rows of triangles (above and below the horizontal line) adjoining the connection are removed. Triangles can be arranged in many ways to form a connection. Figure 11-3 shows four possible arrangements. All the triangles in the rows adjoining the connection are always removed, even if one of the rows does not contribute to the connection, as seen in the third arrangement in Figure 11-3.

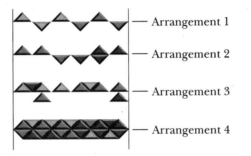

Figure 11-3.
Some examples of connections in TriPack.

Note: A connection that lies at the very bottom of the playing area does not cause the row of triangles adjoining the connection to be removed.

Each time you form a connection, you are awarded points as follows: If six triangles are removed, you are given 6 points for each triangle; if seven triangles are removed, you are given 7 points for each triangle; and so on. In other words, the total number of points awarded equals the *square* of the number of triangles removed. This method for assigning points strongly rewards well-packed rows of triangles.

Notice that the first arrangement shown in Figure 11-3 contains six triangles, which is the minimum number of triangles needed to form a connection (for which 36 points would be awarded). The fourth arrangement shown in this figure contains 22 triangles, which is the maximum number of triangles that can adjoin a connection (for which 484 points would be awarded).

The game ends when the next generated block of triangles will not fit at the top of the playing area. The program then displays your current score as well as your highest previous score (if any). Figure 11-4 shows a game that has been completed. (The message box—a dialog box created with Visual Basic's *MsgBox* statement—with the scores has been removed.)

Figure 11-4.
A completed TriPack game.

To start a new game, choose the New Game command from the Game menu. If you choose this command while a game is already in progress, the current game will be terminated and a new one will be started.

Strategy and Hints

As you play TriPack, you should try to form as many connections as possible to keep the game going. You should also try to pack as many triangles as possible into each connection to maximize your score.

Keep in mind that the playing area is 6 triangles wide and that many of the blocks are 3 triangles wide. The easiest way to form a

> **T I P**
>
> TriPack saves your highest score to date in the Windows initialization file (WIN.INI) and displays it each time you complete a game. To erase this score, choose the Reset Hi Score command from the Options menu; the program will then begin saving the highest score attained *after* resetting.

connection is to place two such blocks side by side. Accordingly, when you get one of these blocks, place it against one side of the playing area; with any luck, you will soon get a second block that is also 3 triangles wide to place next to the first block. While waiting for the second block, try to reserve space for it; you might be able to pack smaller blocks around the space occupied by the two 3-triangle–wide blocks. Figure 11-5 shows an example of this general strategy.

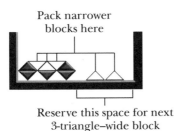

Figure 11-5.
TriPack strategy: reserving space for a 3-triangle–wide block.

Coding TriPack

The source code for the TriPack program is contained in the files listed in the following table.

File	Purpose
GLOBALTP.BAS	Contains global type definitions
TP.FRM	Defines the main form, FormMain, and the controls it contains
TPABOUT.FRM	Defines the ABOUT form, FormAbout, and the controls it contains
TP.MAK	Contains the TriPack project file

Figures 11-6 through 11-11 beginning on the following page present the form designs, properties, menu commands, and source code for the TriPack program.

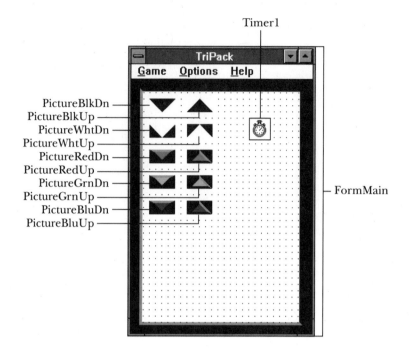

Figure 11-6.
TP.FRM at design time.

Object Name	Object Type	Property	Setting
FormMain	Form	AutoRedraw	True
		BackColor	&H00800000& [dark blue]
		BorderStyle	1 - Fixed Single
		Caption	TriPack
		FormName	FormMain
		Grid Height	8 [pixels]
		Grid Width	8 [pixels]
		Height	5460 [twips]
		Icon	(Icon) [TP.ICO]
		Left	1035 [twips]
		MaxButton	False
		Picture	(Bitmap) [TP.BMP]

Figure 11-7.   *(continued)*
TP.FRM form and control properties.

Figure 11-7 *continued*

Object Name	Object Type	Property	Setting
		ScaleMode	3 - Pixel
		Top	1095 [twips]
		Width	3630 [twips]
PictureBlkDn	Picture box	AutoRedraw	True
		AutoSize	True
		BorderStyle	0 - None
		CtlName	PictureBlkDn
		Height	17 [pixels]
		Left	24 [pixels]
		Picture	(Bitmap) [BLKDN.BMP]
		ScaleMode	3 - Pixel
		Top	24 [pixels]
		Visible	False
		Width	33 [pixels]
PictureBlkUp	Picture box	AutoRedraw	True
		AutoSize	True
		BorderStyle	0 - None
		CtlName	PictureBlkUp
		Height	17 [pixels]
		Left	72 [pixels]
		Picture	(Bitmap) [BLKUP.BMP]
		ScaleMode	3 - Pixel
		Top	24 [pixels]
		Visible	False
		Width	33 [pixels]
PictureBluDn	Picture box	AutoRedraw	True
		AutoSize	True
		BorderStyle	0 - None
		CtlName	PictureBluDn
		Height	17 [pixels]
		Left	24 [pixels]
		Picture	(Bitmap) [BLUDN.BMP]

(continued)

Figure 11-7 *continued*

Object Name	Object Type	Property	Setting
		ScaleMode	3 - Pixel
		Top	184 [pixels]
		Visible	False
		Width	33 [pixels]
PictureBluUp	Picture box	AutoRedraw	True
		AutoSize	True
		BorderStyle	0 - None
		CtlName	PictureBluUp
		Height	17 [pixels]
		Left	72 [pixels]
		Picture	(Bitmap) [BLUUP.BMP]
		ScaleMode	3 - Pixel
		Top	184 [pixels]
		Visible	False
		Width	33 [pixels]
PictureGrnDn	Picture box	AutoRedraw	True
		AutoSize	True
		BorderStyle	0 - None
		CtlName	PictureGrnDn
		Height	17 [pixels]
		Left	24 [pixels]
		Picture	(Bitmap) [BRNDN.BMP]
		ScaleMode	3 - Pixel
		Top	144 [pixels]
		Visible	False
		Width	33 [pixels]
PictureGrnUp	Picture box	AutoRedraw	True
		AutoSize	True
		BorderStyle	0 - None
		CtlName	PictureGrnUp
		Height	17 [pixels]
		Left	72 [pixels]

(continued)

Figure 11-7 *continued*

Object Name	Object Type	Property	Setting
		Picture	(Bitmap) [GRNUP.BMP]
		ScaleMode	3 - Pixel
		Top	144 [pixels]
		Visible	False
		Width	33 [pixels]
PictureRedDn	Picture box	AutoRedraw	True
		AutoSize	True
		BorderStyle	0 - None
		CtlName	PictureRedDn
		Height	17 [pixels]
		Left	24 [pixels]
		Picture	(Bitmap) [REDDN.BMP]
		ScaleMode	3 - Pixel
		Top	104 [pixels]
		Visible	False
		Width	33 [pixels]
PictureRedUp	Picture box	AutoRedraw	True
		AutoSize	True
		BorderStyle	0 - None
		CtlName	PictureRedUp
		Height	17 [pixels]
		Left	72 [pixels]
		Picture	(Bitmap) [REDUP.BMP]
		ScaleMode	3 - Pixel
		Top	104 [pixels]
		Visible	False
		Width	33 [pixels]
PictureWhtDn	Picture box	AutoRedraw	True
		AutoSize	True
		BorderStyle	0 - None
		CtlName	PictureWhtDn
		Height	17 [pixels]

(continued)

Figure 11-7 *continued*

Object Name	Object Type	Property	Setting
		Left	24 [pixels]
		Picture	(Bitmap) [WHTDN.BMP]
		ScaleMode	3 - Pixel
		Top	64 [pixels]
		Visible	False
		Width	33 [pixels]
PictureWhtUp	Picture box	AutoRedraw	True
		AutoSize	True
		BorderStyle	0 - None
		CtlName	PictureWhtUp
		Height	17 [pixels]
		Left	72 [pixels]
		Picture	(Bitmap) [WHTUP.BMP]
		ScaleMode	3 - Pixel
		Top	64 [pixels]
		Visible	False
		Width	33 [pixels]
Timer1	Timer	Enabled	False
		Interval	5400 [milliseconds]

Indentation/Caption	Control Name	Other Features
&Game	MenuGame	
....&New Game	MenuNew	
....-	MenuSep1	
....E&xit	MenuExit	
&Options	MenuOptions	
....&Reset Hi Score	MenuReset	
&Help	MenuHelp	
....&Index	MenuIndex	Accelerator = F1
....&How to Play	MenuHowTo	

Figure 11-8.
TP.FRM menu design.

(continued)

Figure 11-8 *continued*

Indentation/Caption	Control Name	Other Features
....&Commands	MenuCommands	
....&Using Help	MenuUsingHelp	
....-	MenuSep2	
....&About TriPack...	MenuAbout	

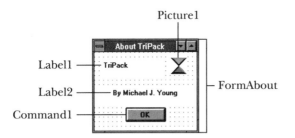

Figure 11-9.
TPABOUT.FRM at design time.

Object Name	Object Type	Property	Setting
Command1	Command button	Caption	OK
		Default	True
		Height	375 [twips]
		Left	840 [twips]
		Top	1440 [twips]
		Width	1095 [twips]
FormAbout	Form	BorderStyle	3 - Fixed Double
		Caption	About TriPack
		FormName	FormAbout
		Grid Height	120 [twips]
		Grid Width	120 [twips]
		Height	2445 [twips]
		Left	1140 [twips]

Figure 11-10. (continued)
TPABOUT.FRM form and control properties.

Figure 11-10 *continued*

Object Name	Object Type	Property	Setting
		MaxButton	False
		MinButton	False
		Top	1440 [twips]
		Width	2880 [twips]
Label1	Label	Caption	TriPack
		Height	375 [twips]
		Left	240 [twips]
		Top	240 [twips]
		Width	1575 [twips]
Label2	Label	Alignment	2 - Center
		Caption	By Michael J. Young
		Height	375 [twips]
		Left	0 [twips]
		Top	960 [twips]
		Width	2745 [twips]
Picture1	Picture box	AutoSize	True
		BorderStyle	0 - None
		Height	480 [twips]
		Left	2040 [twips]
		Picture	(Icon) [TP.ICO]
		Top	120 [twips]
		Width	480 [twips]

GLOBALTP.BAS code

```
Type RECT
    Left As Integer
    Top As Integer
    Right As Integer
    Bottom As Integer
End Type
```

Figure 11-11. *(continued)*

Source code for the TriPack program. (Notice that long program lines are wrapped to the next line and indented one space.)

376

Figure 11-11 *continued*

```
Type TRI
    X As Integer
    Y As Integer
    State As Integer
    Color As Integer
End Type
```

TP.FRM code

```
'Help Section:
'Help file:
Const HELP_FILE = "TP.HLP"
'WinHelp wCommand values:
Const HELP_CONTEXT = &H1
Const HELP_HELPONHELP = &H4
Const HELP_INDEX = &H3
Const HELP_QUIT = &H2
'WinHelp dwData values (help topics):
Const HELP_HOWTOPLAY = 10&
Const HELP_COMMANDS = 20&
'Windows help API:
Declare Sub WinHelp Lib "USER" (ByVal hWnd As Integer,
 ByVal lpHelpFile As String, ByVal wCommand As Integer,
 ByVal dwData As Long)

Const CLIENTRIGHT = 232 'coordinates of LR corner of inside of
 form
Const CLIENTBOTTOM = 319
Const OFFX = 15          'offset of UL corner of playing area
Const OFFY = 15
Const NONE = 0           'constants for 'State' field
Const UP = 1
Const DOWN = 2
Const RED = 1            'constants for 'Color' field
Const GRN = 2
Const BLU = 3

Dim CellTable(0 To 17, -3 To 11) As TRI
Dim CurCol As Integer
Dim CurRow As Integer
Dim Score As Integer
Dim TriTable(1 To 2, 1 To 3) As TRI
```

(continued)

Figure 11-11 *continued*

```
Const WS_CAPTION = &HC00000              'dwStyle values
Const WS_THICKFRAME = &H40000
Declare Sub AdjustWindowRect Lib "USER" (lpRect As RECT,
 ByVal dwStyle&, ByVal bMenu%)

Const SRCAND = &H8800C6      'dest = source AND dest
Const SRCCOPY = &HCC0020      'dest = source
Const SRCINVERT = &H660046  'dest = source XOR dest
Declare Sub BitBlt Lib "GDI" (ByVal HDestDC%, ByVal X%,
 ByVal Y%, ByVal nWidth%, ByVal nHeight%, ByVal HSrcDC%,
 ByVal XSrc%, ByVal YSrc%, ByVal ROP&)

Const LOGPIXELSX = 88
Const LOGPIXELSY = 90
Declare Function GetDeviceCaps Lib "GDI" (ByVal hDC%,
 ByVal Index%) As Integer

Declare Function GetProfileInt Lib "Kernel" (ByVal lpAppName$,
 ByVal lpKeyName$, ByVal nDefault%) As Integer
Declare Sub WriteProfileString Lib "Kernel" (ByVal
 lpApplicationName$, ByVal lpKeyName$, ByVal lpString$)

Sub DrawBlock ()
    Dim Col As Integer
    Dim HDCBlack As Integer
    Dim HDCColor As Integer
    Dim Row As Integer

    For Row = 1 To 2
        For Col = 1 To 3
            If TriTable(Row, Col).State = UP Then
                HDCBlack = PictureBlkUp.hDC
                Select Case TriTable(Row, Col).Color
                    Case RED
                        HDCColor = PictureRedUp.hDC
                    Case GRN
                        HDCColor = PictureGrnUp.hDC
                    Case BLU
                        HDCColor = PictureBluUp.hDC
                End Select
            ElseIf TriTable(Row, Col).State = DOWN Then
                HDCBlack = PictureBlkDn.hDC
```

(continued)

Figure 11-11 *continued*

```
                        Select Case TriTable(Row, Col).Color
                            Case RED
                                HDCColor = PictureRedDn.hDC
                            Case GRN
                                HDCColor = PictureGrnDn.hDC
                            Case BLU
                                HDCColor = PictureBluDn.hDC
                        End Select
                    End If
                    If TriTable(Row, Col).State <> NONE Then
                        BitBlt hDC, TriTable(Row, Col).X +
CellTable(CurRow, CurCol).X, TriTable(Row, Col).Y +
CellTable(CurRow, CurCol).Y, 33, 17, HDCBlack, 0, 0, SRCAND
                        BitBlt hDC, TriTable(Row, Col).X +
CellTable(CurRow, CurCol).X, TriTable(Row, Col).Y +
CellTable(CurRow, CurCol).Y, 33, 17, HDCColor, 0, 0,
SRCINVERT
                    End If
                Next Col
        Next Row
        Refresh
End Sub

Sub DrawBoard ()
    Dim Col As Integer
    Dim HDCBlack As Integer
    Dim HDCColor As Integer
    Dim Row As Integer

    Cls
    For Row = 1 To 17
        For Col = 1 To 11
            If CellTable(Row, Col).State = UP Then
                HDCBlack = PictureBlkUp.hDC
                Select Case CellTable(Row, Col).Color
                    Case RED
                        HDCColor = PictureRedUp.hDC
                    Case GRN
                        HDCColor = PictureGrnUp.hDC
                    Case BLU
                        HDCColor = PictureBluUp.hDC
                End Select
            ElseIf CellTable(Row, Col).State = DOWN Then
                HDCBlack = PictureBlkDn.hDC
```

(continued)

Figure 11-11 *continued*

```
                Select Case CellTable(Row, Col).Color
                    Case RED
                        HDCColor = PictureRedDn.hDC
                    Case GRN
                        HDCColor = PictureGrnDn.hDC
                    Case BLU
                        HDCColor = PictureBluDn.hDC
                End Select
            End If
            If CellTable(Row, Col).State <> NONE Then
                BitBlt hDC, CellTable(Row, Col).X,
 CellTable(Row, Col).Y, 33, 17, HDCBlack, 0, 0, SRCAND
                BitBlt hDC, CellTable(Row, Col).X,
 CellTable(Row, Col).Y, 33, 17, HDCColor, 0, 0, SRCINVERT
            End If
        Next Col
    Next Row
End Sub

Function DropOK ()
    Dim CellTableCol As Integer
    Dim Col As Integer

    DropOK = 0
    CellTableCol = CurCol
    For Col = 1 To 3
        If TriTable(1, Col).State = UP Then
            If CurRow = 17 Then Exit Function
            If CellTable(CurRow + 1, CellTableCol).State
<> NONE Then
                Exit Function
            End If
            If CellTableCol > 1 Then
                If CellTable(CurRow + 1, CellTableCol -
1).State <> NONE Then Exit Function
            End If
            If CellTableCol < 11 Then
                If CellTable(CurRow + 1, CellTableCol +
1).State <> NONE Then Exit Function
            End If
        End If
        CellTableCol = CellTableCol + 2
    Next Col
    CellTableCol = CurCol
```

(continued)

Figure 11-11 *continued*

```
    For Col = 1 To 3
        If TriTable(2, Col).State = DOWN Then
            If CurRow + 1 = 17 Then Exit Function
            If CellTable(CurRow + 2, CellTableCol).State
<> NONE Then
                Exit Function
            End If
            If CellTableCol > 1 Then
                If CellTable(CurRow + 1, CellTableCol - 1)
.State = UP Then Exit Function
                If CellTable(CurRow + 2, CellTableCol -
1).State = DOWN Then Exit Function
            End If
            If CellTableCol < 11 Then
                If CellTable(CurRow + 1, CellTableCol +
1).State = UP Then Exit Function
                If CellTable(CurRow + 2, CellTableCol +
1).State = DOWN Then Exit Function
            End If
        End If
        CellTableCol = CellTableCol + 2
    Next Col
    DropOK = -1
End Function

Sub EraseBlock ()
    Dim Col As Integer
    Dim Row As Integer

    For Row = 1 To 2
        For Col = 1 To 3
            If TriTable(Row, Col).State = UP Then
                BitBlt hDC, TriTable(Row, Col).X +
CellTable(CurRow, CurCol).X, TriTable(Row, Col).Y +
CellTable(CurRow, CurCol).Y, 33, 17, PictureBlkUp.hDC, 0, 0,
SRCAND
                BitBlt hDC, TriTable(Row, Col).X +
CellTable(CurRow, CurCol).X, TriTable(Row, Col).Y +
CellTable(CurRow, CurCol).Y, 33, 17, PictureWhtUp.hDC, 0, 0,
SRCINVERT
            ElseIf TriTable(Row, Col).State = DOWN Then
                BitBlt hDC, TriTable(Row, Col).X +
CellTable(CurRow, CurCol).X, TriTable(Row, Col).Y +
CellTable(CurRow, CurCol).Y, 33, 17, PictureBlkDn.hDC, 0, 0,
```

(continued)

Figure 11-11 *continued*

```
    SRCAND
                    BitBlt hDC, TriTable(Row, Col).X +
    CellTable(CurRow, CurCol).X, TriTable(Row, Col).Y +
    CellTable(CurRow, CurCol).Y, 33, 17, PictureWhtDn.hDC, 0, 0,
    SRCINVERT
            End If
        Next Col
    Next Row
End Sub

Sub FlipH ()
    Dim Col As Integer
    Dim Hi As Integer
    Dim Hold As Integer
    Dim Lo As Integer
    Dim Row As Integer

    Hi = 0
    Lo = 4
    For Row = 1 To 2
        For Col = 1 To 3
            If TriTable(Row, Col).State <> NONE Then
                If Col < Lo Then Lo = Col
                If Col > Hi Then Hi = Col
            End If
        Next Col
    Next Row
    For Row = 1 To 2
        Hold = TriTable(Row, Lo).State
        TriTable(Row, Lo).State = TriTable(Row, Hi).State
        TriTable(Row, Hi).State = Hold
    Next Row
End Sub

Sub FlipV ()
    Dim Col As Integer
    Dim Hold As Integer

    For Col = 1 To 3
        Hold = TriTable(1, Col).State
        If TriTable(2, Col).State = DOWN Then
            TriTable(1, Col).State = UP
        Else
            TriTable(1, Col).State = NONE
```

(continued)

Figure 11-11 *continued*

```
            End If
            If Hold = UP Then
                TriTable(2, Col).State = DOWN
            Else
                TriTable(2, Col).State = NONE
            End If
        Next Col
End Sub

Sub MarkCellTable ()
    Dim CellTableCol As Integer
    Dim Col As Integer
    Dim Count As Integer
    Dim I As Integer
    Dim Row As Integer
    Dim Thru As Integer

    'record final coordinates of each triangle in block:
    For Row = 1 To 2
        If CurRow + Row - 1 >= 18 Then Exit For
        CellTableCol = CurCol
        For Col = 1 To 3
            If CellTableCol >= 12 Then Exit For
            If TriTable(Row, Col).State <> NONE Then
                CellTable(CurRow + Row - 1,
CellTableCol).State = TriTable(Row, Col).State
                CellTable(CurRow + Row - 1,
CellTableCol).Color = TriTable(Row, Col).Color
            End If
            CellTableCol = CellTableCol + 2
        Next Col
    Next Row

    'test for a connection:
    Thru = 1
    If CurRow = 17 Then Exit Sub
    For Col = 1 To 11
        If CellTable(CurRow, Col).State = UP Or
CellTable(CurRow + 1, Col).State = DOWN Then
            Thru = Col + 2
        End If
        If Col >= Thru Or Col = 11 And Thru < 13 Then Exit Sub
```

(continued)

Figure 11-11 *continued*

```
            If CellTable(CurRow, Col).State <> NONE Then
                Count = Count + 1
            End If
            If CellTable(CurRow + 1, Col).State <> NONE Then
                Count = Count + 1
            End If
        Next Col
        Score = Score + Count * Count
        RemoveRow CurRow
        RemoveRow CurRow + 1
        For I = 1 To Count
            Beep
        Next I
        DrawBoard
End Sub

Function PositionOK ()
    Dim CellTableCol As Integer
    Dim Col As Integer
    Dim Row As Integer

    PositionOK = 0
    For Row = 1 To 2
        CellTableCol = CurCol
        For Col = 1 To 3
            If TriTable(Row, Col).State = UP Then
                If CellTable(CurRow + Row - 1,
 CellTableCol).State <> NONE Then Exit Function
                If CellTable(CurRow + Row - 1,
 CellTableCol - 1).State = UP Then Exit Function
                If CellTableCol < 11 Then
                    If CellTable(CurRow + Row - 1,
 CellTableCol + 1).State = UP Then Exit Function
                End If
            ElseIf TriTable(Row, Col).State = DOWN Then
                If CellTable(CurRow + Row - 1,
 CellTableCol).State <> NONE Then Exit Function
                If CellTable(CurRow + Row - 1,
 CellTableCol - 1).State = DOWN Then Exit Function
                If CellTableCol < 11 Then
                    If CellTable(CurRow + Row - 1,
 CellTableCol + 1).State = DOWN Then Exit Function
                End If
            End If
```

(continued)

Figure 11-11 *continued*

```
            CellTableCol = CellTableCol + 2
        Next Col
    Next Row
    PositionOK = -1
End Function


Sub RemoveRow (RowToGo As Integer)
    Dim Col As Integer
    Dim Row As Integer

    For Row = RowToGo - 1 To 1 Step -1
        For Col = 1 To 11
            CellTable(Row + 1, Col).State = CellTable(Row, Col).State
            CellTable(Row + 1, Col).Color = CellTable(Row, Col).Color
        Next Col
    Next Row
    For Col = 1 To 11
        CellTable(1, Col).State = NONE
    Next Col
End Sub


Sub Form_KeyDown (KeyCode As Integer, Shift As Integer)
    Dim CellTableCol As Integer
    Dim Col As Integer

    If Not Timer1.Enabled Or Timer1.Interval = 5 Or CurRow = -1 Then Exit Sub
    Select Case KeyCode
        Case &H25, &H64      'Left arrow (4): move block left
            CellTableCol = CurCol
            For Col = 1 To 3
                If TriTable(1, Col).State = UP Then
                    If CellTableCol = 1 Then Exit Sub
                    If CellTableCol > 1 Then
                        If CellTable(CurRow, CellTableCol - 1).State <> NONE Then Exit Sub
                    End If
                    If CellTableCol > 2 Then
                        If CellTable(CurRow, CellTableCol - 2).State = UP Then Exit Sub
                    End If
                    Exit For
```

(continued)

Figure 11-11 *continued*

```
            End If
            CellTableCol = CellTableCol + 2
        Next Col
        CellTableCol = CurCol
        For Col = 1 To 3
            If TriTable(2, Col).State = DOWN Then
                If CellTableCol = 1 Then Exit Sub
                If CellTableCol > 1 Then
                    If CellTable(CurRow + 1, CellTableCol
- 1).State <> NONE Then Exit Sub
                End If
                If CellTableCol > 2 Then
                    If CellTable(CurRow + 1, CellTableCol
- 2).State = DOWN Then Exit Sub
                End If
                Exit For
            End If
            CellTableCol = CellTableCol + 2
        Next Col
        EraseBlock
        CurCol = CurCol - 1
        DrawBlock
    Case &H26, &H68       'Up arrow (8): flip block
                          'vertically
        FlipV
        If PositionOK() Then
            FlipV
            EraseBlock
            FlipV
            DrawBlock
        Else
            FlipV
        End If
    Case &H27, &H66       'Right arrow (6): move block right
        CellTableCol = CurCol + 4
        For Col = 3 To 1 Step -1
            If TriTable(1, Col).State = UP Then
                If CellTableCol = 11 Then Exit Sub
                If CellTableCol <= 10 Then
                    If CellTable(CurRow, CellTableCol
+ 1).State <> NONE Then Exit Sub
                End If
                If CellTableCol <= 9 Then
                    If CellTable(CurRow, CellTableCol
+ 2).State = UP Then Exit Sub
```

(continued)

Figure 11-11 *continued*

```
                         End If
                         Exit For
                     End If
                     CellTableCol = CellTableCol - 2
                 Next Col
                 CellTableCol = CurCol + 4
                 For Col = 3 To 1 Step -1
                     If TriTable(2, Col).State = DOWN Then
                         If CellTableCol = 11 Then Exit Sub
                         If CellTableCol <= 10 Then
                             If CellTable(CurRow + 1, CellTableCol
+ 1).State <> NONE Then Exit Sub
                         End If
                         If CellTableCol <= 9 Then
                             If CellTable(CurRow + 1, CellTableCol
+ 2).State = DOWN Then Exit Sub
                         End If
                         Exit For
                     End If
                     CellTableCol = CellTableCol - 2
                 Next Col
                 EraseBlock
                 CurCol = CurCol + 1
                 DrawBlock
            Case &H28, &H62      'Down arrow (2): accelerate drop
                 Timer1.Interval = 5
                 Exit Sub
            Case &HC, &H65       'center key (5): flip block
                                 'horizontally
                 FlipH
                 If PositionOK() Then
                     FlipH
                     EraseBlock
                     FlipH
                     DrawBlock
                 Else
                     FlipH
                 End If
        End Select
        If Not DropOK() Then
            MarkCellTable
            CurRow = -1
        End If
End Sub
```

(continued)

Figure 11-11 *continued*

```
Sub Form_Load ()
    Dim Col As Integer
    Dim Rec As RECT
    Dim Row As Integer
    Dim X As Integer, Y As Integer

    'code for display device independence:
    FormMain.Left = 5 * (1440 / GetDeviceCaps(hDC,
LOGPIXELSX))
    FormMain.Top = 5 * (1440 / GetDeviceCaps(hDC, LOGPIXELSY))
    Rec.Left = 0
    Rec.Top = 0
    Rec.Right = CLIENTRIGHT
    Rec.Bottom = CLIENTBOTTOM
    AdjustWindowRect Rec, WS_CAPTION, -1
    FormMain.Width = (Rec.Right - Rec.Left + 1) * (1440 /
GetDeviceCaps(hDC, LOGPIXELSX))
    FormMain.Height = (Rec.Bottom - Rec.Top + 1) * (1440 /
GetDeviceCaps(hDC, LOGPIXELSY))

    Y = OFFY
    For Row = 1 To 17
        X = OFFX - 4 * 17
        For Col = -3 To 11
            CellTable(Row, Col).X = X
            CellTable(Row, Col).Y = Y
            X = X + 17
        Next Col
        Y = Y + 17
    Next Row
    TriTable(1, 1).X = 0
    TriTable(1, 1).Y = 0
    TriTable(1, 2).X = 34
    TriTable(1, 2).Y = 0
    TriTable(1, 3).X = 68
    TriTable(1, 3).Y = 0
    TriTable(2, 1).X = 0
    TriTable(2, 1).Y = 17
    TriTable(2, 2).X = 34
    TriTable(2, 2).Y = 17
    TriTable(2, 3).X = 68
    TriTable(2, 3).Y = 17
    Randomize
End Sub
```

(continued)

Figure 11-11 *continued*

```
Sub Form_Unload (Cancel As Integer)
    WinHelp hWnd, HELP_FILE, HELP_QUIT, 0
End Sub

Sub MenuAbout_Click ()
    FormAbout.Show 1
End Sub

Sub MenuCommands_Click ()
    WinHelp hWnd, HELP_FILE, HELP_CONTEXT, HELP_COMMANDS
End Sub

Sub MenuExit_Click ()
    WinHelp hWnd, HELP_FILE, HELP_QUIT, 0
    End
End Sub

Sub MenuHowTo_Click ()
    WinHelp hWnd, HELP_FILE, HELP_CONTEXT, HELP_HOWTOPLAY
End Sub

Sub MenuIndex_Click ()
    WinHelp hWnd, HELP_FILE, HELP_INDEX, 0
End Sub

Sub MenuNew_Click ()
    Dim Col As Integer
    Dim Row As Integer

    For Row = 0 To 17
        For Col = -3 To 11
            CellTable(Row, Col).State = NONE
        Next Col
    Next Row
    Cls
    CurRow = -1
    Score = 0
    Timer1.Enabled = -1
End Sub

Sub MenuUsingHelp_Click ()
    WinHelp hWnd, HELP_FILE, HELP_HELPONHELP, 0
End Sub
```

(continued)

Figure 11-11 *continued*

```
Sub MenuReset_Click ()
    Dim Result As Integer

    'display message box with question mark and
    'Yes/No buttons:
    Result = MsgBox("Are you sure you want to erase your
 highest previous score?", 32 + 4, "TriPack")
    If Result = 6 Then   'user clicked Yes button
        WriteProfileString "TriPack", "HiScore", ""
    End If
End Sub

Sub Timer1_Timer ()
    Dim Col As Integer
    Dim ColorVal As Integer
    Dim HiScore As Integer
    Dim Mand As Integer
    Dim Message As String
    Dim Row As Integer

    If CurRow = -1 Then      'create a new block
        Timer1.Interval = 500
        CurCol = 4
        ColorVal = Int(3 * Rnd + 1)
        For Row = 1 To 2
            For Col = 1 To 3
                TriTable(Row, Col).Color = ColorVal
            Next Col
        Next Row
        For Col = 1 To 3
            If Int(2 * Rnd) Then
                TriTable(1, Col).State = UP
            Else
                TriTable(1, Col).State = NONE
            End If
        Next Col
        If Int(2 * Rnd) Then
            TriTable(2, 1).State = DOWN
        Else
            TriTable(2, 1).State = NONE
        End If
        If Int(2 * Rnd) Then
            TriTable(2, 3).State = DOWN
```

(continued)

Figure 11-11 *continued*

```
    Else
        TriTable(2, 3).State = NONE
    End If
    TriTable(2, 2).State = NONE
    Mand = -1
    For Row = 1 To 2
        For Col = 1 To 3
            If TriTable(Row, Col).State <> NONE Then Mand
= 0
        Next Col
    Next Row
    If TriTable(1, 2).State = NONE Then
        If TriTable(1, 1).State <> NONE Or TriTable(2,
1).State <> NONE Then
            If TriTable(1, 3).State <> NONE Or TriTable(2,
3).State <> NONE Then Mand = -1
        End If
    End If
    If Mand Or Int(2 * Rnd) Then
        TriTable(2, 2).State = DOWN
    End If
    If DropOK() Then
        CurRow = 0
        If DropOK() Then CurRow = 1
    End If
    If CurRow <> 1 Then        'game over
        Beep: Beep: Beep: Beep: Beep: Beep
        Timer1.Enabled = 0
        HiScore = GetProfileInt("TriPack", "HiScore", 0)
        Message = "Game Over" + Chr$(13) + Chr$(10) +
Chr$(13) + Chr$(10)
        If HiScore > 0 Then
            Message = Message + "Highest Previous Score: "
+ Str$(HiScore) + Chr$(13) + Chr$(10)
        End If
        Message = Message + "Current Score: "
+ Str$(Score)
        If HiScore > 0 And Score > HiScore Then
            Message = Message + Chr$(13) + Chr$(10) +
"Record Broken! Congratulations!"
        End If
        MsgBox Message, 0, "TriPack"
        If Score > HiScore Then
            WriteProfileString "TriPack", "HiScore",
```

(continued)

Figure 11-11 *continued*

```
Str$(Score)
            End If
            Exit Sub
        End If
    Else                        'move existing block down 1 row
        EraseBlock
        CurRow = CurRow + 1
    End If
    DrawBlock
    If Not DropOK() Then        'test whether another drop is
                                'possible
        MarkCellTable           'record final position of block
        CurRow = -1             'signal Timer1_Timer that a new
                                'block is needed
    End If
End Sub
```

TPABOUT.FRM code

```
Sub Command1_Click ()
    Unload FormAbout
End Sub
```

Programming Techniques

As is the case with several of the games you have seen, the background for TriPack consists of a bitmap that was created in Paintbrush and then assigned to the main form's Picture property. The individual triangles are drawn on top of this bitmap by using the *BitBlt* Windows API function, employing the same technique used in the previous three games. With this technique, the image is transferred from two separate bitmaps: a mask bitmap and an image bitmap. The technique permits drawing (or erasing) a single triangle without disturbing adjoining triangles.

TriPack also uses the Visual Basic random-number generator to create random arrangements of blocks; this facility has been used in most of the games presented so far.

Additionally, TriPack introduces several new programming techniques. All the previous games have moved the playing objects in response to movements of the mouse. TriPack, however, moves the game objects (that is, the falling blocks of triangles) in response to timer and keyboard events. Accordingly, the TriPack program includes not only a timer event handler but also a low-level keyboard handler. In addition, TriPack includes code for saving game information in the Windows initialization file, so this information will be available the next time the player runs the program.

Program Overview

After a new game starts, all actions in TriPack are triggered by timer and keyboard events. A timer event occurs every 500 milliseconds and signals the program that it is time to drop the falling block another row. A keyboard event occurs whenever the player presses a key on the numeric keypad to manipulate the falling block.

Here is a summary of the main sequence of events in the TriPack program.

- When the program first starts running, *Form_Load* performs the one-time initialization tasks.

- When the player chooses the NewGame command from the Game menu, the *MenuNew_Click* event procedure assigns values to all variables that must be initialized for each new game and enables the timer so that timer events begin.

- When a timer event occurs, the *Timer1_Timer* event procedure moves the falling block down by one row. This procedure also creates a new block when needed, removes rows of triangles as connections are made, and terminates the game when no more blocks will fit within the window.

- When the player presses a key on the numeric keypad, the *Form_KeyDown* event procedure moves the block sideways or flips it, depending on the key pressed.

Initializing the Program

The *Form_Load* and *MenuNew_Click* procedures perform the program initialization tasks.

The *Form_Load* Procedure

The *Form_Load* event procedure begins with the device-independent code used for positioning and sizing the form. The form is placed quite near top of the screen to ensure that the entire playing area is initially visible on an EGA system.

Form_Load then initializes the coordinate values stored within two important program arrays, CellTable and TriTable.

CellTable stores information on each possible position of a triangle resting within the playing area. The playing area is high enough to hold 17 rows of triangles. Although the playing area is wide enough to hold only 6 triangles side by side, 11 possible horizontal positions are actually possible because triangles are allowed to overlap. (A downward-pointing triangle can overlap an upward-pointing one.) Accordingly, CellTable must be large enough to accommodate 17 rows and 11 columns. Several additional elements are included to simplify some of the tests that the program performs, resulting in the following declaration:

```
Dim CellTable(0 To 17, -3 To 11) As TRI
```

The TriTable array stores information about each triangle position within the current falling block. TriTable is declared large enough to hold the largest possible block, which is 2 triangles high and 3 triangles wide:

```
Dim TriTable(1 To 2, 1 To 3) As TRI
```

The base type of both of these arrays is TRI, which is defined in the global module as follows:

```
Type TRI
    X As Integer        'horizontal coordinate of upper left
                        'corner of triangle position
    Y As Integer        'vertical coordinate of upper left corner
    State As Integer    'type of triangle at the position:
                        'UP, DOWN, or NONE
    Color As Integer    'color of triangle: RED, GRN, BLU
End Type
```

The coordinates stored in CellTable are relative to the upper left corner of the form, and those stored in TriTable are relative to the upper left corner of the falling block.

The *MenuNew_Click* Procedure

The *MenuNew_Click* event procedure initializes a new game. It first clears the playing area by setting all of the *State* fields of CellTable to the value NONE, indicating that no triangles are currently positioned in the playing area, and by calling the *Cls* method to erase the images of any triangles currently displayed in the form.

Next, *MenuNew_Click* sets the form-level variable *CurRow* to −*1*. *CurRow* stores the number of the row within the playing area that currently contains the top row of the falling block. The special value −*1* indicates that *no* block is falling—that is, either a new game is starting or the previous falling block has reached its final resting position.

Next, *MenuNew_Click* assigns *0* to *Score*, which is a form-level variable that stores the total score for the current game.

Finally, the procedure enables the timer:

```
Timer1.Enabled = -1
```

Note: At design time, the Enabled property of the timer was set to False.

The *Timer1_Timer* Procedure

After the timer is enabled, the *Timer1_Timer* event procedure receives control every 500 milliseconds. (At design time, the timer's Interval property was set to 500.) This procedure performs the following two primary tasks:

- If no block is falling, the procedure creates a new block and places it at the top of the playing area.

- If a block *is* falling, the procedure moves it down by one row.

Creating a Block

At the beginning of a game, or whenever the currently falling block has reached its final position, the variable *CurRow* is set to −*1*. This value signals *Timer1_Timer* to create a new block. To do so, *Timer1_Timer* first sets the Interval property of the timer to 500 milliseconds, which is the normal time between each drop of the block. This step is necessary because the player might have pressed the Down arrow key, which causes the keyboard handler to temporarily set the interval to 5 milliseconds to accelerate the block's descent.

Timer1_Timer then sets *CurCol* to *4. CurCol* is analogous to *CurRow*; it is a form-level variable that stores the current column position of the leftmost triangle in the falling block.

Next, the procedure assigns a random color to all triangles in the block, using the Visual Basic *Rnd* function, as follows:

```
ColorVal = Int(3 * Rnd + 1)
For Row = 1 To 2
    For Col = 1 To 3
        TriTable(Row, Col).Color = ColorVal
    Next Col
Next Row
```

Remember that TriTable stores information on each of the six possible triangles within the falling block. The expression *Int(3 * Rnd + 1)* returns a random integer from 1 through 3. Each value indicates one of three possible colors (red, green, or blue). You will later see how the color values are used by the procedures that draw the triangles.

Timer1_Timer also uses the *Rnd* function to randomly select which positions within the block will contain triangles. To determine whether a given position will contain a triangle, it uses the expression

```
Int(2 * Rnd)
```

which returns either *0* or *1*. When assigning triangles, the procedure employs several additional guidelines. First, all triangles in the first (top) row must point up, and all those in the second (bottom) row must point down. Also, no gap can exist between triangles—that is, all triangles must touch along an edge or vertex. Finally, the block must contain at least one triangle.

The procedure assigns a code to the *State* field of each element of TriTable to indicate the triangle assigned to that position: UP (1) for an up-pointing triangle, DOWN (2) for a down-pointing triangle, or NONE (0) to indicate *no* triangle.

After assigning values to all fields of TriTable, *Timer1_Timer* calls the general procedure *DropOK* to determine whether the newly created block will fit at the top of the window:

```
If DropOK() Then
    CurRow = 0
    If DropOK() Then CurRow = 1
End If
```

Each call to *DropOK* checks whether the block can be dropped one row. *DropOK* is called twice because, conceptually, the new block is initially positioned *above* the playing area and is then dropped two rows so that it becomes completely visible. Notice that this code also sets *CurRow* to its initial value.

If the new block fits within the playing area, *Timer1_Timer* calls *DrawBlock* to draw the newly created block at the top of the playing area. The procedure then calls *DropOK* again to determine whether another drop is possible or whether the block has reached its final position. These steps are explained later, in the section "Dropping a Block."

If the new block does not fit within the playing area, *Timer1-_Timer* terminates the game. To terminate the game, the procedure first beeps, and then disables the timer so that the system will not call *Timer1-_Timer* again:

```
Timer1.Enabled = 0
```

The procedure then displays the total score for the game (stored in *Score*), as well as the highest previous score, with the Visual Basic *MsgBox* statement:

```
MsgBox Message, 0, "TriPack"
```

Saving and Retrieving the Highest Score

To preserve a record of the highest score to date, even after the program exits, TriPack writes this information to the WIN.INI file if the score for the current game is greater than the highest previous score (or if no score is currently saved in WIN.INI). In either case, *Timer1_Timer* writes the score to a private section of WIN.INI using the *WriteProfileString* Windows API function:

```
WriteProfileString("TriPack", "HiScore", Str$(Score))
```

Each piece of information in WIN.INI is stored as a *key* string, followed by an equal sign (=), followed by a *value* field. The first parameter in the call to *WriteProfileString* specifies the title of the private section of WIN.INI (if the section does not exist, Windows creates it), the second parameter specifies the key, and the third parameter specifies the value of this key. For example, if the current highest score is 1000, the function call shown above would result in the following entry in WIN.INI:

```
[TriPack]
HiScore=1000
```

WriteProfileString is described in Figure 11-12 on the following page.

Windows API Function: *WriteProfileString*

Purpose Writes information to a private section of the Windows initialization file, WIN.INI.

Declaration
```
Declare Sub WriteProfileString Lib "Kernel" (ByVal
  lpApplicationName$, ByVal lpKeyName$, ByVal lpString$)
```

Parameter	Description
lpApplicationName$	Title of the section of the WIN.INI file in which you want to write the information; usually, the name of the calling program.
lpKeyName$	The *key* portion of the information. (See "Comments," below.)
lpString$	The *value* of the key. (See "Comments," below.)

Comments Each item of information written to WIN.INI consists of a key followed by an equal sign (=), followed by a value.

WriteProfileString creates an entry in WIN.INI that has the following format:

[*lpApplicationName$*]
lpKeyName$*=*lpString$

Figure 11-12.
The WriteProfileString *Windows API function.*

The *Timer1_Timer* procedure retrieves the score from WIN.INI by calling the Windows API function *GetProfileInt*:

```
HiScore = GetProfileInt("TriPack", "HiScore", 0)
```

The first parameter specifies the title of the private section of the WIN.INI file, and the second parameter specifies the key. The third parameter is the desired default return value; if the key is not found, *GetProfileInt* will return this value. If the key is found, *GetProfileInt* will return its numeric value. For example, if no score is saved in WIN.INI, this function call would return 0. If, however, the entry shown above is contained in WIN.INI, the function call would return the numeric value 1000. *GetProfileInt* is described in Figure 11-13.

Windows API Function: *GetProfileInt*

Purpose Retrieves the numeric value of a specified key from the Windows initialization file, WIN.INI.

Declaration
```
Declare Function GetProfileInt Lib "Kernel" (ByVal
 lpAppName$, ByVal lpKeyName$, ByVal nDefault%) As Integer
```

Parameter	Description
lpAppName$	The title of the section of WIN.INI containing the key; usually, the name of the calling program.
lpKeyName$	The name of the key whose value you want to obtain.
nDefault%	The value you want *GetProfileInt* to return if the specified key is not found.

Return Value If the function is successful, the numeric value of the key. If the value of the key is not numeric (or if the value is negative), it returns *0*. If the key is not found, it returns the value you passed as the *nDefault%* parameter.

Comment See also *WriteProfileString* (Figure 11-12).

Figure 11-13.
The GetProfileInt *Windows API function.*

If the player chooses the Reset Hi Score command from the Options menu, the *MenuReset_Click* event procedure receives control. This procedure first displays a dialog box created with Visual Basic's *MsgBox* statement, to confirm that the player wants to erase the previous score. If the player clicks on Yes, the procedure calls *WriteProfileString*, passing an empty string as the value parameter:

```
WriteProfileString("TriPack", "HiScore", "")
```

As a result, the score saved in WIN.INI is erased. The next time a game is completed, the call to *GetProfileInt* will return *0*, and TriPack will call *WriteProfileString* to save the current score (provided the score is greater than *0*).

You can use *WriteProfileString* and *GetProfileInt* to save and retrieve a wide variety of game information as long as the information fits into the *key=value* format.

T I P

To read a string value from WIN.INI, you can use the Windows API function *GetProfileString*.

Dropping a Block

If a falling block already exists (that is, *CurRow* is not set to −*1*), the *Timer1_Timer* event procedure moves this block down one row. To do so, it first calls *EraseBlock* to erase the block at its current position. It then increments *CurRow*, and calls *DrawBlock* to draw the block at the new location.

DrawBlock draws a triangle at every position indicated in the Tri-Table array. It draws each triangle by making two calls to *BitBlt*, first to transfer a mask bitmap from one picture box, and then to transfer an image bitmap from another picture box. This technique is identical to the one used for drawing the playing pieces in the previous three games and is fully explained in Chapter 8, in the section titled ''The Drawing Technique.'' Recall that this technique allows you to rapidly draw a nonrectangular image, without disturbing the existing graphics surrounding the image. This technique is used in TriPack because a given triangle can be surrounded by one or more other triangles. The specific picture boxes that are used for drawing a given triangle depend on the direction of the triangle (UP or DOWN, which is stored in the *State* field of TriTable) and its color (RED, GRN, or BLU, which is stored in the *Color* field).

The *EraseBlock* general procedure uses the same bitmap technique as *DrawBlock*, except that it draws a *white* triangle on top of each existing triangle, which effectively erases the entire block (because the background color of the playing area is white).

Note: See Figures 11-6 and 11-7 for an illustration and description of each picture box used to store the bitmaps for drawing and erasing triangles.

Notice that the *DrawBlock* procedure ends with a call to the Visual Basic *Refresh* method. This call is necessary because the form's AutoRedraw property has been set to True. As explained in Chapter 9, if Auto-Redraw is enabled, you must call *Refresh* to make an image drawn with *BitBlt* visible (unless the procedure calling *BitBlt* also contains a call to a standard Visual Basic drawing method). Notice also that *EraseBlock* does *not* call *Refresh*, because *DrawBlock* is always called immediately afterwards, causing the form to be refreshed. (Calling *Refresh* from both procedures would produce an unnecessary flicker, as the erased drawing board momentarily flashes into view.)

After the dropped block has been redrawn in its new location, *Timer1_Timer* calls *DropOK* to determine whether another drop is possible or whether the block has reached its final resting position. *DropOK* returns TRUE if the block can be dropped another row, and it returns FALSE if the block is at the bottom of the playing area or if the block has landed on one or more triangles outside the block.

If *DropOK* returns FALSE, the *Timer1_Timer* procedure calls the *MarkCellTable* procedure to record the final position of the block. It then sets *CurRow* to −1 so that *Timer1_Timer* will create a new block the next time it is called.

The *MarkCellTable* procedure performs two important tasks:

1. It stores the final coordinates of each triangle within the block in the array CellTable. CellTable stores the coordinates, type (up-pointing or down-pointing), and the color of all triangles that are at rest within the playing area.

2. It tests to see whether a *connection* has been formed by the newly placed block. As you saw in the instructions for playing the game, a connection is an arrangement of triangles that forms a continuous horizontal link between the two sides of the playing area. (See Figure 11-3 for examples.)

If a connection is present, *MarkCellTable* removes both rows of triangles adjoining the connection and adds the appropriate number of points to the variable *Score*. Each row is removed by calling the general procedure *RemoveRow*, which simply deletes rows from the CellTable array. *MarkCellTable* then calls *DrawBoard* to redraw the playing area.

DrawBoard first erases all triangle images by calling Visual Basic's *Cls* method. *Cls* removes all images that were drawn with the *BitBlt* function but does *not* remove the underlying bitmap assigned to the form. *DrawBoard* then draws all the resting triangles in their current positions (as stored in CellTable), using the same calls to the *BitBlt* technique described previously.

The *Form_KeyDown* Procedure

The *Form_KeyDown* event procedure receives control whenever the player presses one of the numeric-keypad keys or one of the stand-alone arrow keys to manipulate the falling block.

Note: The keystrokes must be processed in a *KeyDown* event procedure rather than a *KeyPress* event procedure, because *KeyPress* events are not generated by stand-alone arrow keys or by numeric-keypad keys when NumLock is off.

The *Form_KeyDown* procedure exits immediately if any one of the following conditions is true:

- The timer is not enabled, indicating that a game is not in progress.

- The timer interval is set to 5 milliseconds, indicating that the player pressed the Down arrow key to drop the block. After pressing this key, the player loses the privilege of manipulating the block.

- *CurRow* is set to −1, indicating that there is currently no falling block.

If none of these conditions is true, the *Form_KeyDown* procedure continues as follows. If the user has pressed a Left or Right arrow key, the procedure first tests whether the block can be moved in the indicated direction. (The edge of the playing area, or a fixed triangle in the playing area, might prohibit the movement.) If the movement is possible, the procedure calls *EraseBlock* to erase the block in its original position, increments or decrements *CurCol*, and then calls *DrawBlock* to draw the block in the new position.

If the player has pressed the Up arrow key, the procedure calls *FlipV* to flip the block on the vertical direction. *FlipV* merely changes the arrangement of the elements of the TriTable, without redrawing the triangles. The procedure then calls *PositionOK* to see whether the new arrangement of the block is valid (that is, none of the triangles has landed outside of the playing area or overlaps a fixed triangle). If the new arrangement is valid, *Form_KeyDown* calls *FlipV* and *EraseBlock* to erase the original block configuration and then calls *FlipV* and *EraseBlock* to draw the block's new configuration.

If the block's new configuration is not valid, the procedure merely calls *FlipV* to restore the elements of TriTable; in this case, the player sees no change.

Notice that each branch of the *Select* statement lists several key codes. For example, the following branch receives control when the player presses the Left arrow key:

```
Case &H25, &H64
```

The first code is passed to *Form_KeyDown* if the player presses a Left arrow key that is not on the numeric keypad or presses the Left arrow key on the numeric keypad with NumLock off. The second code results from the player pressing the Left arrow key on the numeric keypad with NumLock on.

I obtained the code values by placing the following statement at the top of the *Form_KeyDown* procedure:

```
Debug.Print Hex$(KeyCode)
```

I then pressed each key and wrote down the code that was displayed.

If the player has pressed the center key (the 5 key on the numeric keypad), *Form_KeyDown* flips the block on the horizontal direction, if possible, using the same technique just described (except that it calls *FlipH* rather than *FlipV* to rearrange the elements of TriTable).

Finally, if the player has pressed the Down arrow key, *Form_Key-Down* sets the timer interval to 5 milliseconds to accelerate the block's descent:

```
Timer1.Interval = 5
```

Before terminating, *Form_KeyPress* calls *DropOK* to ensure that the block—in its new position—is still free to fall. If the block is *not* free to fall, *Form_KeyPress* calls *MarkCellTable* and sets *CurRow* to −1, exactly as for the *Timer1_Timer* procedure, described previously.

Enhancing the Game

Here are some suggestions for enhancing the TriPack program.

- In TriPack's current form, connections can be formed with relative ease. Consequently, games tend to last a long time. One reason for this is that the playing area is exactly wide enough to accommodate 6 triangles, and, conveniently, many of the blocks are 3 triangles wide. As you become an experienced player, you might want to make it more difficult to form connections. One way to do this would be to generate blocks that are from 1 through 4 triangles wide. Another way would be to change the width of the playing area. You can adjust these factors until you obtain a game that is suitably challenging. You could even allow the player to freely adjust these parameters by choosing a menu command.

- Provide various playing levels. At each higher level, the blocks would drop faster; the greater speed is achieved simply by decreasing the Interval property of the timer. You could have the program automatically move to higher (more difficult) levels as the game progresses, or you could allow the player to choose the level of difficulty before starting a game.

- Award bonus points whenever the player presses the Down arrow key, which makes the block fall more rapidly. Currently, the only reason for pressing this key is to make the game move along faster.

- When the program removes a pair of rows, it does not check whether another connection has been formed in the process. The player might see this connection and feel cheated. You might therefore want to repeat the test for a connection immediately after removing rows (in the procedure *Mark-CellTable*), and then remove two more rows if another connection is discovered.

- Add a text box to the form to provide a continuous display of the current score.

CHAPTER TWELVE

GRID WAR

In the Grid War game, you engage in combat against an enemy spaceship. Destroying the enemy ship requires precise maneuvering and the well-timed firing of a torpedo. You must also avoid colliding with the enemy ship or being hit by one of its torpedoes. The game seems to start slowly, but you will soon learn that the enemy is a formidable opponent.

The code for Grid War shows how to animate game objects using Visual Basic picture boxes, the *Move* method, and a timer object. You will also learn how to use the *IntersectRect* Windows API function for easily detecting collisions between game objects.

Playing Grid War

When you run Grid War (GW.EXE), the program starts a game. You can later start a new game—even before the current game is over—by choosing the New Game command from the Game menu. At the beginning of a game, two spaceships appear within the grid: Your ship is the yellow one, located in the upper left corner. The enemy ship is the red one, located in the lower right corner. Figure 12-1 shows Grid War at the beginning of a game.

your ship ——

—— the enemy ship

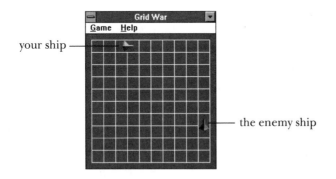

Figure 12-1.
Grid War at the beginning of a game.

405

The enemy ship pursues your ship doggedly throughout the game. Also, as soon as it begins moving within the same row or column as your ship, it fires a torpedo at you. If your ship collides with the enemy ship or is struck by one of the enemy's torpedoes, your ship is destroyed and the game is over.

Use the arrow keys in the numeric keypad (or in the stand-alone four-key arrow keypad) to maneuver your ship through the white grid. You can move only through the marked rows and columns. To fire a torpedo, press the key in the center of the numeric keypad (the 5 key). If you hit the enemy ship with a torpedo, the enemy ship is destroyed and you score 1 point. If a torpedo reaches the edge of the grid, it disappears; and if it collides with a torpedo fired by the enemy, the two torpedoes neutralize each other and vanish.

Note: A torpedo travels in a straight path at twice the speed of a spaceship. (See the section titled "Creating Different Object Speeds," later in this chapter.) If a ship fires a torpedo, it cannot fire another one while the original torpedo is still within the playing grid.

If your ship destroys the enemy ship by colliding with it, you will score a point. This point, however, will be your last in the game—because your ship will also be destroyed!

If you destroy the enemy ship, the program pauses for a few seconds…and then creates another enemy ship. This time, however, the ship does not necessarily appear in the lower right corner. Rather, it can arrive within any of the squares along the outside edges of the grid. It can even appear within the same square that contains your ship; in this case, the game will be over quickly. (Yes, there is an element of luck in this game.)

The game will continue in this manner as long as you keep obliterating enemy ships. The object is to defeat as many of these ships as you can. If your ship is destroyed, Grid War ends the game and displays your score, which equals the total number of enemy ships you have destroyed.

Strategy and Hints

You can defeat the first enemy ship through skill alone. However, as soon as each new enemy ship appears at a random location along the edge of the grid, luck will play an important part in your success. (In fact, if an enemy ship materializes in the square your ship is currently occupying, your ship's destruction is inescapable.)

The primary defensive strategy is to keep your ship as far in front of the enemy ship as possible. You can defend your ship against a torpedo using one of the following two strategies:

- Make a right angle turn out of your current row or column. The torpedo will continue to move in a straight line and will miss your ship.

- Fire one of your torpedoes directly at the approaching enemy torpedo. When the two torpedoes collide, they destroy each other. Be aware, however, that if you keep approaching the enemy while firing away, hoping to ward off all approaching torpedoes, you will lose the battle because the enemy's torpedo technology is slightly better than yours! (Note: As explained later in this chapter in the section titled "Moving the Torpedoes," the red torpedo is moved before the yellow one.)

The only way I have found to destroy the enemy ship is to fire a torpedo at it from a direction that is at a right angle to the enemy's direction of travel. You must time the release of the torpedo so that it hits the enemy ship just as the enemy ship reaches your ship's row or column location. It you fire a bit early, you will miss the ship; if you fire a bit late, the enemy will destroy your torpedo with one of its own. Figure 12-2 shows this strategy.

fire when your ship is here...

...and you will hit the enemy ship when it arrives here (before it turns toward you)

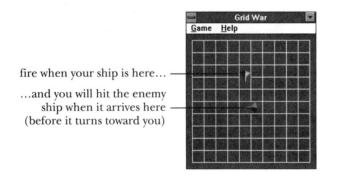

Figure 12-2.
A strategy for destroying the enemy ship.

Coding Grid War

The source code for the Grid War program is contained in the files listed in the following table.

File	Purpose
GLOBALGW.BAS	Contains global type definitions
GW.FRM	Defines the main form, FormMain, and the controls it contains
GWABOUT.FRM	Defines the ABOUT form, FormAbout, and the controls it contains
GW.MAK	Contains the Grid War project file

Figures 12-3 through 12-8 present the form designs, properties, menu commands, and source code for the Grid War program.

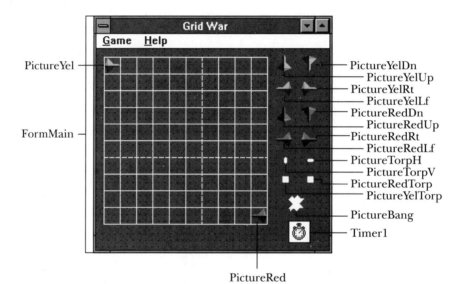

Figure 12-3.
GW.FRM at design time.

Object Name	Object Type	Property	Setting
FormMain	Form	BackColor	&H00800000& [dark blue]
		BorderStyle	1 - Fixed Single
		Caption	Grid War

Figure 12-4.
GW.FRM form and control properties.

(continued)

Figure 12-4 *continued*

Object Name	Object Type	Property	Setting
		FormName	FormMain
		Grid Height	8 [pixels]
		Grid Width	8 [pixels]
		Height	4485 [twips]
		Icon	(Icon) [GW.ICO]
		Left	1020 [twips]
		MaxButton	False
		Picture	(Bitmap) [GW.BMP]
		ScaleMode	3 - Pixel
		Top	1110 [twips]
		Width	4620 [twips]
PictureBang	Picture box	AutoSize	True
		BorderStyle	0 - None
		CtlName	PictureBang
		Height	20 [pixels]
		Left	248 [pixels]
		Picture	(Bitmap) [BANG.BMP]
		Top	184 [pixels]
		Visible	False
		Width	20 [pixels]
PictureRed	Picture box	AutoSize	True
		BorderStyle	0 - None
		CtlName	PictureRed
		Enabled	False
		Height	20 [pixels]
		Left	200 [pixels]
		Picture	(Bitmap) [REDLF.BMP]
		Top	200 [pixels]
		Width	20 [pixels]
PictureRedDn	Picture box	AutoSize	True
		BorderStyle	0 - None
		CtlName	PictureRedDn

(continued)

Figure 12-4 *continued*

Object Name	Object Type	Property	Setting
		Height	20 [pixels]
		Left	264 [pixels]
		Picture	(Bitmap) [REDDN.BMP]
		Top	72 [pixels]
		Visible	False
		Width	20 [pixels]
PictureRedLf	Picture box	AutoSize	True
		BorderStyle	0 - None
		CtlName	PictureRedLf
		Height	20 [pixels]
		Left	232 [pixels]
		Picture	(Bitmap) [REDLF.BMP]
		Top	104 [pixels]
		Visible	False
		Width	20 [pixels]
PictureRedRt		AutoSize	True
		BorderStyle	0 - None
		CtlName	PictureRedRt
		Height	20 [pixels]
		Left	264 [pixels]
		Picture	(Bitmap) [REDRT.BMP]
		Top	104 [pixels]
		Visible	False
		Width	20 [pixels]
PictureRedTorp	Picture box	AutoSize	True
		BorderStyle	0 - None
		CtlName	PictureRedTorp
		Enabled	False
		Height	8 [pixels]
		Left	272 [pixels]

(continued)

Figure 12-4 *continued*

Object Name	Object Type	Property	Setting
		Top	160 [pixels]
		Visible	False
		Width	8 [pixels]
PictureRedUp		AutoSize	True
		BorderStyle	0 - None
		CtlName	PictureRedUp
		Height	20 [pixels]
		Left	232 [pixels]
		Picture	(Bitmap)[REDUP.BMP]
		Top	72 [pixels]
		Visible	False
		Width	20 [pixels]
PictureTorpH	Picture box	AutoSize	True
		BorderStyle	0 - None
		CtlName	PictureTorpH
		Height	8 [pixels]
		Left	272 [pixels]
		Picture	(Bitmap) [TORPH.BMP]
		Top	136 [pixels]
		Visible	False
		Width	8 [pixels]
PictureTorpV	Picture box	AutoSize	True
		BorderStyle	0 - None
		CtlName	PictureTorpV
		Height	8 [pixels]
		Left	240 [pixels]
		Picture	(Bitmap) [TORPV.BMP]
		Top	136 [pixels]
		Visible	False
		Width	8 [pixels]

(continued)

411

Figure 12-4 *continued*

Object Name	Object Type	Property	Setting
PictureYel	Picture box	AutoSize	True
		BorderStyle	0 - None
		CtlName	PictureYel
		Enabled	False
		Height	20 [pixels]
		Left	11 [pixels]
		Picture	(Bitmap) [YELRT.BMP]
		Top	11 [pixels]
		Width	20 [pixels]
PictureYelDn	Picture box	AutoSize	True
		BorderStyle	0 - None
		CtlName	PictureYelDn
		Height	20 [pixels]
		Left	264 [pixels]
		Picture	(Bitmap) [YELDN.BMP]
		Top	8 [pixels]
		Visible	False
		Width	20 [pixels]
PictureYelLf	Picture box	AutoSize	True
		BorderStyle	0 - None
		CtlName	PictureYelLf
		Height	20 [pixels]
		Left	232 [pixels]
		Picture	(Bitmap) [YELLF.BMP]
		Top	40 [pixels]
		Visible	False
		Width	20 [pixels]
PictureYelTorp	Picture box	AutoSize	True
		BorderStyle	0 - None
		CtlName	PictureYelTorp
		Enabled	False
		Height	8 [pixels]

(continued)

Figure 12-4 *continued*

Object Name	Object Type	Property	Setting
		Left	240 [pixels]
		Top	160 [pixels]
		Visible	False
		Width	8 [pixels]
PictureYelRt	Picture box	AutoSize	True
		BorderStyle	0 - None
		CtlName	PictureYelRt
		Height	20 [pixels]
		Left	264 [pixels]
		Picture	(Bitmap) [YELRT.BMP]
		Top	40 [pixels]
		Visible	False
		Width	20 [pixels]
PictureYelUp	Picture box	AutoSize	True
		BorderStyle	0 - None
		CtlName	PictureYelUp
		Height	20 [pixels]
		Left	232 [pixels]
		Picture	(Bitmap) [YELUP.BMP]
		Top	8 [pixels]
		Visible	False
		Width	20 [pixels]
Timer1	Timer	Enabled	False
		Interval	10 [milliseconds]

Indentation/Caption	Control Name	Other Features
&Game	MenuGame	
....&New Game	MenuNew	
....-	MenuSep1	
....E&xit	MenuExit	

Figure 12-5.
GW.FRM menu design.

(continued)

Figure 12-5 *continued*

Indentation/Caption	Control Name	Other Features
&Help	MenuHelp	
....&Index	MenuIndex	Accelerator = F1
....&How to Play	MenuHowTo	
....&Commands	MenuCommands	
....&Using Help	MenuUsingHelp	
....-	MenuSep2	
....&About Grid War...	MenuAbout	

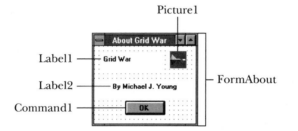

Figure 12-6.
GWABOUT.FRM at design time.

Object Name	Object Type	Property	Setting
Command1	Command button	Caption	OK
		Default	True
		Height	375 [twips]
		Left	840 [twips]
		Top	1440 [twips]
		Width	1095 [twips]
FormAbout	Form	BorderStyle	3 - Fixed Double
		Caption	About Grid War
		FormName	FormAbout
		Grid Height	120 [twips]

Figure 12-7.   *(continued)*
GWABOUT.FRM form and control properties.

414

Figure 12-7 *continued*

Object Name	Object Type	Property	Setting
		Grid Width	120 [twips]
		Height	2445 [twips]
		Left	1140 [twips]
		MaxButton	False
		MinButton	False
		Top	1440 [twips]
		Width	2880 [twips]
Label1	Label	Caption	Grid War
		Height	375 [twips]
		Left	240 [twips]
		Top	240 [twips]
		Width	1575 [twips]
Label2	Label	Alignment	2 - Center
		Caption	By Michael J. Young
		Height	375 [twips]
		Left	0 [twips]
		Top	960 [twips]
		Width	2745 [twips]
Picture1	Picture box	AutoSize	True
		BorderStyle	0 - None
		Height	480 [twips]
		Left	2040 [twips]
		Picture	(Icon) [GW.ICO]
		Top	120 [twips]
		Width	480 [twips]

GLOBALGW.BAS code

```
Type RECT
    Left As Integer
    Top As Integer
```

Figure 12-8.   *(continued)*

Source code for the Grid War program. (Notice that long lines are wrapped to the next line and indented one space.)

Figure 12-8 *continued*

```
      Right As Integer
      Bottom As Integer
End Type
```

GW.FRM code

```
'Help Section:
'Help file:
Const HELP_FILE = "GW.HLP"
'WinHelp wCommand values:
Const HELP_CONTEXT = &H1
Const HELP_HELPONHELP = &H4
Const HELP_INDEX = &H3
Const HELP_QUIT = &H2
'WinHelp dwData values (help topics):
Const HELP_HOWTOPLAY = 10&
Const HELP_COMMANDS = 20&
'Windows help API:
Declare Sub WinHelp Lib "USER" (ByVal hWnd As Integer,
 ByVal lpHelpFile As String, ByVal wCommand As Integer,
 ByVal dwData As Long)

Const CLIENTRIGHT = 230 'coordinates of lower right
                        'corner of inside of form
Const CLIENTBOTTOM = 231
Const DIRLEFT = 1
Const DIRUP = 2
Const DIRRIGHT = 3
Const DIRDOWN = 4

Dim FireYelTorp As Integer
Dim GridRect As RECT
Dim RedCol As Integer
Dim RedDir As Integer
Dim RedMoves As Integer
Dim RedTorpDir As Integer
Dim RedRow As Integer
Dim Score As Integer
Dim TimerToggle As Integer
Dim WaitCount As Integer
Dim YelCol As Integer
Dim YelDir As Integer
```

(continued)

Figure 12-8 *continued*

```
Dim YelMoves As Integer
Dim YelNextDir As Integer
Dim YelRow As Integer
Dim YelTorpCol As Integer
Dim YelTorpDir As Integer
Dim YelTorpRow As Integer


Const WS_CAPTION = &HC00000
Const WS_THICKFRAME = &H40000
Declare Sub AdjustWindowRect Lib "USER" (lpRect As RECT,
 ByVal dwStyle&, ByVal bMenu%)


Const LOGPIXELSX = 88
Const LOGPIXELSY = 90
Declare Function GetDeviceCaps Lib "GDI" (ByVal hDC%,
 ByVal Index%) As Integer


Declare Function IntersectRect Lib "USER" (lpDestRect As RECT,
 lpSrc1Rect As RECT, lpSrc2Rect As RECT) As Integer


Function Collision ()
    Dim IntRect As RECT
    Dim YelRect As RECT
    Dim RedRect As RECT

    YelRect.Left = PictureYel.Left
    YelRect.Top = PictureYel.Top
    YelRect.Right = PictureYel.Left + PictureYel.Width - 1
    YelRect.Bottom = PictureYel.Top + PictureYel.Height - 1
    RedRect.Left = PictureRed.Left
    RedRect.Top = PictureRed.Top
    RedRect.Right = PictureRed.Left + PictureRed.Width - 1
    RedRect.Bottom = PictureRed.Top + PictureRed.Height - 1
    If IntersectRect(IntRect, YelRect, RedRect) Then
        Collision = -1
    Else
        Collision = 0
    End If
End Function

Sub EndGame ()
    Dim Message As String

    Timer1.Enabled = 0
    Beep: Beep: Beep: Beep: Beep: Beep
```

(continued)

Figure 12-8 *continued*

```
      PictureYelTorp.Visible = 0
      PictureRedTorp.Visible = 0
      Message = "Game Over" + Chr$(13) + Chr$(10) + Chr$(13) +
  Chr$(10)
      Message = Message + "Score: " + Str$(Score)
      MsgBox Message, 0, "Grid War"
  End Sub

  Sub GetRandomStart (Col As Integer, Row As Integer,
   X As Integer, Y As Integer)
      Dim Edge As Integer
      Dim Square As Integer

      Edge = Int(4 * Rnd + 1)      '1 to 4
      Square = Int(10 * Rnd + 1)  '1 to 10
      Select Case Edge
          Case 1            'left edge
              Col = 1
              Row = Square
              X = 11
              Y = 11 + (Square - 1) * 21
          Case 2            'top edge
              Col = Square
              Row = 1
              X = 11 + (Square - 1) * 21
              Y = 11
          Case 3            'right edge
              Col = 10
              Row = Square
              X = 200
              Y = 11 + (Square - 1) * 21
          Case 4            'bottom edge
              Col = Square
              Row = 10
              X = 11 + (Square - 1) * 21
              Y = 200
      End Select
  End Sub

  Function GetRedDir ()
      If YelDir = DIRLEFT Or YelDir = DIRRIGHT Then
          If YelRow < RedRow Then
              GetRedDir = DIRUP
```

(continued)

Figure 12-8 *continued*

```
        ElseIf YelRow > RedRow Then
            GetRedDir = DIRDOWN
        Else
            If YelCol < RedCol Then
                GetRedDir = DIRLEFT
            Else
                GetRedDir = DIRRIGHT
            End If
        End If
    Else
        If YelCol < RedCol Then
            GetRedDir = DIRLEFT
        ElseIf YelCol > RedCol Then
            GetRedDir = DIRRIGHT
        Else
            If YelRow < RedRow Then
                GetRedDir = DIRUP
            Else
                GetRedDir = DIRDOWN
            End If
        End If
    End If
End Function

Sub InitNewGame ()
    FireYelTorp = 0
    RedCol = 10
    RedMoves = 7
    RedRow = 10
    Score = 0
    YelCol = 1
    YelDir = DIRRIGHT
    YelMoves = 0
    YelNextDir = DIRRIGHT
    YelRow = 1
    PictureYel.Picture = PictureYelRt.Picture
    PictureYelTorp.Visible = 0
    PictureRedTorp.Visible = 0
    PictureYel.Move 11, 11
    PictureRed.Move 200, 200
    Timer1.Enabled = -1
End Sub
```

(continued)

419

Figure 12-8 *continued*

```
Function OutOfBounds (ByVal LeftEdge As Single,
  ByVal TopEdge As Single)
    OutOfBounds = 0
    If LeftEdge <= GridRect.Left Then OutOfBounds = -1
    If TopEdge <= GridRect.Top Then OutOfBounds = -1
    If LeftEdge + 7 >= GridRect.Right Then OutOfBounds = -1
    If TopEdge + 7 >= GridRect.Bottom Then OutOfBounds = -1
End Function

Function TorpCollision ()
    Dim IntRect As RECT
    Dim YelTorpRect As RECT
    Dim RedTorpRect As RECT

    If PictureYelTorp.Visible = 0 Or PictureRedTorp.Visible
= 0 Then
        TorpCollision = 0
        Exit Function
    End If
    YelTorpRect.Left = PictureYelTorp.Left
    YelTorpRect.Top = PictureYelTorp.Top
    YelTorpRect.Right = PictureYelTorp.Left +
 PictureYelTorp.Width - 1
    YelTorpRect.Bottom = PictureYelTorp.Top +
 PictureYelTorp.Height - 1
    RedTorpRect.Left = PictureRedTorp.Left
    RedTorpRect.Top = PictureRedTorp.Top
    RedTorpRect.Right = PictureRedTorp.Left +
 PictureRedTorp.Width - 1
    RedTorpRect.Bottom = PictureRedTorp.Top +
 PictureRedTorp.Height - 1
    If IntersectRect(IntRect, YelTorpRect, RedTorpRect) Then
        TorpCollision = -1
    Else
        TorpCollision = 0
    End If
End Function

Function RedHit ()
    Dim IntRect As RECT
    Dim RedRect As RECT
    Dim YelTorpRect As RECT
```

(continued)

Figure 12-8 *continued*

```
    RedRect.Left = PictureRed.Left
    RedRect.Top = PictureRed.Top
    RedRect.Right = PictureRed.Left + PictureRed.Width - 1
    RedRect.Bottom = PictureRed.Top + PictureRed.Height - 1
    YelTorpRect.Left = PictureYelTorp.Left
    YelTorpRect.Top = PictureYelTorp.Top
    YelTorpRect.Right = PictureYelTorp.Left +
PictureYelTorp.Width - 1
    YelTorpRect.Bottom = PictureYelTorp.Top +
PictureYelTorp.Height - 1
    If IntersectRect(IntRect, RedRect, YelTorpRect) Then
        RedHit = -1
    Else
        RedHit = 0
    End If
End Function

Function YelHit ()
    Dim IntRect As RECT
    Dim YelRect As RECT
    Dim RedTorpRect As RECT

    YelRect.Left = PictureYel.Left
    YelRect.Top = PictureYel.Top
    YelRect.Right = PictureYel.Left + PictureYel.Width - 1
    YelRect.Bottom = PictureYel.Top + PictureYel.Height - 1
    RedTorpRect.Left = PictureRedTorp.Left
    RedTorpRect.Top = PictureRedTorp.Top
    RedTorpRect.Right = PictureRedTorp.Left +
PictureRedTorp.Width - 1
    RedTorpRect.Bottom = PictureRedTorp.Top +
PictureRedTorp.Height - 1
    If IntersectRect(IntRect, YelRect, RedTorpRect) Then
        YelHit = -1
    Else
        YelHit = 0
    End If
End Function

Sub Form_KeyDown (KeyCode As Integer, Shift As Integer)
    If Timer1.Enabled = 0 Then Exit Sub
    Select Case KeyCode
        Case &H25, &H64      'Left arrow (4)
            YelNextDir = DIRLEFT
```

(continued)

Figure 12-8 *continued*

```
        Case &H26, &H68      'Up arrow (8)
            YelNextDir = DIRUP
        Case &H27, &H66      'Right arrow (6)
            YelNextDir = DIRRIGHT
        Case &H28, &H62      'Down arrow (2)
            YelNextDir = DIRDOWN
        Case &HC, &H65       'center key (5): fire torpedo
            If PictureYelTorp.Visible = 0 Then FireYelTorp
= -1
    End Select
End Sub


Sub Form_Load ()
    Dim Rec As RECT

    'code for display device independence:
    Rec.Left = 0
    Rec.Top = 0
    Rec.Right = CLIENTRIGHT
    Rec.Bottom = CLIENTBOTTOM
    AdjustWindowRect Rec, WS_CAPTION, -1
    FormMain.Width = (Rec.Right - Rec.Left + 1) * (1440 /
GetDeviceCaps(hDC, LOGPIXELSX))
    FormMain.Height = (Rec.Bottom - Rec.Top + 1) * (1440 /
GetDeviceCaps(hDC, LOGPIXELSY))

    GridRect.Left = 10
    GridRect.Top = 10
    GridRect.Right = 220
    GridRect.Bottom = 220
    Randomize
    InitNewGame
End Sub


Sub Form_Unload (Cancel As Integer)
    WinHelp hWnd, HELP_FILE, HELP_QUIT, 0
End Sub


Sub MenuAbout_Click ()
    FormAbout.Show 1
End Sub


Sub MenuCommands_Click ()
    WinHelp hWnd, HELP_FILE, HELP_CONTEXT, HELP_COMMANDS
End Sub
```

(continued)

Figure 12-8 *continued*

```
Sub MenuExit_Click ()
    WinHelp hWnd, HELP_FILE, HELP_QUIT, 0
    End
End Sub

Sub MenuHowTo_Click ()
    WinHelp hWnd, HELP_FILE, HELP_CONTEXT, HELP_HOWTOPLAY
End Sub

Sub MenuIndex_Click ()
    WinHelp hWnd, HELP_FILE, HELP_INDEX, 0
End Sub

Sub MenuNew_Click ()
    InitNewGame
End Sub

Sub MenuUsingHelp_Click ()
    WinHelp hWnd, HELP_FILE, HELP_HELPONHELP, 0
End Sub

Sub Timer1_Timer ()
    Dim Col As Integer
    Dim FireRedTorp As Integer
    Dim Moved As Integer
    Dim Row As Integer
    Dim X As Integer
    Dim Y As Integer

    'wait after a red ship is hit:
    If WaitCount > 0 Then
        WaitCount = WaitCount - 1
        If WaitCount = 0 Then    'reinitialize red ship
            RedMoves = 7
            GetRandomStart Col, Row, X, Y
            RedCol = Col
            RedRow = Row
            PictureRed.Move X, Y
        Else
            Exit Sub
        End If
    End If
```

(continued)

Figure 12-8 *continued*

```
'move red torpedo:
If PictureRedTorp.Visible Then
    Select Case RedTorpDir
        Case DIRLEFT
            PictureRedTorp.Move PictureRedTorp.Left - 3,
PictureRedTorp.Top
        Case DIRUP
            PictureRedTorp.Move PictureRedTorp.Left,
PictureRedTorp.Top - 3
        Case DIRRIGHT
            PictureRedTorp.Move PictureRedTorp.Left + 3,
PictureRedTorp.Top
        Case DIRDOWN
            PictureRedTorp.Move PictureRedTorp.Left,
PictureRedTorp.Top + 3
    End Select
    If TorpCollision() Then
        Beep: Beep: Beep
        PictureYelTorp.Visible = 0
        PictureRedTorp.Visible = 0
    ElseIf YelHit() Then
        PictureYel.Picture = PictureBang.Picture
        EndGame
        Exit Sub
    ElseIf OutOfBounds(PictureRedTorp.Left,
PictureRedTorp.Top) Then
        PictureRedTorp.Visible = 0
    End If
End If

'move yellow torpedo:
If PictureYelTorp.Visible Then
    Select Case YelTorpDir
        Case DIRLEFT
            PictureYelTorp.Move PictureYelTorp.Left - 3,
PictureYelTorp.Top
        Case DIRUP
            PictureYelTorp.Move PictureYelTorp.Left,
PictureYelTorp.Top - 3
        Case DIRRIGHT
            PictureYelTorp.Move PictureYelTorp.Left + 3,
PictureYelTorp.Top
        Case DIRDOWN
```

(continued)

Figure 12-8 *continued*

```
                PictureYelTorp.Move PictureYelTorp.Left,
    PictureYelTorp.Top + 3
        End Select
        If TorpCollision() Then
            Beep: Beep: Beep
            PictureYelTorp.Visible = 0
            PictureRedTorp.Visible = 0
        ElseIf RedHit() Then
            Beep: Beep: Beep
            Score = Score + 1
            PictureRed.Picture = PictureBang.Picture
            PictureYelTorp.Visible = 0
            PictureRedTorp.Visible = 0
            WaitCount = 25
            Exit Sub
        ElseIf OutOfBounds(PictureYelTorp.Left,
    PictureYelTorp.Top) Then
            PictureYelTorp.Visible = 0
        End If
    End If

    'exit on every other timer event:
    TimerToggle = TimerToggle Xor -1
    If TimerToggle Then Exit Sub

    'move yellow ship:
    If YelMoves >= 7 Then
        Select Case YelNextDir
            Case DIRLEFT
                If YelCol > 1 Then
                    PictureYel.Picture = PictureYelLf.Picture
                    YelDir = DIRLEFT
                End If
            Case DIRUP
                If YelRow > 1 Then
                    PictureYel.Picture = PictureYelUp.Picture
                    YelDir = DIRUP
                End If
            Case DIRRIGHT
                If YelCol < 10 Then
                    PictureYel.Picture = PictureYelRt.Picture
                    YelDir = DIRRIGHT
                End If
```

(continued)

Figure 12-8 *continued*

```
            Case DIRDOWN
                If YelRow < 10 Then
                    PictureYel.Picture = PictureYelDn.Picture
                    YelDir = DIRDOWN
                End If
        End Select
        YelMoves = 0
    End If
    Select Case YelDir
        Case DIRLEFT
            If YelCol > 1 Then
                PictureYel.Move PictureYel.Left - 3,
PictureYel.Top
                Moved = -1
            End If
        Case DIRUP
            If YelRow > 1 Then
                PictureYel.Move PictureYel.Left,
PictureYel.Top - 3
                Moved = -1
            End If
        Case DIRRIGHT
            If YelCol < 10 Then
                PictureYel.Move PictureYel.Left + 3,
PictureYel.Top
                Moved = -1
            End If
        Case DIRDOWN
            If YelRow < 10 Then
                PictureYel.Move PictureYel.Left,
PictureYel.Top + 3
                Moved = -1
            End If
    End Select
    If Moved Then
        If Collision() Then
            PictureYel.Picture = PictureBang.Picture
            PictureRed.Picture = PictureBang.Picture
            Score = Score + 1
            EndGame
            Exit Sub
        End If
```

(continued)

Figure 12-8 *continued*

```
        YelMoves = YelMoves + 1
        If YelMoves >= 7 Then
            Select Case YelDir
                Case DIRLEFT
                    YelCol = YelCol - 1
                Case DIRUP
                    YelRow = YelRow - 1
                Case DIRRIGHT
                    YelCol = YelCol + 1
                Case DIRDOWN
                    YelRow = YelRow + 1
            End Select
        End If
    Else
        YelMoves = 7
    End If


    'fire yellow torpedo if needed:
    If FireYelTorp Then        'FireYelTorp set by Form_KeyDown
        Select Case YelDir
            Case DIRLEFT
                PictureYelTorp.Picture = PictureTorpH.Picture
                PictureYelTorp.Move PictureYel.Left - 8,
PictureYel.Top + 6
            Case DIRUP
                PictureYelTorp.Picture = PictureTorpV.Picture
                PictureYelTorp.Move PictureYel.Left + 6,
PictureYel.Top - 8
            Case DIRRIGHT
                PictureYelTorp.Picture = PictureTorpH.Picture
                PictureYelTorp.Move PictureYel.Left +
PictureYel.Width, PictureYel.Top + 6
            Case DIRDOWN
                PictureYelTorp.Picture = PictureTorpV.Picture
                PictureYelTorp.Move PictureYel.Left + 6,
PictureYel.Top + PictureYel.Height
        End Select
        YelTorpCol = YelCol
        YelTorpRow = YelRow
        YelTorpDir = YelDir
        PictureYelTorp.Visible = -1
        FireYelTorp = 0
    End If
```

(continued)

Figure 12-8 *continued*

```
'move red ship:
If RedMoves >= 7 Then
    RedDir = GetRedDir()
    Select Case RedDir
        Case DIRLEFT
            PictureRed.Picture = PictureRedLf.Picture
        Case DIRUP
            PictureRed.Picture = PictureRedUp.Picture
        Case DIRRIGHT
            PictureRed.Picture = PictureRedRt.Picture
        Case DIRDOWN
            PictureRed.Picture = PictureRedDn.Picture
    End Select
    RedMoves = 0
End If
Select Case RedDir
    Case DIRLEFT
        PictureRed.Move PictureRed.Left - 3,
PictureRed.Top
    Case DIRUP
        PictureRed.Move PictureRed.Left,
PictureRed.Top - 3
    Case DIRRIGHT
        PictureRed.Move PictureRed.Left + 3,
PictureRed.Top
    Case DIRDOWN
        PictureRed.Move PictureRed.Left,
PictureRed.Top + 3
End Select
If Collision() Then
    PictureYel.Picture = PictureBang.Picture
    PictureRed.Picture = PictureBang.Picture
    Score = Score + 1
    EndGame
    Exit Sub
End If
RedMoves = RedMoves + 1
If RedMoves >= 7 Then
    Select Case RedDir
        Case DIRLEFT
            RedCol = RedCol - 1
        Case DIRUP
            RedRow = RedRow - 1
        Case DIRRIGHT
```

(continued)

Figure 12-8 *continued*

```
                RedCol = RedCol + 1
            Case DIRDOWN
                RedRow = RedRow + 1
        End Select
   End If


   'fire red torpedo if needed:
   If PictureRedTorp.Visible = 0 Then
       If (RedDir = DIRLEFT Or RedDir = DIRRIGHT) And (YelDir
= DIRLEFT Or YelDir = DIRRIGHT) And YelRow = RedRow Then
           FireRedTorp = -1
       ElseIf (RedDir = DIRUP Or RedDir = DIRDOWN) And (YelDir
= DIRUP Or YelDir = DIRDOWN) And YelCol = RedCol Then
           FireRedTorp = -1
       ElseIf PictureYelTorp.Visible Then
           If (RedDir = DIRLEFT Or RedDir = DIRRIGHT) And
(YelTorpDir = DIRLEFT Or YelTorpDir = DIRRIGHT) And
YelTorpRow = RedRow Then
               FireRedTorp = -1
           End If
           If (RedDir = DIRUP Or RedDir = DIRDOWN) And
(YelTorpDir = DIRUP Or YelTorpDir = DIRDOWN) And YelTorpCol =
RedCol Then
               FireRedTorp = -1
           End If
       End If
       If FireRedTorp Then
           Select Case RedDir
               Case DIRLEFT
                   PictureRedTorp.Picture =
PictureTorpH.Picture
                   PictureRedTorp.Move PictureRed.Left - 8,
PictureRed.Top + 6
               Case DIRUP
                   PictureRedTorp.Picture =
PictureTorpV.Picture
                   PictureRedTorp.Move PictureRed.Left + 6,
PictureRed.Top - 8
               Case DIRRIGHT
                   PictureRedTorp.Picture =
PictureTorpH.Picture
                   PictureRedTorp.Move PictureRed.Left +
PictureRed.Width, PictureRed.Top + 6
```

(continued)

Figure 12-8 *continued*

```
                Case DIRDOWN
                       PictureRedTorp.Picture =
  PictureTorpV.Picture
                       PictureRedTorp.Move PictureRed.Left + 6,
  PictureRed.Top + PictureRed.Height
              End Select
              RedTorpDir = RedDir
              PictureRedTorp.Visible = -1
          End If
      End If
  End Sub
```

GWABOUT.FRM code

```
Sub Command1_Click ()
    Unload FormAbout
End Sub
```

Programming Techniques

As with many of the games presented in this book, the background for the Grid War game consists of a bitmap, which was created in Paint-brush, saved in a file, and then assigned to the main form's Picture property.

All the movable objects in Grid War (namely, the spaceships and torpedoes) are created using Visual Basic picture boxes. As the game progresses, the appearance of a given object is changed as necessary by assigning an appropriate bitmap to the picture box's Picture property. For example, when a ship is moving to the right, the picture box is assigned a bitmap depicting a ship pointing right; if the ship is hit by a torpedo, the picture box is then assigned a bitmap depicting an explosion. (The bitmaps used for this purpose were created in Paintbrush; they are stored in a set of invisible picture boxes so that they can be copied to the visible picture boxes whenever needed.)

Picture boxes are an ideal medium for the game objects in Grid War because the game objects are moved across a plain background and do not overlap. In contrast, the Ludo and TriPack programs had to use the *BitBlt* Windows API function to draw the game objects because these objects overlapped and—in the case of Ludo—because they were drawn on top of a heterogeneous background that had to be preserved.

430

The game objects are moved at a regular rate using a Visual Basic timer control. Each time the timer event handler is activated, it uses the *Move* method to move each object forward a fixed small amount. The program also includes a low-level keyboard handler so that the player can change the direction of the yellow ship or fire a torpedo by pressing the appropriate key.

The code for Grid War introduces the *IntersectRect* Windows API function. This function provides an easy way to determine whether two picture boxes have intersected. (Picture boxes intersect whenever a collision has taken place between two ships, two torpedoes, or between a ship and a torpedo.)

Finally, Grid War uses Visual Basic's random-number generator to assign random starting positions to each new enemy ship that appears during the game.

Program Overview

Here is a summary of the sequence of events in the Grid War program.

- When the program starts running, the *Form_Load* event procedure performs one-time initialization tasks and then calls *InitNewGame* to start a game.

- Whenever the player chooses the New Game command from the Game menu, the *MenuNew_Click* event procedure also calls *InitNewGame* to start a game.

- The *InitNewGame* general procedure initializes all variables for a new game and then enables the timer so that timer events start occurring.

- Whenever a timer event occurs, the *Timer1_Timer* event procedure receives control. This procedure moves the ships and torpedoes, changes the direction of ships as necessary, launches torpedoes when appropriate, tests for collisions between objects, and takes the required action when collisions occur.

- When the player presses a key to change the ship's direction or to fire a torpedo, the *Form_KeyDown* procedure receives control. This procedure merely records the keystroke; the required action is performed by *Timer1_Timer* when the next timer event occurs.

Initializing the Program

The *Form_Load* and *InitNewGame* procedures perform the program initialization tasks.

The *Form_Load* Procedure

The *Form_Load* event procedure begins with the standard code for assuring video-device independence. It then initializes the fields of the *GridRect* variable, which store the coordinates of the white grid that defines the playing area. The *OutOfBounds* general procedure (called by *Timer1_Timer*) uses this variable to determine whether a torpedo has reached one of the outside edges of the grid.

Form_Load then calls *Randomize* to seed the Visual Basic random-number generator and calls *InitNewGame* to start a new game.

The *InitNewGame* Procedure

The *InitNewGame* event procedure starts a new game. It is called by *Form_Load* at the beginning of the program, and it is called by *MenuNew_Click* whenever the player chooses the New Game command from the Game menu.

InitNewGame first initializes all form-level variables that must be reset at the beginning of a new game. The program uses quite a few of these variables; the following table will help you understand their purposes. (Remember: The yellow ship belongs to the player, and the red ship belongs to the enemy.) Not all the variables listed in the table are initialized by *InitNewGame*, but they are included to provide a complete reference.

Variable	Purpose
FireYelTorp	*Form_KeyDown* sets this variable to TRUE when the player presses the 5 key on the numeric keypad, to signal *Timer1_Timer* to fire the torpedo belonging to the yellow ship.
RedCol	The column within the playing grid currently containing the red ship. The columns are numbered from 1 through 10.
RedDir	The direction of the red ship (assigned one of the symbolic constants DIRLEFT, DIRRIGHT, DIRUP, or DIRDOWN). *Timer1_Timer* updates this variable whenever the red ship reaches a crossroads in the grid. (See the section titled "Moving the Ships," later in this chapter.)

(continued)

continued

Variable	Purpose
RedMoves	The number of times the red ship has been moved since leaving the last row (if moving vertically) or the last column (if moving horizontally). The values of this variable range from 0 through 7 because it takes exactly seven moves to go from one row or column to the next.
RedRow	The playing grid row containing the red ship.
RedTorpDir	The direction of the red ship's torpedo (if it is in motion). *Timer1_Timer* assigns a value to this variable when it launches the torpedo.
Score	The player's total score (equal to the number of enemy ships destroyed).
TimerToggle	A variable used by *Timer1_Timer* so that the procedure moves the torpedoes on every timer event but moves the ships on every *other* timer event.
WaitCount	A counter used by *Timer1_Timer* to create a delay after an enemy ship has been destroyed.
YelCol	The playing grid column containing the yellow ship.
YelDir	The direction of the yellow ship.
YelMoves	The number of times the yellow ship has been moved since leaving the last row (if moving vertically) or the last column (if moving horizontally).
YelNextDir	This variable tells *Timer1_Timer* the direction that the yellow ship should take when it reaches the next row (if moving vertically) or the next column (if moving horizontally).
YelRow	The playing grid row containing the yellow ship.
YelTorpCol	The playing grid column containing the yellow ship's torpedo (if it is in motion). *Timer1_Timer* assigns a value to this variable when it launches the torpedo.
YelTorpDir	The direction of the yellow ship's torpedo (if it is in motion). *Timer1_Timer* assigns a value to this variable when it launches the torpedo.
YelTorpRow	The playing grid row containing the yellow ship's torpedo (if it is in motion). *Timer1_Timer* assigns a value to this variable when it launches the torpedo.

After initializing program variables, *InitNewGame* assigns initial property settings to three of the four picture boxes that are used to display the visible game objects:

```
PictureYel.Picture = PictureYelRt.Picture
PictureYelTorp.Visible = 0
PictureRedTorp.Visible = 0
```

The PictureYel picture box displays the yellow ship; it is assigned a bitmap depicting a yellow ship headed to the right, which is the initial direction of this ship. (The red ship is displayed by the PictureRed picture box, which is assigned its initial Picture property in the *Timer1-_Timer* procedure.) PictureYelTorp and PictureRedTorp display the torpedoes that belong to the yellow and red ships; they are kept invisible until a torpedo is launched.

Next, *InitNewGame* moves the picture boxes displaying the two ships to their initial locations on the playing grid:

```
PictureYel.Move 11, 11
PictureRed.Move 200, 200
```

Finally, *InitNewGame* enables the program timer:

```
Timer1.Enabled = -1
```

The *Timer1_Timer* Procedure

At design time, the Timer1 timer control is disabled. At runtime, whenever a new game is started, the timer is enabled (*Timer1.Enabled* is set to TRUE); whenever a game is terminated, it is disabled (*Timer1.Enabled* is set to FALSE). While the timer is enabled, the *Timer1_Timer* procedure receives control as each timer event occurs.

As you have seen, the amount of time between timer events is specified by assigning a number of milliseconds to the timer's Interval property. The Interval property of Timer1 is set to 10 milliseconds. This does not mean, however, that the *Timer1_Timer* event procedure is actually called every 10 milliseconds. In fact, because this procedure is fairly complex, it typically takes longer than 10 milliseconds to execute. Consequently, the actual time between timer events is longer than 10 milliseconds, and decreasing the value of the Interval property would not speed up the movement of game objects. The 10-millisecond value is simply a safe number to assure that *Timer1_Timer* is called at the maximum frequency.

Timer1_Timer begins by testing to see whether the form-level variable *WaitCount* is greater than 0:

```
If WaitCount > 0 Then
    'decrement WaitCount
    'initialize new red ship when WaitCount reaches 0
```

Whenever a red ship is destroyed, *WaitCount* is set to *25* to create a pause before the next enemy ship appears. When the procedure discovers that this variable is greater than 0, it decrements the variable by 1. When the value finally reaches *0*, it initializes a new red ship. Rather than simply placing the ship within the lower right square of the grid, however, it calls the general procedure *GetRandomStart* to obtain a random starting position:

```
GetRandomStart Col, Row, X, Y
```

GetRandomStart uses Visual Basic's random-number generator to select a random starting position within one of the squares along the outside edges of the grid.

Moving the Torpedoes

Timer1_Timer then tests whether the torpedo belonging to the red ship is visible:

```
If PictureRedTorp.Visible Then
    'move red torpedo
```

If the torpedo is visible, it must be in motion. In this case, the procedure uses Visual Basic's *Move* method to move the torpedo 3 pixels forward along its current path. After moving the torpedo, the procedure performs the following important tests:

1. It calls the general function procedure *TorpCollision* to see whether the torpedo has collided with the yellow ship's torpedo. If *TorpCollision* returns TRUE, *Timer1_Timer* takes both torpedoes out of action by making them invisible. If *TorpCollision* returns FALSE, then *Timer1_Timer* proceeds with the following test.

2. It calls the general function procedure *YelHit* to determine whether the red ship's torpedo has hit the yellow ship. If *YelHit* returns TRUE, then *Timer1_Timer* replaces the bitmap in the yellow ship's picture box with a bitmap depicting an explosion:

   ```
   PictureYel.Picture = PictureBang.Picture
   ```

   and then calls the general procedure *EndGame* to terminate the current game. *EndGame* stops all action by disabling the timer; *EndGame* then makes the torpedoes invisible and displays the player's score. If *YelHit* returns FALSE, then *Timer1-_Timer* proceeds with the following test.

435

3. It calls the general function procedure *OutOfBounds* to determine whether the torpedo has reached an outside edge of the grid. *OutOfBounds* compares the torpedo position (which is passed in the two parameters) with the dimensions of the grid stored in *GridRect* (described previously). If *OutOfBounds* returns TRUE, then *Timer1_Timer* takes the torpedo out of play by making it invisible.

Both *TorpCollision* and *YelHit* call the *IntersectRect* Windows API function to determine whether the objects have collided. For example, *YelHit* makes the following call:

```
If IntersectRect(IntRect, YelRect, RedTorpRect) Then
    YelHit = -1
Else
    YelHit = 0
End If
```

All three parameters passed to *IntersectRect* have the type RECT, which is defined as follows in the global module:

```
Type RECT
    Left As Integer
    Top As Integer
    Right As Integer
    Bottom As Integer
End Type
```

In this call, *YelRect* is assigned the coordinates of the yellow ship's picture box, and *RedTorpRect* is assigned the coordinates of the picture box for the red ship's torpedo. If the two picture boxes intersect, *IntersectRect* returns a nonzero value (and assigns the coordinates of the intersection to the *IntRect* parameter, which the program does not use). If the picture boxes do not intersect, *IntersectRect* returns 0. *IntersectRect* is described in Figure 12-9.

After moving the red ship's torpedo, *Timer1_Timer* proceeds to move the yellow ship's torpedo if it is visible (and therefore in motion):

```
If PictureYelTorp.Visible Then
    'move yellow torpedo
```

Note: Moving the yellow ship's torpedo *after* the red ship's torpedo gives the red ship a slight advantage in a situation where the ships are facing each other and firing repeatedly. This provision eliminates a way that the player could destroy enemy ships too easily.

Windows API Function: *IntersectRect*

Purpose Reports whether two rectangular areas intersect. If they intersect, it supplies the coordinates of the intersection.

Declaration
```
Declare Function IntersectRect Lib "USER" (lpDestRect As
  RECT, lpSrc1Rect As RECT, lpSrc2Rect As RECT) As Integer
```

Parameter	Description

lpDestRect	A RECT type variable that is assigned the coordinates of the intersection *if* the rectangles specified by the next two parameters intersect. The RECT type is defined as follows:
	
	```Type RECT```
	`    Left As Integer`
	`    Top As Integer`
	`    Right As Integer`
	`    Bottom As Integer`
	`End Type`

lpSrc1Rect	A RECT type variable containing the coordinates of one of the rectangles to be tested.
lpSrc2Rect	A RECT type variable containing the coordinates of the other rectangle to be tested.

Return Value A nonzero value if the rectangles specified by the second two parameters intersect, or 0 if these rectangles do not intersect.

Figure 12-9.
The IntersectRect *Windows API function.*

Timer1_Timer uses the same method that it used for moving the red torpedo, except for the following two differences:

- Rather than calling *YelHit*, it calls *RedHit* to see whether the yellow ship's torpedo hit the red ship. (*RedHit* works in the same manner as *YelHit*.)

- If the torpedo scored a hit, rather than terminating the game, the procedure adds 1 point to the player's score, hides the torpedoes, and sets *WaitCount* to *25*. As you have seen, setting *WaitCount* to a nonzero value generates a pause and then causes *Timer1_Timer* to initialize a new red ship.

Creating Different Object Speeds

After moving any visible torpedoes, the *Timer1_Timer* procedure executes the following statements:

```
'exit on every other timer event:
TimerToggle = TimerToggle Xor -1
If TimerToggle Then Exit Sub
```

The effect of these statements is to exit from the procedure every other time it is called. Because the torpedoes have already been moved and because the two ships are not moved until later in the procedure, the result is that the torpedoes travel at twice the speed of the ships.

Moving the Ships

Timer1_Timer now proceeds to move the yellow ship. As the first step, it checks whether this ship has been moved seven times since leaving the last column or row:

```
If YelMoves >= 7 Then
    'adjust direction
```

It requires exactly seven moves to advance the ship one column (if the ship is moving horizontally) or one row (if the ship is moving vertically). This number results from the facts that columns and rows measure 21 pixels from center to center (in the horizontal and vertical directions) and that a ship is advanced 3 pixels with each move. *YelMoves* is initialized to *0*; it is then incremented with each move of the yellow ship. When *YelMoves* reaches *7*, the ship must have moved completely into the next column or row, and the direction of the ship can be adjusted. (As you can see when you play the game, a ship always moves *between* grid lines. Therefore, a ship cannot turn until it reaches a "crossroads," where the centers of a column and a row intersect.)

Consequently, if *YelMoves* has reached *7*, the procedure adjusts the Picture property of PictureYel and the value of *YelDir* (which stores the current ship direction), according to the value of *YelNextDir*. *YelNextDir* is initialized to DIRRIGHT because this is the initial direction of the yellow ship. If the player presses an arrow key to change the ship's direction, the *Form_KeyDown* procedure assigns the specified direction to *YelNextDir*. (This occurs *between* timer events.)

For example, if the player has pressed the Left arrow key since the ship left the last column or row, the procedure turns the ship to the left (provided that the ship is not in column 1), using the following code:

```
Select Case YelNextDir
    Case DIRLEFT                    'player pressed Left arrow key
        If YelCol > 1 Then
            PictureYel.Picture = PictureYelLf.Picture  'bitmap
of ship heading left
            YelDir = DIRLEFT  'stores current direction of
yellow ship
        End If

    'other directions
```

Also, when *YelMoves* has reached *7*, it is set back to *0* to begin the count toward the next column or row.

Next, *Timer1_Timer* calls the *Move* method to move the ship 3 pixels in the direction indicated by the current value of *YelDir*:

```
Select Case YelDir
    Case DIRLEFT
        If YelCol > 1 Then
            PictureYel.Move PictureYel.Left - 3, PictureYel.Top
            Moved = -1
        End If

    'other directions
```

The ship is moved only if it has not reached the outside edge of the grid. If a move is made, the procedure then performs the following steps:

- If the general function *Collision* returns TRUE, indicating that the two ships have collided, *Timer1_Timer* assigns the "explosion" bitmap to both picture boxes, adds 1 to *Score*, and calls *EndGame* to terminate the game:

```
If Collision() Then
    PictureYel.Picture = PictureBang.Picture
    PictureRed.Picture = PictureBang.Picture
    Score = Score + 1
    EndGame
    Exit Sub
End If
```

  Notice that the *Collision* procedure uses the *IntersectRect* Windows API function in the same manner as did the *TorpCollision* and *YelHit* functions, described previously.

- It adds 1 to *YelMoves*.

- If *YelMoves* has now reached 7, the procedure adjusts the current column, *YelCol* (if the ship is moving horizontally), or the current row, *YelRow* (if the ship is moving vertically).

Note: If a move is *not* possible (because the ship is abutting an edge of the grid), *YelMoves* is set to 7 so that the player can immediately begin moving the ship again by pressing an appropriate arrow key.

After it has moved the yellow ship, the *Timer1_Timer* procedure launches the yellow ship's torpedo, if necessary. (This process will be described later in the chapter.)

The procedure next moves the red ship. The method the procedure uses for moving the red ship is quite similar to that used for moving the yellow ship. However, rather than allowing the player to determine the new direction of the red ship when it reaches a crossroads, the procedure obtains the new direction from the *GetRedDir* general function procedure.

The *GetRedDir* Function Procedure

The *GetRedDir* general function procedure calculates the next move for the red ship based upon the current position of the yellow ship. The goal is to move the red ship systematically and relentlessly toward the yellow ship.

If the yellow ship is moving horizontally, *GetRedDir* selects a direction (DIRUP or DIRDOWN) so that the red ship immediately moves toward the yellow ship's row. If, however, the red ship is already within the yellow ship's row, the function selects a direction (DIRLEFT or DIRRIGHT) so that the red ship moves toward the yellow ship itself.

Similarly, if the yellow ship is moving vertically, the function selects a direction (DIRLEFT or DIRRIGHT) to move the red ship toward the yellow ship's column. If the red ship is already in that column, the function selects a direction (DIRUP or DIRDOWN) to move the red ship toward the yellow ship.

```
If YelDir = DIRLEFT Or YelDir = DIRRIGHT Then
    'move toward yellow ship's row,
    'or toward yellow ship within same row
Else
    'move toward yellow ship's column,
    'or toward yellow ship within same column
```

Launching the Yellow Ship's Torpedo

If the player presses the center key on the numeric keypad (the 5), the *Form_KeyDown* procedure sets the *FireYelTorp* variable to TRUE, provided that the yellow ship's torpedo is not already visible and therefore already in motion. When the next timer event occurs, the *Timer1_Timer* procedure tests this variable immediately after moving the yellow ship. If the variable is TRUE, *Timer1_Timer* proceeds to fire the torpedo:

```
If FireYelTorp Then
    'fire yellow torpedo
```

The torpedo is always fired in the direction that the ship is currently moving. To launch the torpedo, *Timer1_Timer* performs the following steps:

1. If the ship is moving horizontally, the procedure assigns the bitmap depicting a horizontal torpedo to the picture box used for displaying the yellow ship's torpedo:

   ```
   PictureYelTorp.Picture = PictureTorpH.Picture
   ```

   If the ship is moving vertically, the procedure assigns the bitmap depicting a vertical torpedo to this picture box:

   ```
   PictureYelTorp.Picture = PictureTorpV.Picture
   ```

2. It moves the torpedo's picture box to its initial position immediately in front of the ship's picture box. For example, if the ship is moving left, it makes the following call to the *Move* method:

   ```
   PictureYelTorp.Move PictureYel.Left - 8,
    PictureYel.Top + 6
   ```

3. It saves the row, column, and direction of the ship in the variables that store these values for the torpedo:

   ```
   YelTorpCol = YelCol
   YelTorpRow = YelRow
   YelTorpDir = YelDir
   ```

   This step is necessary because the ship may change direction, row, or column while the torpedo is still in motion. (And, as you will see in the next section, *Timer1_Timer* needs to know the location and direction of this torpedo.)

4. It makes visible the picture box displaying the torpedo:

   ```
   PictureYelTorp.Visible = -1
   ```

5. It resets the *FireYelTorp* flag to *0* so that another torpedo is not inadvertently fired:

```
FireYelTorp = 0
```

Launching the Red Ship's Torpedo

The method for launching the red ship's torpedo is basically the same as that used for launching the yellow ship's torpedo. Before launching the red ship's torpedo, however, *Timer1_Timer* performs a series of tests to determine whether it should proceed with the launch. These tests come immediately after the code for moving the red ship.

1. *Timer1_Timer* tests whether the torpedo is currently visible.

```
If PictureRedTorp.Visible = 0 Then
     'proceed with remaining tests
```

If it is visible, the torpedo is already in motion and a new torpedo cannot be launched.

2. If the torpedo is *not* visible, the procedure continues with the launching if any one of the following conditions is true:

□ The red ship and the yellow ship are both moving in the same row.

□ The red ship and the yellow ship are both moving in the same column.

□ The yellow ship's torpedo is moving in the same row or column as the red ship.

The *Form_KeyDown* Procedure

Whenever the player presses a key, the *Form_KeyDown* event procedure receives control.

Form_KeyDown exits immediately if the timer is disabled, indicating that a game is not in progress:

```
If Timer1.Enabled = 0 Then Exit Sub
```

Otherwise, it proceeds to process the keystroke if the player has pressed either an arrow key or the center key on the numeric keypad (the 5).

> ## T I P
>
> To ensure that the *Form_KeyDown* event procedure processes all keystrokes, rather than a *KeyDown* event procedure belonging to only one of the visible picture boxes, the Enabled property of all visible picture boxes was set to False at design time.

Note: See Chapter 11, the section titled "The *Form_KeyDown* Procedure," for a description of how the key codes were derived and for other information on implementing a low-level keyboard handler.

If the player has pressed an arrow key, *Form_KeyDown* assigns the appropriate value to the form-level variable *YelNextDir.* As you have seen, this variable tells the timer event handler which direction to move the yellow ship the next time this ship reaches a crossroads within the grid.

If the player has pressed the center numeric-keypad key, the procedure sets the *FireYelTorp* variable to TRUE, provided that a yellow torpedo is not already in motion:

```
Case &HC, &H65      'center key (5): fire torpedo
    If PictureYelTorp.Visible = 0 Then FireYelTorp = -1
```

As explained previously, setting this variable to TRUE causes the timer event handler to launch the yellow ship's torpedo when the next timer event occurs.

Enhancing the Game

Here are a few suggestions for enhancing the Grid War program.

- Explore some alternative algorithms for guiding the red ship in its pursuit of the yellow ship. The *GetRedDir* function currently plots a simple, rectangular path toward the yellow ship. As an alternative method, the function could calculate the shortest path to the yellow ship.

- Add one or more other weapons to the ships' arsenals. For example, the ships could be equipped with a second class of torpedoes, which are faster than the standard torpedoes but whose range is shorter.

- Save the highest score to date in the WIN.INI file. (See Chapter 11, the section titled "Saving and Retrieving the Highest Score," for a description of how to implement such a feature.)

CHAPTER THIRTEEN

BOULE

Boule is a simple form of roulette. As you play the computer version of the game presented here, you will discover that the odds are strongly in favor of the house, and you will probably be glad you are not playing the actual game in a European casino.

The Boule program uses a variety of techniques to move playing objects, both automatically and in response to movements of the mouse. Although in previous chapters you have seen the basic animation techniques used here, this chapter shows you how to plot a complex path for a moving object using Visual Basic trigonometric functions.

About Boule

Boule originated in the eighteenth century and is currently played in Europe. It is considerably simpler than the standard versions of roulette, and the minimum bet is typically lower. Boule is played on a table with a recessed bowl at one end and one or two betting layouts at the other end. The table top and the bowl are commonly made of polished wood; the betting layout consists of green baize, with gold letters and markings.

Players bet by placing chips within marked areas on the betting layout. Players can bet on a single number (from 1 through 9) or on a characteristic of the number (high or low, odd or even, or red or black). Unlike the roulette wheel, the bowl is stationary. After all bets have been placed, the croupier (the casino employee in charge of running the game) throws a rubber ball into a groove that runs around the outside edge of the bowl. The ball circles within this groove; as it loses speed, it spirals toward the bottom of the bowl, eventually coming to rest in one of the numbered indentations that surround the raised hub at the center of the bowl. There are 18 indentations, numbered clockwise from 1 through 9 twice; accordingly, the result of throwing the ball is a random number from 1 through 9.

After the throw, the croupier collects the losses and then pays the winnings.

Playing Boule

When you run Boule (BL.EXE), the program initializes a new game. Figure 13-1 shows the form at the beginning of a game.

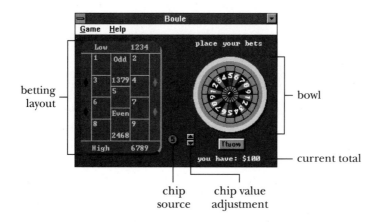

Figure 13-1.
Boule at the beginning of a game.

At the start of a game, you have $100. As you play, the program displays your current total at the bottom of the form. Boule is played in two stages: placing bets and throwing the ball.

Placing Bets

In Boule, you bet by placing one or more chips on the betting layout. Each of the rectangular areas marked on this layout represents a possible outcome of throwing the ball. These areas are labeled and explained in Figure 13-2.

To place a bet, simply drag the chip from the chip source (labeled in Figure 13-1) to the target area on the betting layout. The initial value of the chip at the source is $5. Before dragging the chip, you can adjust its value by clicking the up arrow or down arrow located to the right of the chip. The minimum value of a chip is $1; the maximum value is $99 or the total amount of money you have available for betting, whichever is smaller.

If you place a chip on area…	you are betting on…
a	an individual number
b	a low number: 1, 2, 3, or 4
c	a high number: 6, 7, 8, 9
d	a black number: 2, 4, 7, or 9
e	a red number: 1, 3, 6, or 8
f	an odd number: 1, 3, 7, or 9 (not 5)
g	an even number: 2, 4, 6, or 8

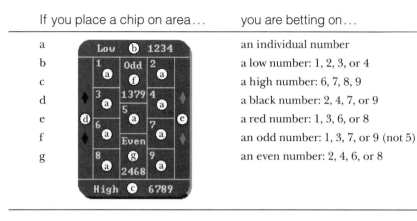

Figure 13-2.

The Boule betting layout.

Note: Chips can be placed only within the marked areas on the betting layout. Unlike roulette, Boule does not allow you to bet on more than one number by placing a chip on a dividing line.

When you drop the chip on a valid position within the betting layout, another chip appears immediately at the chip source. The new chip's initial value is the same as the previous chip's value; however, you can adjust the value. If you want to bet another chip, you can now drag the chip from the chip source to the target area on the layout.

Note: You cannot place another chip within an area on the betting layout that is already occupied by a chip. However, you can change the value of a chip already placed on the layout, as explained shortly.

You can continue placing chips in this manner until no open areas are left on the layout or until you run out of money.

After you have placed a chip within a particular area on the layout, you can move it to another open area, change its value, or remove it from the layout. To move the chip to another open area, simply drag it to this area from its current location. To change the value of a chip, drag the chip back to the chip source, use the up or down arrow to adjust the value, and then drag the chip back to its original location. To remove a chip from the layout, drag it back to the chip source and leave it there.

Note: If you drop a chip on an invalid position, the program returns it to its original location.

Throwing the Ball

After you have placed one or more chips on the layout, the Throw button is enabled, and you can throw the ball at any time by clicking this button. When you click the Throw button, the ball starts "rolling" around the bowl, eventually coming to rest within one of the eighteen indentations near the center. During this time, the program displays the *no more bets* message.

When the ball has stopped rolling, the program displays the result of the throw at the top of the form. The program then removes all chips for losing bets and pays all winning bets according to the guidelines in the following table.

Type of Winning Bet	Payment
Single number	7 to 1
Characteristic (high, low, even, odd, red, or black)	1 to 1

For example, if you win a $1 bet on a single number, you win $7.

Winning bets are paid by adding the amount won to the current value of the chip; the chip is left in its present location on the layout (so that you will be tempted to bet the chip again). If, however, the resulting value of the chip would be greater than $99 (which is the maximum chip value), the chip is assigned only $99, but the full amount won is added to your total.

After paying bets and removing chips, the program adds to your total the amount won or subtracts from your total the amount lost and displays the new total at the bottom of the form. If this amount is greater than $0, you can begin placing bets again.

Note: After the ball is thrown, the ball and the result of the throw remain visible until you click within the form.

If your total is reduced to $0, the game is terminated. You can then start a new game by choosing the New Game command from the Game menu. (If you choose this command before going broke, the program terminates the current game and starts a new one.)

Strategy and Hints

Boule is designed so that the payouts—or the *expected value*, to use a term from statistics—are the same for any type of bet; it does not matter whether you bet on a single number or bet on a characteristic (such as *even* or *red*). The odds are strongly in favor of the house; in fact, the house's advantage is more than twice that of American roulette. For example, the *expected value* of a bet of $1 in Boule is $-0.111. In other words, on the average, you can expect to lose about $.11 for every $1 bet. For a bet on a single number, the expected value is derived as follows:

expected value = probability of winning * value of winning + probability of losing * value of losing
expected value = $(1/9) * (7) + (8/9) * (-1)$
expected value = -0.111

The expected value for betting $1 on a characteristic is the same:

expected value = $(4/9) * (1) + (5/9) * (-1) = -0.111$

In contrast, the expected value for betting $1 on a single number in American roulette is $-0.0526, which is about half the loss for Boule. (In versions of roulette without the 00 indentation, the loss is even less.)

The moral is: Enjoy the computer game, but stay away from Boule if you travel in Europe!

Coding Boule

The source code for the Boule program is contained in the files listed in the following table.

File	Purpose
GLOBALBL.BAS	Contains global type definitions
BL.FRM	Defines the main form, FormMain, and the controls it contains
BLABOUT.FRM	Defines the ABOUT form, FormAbout, and the controls it contains
BL.MAK	Contains the Boule project file

Figures 13-3 through 13-8 present the form designs, properties, menu commands, and source code for the Boule program.

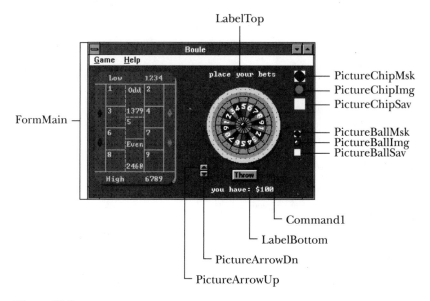

Figure 13-3.
BL.FRM at design time.

Object Name	Object Type	Property	Setting
Command1	Command button	BackColor	&H00008080& [dark yellow]
		Caption	Throw
		Default	True
		Height	22 [pixels]
		Left	256 [pixels]
		Top	178 [pixels]
		Width	49 [pixels]
FormMain	Form	AutoRedraw	True
		BackColor	&H00008080& [dark yellow]

Figure 13-4. *(continued)*
BL.FRM form and control properties.

450

Figure 13-4 *continued*

Object Name	Object Type	Property	Setting
		BorderStyle	1 - Fixed Single
		Caption	Boule
		FormName	FormMain
		Grid Height	8 [pixels]
		Grid Width	8 [pixels]
		Height	4110 [twips]
		Icon	(Icon) [BL.ICO]
		Left	1035 [twips]
		MaxButton	False
		Picture	(Bitmap) [BL.BMP]
		ScaleMode	3 - Pixel
		Top	1140 [twips]
		Width	6135 [twips]
LabelBottom		Alignment	2 - Center
		BackColor	&H00008080& [dark yellow]
		Caption	you have: $100
		CtlName	LabelBottom
		ForeColor	&H00FFFFFF& [white]
		Height	17 [pixels]
		Left	208 [pixels]
		Top	208 [pixels]
		Width	137 [pixels]
LabelTop		Alignment	2 - Center
		BackColor	&H00008080& [dark yellow]
		Caption	place your bets
		CtlName	LabelTop
		ForeColor	&H00FFFFFF& [white]
		Height	25 [pixels]
		Left	200 [pixels]
		Top	8 [pixels]
		Width	153 [pixels]

(continued)

Figure 13-4 *continued*

Object Name	Object Type	Property	Setting
PictureArrowDn		AutoSize	True
		BorderStyle	0 - None
		CtlName	PictureArrowDn
		Height	12 [pixels]
		Left	200 [pixels]
		Picture	(Bitmap) [ARROWDN.BMP]
		Top	181 [pixels]
		Width	15 [pixels]
PictureArrowUp		AutoSize	True
		BorderStyle	0 - None
		CtlName	PictureArrowUp
		Height	12 [pixels]
		Left	200 [pixels]
		Picture	(Bitmap) [ARROWUP.BMP]
		Top	170 [pixels]
		Width	15 [pixels]
PictureBallImg		AutoRedraw	True
		AutoSize	True
		BorderStyle	0 - None
		CtlName	PictureBallImg
		Height	11 [pixels]
		Left	368 [pixels]
		Picture	(Bitmap) [BALLIMG.BMP]
		ScaleMode	3 - Pixel
		Top	128 [pixels]
		Visible	False
		Width	11 [pixels]
PictureBallMsk		AutoRedraw	True
		AutoSize	True
		BorderStyle	0 - None

(continued)

Figure 13-4 *continued*

Object Name	Object Type	Property	Setting
		CtlName	PictureBallMsk
		Height	11 [pixels]
		Left	368 [pixels]
		Picture	(Bitmap) [BALLMSK.BMP]
		ScaleMode	3 - Pixel
		Top	112 [pixels]
		Visible	False
		Width	11 [pixels]
PictureBallSav		AutoRedraw	True
		AutoSize	True
		BorderStyle	0 - None
		CtlName	PictureBallSav
		Height	11 [pixels]
		Left	368 [pixels]
		ScaleMode	3 - Pixel
		Top	144 [pixels]
		Visible	False
		Width	11 [pixels]
PictureChipImg		AutoRedraw	True
		AutoSize	True
		BorderStyle	0 - None
		CtlName	PictureChipImg
		Height	19 [pixels]
		Left	368 [pixels]
		Picture	(Bitmap) [CHIPIMG.BMP]
		ScaleMode	3 - Pixel
		Top	32 [pixels]
		Visible	False
		Width	19 [pixels]
PictureChipMsk		AutoRedraw	True
		AutoSize	True

(continued)

Figure 13-4 *continued*

Object Name	Object Type	Property	Setting
		BorderStyle	0 - None
		CtlName	PictureChipMsk
		Height	19 [pixels]
		Left	368 [pixels]
		Picture	(Bitmap) [CHIPMSK.BMP]
		ScaleMode	3 - Pixel
		Top	8 [pixels]
		Visible	False
		Width	19 [pixels]
PictureChipSav		AutoRedraw	True
		AutoSize	True
		BorderStyle	0 - None
		CtlName	PictureChipSav
		Height	19 [pixels]
		Left	368 [pixels]
		ScaleMode	3 - Pixel
		Top	56 [pixels]
		Visible	False
		Width	19 [pixels]

Indentation/Caption	Control Name	Other Features
&Game	MenuGame	
....&New Game	MenuNew	
....-	MenuSep1	
....E&xit	MenuExit	
&Help	MenuHelp	
....&Index	MenuIndex	Accelerator = F1
....&How to Play	MenuHowTo	

Figure 13-5.
BL.FRM menu design.

(continued)

Figure 13-5 *continued*

Indentation/Caption	Control Name	Other Features
....&Commands	MenuCommands	
....&Using Help	MenuUsingHelp	
....-	MenuSep2	
....&About Boule...	MenuAbout	

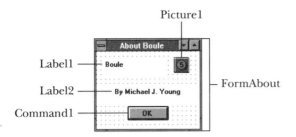

Figure 13-6.
BLABOUT.FRM at design time.

Object Name	Object Type	Property	Setting
Command1	Command button	Caption	OK
		Default	True
		Height	375 [twips]
		Left	840 [twips]
		Top	1440 [twips]
		Width	1095 [twips]
FormAbout	Form	BorderStyle	3 - Fixed Double
		Caption	About Boule
		FormName	FormAbout
		Grid Height	120 [twips]
		Grid Width	120 [twips]
		Height	2445 [twips]

Figure 13-7.   *(continued)*
BLABOUT.FRM form and control properties.

Figure 13-7 *continued*

Object Name	Object Type	Property	Setting
		Left	1140 [twips]
		MaxButton	False
		MinButton	False
		Top	1440 [twips]
		Width	2880 [twips]
Label1	Label	Caption	Boule
		Height	375 [twips]
		Left	240 [twips]
		Top	240 [twips]
		Width	1575 [twips]
Label2	Label	Alignment	2 - Center
		Caption	By Michael J. Young
		Height	375 [twips]
		Left	0 [twips]
		Top	960 [twips]
		Width	2745 [twips]
Picture1	Picture box	AutoSize	True
		BorderStyle	0 - None
		Height	480 [twips]
		Left	2040 [twips]
		Picture	(Icon) [BL.ICO]
		Top	120 [twips]
		Width	480 [twips]

GLOBALBL.BAS code

```
Type APIPOINT
    X As Integer
    Y As Integer
End Type
```

Figure 13-8.   *(continued)*

Source code for the Boule program. (Notice that long program lines are wrapped to the next line and indented one space.)

Figure 13-8 *continued*

```
Type RECT
    Left As Integer
    Top As Integer
    Right As Integer
    Bottom As Integer
End Type

Type SQUARE
    Outer As RECT
    Inner As RECT
    ChipVal As Integer
End Type
```

BL.FRM code

```
'Help Section:
'Help file:
Const HELP_FILE = "BL.HLP"
'WinHelp wCommand values:
Const HELP_CONTEXT = &H1
Const HELP_HELPONHELP = &H4
Const HELP_INDEX = &H3
Const HELP_QUIT = &H2
'WinHelp dwData values (help topics):
Const HELP_HOWTOPLAY = 10&
Const HELP_COMMANDS = 20&
'Windows help API:
Declare Sub WinHelp Lib "USER" (ByVal hWnd As Integer,
 ByVal lpHelpFile As String, ByVal wCommand As Integer,
 ByVal dwData As Long)

Const CLIENTBOTTOM = 228
Const CLIENTRIGHT = 360
Const PI = 3.14159265

Dim GameOver As Integer
Dim MoneyBet As Integer
Dim MoneyTotal As Integer
Dim MoveOrigin As Integer
Dim MoveValue As Integer
Dim PrevX As Integer
Dim PrevY As Integer
```

(continued)

Figure 13-8 *continued*

```
Dim SquareTable(0 To 15) As SQUARE
Dim ThrowDone As Integer
Dim XOffset As Integer
Dim YOffset As Integer

Const WS_CAPTION = &HC00000
Const WS_THICKFRAME = &H40000
Declare Sub AdjustWindowRect Lib "USER" (lpRect As RECT,
 ByVal dwStyle&, ByVal bMenu%)

Const SRCAND = &H8800C6      'dest = source AND dest
Const SRCCOPY = &HCC0020     'dest = source
Const SRCINVERT = &H660046   'dest = source XOR dest
Declare Sub BitBlt Lib "GDI" (ByVal HDestDC%, ByVal X%,
 ByVal Y%, ByVal nWidth%, ByVal nHeight%, ByVal HSrcDC%,
 ByVal XSrc%, ByVal YSrc%, ByVal ROP&)

Const LOGPIXELSX = 88
Const LOGPIXELSY = 90
Declare Function GetDeviceCaps Lib "GDI" (ByVal hDC%,
 ByVal Index%) As Integer

Declare Sub ClientToScreen Lib "USER" (ByVal hWnd As Integer,
 Pt As APIPOINT)
Declare Sub ClipCursor Lib "USER" (Rec As Any)
Declare Sub ReleaseCapture Lib "USER" ()
Declare Sub SetCapture Lib "USER" (ByVal hWnd As Integer)
Declare Sub ShowCursor Lib "USER" (ByVal ShowIt As Integer)

Sub DoLose (Idx As Integer)
    MoneyTotal = MoneyTotal - SquareTable(Idx).ChipVal
    MoneyBet = MoneyBet - SquareTable(Idx).ChipVal
    SquareTable(Idx).ChipVal = -1
    PictureChipSav.BackColor = &H8000&
    BitBlt hDC, SquareTable(Idx).Inner.Left,
 SquareTable(Idx).Inner.Top, 19, 19, PictureChipSav.hDC, 0, 0,
 SRCCOPY
End Sub

Sub DoWin (Idx As Integer)
    Dim Winning As Integer

    If Idx <= 9 Then
        Winning = 7 * SquareTable(Idx).ChipVal
```

(continued)

Figure 13-8 *continued*

```
    Else
        Winning = SquareTable(Idx).ChipVal
    End If
    MoneyTotal = MoneyTotal + Winning
    MoneyBet = MoneyBet - SquareTable(Idx).ChipVal
    SquareTable(Idx).ChipVal = SquareTable(Idx).ChipVal
+ Winning
    If SquareTable(Idx).ChipVal > 99 Then
SquareTable(Idx).ChipVal = 99
    MoneyBet = MoneyBet + SquareTable(Idx).ChipVal
    PrintImgValue (SquareTable(Idx).ChipVal)
    BitBlt hDC, SquareTable(Idx).Inner.Left,
SquareTable(Idx).Inner.Top, 19, 19, PictureChipMsk.hDC, 0, 0,
SRCAND
    BitBlt hDC, SquareTable(Idx).Inner.Left,
SquareTable(Idx).Inner.Top, 19, 19, PictureChipImg.hDC, 0, 0,
SRCINVERT
End Sub

Sub InitNewGame ()
    Dim I As Integer

    GameOver = 0
    MoneyBet = 0
    MoneyTotal = 100
    MoveValue = -1
    ThrowDone = 0
    SquareTable(0).ChipVal = 5
    For I = 1 To 15
        SquareTable(I).ChipVal = -1
    Next I
    Command1.Enabled = 0
    LabelBottom.Caption = "you have: $100"
    LabelTop.Caption = "place your bets"
    Cls
    PrintImgValue (SquareTable(0).ChipVal)
    BitBlt hDC, SquareTable(0).Inner.Left,
SquareTable(0).Inner.Top, 19, 19, PictureChipMsk.hDC, 0, 0,
SRCAND
    BitBlt hDC, SquareTable(0).Inner.Left,
SquareTable(0).Inner.Top, 19, 19, PictureChipImg.hDC, 0, 0,
SRCINVERT
End Sub
```

(continued)

Figure 13-8 *continued*

```
Function InnerSquareHit (X As Integer, Y As Integer,
 XOffset As Integer, YOffset As Integer)
    Dim I As Integer

    For I = 0 To 15
        If X >= SquareTable(I).Inner.Left And X <=
SquareTable(I).Inner.Right Then
            If Y >= SquareTable(I).Inner.Top And Y <=
SquareTable(I).Inner.Bottom Then
                InnerSquareHit = I
                XOffset = X - SquareTable(I).Inner.Left
                YOffset = Y - SquareTable(I).Inner.Top
                Exit Function
            End If
        End If
    Next I
    InnerSquareHit = -1
End Function

Function OuterSquareHit (X As Integer, Y As Integer)
    Dim I As Integer

    For I = 0 To 15
        If X >= SquareTable(I).Outer.Left And X <=
SquareTable(I).Outer.Right Then
            If Y >= SquareTable(I).Outer.Top And Y <=
SquareTable(I).Outer.Bottom Then
                OuterSquareHit = I
                Exit Function
            End If
        End If
    Next I
    OuterSquareHit = -1
End Function

Sub PrintImgValue (Value As Integer)
    Dim Number As String

    If Value < 10 Then Number = " "
    Number = Number + Format$(Value, "")
    PictureChipImg.Cls
    PictureChipImg.CurrentX = 1
    PictureChipImg.CurrentY = 2
    PictureChipImg.Print Number
End Sub
```

(continued)

460

Figure 13-8 *continued*

```
Sub Command1_Click ()
    Dim DeltaTheta As Single
    Dim I As Integer
    Dim Message As String
    Dim Radius As Integer
    Dim Result As Integer
    Dim Theta As Single
    Dim X As Integer
    Dim XCenter As Integer
    Dim Y As Integer
    Dim YCenter As Integer

    Command1.Enabled = 0
    If ThrowDone Then
        BitBlt hDC, PrevX, PrevY, 11, 11, PictureBallSav.hDC,
0, 0, SRCCOPY
        Refresh
        ThrowDone = 0
    End If
    LabelTop.Caption = "no more bets"

    'simulate throw of ball:

    XCenter = 277    'center of bowl
    YCenter = 102
    Radius = 53      'initial radius of path of ball

    'initialize ball position & PictureBallSav:
    X = XCenter + Radius - 5
    Y = YCenter - 5
    BitBlt PictureBallSav.hDC, 0, 0, 11, 11, hDC, X, Y, SRCCOPY

    'roll ball around outer edge of bowl, steadily decreasing
    'speed:
    For DeltaTheta = .75 To .3 Step -.01
        BitBlt hDC, X, Y, 11, 11, PictureBallSav.hDC, 0, 0,
SRCCOPY
        X = XCenter + Radius * Cos(Theta) - 5
        Y = YCenter - Radius * Sin(Theta) - 5
        BitBlt PictureBallSav.hDC, 0, 0, 11, 11, hDC, X, Y,
SRCCOPY
        BitBlt hDC, X, Y, 11, 11, PictureBallMsk.hDC, 0, 0,
SRCAND
        BitBlt hDC, X, Y, 11, 11, PictureBallImg.hDC, 0, 0,
```

(continued)

Figure 13-8 *continued*

```
SRCINVERT
        Refresh
        Theta = Theta + DeltaTheta
    Next DeltaTheta

    'move ball toward center of bowl in helical path:
    For Radius = 53 To 11 Step -1
        BitBlt hDC, X, Y, 11, 11, PictureBallSav.hDC, 0, 0,
SRCCOPY
        X = XCenter + Radius * Cos(Theta) - 5
        Y = YCenter - Radius * Sin(Theta) - 5
        BitBlt PictureBallSav.hDC, 0, 0, 11, 11, hDC, X, Y,
SRCCOPY
        BitBlt hDC, X, Y, 11, 11, PictureBallMsk.hDC, 0, 0,
SRCAND
        BitBlt hDC, X, Y, 11, 11, PictureBallImg.hDC, 0, 0,
SRCINVERT
        Refresh
        Theta = Theta + DeltaTheta
    Next Radius

    'move ball to final, random, stopping point on inner
    'circumference of bowl:
    Result = Int(18 * Rnd + 1)
    For Theta = 31 * PI / 18 To ((71 + 2 * Result) * PI) / 18
Step PI / 9
        BitBlt hDC, X, Y, 11, 11, PictureBallSav.hDC, 0, 0,
SRCCOPY
        X = XCenter + Radius * Cos(Theta) - 5
        Y = YCenter - Radius * Sin(Theta) - 5
        BitBlt PictureBallSav.hDC, 0, 0, 11, 11, hDC, X, Y,
SRCCOPY
        BitBlt hDC, X, Y, 11, 11, PictureBallMsk.hDC, 0, 0,
SRCAND
        BitBlt hDC, X, Y, 11, 11, PictureBallImg.hDC, 0, 0,
SRCINVERT
        Refresh
        Beep
    Next Theta
    PrevX = X: PrevY = Y

    'print result of spin:
    Result = (18 - Result) Mod 9 + 1
    Message = "result: " + Str$(Result)
    If Result <> 5 Then
```

(continued)

Figure 13-8 *continued*

```
        If Result >= 6 Then
            Message = Message + ", high, "
        Else
            Message = Message + ", low, "
        End If
        If Result Mod 2 Then
            Message = Message + "odd, "
        Else
            Message = Message + "even, "
        End If
        If Result = 1 Or Result = 3 Or Result = 6 Or Result =
8 Then
            Message = Message + "red"
        Else
            Message = Message + "black"
        End If
    End If
    LabelTop.Caption = Message

    'remove lost chips/award winnings:
    For I = 1 To 9
        If SquareTable(I).ChipVal <> -1 Then
            If I = Result Then
                DoWin (I)
            Else
                DoLose (I)
            End If
        End If
    Next I
    If SquareTable(10).ChipVal <> -1 Then
        If Result < 5 Then
            DoWin (10)
        Else
            DoLose (10)
        End If
    End If
    If SquareTable(11).ChipVal <> -1 Then
        If Result = 2 Or Result = 4 Or Result = 7 Or Result =
9 Then
            DoWin (11)
        Else
            DoLose (11)
        End If
    End If
```

(continued)

Figure 13-8 *continued*

```
    If SquareTable(12).ChipVal <> -1 Then
        If Result = 1 Or Result = 3 Or Result = 6 Or Result =
8 Then
            DoWin (12)
        Else
            DoLose (12)
        End If
    End If
    If SquareTable(13).ChipVal <> -1 Then
        If Result > 5 Then
            DoWin (13)
        Else
            DoLose (13)
        End If
    End If
    If SquareTable(14).ChipVal <> -1 Then
        If Result = 1 Or Result = 3 Or Result = 7 Or Result =
9 Then
            DoWin (14)
        Else
            DoLose (14)
        End If
    End If
    If SquareTable(15).ChipVal <> -1 Then
        If Result Mod 2 = 0 Then
            DoWin (15)
        Else
            DoLose (15)
        End If
    End If

    'update controls:
    If MoneyBet > 0 Then Command1.Enabled = -1
    LabelBottom.Caption = "you have: $" +
Format$(MoneyTotal, "")
    If MoneyTotal = 0 Then
        GameOver = -1
        Command1.Enabled = 0
        LabelTop.Caption = "you're broke: game over!"
    End If

    Refresh
    ThrowDone = -1
End Sub
```

(continued)

Figure 13-8 *continued*

```
Sub Form_Load ()
    Dim Rec As RECT

    'code for display-device independence:
    Rec.Left = 0
    Rec.Top = 0
    Rec.Right = CLIENTRIGHT
    Rec.Bottom = CLIENTBOTTOM
    AdjustWindowRect Rec, WS_CAPTION, -1
    FormMain.Width = (Rec.Right - Rec.Left + 1) * (1440 /
  GetDeviceCaps(hDC, LOGPIXELSX))
    FormMain.Height = (Rec.Bottom - Rec.Top + 1) * (1440 /
  GetDeviceCaps(hDC, LOGPIXELSY))
    Command1.Left = 256: Command1.Top = 178
    Command1.Width = 49: Command1.Height = 22
    LabelBottom.Left = 208: LabelBottom.Top = 208
    LabelBottom.Width = 137: LabelBottom.Height = 17
    LabelTop.Left = 200: LabelTop.Top = 8
    LabelTop.Width = 153: LabelTop.Height = 25
    PictureArrowDn.Left = 200: PictureArrowDn.Top = 181
    PictureArrowUp.Left = 200: PictureArrowUp.Top = 170
    PictureBallSav.Width = 11: PictureBallSav.Height = 11
    PictureChipSav.Width = 19: PictureChipSav.Height = 19

    SquareTable(0).Outer.Left = 167
    SquareTable(0).Outer.Top = 172
    SquareTable(0).Outer.Right = 185
    SquareTable(0).Outer.Bottom = 190
    SquareTable(0).Inner.Left = 167
    SquareTable(0).Inner.Top = 172
    SquareTable(0).Inner.Right = 185
    SquareTable(0).Inner.Bottom = 190
    SquareTable(1).Outer.Left = 29
    SquareTable(1).Outer.Top = 31
    SquareTable(1).Outer.Right = 63
    SquareTable(1).Outer.Bottom = 68
    SquareTable(1).Inner.Left = 40
    SquareTable(1).Inner.Top = 44
    SquareTable(1).Inner.Right = 58
    SquareTable(1).Inner.Bottom = 62
    SquareTable(2).Outer.Left = 99
    SquareTable(2).Outer.Top = 31
    SquareTable(2).Outer.Right = 133
    SquareTable(2).Outer.Bottom = 68
```

(continued)

465

Figure 13-8 *continued*

```
SquareTable(2).Inner.Left = 110
SquareTable(2).Inner.Top = 44
SquareTable(2).Inner.Right = 128
SquareTable(2).Inner.Bottom = 62
SquareTable(3).Outer.Left = 29
SquareTable(3).Outer.Top = 69
SquareTable(3).Outer.Right = 63
SquareTable(3).Outer.Bottom = 106
SquareTable(3).Inner.Left = 40
SquareTable(3).Inner.Top = 82
SquareTable(3).Inner.Right = 58
SquareTable(3).Inner.Bottom = 100
SquareTable(4).Outer.Left = 99
SquareTable(4).Outer.Top = 69
SquareTable(4).Outer.Right = 133
SquareTable(4).Outer.Bottom = 106
SquareTable(4).Inner.Left = 110
SquareTable(4).Inner.Top = 82
SquareTable(4).Inner.Right = 128
SquareTable(4).Inner.Bottom = 100
SquareTable(5).Outer.Left = 64
SquareTable(5).Outer.Top = 88
SquareTable(5).Outer.Right = 98
SquareTable(5).Outer.Bottom = 125
SquareTable(5).Inner.Left = 75
SquareTable(5).Inner.Top = 101
SquareTable(5).Inner.Right = 93
SquareTable(5).Inner.Bottom = 119
SquareTable(6).Outer.Left = 29
SquareTable(6).Outer.Top = 107
SquareTable(6).Outer.Right = 63
SquareTable(6).Outer.Bottom = 144
SquareTable(6).Inner.Left = 40
SquareTable(6).Inner.Top = 120
SquareTable(6).Inner.Right = 58
SquareTable(6).Inner.Bottom = 138
SquareTable(7).Outer.Left = 99
SquareTable(7).Outer.Top = 107
SquareTable(7).Outer.Right = 133
SquareTable(7).Outer.Bottom = 144
SquareTable(7).Inner.Left = 110
SquareTable(7).Inner.Top = 120
SquareTable(7).Inner.Right = 128
SquareTable(7).Inner.Bottom = 138
```

(continued)

Figure 13-8 *continued*

```
SquareTable(8).Outer.Left = 29
SquareTable(8).Outer.Top = 145
SquareTable(8).Outer.Right = 63
SquareTable(8).Outer.Bottom = 182
SquareTable(8).Inner.Left = 40
SquareTable(8).Inner.Top = 158
SquareTable(8).Inner.Right = 58
SquareTable(8).Inner.Bottom = 176
SquareTable(9).Outer.Left = 99
SquareTable(9).Outer.Top = 145
SquareTable(9).Outer.Right = 133
SquareTable(9).Outer.Bottom = 182
SquareTable(9).Inner.Left = 110
SquareTable(9).Inner.Top = 158
SquareTable(9).Inner.Right = 128
SquareTable(9).Inner.Bottom = 176
SquareTable(10).Outer.Left = 10
SquareTable(10).Outer.Top = 10
SquareTable(10).Outer.Right = 153
SquareTable(10).Outer.Bottom = 30
SquareTable(10).Inner.Left = 72
SquareTable(10).Inner.Top = 11
SquareTable(10).Inner.Right = 90
SquareTable(10).Inner.Bottom = 29
SquareTable(11).Outer.Left = 10
SquareTable(11).Outer.Top = 31
SquareTable(11).Outer.Right = 28
SquareTable(11).Outer.Bottom = 182
SquareTable(11).Inner.Left = 10
SquareTable(11).Inner.Top = 98
SquareTable(11).Inner.Right = 28
SquareTable(11).Inner.Bottom = 116
SquareTable(12).Outer.Left = 134
SquareTable(12).Outer.Top = 31
SquareTable(12).Outer.Right = 153
SquareTable(12).Outer.Bottom = 182
SquareTable(12).Inner.Left = 135
SquareTable(12).Inner.Top = 98
SquareTable(12).Inner.Right = 153
SquareTable(12).Inner.Bottom = 116
SquareTable(13).Outer.Left = 10
SquareTable(13).Outer.Top = 183
SquareTable(13).Outer.Right = 153
SquareTable(13).Outer.Bottom = 204
```

(continued)

Figure 13-8 *continued*

```
    SquareTable(13).Inner.Left = 72
    SquareTable(13).Inner.Top = 185
    SquareTable(13).Inner.Right = 90
    SquareTable(13).Inner.Bottom = 203
    SquareTable(14).Outer.Left = 64
    SquareTable(14).Outer.Top = 31
    SquareTable(14).Outer.Right = 98
    SquareTable(14).Outer.Bottom = 87
    SquareTable(14).Inner.Left = 75
    SquareTable(14).Inner.Top = 53
    SquareTable(14).Inner.Right = 93
    SquareTable(14).Inner.Bottom = 71
    SquareTable(15).Outer.Left = 64
    SquareTable(15).Outer.Top = 126
    SquareTable(15).Outer.Right = 98
    SquareTable(15).Outer.Bottom = 182
    SquareTable(15).Inner.Left = 75
    SquareTable(15).Inner.Top = 148
    SquareTable(15).Inner.Right = 93
    SquareTable(15).Inner.Bottom = 166

    Randomize
    InitNewGame
End Sub

Sub Form_MouseDown (Button As Integer, Shift As Integer,
 X As Single, Y As Single)
    Dim NumSquare As Integer
    Dim Pt As APIPOINT
    Dim Rec As RECT

    If GameOver Then Exit Sub
    If ThrowDone Then
        LabelTop.Caption = "place your bets"
        BitBlt hDC, PrevX, PrevY, 11, 11, PictureBallSav.hDC,
0, 0, SRCCOPY
        Refresh
        ThrowDone = 0
    End If
    NumSquare = InnerSquareHit(Int(X), Int(Y), XOffset, YOffset)
    If NumSquare = -1 Then Exit Sub
    If SquareTable(NumSquare).ChipVal < 1 Then Exit Sub
```

(continued)

Figure 13-8 *continued*

```
    ShowCursor 0
    SetCapture hWnd
    Pt.X = 0
    Pt.Y = 0
    ClientToScreen hWnd, Pt
    Rec.Left = Pt.X
    Rec.Top = Pt.Y
    Pt.X = 182
    Pt.Y = ScaleHeight
    ClientToScreen hWnd, Pt
    Rec.Right = Pt.X
    Rec.Bottom = Pt.Y
    ClipCursor Rec
    MoveOrigin = NumSquare
    MoveValue = SquareTable(NumSquare).ChipVal
    PrintImgValue (SquareTable(NumSquare).ChipVal)
    PrevX = SquareTable(NumSquare).Inner.Left
    PrevY = SquareTable(NumSquare).Inner.Top
    If NumSquare = 0 Then
        PictureChipSav.BackColor = &H8080&
    Else
        PictureChipSav.BackColor = &H8000&
        MoneyBet = MoneyBet - SquareTable(NumSquare).ChipVal
        If MoneyBet = 0 Then Command1.Enabled = 0
        SquareTable(NumSquare).ChipVal = -1
    End If
End Sub

Sub Form_MouseMove (Button As Integer, Shift As Integer,
 X As Single, Y As Single)
    If MoveValue = -1 Then Exit Sub
    BitBlt hDC, PrevX, PrevY, 19, 19, PictureChipSav.hDC,
 0, 0, SRCCOPY
    PrevX = X - XOffset
    PrevY = Y - YOffset
    BitBlt PictureChipSav.hDC, 0, 0, 19, 19, hDC, PrevX,
 PrevY, SRCCOPY
    BitBlt hDC, PrevX, PrevY, 19, 19, PictureChipMsk.hDC,
 0, 0, SRCAND
    BitBlt hDC, PrevX, PrevY, 19, 19, PictureChipImg.hDC,
 0, 0, SRCINVERT
    Refresh
End Sub
```

(continued)

469

Figure 13-8 *continued*

```
Sub Form_MouseUp (Button As Integer, Shift As Integer,
 X As Single, Y As Single)
    Dim NumSquare As Integer

    If MoveValue = -1 Then Exit Sub
    ShowCursor -1
    ReleaseCapture
    ClipCursor ByVal 0&
    BitBlt hDC, PrevX, PrevY, 19, 19, PictureChipSav.hDC,
0, 0, SRCCOPY
    NumSquare = OuterSquareHit(PrevX + 9, PrevY + 9)
    If NumSquare = 0 Then
        SquareTable(0).ChipVal = MoveValue
    ElseIf NumSquare > 0 Then
        If SquareTable(NumSquare).ChipVal = -1 Then
            BitBlt hDC, SquareTable(NumSquare).Inner.Left,
SquareTable(NumSquare).Inner.Top, 19, 19, PictureChipMsk.hDC,
0, 0, SRCAND
            BitBlt hDC, SquareTable(NumSquare).Inner.Left,
SquareTable(NumSquare).Inner.Top, 19, 19, PictureChipImg.hDC,
0, 0, SRCINVERT
            SquareTable(NumSquare).ChipVal = MoveValue
            MoneyBet = MoneyBet + MoveValue
            Command1.Enabled = -1
        Else
            NumSquare = -1
        End If
    End If
    If NumSquare = -1 Then
        BitBlt hDC, SquareTable(MoveOrigin).Inner.Left,
SquareTable(MoveOrigin).Inner.Top, 19, 19, PictureChipMsk.hDC,
0, 0, SRCAND
        BitBlt hDC, SquareTable(MoveOrigin).Inner.Left,
SquareTable(MoveOrigin).Inner.Top, 19, 19, PictureChipImg.hDC,
0, 0, SRCINVERT
        If MoveOrigin <> 0 Then
            SquareTable(MoveOrigin).ChipVal = MoveValue
            MoneyBet = MoneyBet + MoveValue
            Command1.Enabled = -1
        End If
    End If
    If SquareTable(0).ChipVal + MoneyBet > MoneyTotal Then
        SquareTable(0).ChipVal = MoneyTotal - MoneyBet
```

(continued)

Figure 13-8 *continued*

```
    End If
    If SquareTable(0).ChipVal > 99 Then
        SquareTable(0).ChipVal = 99
    End If
    PrintImgValue (SquareTable(0).ChipVal)
    BitBlt hDC, SquareTable(0).Inner.Left,
 SquareTable(0).Inner.Top, 19, 19, PictureChipMsk.hDC, 0, 0,
 SRCAND
    BitBlt hDC, SquareTable(0).Inner.Left,
 SquareTable(0).Inner.Top, 19, 19, PictureChipImg.hDC, 0, 0,
 SRCINVERT
    Refresh
    MoveValue = -1
End Sub

Sub Form_Unload (Cancel As Integer)
    WinHelp hWnd, HELP_FILE, HELP_QUIT, 0
End Sub

Sub MenuAbout_Click ()
    FormAbout.Show 1
End Sub

Sub MenuCommands_Click ()
    WinHelp hWnd, HELP_FILE, HELP_CONTEXT, HELP_COMMANDS
End Sub

Sub MenuExit_Click ()
    WinHelp hWnd, HELP_FILE, HELP_QUIT, 0
    End
End Sub

Sub MenuHowTo_Click ()
    WinHelp hWnd, HELP_FILE, HELP_CONTEXT, HELP_HOWTOPLAY
End Sub

Sub MenuIndex_Click ()
    WinHelp hWnd, HELP_FILE, HELP_INDEX, 0
End Sub

Sub MenuNew_Click ()
    InitNewGame
End Sub
```

(continued)

Figure 13-8 *continued*

```
Sub MenuUsingHelp_Click ()
    WinHelp hWnd, HELP_FILE, HELP_HELPONHELP, 0
End Sub

Sub PictureArrowDn_MouseUp (Button As Integer, Shift As Integer,
 X As Single, Y As Single)
    If GameOver Then Exit Sub
    If SquareTable(0).ChipVal > 1 Then
        SquareTable(0).ChipVal = SquareTable(0).ChipVal - 1
        PrintImgValue (SquareTable(0).ChipVal)
        BitBlt hDC, SquareTable(0).Inner.Left,
SquareTable(0).Inner.Top, 19, 19, PictureChipMsk.hDC, 0, 0,
SRCAND
        BitBlt hDC, SquareTable(0).Inner.Left,
SquareTable(0).Inner.Top, 19, 19, PictureChipImg.hDC, 0, 0,
SRCINVERT
        Refresh
    End If
End Sub

Sub PictureArrowUp_MouseUp (Button As Integer, Shift As Integer,
 X As Single, Y As Single)
    If GameOver Then Exit Sub
    If SquareTable(0).ChipVal < 99 And SquareTable(0).ChipVal +
MoneyBet < MoneyTotal Then
        SquareTable(0).ChipVal = SquareTable(0).ChipVal + 1
        PrintImgValue (SquareTable(0).ChipVal)
        BitBlt hDC, SquareTable(0).Inner.Left,
SquareTable(0).Inner.Top, 19, 19, PictureChipMsk.hDC, 0, 0,
SRCAND
        BitBlt hDC, SquareTable(0).Inner.Left,
SquareTable(0).Inner.Top, 19, 19, PictureChipImg.hDC, 0, 0,
SRCINVERT
        Refresh
    End If
End Sub
```

BLABOUT.FRM code

```
Sub Command1_Click ()
    Unload FormAbout
End Sub
```

Programming Techniques

The Boule program uses the same basic animation technique to move both the betting chips and the ball. The program moves the chips in response to movements of the mouse, and it moves the ball automatically. The animation technique employs the *BitBlt* Windows API function to draw the image in each new location; this technique is the same as that used in the Ludo and Ringo games in Chapters 9 and 10. Boule, however, introduces a technique for moving an object automatically along a calculated path. (TriPack moves triangles automatically, but only along a simple straight path.) When the ball is thrown, the program uses the Visual Basic trigonometric functions *Sin* and *Cos* to plot circular and spiral paths to simulate the movements of an actual ball.

The up arrow and down arrow for adjusting the chip value are created using picture boxes and bitmaps. This method demonstrates how you can effectively create new control objects using Visual Basic, without employing other development tools.

The entire game background—which includes the betting layout, table top, and bowl—consists of a single bitmap. This bitmap was created in Paintbrush, saved in a file (BL.BMP), and assigned to the main form's Picture property. Although most of the other games in this book use this same technique, coding Boule presents a small problem: In VGA and in other high-resolution modes that have "square" pixels, the bowl appears perfectly round. In EGA mode, however, the bowl has a noticeably oval shape because pixels are not "square" in this mode; EGA has fewer pixels per inch in the vertical direction than it has in the horizontal direction, causing the bowl to be elongated vertically. (This topic is discussed in Chapter 3.)

If you have an EGA system, you can eliminate this effect by editing the bitmap to make the bowl round while in EGA mode. If you want the bowl to be perfectly round in every mode, you can create the graphics using Visual Basic drawing commands, as described in Chapters 6 and 10; however, using drawing commands makes your coding task much more complex. (If you use either of these two methods, be sure to set the ScaleMode property of the form to the Twip setting or to one of the other device-independent settings.)

473

Program Overview

Here is a summary of the sequence of events in the Boule program.

- When the program is started, the *Form_Load* event procedure performs one-time initialization tasks and calls *InitNewGame* to start a new game.

- The *MenuNew_Click* event procedure also calls *InitNewGame* whenever the player chooses the New Game command from the Game menu.

- *InitNewGame* assigns values to all variables and properties that need to be initialized with each new game, clears the form, and draws the initial chip at the chip source.

- Whenever the player clicks the up arrow next to the chip source, the *PictureArrowUp_Click* event procedure increments the value displayed in the chip at the chip source. Similarly, whenever, the player clicks the down arrow, the *PictureArrowDn_Click* event procedure decrements this value.

- Whenever the player presses the mouse button while the mouse pointer is on a chip, the *Form_MouseDown* event procedure initiates a move operation, setting *MoveValue* to the value of the chip under the mouse pointer.

- After a move operation has been started (that is, *MoveValue* <> –1), the *Form_MouseMove* event procedure redraws the chip in each new location as the mouse is moved.

- When the player releases the mouse button, the *Form_MouseUp* event procedure stops the move operation. If the mouse pointer is at a valid position, the procedure records the new position of the chip; if the mouse pointer is at an invalid position, the procedure moves the chip back to its starting point. If a bet has been placed, the procedure enables the Throw button (Command1).

- When the player clicks the Throw button, the *Command1_Click* event procedure simulates the throw of the ball, bringing the ball to rest on a randomly selected indentation. The procedure then removes chips and awards winnings. Also, if the player goes broke, the procedure terminates the game.

Initializing the Program

The *Form_Load* event procedure is called once, when the program is first run, and the *InitNewGame* general procedure is called each time a new game is to be started.

The *Form_Load* Procedure

After performing the standard tasks for assuring video-device independence, the *Form_Load* procedure initializes the coordinate values in the SquareTable array. SquareTable stores the coordinates and current contents of each area on the betting layout. It is declared as follows:

```
Dim SquareTable(0 To 15) As SQUARE
```

The base type SQUARE is defined in the global module as follows:

```
Type SQUARE
    Outer As RECT
    Inner As RECT
    ChipVal As Integer
End Type
```

The *Outer* field stores the coordinates of the entire marked area on the betting layout, and the *Inner* field stores the coordinates of the area actually occupied by a chip that has been placed within the marked area. As you will see, when the player drops a chip anywhere within the marked area (specified by the *Outer* field), the program centers the chip by placing it within the coordinates stored in the *Inner* field. Thus, the chip always occupies a standard position within each marked area; this assures that the player can always see the numbers within each area and also makes it easier to detect when the user has started dragging a chip.

The *ChipVal* field stores the value of the chip currently placed within the corresponding area, or the value *–1* if no chip is currently within this area. The *ChipVal* fields are initialized at the beginning of each game, by the *InitNewGame* procedure.

The elements of SquareTable numbered 1 through 15 correspond to each of the 15 areas within the betting layout. SquareTable(0), however, stores the coordinates and current value of the chip source; for this element, the *Inner* and *Outer* fields contain the same coordinate because there is no marked area surrounding the chip at the source. In Figure 13-9 on the following page, the numbers within parentheses show the locations of the elements of SquareTable.

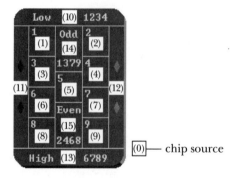

Figure 13-9.
The locations of the elements of the SquareTable array.

The *InitNewGame* Procedure

InitNewGame begins by initializing a variety of variables used during the game:

```
GameOver = 0
MoneyBet = 0
MoneyTotal = 100
MoveValue = -1
ThrowDone = 0
```

The use of these variables is described in the following table.

Variable	Explanation
GameOver	A variable set to TRUE when the game is terminated (that is, when the player's total, *MoneyTotal*, reaches *0*)
MoneyBet	The sum of the values of all chips placed on the betting layout
MoneyTotal	The amount of money that the player possesses
MoveValue	The value of the chip being moved; the value *−1* indicates that no chip is being moved
ThrowDone	A variable set to TRUE immediately after a throw, signaling the program that it must erase the image of the ball and change the label at the top of the form the next time the player presses the mouse button

InitNewGame then initializes the *ChipVal* fields of the SquareTable array. The *ChipVal* field of the chip at the source—SquareTable(0)—is set to *5* so that the player starts with a $5 chip, and the *ChipVal* field of each of the other elements of SquareTable is set to the special value *–1*, which indicates that the area does not contain a chip.

InitNewGame then disables the Throw button; this button is enabled only when at least one chip is on the betting layout. The procedure then initializes the labels at the top and bottom of the form and calls *Cls* to remove any images previously drawn on the form.

Finally, *InitNewGame* draws the chip at the source:

```
PrintImgValue (SquareTable(0).ChipVal)
BitBlt hDC, SquareTable(0).Inner.Left, SquareTable(0).Inner.Top,
  19, 19, PictureChipMsk.hDC, 0, 0, SRCAND
BitBlt hDC, SquareTable(0).Inner.Left, SquareTable(0).Inner.Top,
  19, 19, PictureChipImg.hDC, 0, 0, SRCINVERT
```

BitBlt is called first to transfer a mask drawing and then to transfer an image drawing. As you have seen, this method creates a drawing without disturbing the surrounding graphics at the target location (a technique first explained in Chapter 8, in the section titled "The Drawing Technique"). Before drawing the chip, however, *InitNewGame* calls *PrintImgValue*. This general procedure uses the Visual Basic *Print* method to print the value of the chip directly to the PictureChipImg picture box, which stores the image drawing. Subsequently, this number appears in the center of the chip whenever the drawing is transferred to the form.

Adjusting the Chip Value

The Boule program uses two picture boxes, PictureArrowUp and PictureArrowDn, to create the arrow buttons that allow the player to adjust the value of the chip at the chip source. PictureArrowUp was assigned a bitmap depicting an up arrow (ARROWUP.BMP), and PictureArrowDn was assigned a bitmap depicting a down arrow (ARROWDN.BMP).

Whenever the player clicks on the up arrow box, the *PictureArrowUp_MouseUp* event procedure receives control as soon as the mouse button is released. This procedure exits immediately if the game is over or if incrementing the chip value would cause it to exceed the maximum value (99) or the amount of money the player has available for betting. Otherwise, the procedure increments the value of the chip at the chip source and then redraws the image of the chip displaying the new value.

Similarly, whenever the player clicks the down arrow button, the *PictureArrowDn_MouseUp* event procedure decrements the value of the chip, if appropriate, and then redisplays the image.

Why does the program process MouseUp events rather than Mouse-Down or Click events? The problem with using either the MouseDown or Click event to process clicks is that if the player clicks twice in rapid succession, the second click causes a DblClick event rather than a Mouse-Down and a Click event. However, no matter how rapidly the player clicks a picture box, each click produces exactly one MouseUp event. Therefore, by processing in response to the MouseUp event, no clicks are lost.

Moving the Chips

To permit the player to drag a chip from one location to another, the Boule program uses the same method employed by the Ludo and Ringo programs. (For a complete description of this animation technique, see Chapter 9, the section titled "Moving the Player's Piece.")

Three event procedures control the movement of the chip:

- The *Form_MouseDown* procedure initiates the move operation.

- The *Form_MouseMove* procedure redraws the image of the chip at each new location of the mouse pointer.

- The *Form_MouseUp* procedure terminates the move operation.

The *Form_MouseDown* Procedure

The *Form_MouseDown* event procedure receives control whenever the player presses the mouse button while the mouse pointer is over the form. If the game has ended (that is, if *GameOver* is TRUE), the procedure exits immediately. Otherwise, if necessary, the procedure restores the caption and erases the image of the ball drawn during the previous throw:

```
If ThrowDone Then
    LabelTop.Caption = "place your bets"
    BitBlt hDC, PrevX, PrevY, 11, 11, PictureBallSav.hDC, 0, 0,
SRCCOPY
    Refresh
    ThrowDone = 0
End If
```

As you will see later in the chapter, in the section titled "Simulating the Throw," each time the ball is drawn on the form, the existing graphics underlying the ball are stored in PictureBallSav immediately before the image is drawn. Therefore, transferring the contents of this picture box back to the current location of the ball erases the image.

The procedure then calls the general function *InnerSquareHit* to determine whether the mouse pointer is within one of the possible chip locations (either at the chip source or on the betting layout):

```
NumSquare = InnerSquareHit(Int(X), Int(Y), XOffset, YOffset)
```

If the mouse pointer is within a valid chip location, *InnerSquareHit* returns the index of the corresponding element of SquareTable. In this case, the procedure also assigns to the *XOffset* and *YOffset* parameters the horizontal and vertical offsets of the mouse pointer from the upper left corner of the rectangular chip location. These variables are later used by the *Form_MouseMove* event procedure so that it can properly position the image of the chip.

If the pointer is not on a valid chip location, *InnerSquareHit* returns –1. In this case, the procedure exits immediately:

```
If NumSquare = -1 Then Exit Sub
```

Form_MouseDown also exits if *InnerSquareHit* returns a value greater than –1, but the indicated location does not contain a chip:

```
If SquareTable(NumSquare).ChipVal < 1 Then Exit Sub
```

If the mouse pointer is located over a chip, *Form_MouseDown* proceeds to initiate a move operation. To do this, the procedure first executes a series of statements to control the mouse pointer. Here is a summary of the main steps:

1. *Form_MouseDown* calls *ShowCursor* (see Figure 5-12) to hide the mouse pointer.

2. It calls *SetCapture* (see Figure 5-13) to assure that the main form processes all mouse events.

3. It calls *ClipCursor* (see Figure 5-14) to confine the mouse pointer to the area of the form surrounding the chip source and the betting layout.

Boule confines the mouse to the area of the form immediately surrounding the betting layout. As in the Ludo program (Chapter 9), the player is not permitted to drag the playing piece over one of the other controls within the form because this would cause the chip to appear to "slide under" the control.

Form_MouseDown next sets the value of two variables used by the other procedures that manage the move:

```
MoveOrigin = NumSquare
MoveValue = SquareTable(NumSquare).ChipVal
```

MoveOrigin stores the index of the SquareTable element containing the coordinates of the original location of the moving chip. As explained previously, *MoveValue* stores the value of the moving chip or –1 if no chip is currently being moved.

Next, *Form_MouseDown* calls *PrintImgValue* to print the value of the moving chip within the image drawing used to draw the chip as it is moved:

```
PrintImgValue (SquareTable(NumSquare).ChipVal)
```

The procedure also initializes the variables *PrevX* and *PrevY* with the current location of the chip:

```
PrevX = SquareTable(NumSquare).Inner.Left
PrevY = SquareTable(NumSquare).Inner.Top
```

These variables tell the *Form_MouseMove* procedure the previous location of the chip so that it can erase the chip from this location before it draws the chip at its new location. *Form_MouseDown* also fills the picture box used for erasing the image with the appropriate color:

```
If NumSquare = 0 Then                    'chip at source
    PictureChipSav.BackColor = &H8080&   'dark yellow
Else                                     'chip on betting layout
    PictureChipSav.BackColor = &H8000&   'dark green
```

If the chip is located within the betting layout, the procedure must also adjust the *MoneyBet* variable (explained previously) and set the *ChipVal* field of the SquareTable element to –1 to indicate that the corresponding area is now devoid of a chip:

```
    MoneyBet = MoneyBet - SquareTable(NumSquare).ChipVal
    If MoneyBet = 0 Then Command1.Enabled = 0
    SquareTable(NumSquare).ChipVal = -1
End If
```

The *Form_MouseMove* Procedure

As the player moves the mouse pointer, a series of MouseMove events occur. On each event, the *Form_MouseMove* procedure redraws the image at the new location of the mouse pointer.

If a move operation is in progress (that is, *MoveValue* <> –1), *Form-_MouseMove* redraws the image by taking the following steps:

1. It erases the image of the chip at the previous location by calling *BitBlt* to restore the graphics that were saved in *PictureChipSav*:

```
BitBlt hDC, PrevX, PrevY, 19, 19, PictureChipSav.hDC, 0, 0,
   SRCCOPY
```

2. It sets *PrevX* and *PrevY* to the new location of the chip:

```
PrevX = X - XOffset
PrevY = Y - YOffset
```

3. It saves the underlying graphics at the new location of the chip (so that the image can be restored when the chip moves to the next location):

```
BitBlt PictureChipSav.hDC, 0, 0, 19, 19, hDC, PrevX, PrevY,
   SRCCOPY
```

4. It draws the chip at its new location using *BitBlt* to transfer the mask drawing and then the image drawing:

```
BitBlt hDC, PrevX, PrevY, 19, 19, PictureChipMsk.hDC, 0, 0,
   SRCAND
BitBlt hDC, PrevX, PrevY, 19, 19, PictureChipImg.hDC, 0, 0,
   SRCINVERT
```

5. It calls *Refresh* to make the results of the bit transfers visible. (This step is necessary because the procedure contains no calls to standard Visual Basic graphics methods.)

The *Form_MouseUp* Procedure

When the player finally releases the mouse button to deposit the chip in its new location, the *Form_MouseUp* event procedure receives control. This procedure begins by calling the Windows API *ShowCursor, Release-Capture,* and *ClipCursor* functions to release control of the mouse pointer (explained in Chapter 5, in the section titled "Processing the MouseUp Event"). The procedure then draws the chip in its final location by taking the following steps:

- It calls *BitBlt* to erase the chip from its current position:

```
BitBlt hDC, PrevX, PrevY, 19, 19, PictureChipSav.hDC, 0, 0,
   SRCCOPY
```

■ It calls the general function *OuterSquareHit* to test the location of the center of the chip:

```
NumSquare = OuterSquareHit(PrevX + 9, PrevY + 9)
```

■ If the chip has been dropped on the chip source area, *OuterSquareHit* returns a value of *0.* In this case, the procedure merely updates the value of the chip at the source (redrawing the chip later):

```
SquareTable(0).ChipVal = MoveValue
```

■ If the chip has been dropped within a marked area of the betting layout, *OuterSquareHit* returns a value greater than 1 (specifically, the index of the corresponding SquareTable element). In this case, provided that the area is empty, the procedure draws the chip in the center of the area, updates the chip value in SquareTable, revises *MoneyBet,* and enables the Throw button:

```
BitBlt hDC, SquareTable(NumSquare).Inner.Left,
  SquareTable(NumSquare).Inner.Top, 19, 19,
  PictureChipMsk.hDC, 0, 0, SRCAND
BitBlt hDC, SquareTable(NumSquare).Inner.Left,
  SquareTable(NumSquare).Inner.Top, 19, 19,
  PictureChipImg.hDC, 0, 0, SRCINVERT
SquareTable(NumSquare).ChipVal = MoveValue
MoneyBet = MoneyBet + MoveValue
Command1.Enabled = -1
```

■ If the chip has not been dropped in a valid area, *OuterSquareHit* returns −1. If this happens or if the layout area already contains a chip, the procedure restores the chip to its original position using a set of statements similar to those in the previous step. (The variable *MoveOrigin* stores the SquareTable index of the original position.)

Next, *Form_MouseUp* updates the chip at the source:

```
If SquareTable(0).ChipVal + MoneyBet > MoneyTotal Then
    SquareTable(0).ChipVal = MoneyTotal - MoneyBet
End If
If SquareTable(0).ChipVal > 99 Then
    SquareTable(0).ChipVal = 99
End If
```

(continued)

continued

```
PrintImgValue (SquareTable(0).ChipVal)
BitBlt hDC, SquareTable(0).Inner.Left, SquareTable(0).Inner.Top,
 19, 19, PictureChipMsk.hDC, 0, 0, SRCAND
BitBlt hDC, SquareTable(0).Inner.Left, SquareTable(0).Inner.Top,
 19, 19, PictureChipImg.hDC, 0, 0, SRCINVERT
```

These steps are required because the move operation might have removed the chip from the chip source, altered the chip's value, or changed the amount of money available for the next bet.

Finally, *Form_MouseUp* calls *Refresh* to make all changes visible and resets *MoveOrigin* to *−1* to indicate that the move operation has ended.

Throwing the Ball

When the player clicks the Throw button to get the ball rolling, the *Command1_Click* event procedure receives control. This procedure begins by disabling the Throw button so that the player cannot click it while the simulation is in progress. Also, if an image of the ball is left from a prior throw (that is, *ThrowDone* is TRUE), the procedure erases this image. The procedure also temporarily displays the *no more bets* message at the top of the form. When the simulation is completed, the procedure replaces this message with one showing results of the throw.

Command1_Click then proceeds with its two major tasks:

- Simulating the throw of the ball
- Collecting losing bets and paying winning ones

Simulating the Throw

The simulation routine moves the ball as if it were being thrown into the bowl, eventually bringing it to rest within one of the eighteen indentations around the center of the bowl, selecting the final indentation randomly.

The routine begins by assigning the coordinates of the center of the bowl to *XCenter* and *YCenter*:

```
XCenter = 277    'center of bowl
YCenter = 102
```

The routine sets *Radius* to the radius of the initial circular path of the ball around the outside edge of the bowl:

```
Radius = 53      'initial radius of path of ball
```

Next, it initializes *X* and *Y*:

```
X = XCenter + Radius - 5
Y = YCenter - 5
```

Throughout the routine, *X* and *Y* store the current position of the upper left corner of the bitmap used to draw the ball. This initial assignment places the center of the ball at the three o'clock position along the outside edge of the bowl. (The − 5 term converts the coordinates of the center of the bitmap to the coordinates of the upper left corner, because the bitmap is 11 pixels wide by 11 pixels high.)

The routine then saves the graphics underlying the initial position of the ball so that the ball can be erased from this position when it is first moved:

```
BitBlt PictureBallSav.hDC, 0, 0, 11, 11, hDC, X, Y, SRCCOPY
```

After these preliminary tasks have been completed, the routine moves the ball in three distinct stages:

1. It moves the ball in a circular path around the outside edge of the bowl, with steadily decreasing speed.

2. It moves the ball in a spiral path toward the center of the bowl.

3. It moves the ball in a circular path around the center, bringing it to rest at a randomly selected indentation.

The Outer Circular Path

In an actual game of Boule, the ball is thrown into a groove cut into the outside edge of the bowl. To simulate the movement of the ball in the groove, the program begins by moving the image of the ball in a circular path around the outside circumference of the drawing of the bowl.

To move the ball to each new location along its path, the routine makes a series of calls to *BitBlt*: first to erase the image from its former location, then to save the existing graphics at the new location, and then to draw the ball at the new location. This technique is the same as that used to move the betting chips, and it was described previously in the chapter.

Each location of the ball along the circular path is calculated using the Visual Basic *Sin* and *Cos* functions:

```
X = XCenter + Radius * Cos(Theta) - 5
Y = YCenter - Radius * Sin(Theta) - 5
```

Theta is the angle between the horizontal and a line connecting the center of the circle to the ball. Figure 13-10 illustrates the calculation of the ball's position.

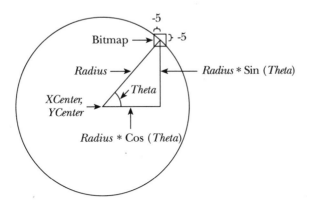

Figure 13-10.
Calculating the position of the ball.

Theta has an initial value of *0* and is incremented each time the ball is drawn, so the ball moves in a counterclockwise direction around the circle. Rather than incrementing *Theta* by a constant amount, it is instead incremented by an amount that constantly decreases, causing the speed of the ball to steadily diminish (simulating the movement of an actual ball). To achieve this, the code for drawing the ball is placed inside the following loop:

```
For DeltaTheta = .75 To .3 Step -.01

    'code for drawing ball at angle Theta

    Theta = Theta + DeltaTheta
Next DeltaTheta
```

The loop repeats often enough to cause the ball to travel several times around the bowl.

The Spiral Path
After the ball has made several revolutions and has lost velocity, the program moves it in a spiral path toward the "bottom" (that is, the center) of the bowl. To create a spiral path, the value of *Radius* is decremented each time the ball is drawn. To achieve this, the drawing statements are placed within the following loop:

```
For Radius = 53 To 11 Step -1

    'code for drawing ball at radius Radius and angle Theta

    Theta = Theta + DeltaTheta
Next Radius
```

Notice that *DeltaTheta* does not change within this loop. Consequently, the ball moves at a constant speed as it spirals ''downward'' (that is, inward).

The Inner Circular Path

Finally, the ball is moved around the center of the bowl, in a circular path and at a constant speed. This time, the final value of *Theta* is selected using the Visual Basic *Rnd* function so that the ball comes to rest at a random indentation. The following code does the trick:

```
Result = Int(18 * Rnd + 1)  'random value from 1 to 18
For Theta = 31 * PI / 18 To ((71 + 2 * Result) * PI) / 18 Step
  PI / 9

    'code for drawing ball

    Beep
Next Theta
```

The initial value of *Theta*,

```
31 * PI / 18
```

places the ball within the center of the indentation that is just beyond the final position of the ball at the end of its spiral path (generated by the previous loop). The symbolic constant PI stores the value of pi. With each repetition of the loop, *Theta* is incremented by *PI / 9*, which moves the ball to the center of the next indentation. (The angle between the centers of adjacent indentations is *PI / 9* radians, because 18 indentations are evenly spaced around the center of the bowl and the number of radians in an entire circle is *2 * PI*.) The starting position of the ball is illustrated in Figure 13-11.

The final value of *Theta*,

```
((71 + 2 * Result) * PI) / 18
```

causes the ball to move to the indentation immediately below the three o'clock position, then around the entire circumference, and then a random distance ranging from 1 through 18 indentations. (The factor *Result* was obtained using the random-number generator.) Notice that the call

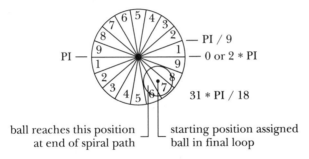

ball reaches this position
at end of spiral path

starting position assigned
ball in final loop

Figure 13-11.
The position of the ball at the start of the final phase of its movement.

to the *Beep* procedure is included in the loop to create a sound as the ball "drops" into an indentation.

After moving the ball to its final resting position, the routine converts the random value stored in *Result* to the numeric value of the final position (that is, the number marked within the bowl):

```
Result = (18 - Result) Mod 9 + 1
```

The procedure then prints a description of the result within the label at the top of the form (*LabelTop*).

Collecting and Paying

Next, the *Command1_Click* procedure examines each of the locations within the betting layout. If a given location contains a chip, the procedure tests whether the bet has been won or lost. If the bet has been won, the procedure calls the general procedure *DoWin* to add the value of the winning bet to the value of the chip. If the bet has been lost, the procedure calls the general procedure *DoLose* to remove the chip. The procedures *DoWin* and *DoLose* not only modify the appearance of the betting layout but also update the SquareTable, *MoneyBet*, and *MoneyTotal* variables.

Command1_Click then reenables the Throw button, provided that at least one chip is left within the betting layout:

```
If MoneyBet > 0 Then Command1.Enabled = -1
```

It also displays the player's current total within the label at the bottom of the form (*LabelBottom*); if this total is *0*, it terminates the game by setting *GameOver* to TRUE, disabling the Throw button, and displaying a message at the top of the form.

487

Finally, *Command1_Click* calls *Refresh* to make visible the changes made to the betting layout and sets *ThrowDone* to TRUE to indicate that a throw has just been completed.

Enhancing the Game

Here are two features you might want to add to the Boule game as well as a suggestion for another game you might want to write.

- Animate the removal of chips from the layout. Currently, chips for losing bets simply disappear. To add visual appeal, you could move them from the betting layout to the dealer's area, simulating the way chips are moved in an actual game. You could move them in a curved or straight path, using the same animation technique currently used to move the ball.

- Allow two or more players to play the game. Each player would have chips of a distinct color. The players would start with the same amount of money, and the program would keep track of each player's bets and money.

- Implement a standard roulette game. Roulette would be a more challenging game to write because of the greater number of betting options and the greater complexity of its rules, and because the roulette wheel rotates as the ball is thrown. To animate the wheel, you could create a series of bitmaps depicting the wheel at various degrees of rotation and store each bitmap in a separate invisible picture box. When the wheel was spun, you could then assign the bitmaps, in succession, to a visible picture box, perhaps inserting a small pause between each assignment. (See Chapter 9, the section titled "Rolling the Die," for a description of a similar technique.)

WINDOWS API FUNCTIONS USED IN THIS BOOK

AdjustWindowRect

Purpose Supplies the outside coordinates of a form based upon the specified inside coordinates.

Declaration
```
Declare Sub AdjustWindowRect Lib "USER" (lpRect As RECT,
ByVal dwStyle&, ByVal bMenu%)
```

Parameter	Description

lpRect	A RECT type variable containing the coordinates of the inside of the form. *AdjustWindowRect* supplies the coordinates of the outside of the form by updating the fields of this variable. RECT has the following form:
	
	```Type RECT```
	``` Left As Integer```
	``` Top As Integer```
	``` Right As Integer```
	``` Bottom As Integer```
	```End Type```

dwStyle&	A code indicating the style of the window. If you have already set the form's BorderStyle property to *1 - Fixed Single*, you should assign *dwStyle* the value
	
	```WS_CAPTION```
	
	If you have already set the BorderStyle property to *2 - Sizable*, you should assign *dwStyle* the value
	
	```WS_CAPTION``` or ```WS_THICKFRAME```
	
	WS_CAPTION and WS_THICKFRAME are constants defined in your program; WS_CAPTION should be set to &HC00000 and WS_THICK-FRAME to &H40000.

bMenu%	A flag that should be set to TRUE if the form has a menu.

Comments The "inside" area refers to the portion of the form inside the borders, title bar, and menu (if present). It is also known as the "client" area.

BitBlt

Purpose Transfers a rectangular block of graphics from one location to another.

Declaration
```
Declare Sub BitBlt Lib "GDI" (ByVal HDestDC%, ByVal X%,
 ByVal Y%, ByVal nWidth%, ByVal nHeight%, ByVal HSrcDC%,
 ByVal XSrc%, ByVal YSrc%, ByVal ROP&)
```

Parameter	Description
HDestDC%	hDC property of destination form, picture box, printer, or other object.
X%	Horizontal coordinate of upper left corner of destination rectangle.
Y%	Vertical coordinate of upper left corner of destination rectangle.
nWidth%	Width of destination and source rectangles.
nHeight%	Height of destination and source rectangles.
HSrcDC%	hDC property of source form, picture box, or other object.
XSrc%	Horizontal coordinate of upper left corner of source rectangle.
YScr%	Vertical coordinate of upper left corner of source rectangle.
ROP&	Code indicating how the bits from the source rectangle are to be combined with the existing bits in the destination rectangle. The following are some typical values:

ROP& Value	Effect
&H00CC0020 (SRCCOPY)	destination = source
&H008800C6 (SRCAND)	destination = source AND destination
&H00EE0086 (SRCPAINT)	destination = source OR destination
&H00660046 (SRCINVERT)	destination = source XOR destination

ClientToScreen

Purpose Converts the coordinates of a point from form coordinates (relative to the origin of the form) to screen coordinates (relative to the upper left corner of the screen).

Declaration

```
Declare Sub ClientToScreen Lib "USER" (ByVal hWnd As
  Integer, Pt As APIPOINT)
```

Parameter	Description
hWnd	The hWnd property of the form.
Pt	A structure giving the coordinates of the point relative to the origin of the form identified by *hWnd*. The structure should have the following format:

```
Type APIPOINT
     X As Integer
     Y As Integer
End Type
```

ClientToScreen converts the coordinates by directly modifying the fields of this structure.

ClipCursor

Purpose Confines the mouse pointer to the inside of the specified rectangle.

Declaration
```
Declare Sub ClipCursor Lib "USER" (Rect As Any)
```

Parameter	Description
Rect	A structure (passed by reference) giving the screen coordinates of the confining rectangle. The structure should have the following format:

```
Type RECT
    Left As Integer
    Top As Integer
    Right As Integer
    Bottom As Integer
End Type
```

If you pass *0* (by value):

```
ClipCursor ByVal 0&
```

the mouse pointer is free to move anywhere on the screen.

GetDeviceCaps

Purpose Supplies device-specific information on a display device.

Declaration
```
Declare Function GetDeviceCaps Lib "GDI"
 (ByVal hDC%, ByVal Index%) As Integer
```

Parameter	Description
hDC%	Handle to the device context.
Index%	Indicates the type of information desired. The following table contains some of the values you can assign to *Index*:

Constant	Value	Meaning
LOGPIXELSX	88	Number of pixels per logical inch in the horizontal direction.
LOGPIXELSY	90	Number of pixels per logical inch in the vertical direction.

GetProfileInt

Purpose Retrieves the numeric value of a specified key from the Windows initialization file, WIN.INI.

Declaration
```
Declare Function GetProfileInt Lib "Kernel" (ByVal
 lpAppName$, ByVal lpKeyName$, ByVal nDefault%) As Integer
```

Parameter	Description
lpAppName$	The title of the section of WIN.INI containing the key; usually, the name of the calling program.
lpKeyName$	The name of the key whose value you want to obtain.
nDefault%	The value you want *GetProfileInt* to return if the specified key is not found.

Return Value If the function is successful, the numeric value of the key. If the value of the key is not numeric (or if the value is negative), it returns *0*. If the key is not found, it returns the value you passed as the *nDefault%* parameter.

Comment See also *WriteProfileString*.

IntersectRect

Purpose Reports whether two rectangular areas intersect. If they intersect, it supplies the coordinates of the intersection.

Declaration

```
Declare Function IntersectRect Lib "USER" (lpDestRect As
RECT, lpSrc1Rect As RECT, lpSrc2Rect As RECT) As Integer
```

Parameter	Description
lpDestRect	A RECT type variable that is assigned the coordinates of the intersection *if* the rectangles specified by the next two parameters intersect. The RECT type is defined as follows:
	``` Type RECT Left As Integer Top As Integer Right As Integer Bottom As Integer End Type ```
lpSrc1Rect	A RECT type variable containing the coordinates of one of the rectangles to be tested.
lpSrc2Rect	A RECT type variable containing the coordinates of the other rectangle to be tested.

Return Value A nonzero value if the rectangles specified by the second two parameters intersect, or 0 if these rectangles do not intersect.

InvertRect

Purpose Inverts all colors within the specified rectangular area of a form or picture box.

Declaration
```
Declare Sub InvertRect Lib "USER" (ByVal hDC As Integer,
Rec As RECT)
```

Parameter	Description
hDC	The hDC property (device context handle) of the form or picture box.
Rec	A structure giving the coordinates of the rectangular area to be inverted. It should have the following format:

```
Type RECT
    Left As Integer
    Top As Integer
    Right As Integer
    Bottom As Integer
End Type
```

Comment If you call this function twice for the same rectangular area, all colors are restored to their original values.

Polygon

Purpose Draws a polygon.

Declaration
```
Declare Sub Polygon Lib "GDI" (ByVal hDC As Integer,
 Points As APIPOINT, ByVal Count As Integer)
```

Parameter	Description
hDC	The hDC property (device context handle) of the form or picture box.
Points	An array of structures that specify each vertex of the desired polygon. The member structures should have the following format:

```
Type APIPOINT
    X As Integer    'Horizontal coordinate
                    'of vertex
    Y As Integer    'Vertical coordinate
                    'of vertex
End Type
```

Count	The number of vertices specified by the Points array.

Comments You can control the drawing style and colors used by *Polygon* by assigning values to the form or picture box properties exactly as you do using a Visual Basic drawing method. For example, if you set the FillStyle property to *0* (solid), the polygon will be filled with the color currently assigned to the FillColor property.

ReleaseCapture

Purpose Frees the mouse from the captured state. After calling this function, mouse events are processed by the object under the mouse pointer.

Declaration
```
Declare Sub ReleaseCapture Lib "USER" ()
```

Comment See also the "Declaration" section of *SetCapture*.

SetCapture

Purpose Forces all future mouse events to be handled by the form specified by the *hWnd* parameter, regardless of the location of the mouse pointer.

Declaration

```
Declare Sub SetCapture Lib "USER" (ByVal hWnd As Integer)
```

Parameter	Description
hWnd	The hWnd property of the form that is to process mouse events.

Comment See also the "Declaration" section of *ReleaseCapture.*

ShowCursor

Purpose Shows or hides the mouse pointer.

Declaration

```
Declare Sub ShowCursor Lib "USER" (ByVal ShowIt As Integer)
```

Parameter	Description
ShowIt	If this value is FALSE (0), the function hides the mouse pointer; if it is TRUE (−1), it shows the mouse pointer. (More accurately, it either decrements or increments an internal counter; the mouse pointer is visible when the counter >= 0.)

WinHelp

Purpose Calls the Windows help facility either to display a help topic or to remove the help window when the program has finished displaying help.

Declaration
```
Declare Sub WinHelp Lib "USER" (ByVal hWnd As Integer,
 ByVal lpHelpFile As String, ByVal wCommand As Integer,
 ByVal dwData As Long)
```

Parameter	Description
hWnd	The hWnd property of the main form.
lpHelpFile	A string containing the name of the HLP file with the help information you want to display. The string must include the full path if the file is neither in the current directory nor in the Windows directory.
wCommand	A code indicating the action wanted. The following are among the values you can pass:

Constant	Value	Meaning
HELP_CONTEXT	1	Display the topic indicated by the *dwData* parameter.
HELP_HELPONHELP	4	Display help on using the help system.
HELP_INDEX	3	Display the help index.
HELP_QUIT	2	Remove the help window.

dwData	If the *wCommand* parameter is set to HELP_CONTEXT, this parameter supplies the identifier of the specific help topic you want to see. (Identifiers are assigned to each help topic when the HLP file is created.) If *wCommand* is not set to HELP_CONTEXT, you should assign *0* to this parameter.

WriteProfileString

Purpose Writes information to a private section of the Windows initialization file, WIN.INI.

Declaration
```
Declare Sub WriteProfileString Lib "Kernel" (ByVal
 lpApplicationName$, ByVal lpKeyName$, ByVal lpString$)
```

Parameter	Description
lpApplicationName$	Title of the section of the WIN.INI file in which you want to write the information; usually, the name of the calling program.
lpKeyName$	The *key* portion of the information. (See "Comments," below.)
lpString$	The *value* of the key. (See "Comments," below.)

Comments Each item of information written to WIN.INI consists of a key followed by an equal sign (=), followed by a value.

WriteProfileString creates an entry in WIN.INI that has the following format:

[*lpApplicationName$*]
lpKeyName$=lpString$

See also *GetProfileInt*.

INDEX

Note: Italicized page numbers refer to tables and figures.

Michael J. Young

Michael J. Young is the author of books on the use of and the programming of computers, including *Inside DOS: A Programmer's Guide*, *Systems Programming in Microsoft C*, *Programmer's Guide to the OS/2 Presentation Manager*, and *Software Tools for OS/2*.

Young was a member of the ANSI committee that developed the standard for the C language. He also developed the Windows shareware application Envelopes & Labels as well as other software applications for Microsoft Windows. He is a graduate of Stanford University and currently lives and works in Mill Valley, California.

The manuscript for this book was prepared and submitted to Microsoft Press in electronic form. Text files were processed and formatted using Microsoft Word.

Principal editorial compositor: Debbie Kem
Principal proofreader/copy editor: Kathleen Atkins
Principal typographer: Katherine Erickson
Interior text designer: Kim Eggleston
Principal illustrator: Lisa Sandburg
Cover designer: Don Baker
Cover color separator: Color Service

Text composition by Microsoft Press in Baskerville with display type in Helvetica Bold, using the Magna composition system and the Linotronic 300 laser imagesetter.

Printed on recycled paper stock.